ITALIAN CUISINE

Arts and Traditions of the Table

ARTS AND TRADITIONS OF THE TABLE:
PERSPECTIVES ON CULINARY HISTORY
Albert Sonnenfeld, *series editor*

Salt: Grain of Life
Pierre Laszlo, translated by Mary Beth Mader

Culture of the Fork
Giovanni Rebora, translated by Albert Sonnenfeld

French Gastronomy: The History and Geography of a Passion
Jean-Robert Pitte, translated by Jody Gladding

Pasta: The Story of a Universal Food
Silvano Serventi and Françoise Sabban,
translated by Antony Shugar

Slow Food: The Case for Taste
Carlo Petrini, translated by William McCuaig

ITALIAN CUISINE
A CULTURAL HISTORY

ALBERTO CAPATTI & MASSIMO MONTANARI

TRANSLATED BY AINE O'HEALY

 COLUMBIA UNIVERSITY PRESS   NEW YORK

COLUMBIA UNIVERSITY PRESS
Publishers Since 1893
New York   Chichester, West Sussex

Copyright © 1999 Gius. Laterza and Figli SpA

This translation of *La cucina Italiana: Storia di una cultura*
is published by arrangement with Gius. Laterza
and Figli SpA, Rome-Bari.

Library of Congress Cataloging-in-Publication Data
Capatti, Alberto, 1944–
[Cucina italiana. English]
Italian cuisine : a cultural history /
Alberto Capatti and Massimo Montanari.
p. cm. — (Arts and traditions of the table)
Includes bibliographical references and index.
ISBN 978-0-231-12232-0 (alk. paper)
1. Cookery, Italian—History. 2. Italy—Social life and customs.
3. Gastronomy—History.
I. Montanari, Massimo, 1949–
II. Title. III. Series.

TX723.C28313   2003
641.5945'09—dc21
2003044009

Printed in the United States of America
Designed by Linda Secondari

c 10 9 8 7 6 5 4

To Libista, a peasant woman from
Cernuschio in Lombardy,
who invented ravioli wrapped in dough

CONTENTS

"What is the glory of Dante compared to spaghetti?" is among the memorable lines in this prodigiously learned yet always readable and entertaining book. The authors have in fact written a veritable diachronic encyclopedia, and how refreshing it is for once to read a chronologically grounded exposition. A chapter devoted to "science and technology in the kitchen" traces cooking techniques, utensils, and devices as they progressed from Roman antiquity through the Middle Ages to the present. In so doing, Capatti and Montanari connect various forms of government, regional topographies, and economies (since Italy's well-documented regionalism leads at times to a specifically local culinary vocabulary and technology).

But what emerges from this book is that, regionalisms aside, there is a national Italian culinary culture. In a compelling study of the linguistic resources of cookbooks and menus, the authors demonstrate how the amazing number of "Italian" cookbooks published from the Middle Ages onward evolved from Latin, at the outset, through the courtly seventeenth-century French (and its on-going snob appeal), into a Tuscan-Italian still burdened by a thick web of gastronomic Gallicisms. In this richly documented chapter (really a history unto itself) recipes from the thirteenth through the sixteenth centuries are adduced to trace the Orphic naming of new products unknown to the early Romans. All this, with a full authorial awareness of political and social developments, makes for a fascinating narrative.

Equally intriguing is the history of military diets: how availability of products in specific locales of conflict and the need to feed troops on the battlefield led to new technologies and tested the limits of culinary availability. At the same time, the military regime, especially during World War I, forged a "national diet" that led to the unity of what we now know as *la cucina italiana*.

Linked to the military is the evolution of chefs', cooks', and servers' attire in restaurants. The absurdity of highly formal tails for headwaiters, say, maintained in our own era of vestimentary informality, reflects the same military hierarchical order found in the emblem of the toque itself. Only the "officers" (maîtres d', executive chefs, et al.) were allowed beards and mustaches; as immediate inferiors, underlings and servers had to be clean-shaven in deference.

Another favorite chapter (chapter nine) traces the history of appetite. How much did medieval Florentine merchants consume to celebrate the prosperity of their nascent bourgeois society [which they themselves called *il popolo grasso* (the stout people)]? What foods constituted a satisfying diet for the glutton? How did this contrast with the regimen in monasteries? And how did the liturgical calendar, with its distinction between "fat" and "lean" days and its repertoire of symbolic foods, affect production, economics, and development of those specifically Italian culinary traditions so easily contaminated by their ancient Roman ancestry?

To be sure, there are other histories of Italian cuisine, but none are as richly documented as the present volume, which nevertheless remains eminently accessible and pleasurable. This monumental grouping of a constellation of culinary histories convinces us incontrovertibly of both the diversity and the unity of *la cucina italiana*.

Albert Sonenfeld

Introduction: Identity as Exchange

Italy, the country with a hundred cities and thousands of bell towers, is also the country with a hundred cuisines and thousands of recipes. Mirroring a history marked by provincial loyalties and political division, a huge variety of gastronomic traditions makes Italy's culinary heritage unimaginably rich and more appealing today than the cuisine of any other country, now that the demand for diversity and for distinctive, "provincial" flavors has become especially keen. Variety is also the element that immediately strikes the visitor's eye and palate. Is this enough to conclude that an *Italian* cuisine in the strict sense has never existed and (fortunately, perhaps) does not exist even today?

This is what one is often led to believe, but the task of this book is to show the contrary, based on a series of considerations that do not strike us as self-evident. Rather, they tend to undermine certain commonplaces, as well as the more usual ways of approaching culinary history. Because this book is entirely organized around a few fundamental themes, we would like to clarify them at the outset.

In the first place, we must restore to culinary history its own particular dimension. The temptation to subordinate this history to the hegemony of literature—regarded for centuries as the highest and most authoritative expression of good taste—has led to contradictory results. On the one hand, there is the attempt to show that patterns of consumption and styles of conviviality reflect an ideal of civility; on the other, there is the ongoing tendency to consider the minor, material arts as subordinate to the major, intellectual ones. To see a baroque stamp on seventeenth-century cuisine, like the rational character attributed to the cuisine of the Enlightenment, has been a means of "ennobling" diet and food, of talking about culinary matters by alluding to something else. But cooking does not require analogies. It has its own history and documentary autonomy, even if it can (and should) be studied by consulting many different sources, including literature.

Another, even stronger, temptation has been to subordinate the history of food to considerations of a very different nature, such as the landmarks of political history, which map out the boundaries of countries and states and assign clearly marked spaces to the population as a whole. Clearly, there are striking connections between these two aspects that go beyond the functional to the symbolic, which we will emphasize in the pages to follow. We will also point out the links between culinary history and the history of economics and modes of production that regulate supply and demand and are in turn related, not insignificantly, to political and institutional events. But again, the history of food cannot be reduced to extraneous dimensions. It is related more closely to the sciences and technologies of everyday material culture, to the rituals and necessities of ordinary life, and to forms of taste than to anything else. If it is true that the problem of "creating Italians" emerged after national unity had been achieved, it is nonetheless also true that the original characteristics of the country called Italy—"*il paese Italia,*" as Ruggiero Romano titled his recent collection of essays[1]—cannot be encapsulated in the short, contentious history of the unified state but must be sought in the dense network of customs, habits, and styles of living that somehow distinguish an "Italian" identity. Culinary practices and the culture of food are essential elements of this identity. It may in fact be useful to reflect on these, perhaps to discover that Italians existed long before Italy,[2] even if only on a few levels of society. But that is another story, and we will come back to it shortly.

A preliminary reflection precisely on the nature of identity thus seems indispensable at this juncture. In the context of culinary traditions, one might assume as self-evident that identity has to do with *belonging* to a particular place and that it involves the products and recipes of a specific location. Thinking about it like this may cause one to forget that identity may also—and perhaps primarily—be defined as *difference,* that is, difference in relation to others. In the case of gastronomy, one thing is quite clear: "local" identity is created as a function of exchange, at the moment when (and to the degree that) a product or recipe is brought into contact with different systems and cultures. Food products are sometimes consumed exclusively at their place of origin. Even in cases where the local economy is only partially self-sufficient, the restriction of local products to local consumption indicates an intimate, ritualized valorization of these foodstuffs, but it also means that the same foods are prevented from reaching the marketplace and from being exposed to public opinion. The "local" product, if consumed only at a local level, is devoid of geographical identity, since identity comes into play through a process of relocation, of "delocalization." Mortadella from Bologna is called "Bologna" only when it leaves the city where it is produced. "Ascoli-style olives" (*olive all'ascolana*) assume this name when they travel beyond the borders of Ascoli, even if they are promptly shipped back there, bearing this name, in a kind of boomerang effect.

What we propose to do in this book is to transfer the concept of identity from the sphere of production (where it is usually placed) to the sphere of exchange. It will thus be relatively easy to distinguish a network of culinary customs, food lore, and cooking practices, dating back to the distant past, that make explicit reference to an "Italian" context. Clearly, it is Italian not on the basis of the uniformity of local cultures (each of which maintains its specific connotations and differences) but on the basis of their diversity, which comes into play at the same moment that food enters into circulation. Cuisine is then revealed for what it actually is and has always been: an unparalleled site of exchange and contamination, beyond its origin. If a product can be the expression of a particular territory, its use in a recipe or on a menu is almost always the result of hybridization.

Clearly, all this applies mainly to the ruling classes. For a long time, the persistence of an "Italian" model of cooking could be observed only in aristocratic circles and among the urban elite, which sometimes coincided with the aristocracy. The middle and lower-middle classes were involved only in a marginal and discontinuous way, depending on developments in the economy and in market prices. To appreciate the unevenness of this model, we must look at its unexpected decline in relatively recent times. Over the past half-century Italy has seen the last of malnutrition and inequality of nutrition, ending a long cycle in the country's culinary history that could be defined as preindustrial. The increase in economic well-being has meant that people in rural areas have adapted to urban ways of living, without this leading to national homogeneity. Instead of translating itself into the large-scale adoption of ready-to-eat foods, often prepared hundreds of miles from the place of purchase, as occurred in England, Germany, and the United States, Italy's increased wealth has led to the new prestige enjoyed by traditional recipes and products, to a preference for small-scale food producers (which enables their survival), and to the cult status of wines and gastronomy. Home cooking has remained an important criterion in culinary matters, whereas the fast-food business supplies meals to less than 3 percent of the population. With the Europeanization of Italy's agriculture and food industry, the nation is now diversifying its image and retrieving the history of its own recent past. Having banished inequalities but not their cultural significance, Italy is reconceptualizing its past with the help of new commercial strategies. The labels "rich" and "poor," "aristocratic" and "peasant" acquire new meanings when applied to today's foods. Even in its relation to modernization, the Italian model presents particular, though easily recognizable, contradictions.

A different but closely related issue now needs to be addressed. Over the course of the centuries, Italian history had revealed a trait that distinguishes it from the history of other countries, namely, the prevalence of strong urban centers throughout the land and the great power wielded by the city-based tradition going back to Roman times and revitalized during the Middle Ages. This power has played itself out in various ways, according to the particularities of each historical region. The points we have argued so far derive their form and meaning from this specific context. In effect, the city constitutes a strategic setting for the creation and transmission of a culinary heritage that is at once local and national.

An unparalleled site of commercial exchange, the city is also (though only in Italy) the administrative center of a territory that, whether large or small, depends on the city in matters of governance, productivity, and culture. For this reason, the city is a decisive element in the interpretive model we are proposing here, since it represents the surrounding territory, and, in a more or less direct and often violent way, it appropriates the area's material resources and culture, including its culinary traditions, adopting them, exporting them, and perpetuating their use. Italy's culinary heritage is usually asserted and recognized through references to city-based identities. This is evident not only in the names of elaborate recipes and food preparations that were devised in urban settings, in the workshops of culinary artisans or, more recently, in industrial establishments (Cremona relish and Neapolitan spaghetti, for example) but also in the names of products originating in the countryside, the mountains, and the sea. When we speak of Treviso chicory, Bitonto oil, Ravenna turbot, Messina swordfish, Sorrento walnuts, or the ewe's-milk cheese called *pecorino romano*, we are highlighting marketing centers rather than the areas where these foods are actually produced. It is understandable that the most successful "typical" products in the history of Italian food are those with the strongest industrial support (we have only to think of pasta, Parmesan cheese, and tomato sauce). These, in effect, are the products that travel best. "Exporting the territory" may seem a provocative expression, but it is clearly an essential key to understanding the history of Italian food down through the centuries. In our account of this history, the city and the surrounding countryside play leading roles, but so does the perception of a common national point of reference. The internal articulations of this model, made up of the urban center, the outlying countryside, and the broader political and cultural territory, can alone convey the complexity of the inventory of dishes and food products, without destroying it. The rural estate functioned as the gateway to the city residence, and in the eyes of the peasants it represented the style of genteel, urban living. In addition to providing increased familiarity with fish and game products, the estate offered peasants opportunities for managing and preserving foodstuffs, as well as experience in raising livestock and growing garden products.

Of how many geographical areas is Italy composed? What are its internal and external boundaries? We will propose a fresh perspective on these questions. Or at least we will offer a few tools to achieve it by pinpointing the complex origins of dishes and food products and by rejecting some commonly held beliefs. We will have to put aside for the moment, at least with respect to the entire span of history preceding the contemporary period, the broader "regional" dimension of the culinary legacy so often stressed today. This is in fact a very recent phenomenon on the cultural and political level, and by its very nature it is foreign to the internal concerns of culinary history. A gastronomic map of Italy must therefore deconstruct or incorporate the administrative divisions of the land, shaping them into more culturally homogeneous and meaningful units.

The dynamic relationship of city and province brings us to another issue that we wish to take into account in this volume: the relationship between the culture of the masses and that of the elite, between "poor" and "rich" culinary traditions. There is no doubt, as we will try to show, that an intense exchange of information and techniques took place between the two social and economic planes. The horizontal exchange that assigns the city the most important role in the diffusion of the culinary culture of the area is constantly supported by a vertical exchange (between the world of the countryside and that of the city) that constitutes its necessary precondition. This obviously involves agricultural production and the raising of livestock, but it also involves recipes.

Only a hasty, preconceived image of so-called subaltern culture can lead us to believe that elaborate culinary preparation is the exclusive prerogative of the ruling classes. Inventiveness thrives not only in circumstances of power and wealth but also in poverty and necessity. At bottom, the most fascinating aspect of studying culinary history is the discovery of how ordinary people, with their physical effort and imagination, sought to transform the pangs of hunger and the anxieties of poverty into potential moments of pleasure. The techniques devised in times of famine to render edible even the smallest, most basic resources of the land—the ability to make bread out of wild berries and grape seeds, recounted in so many medieval and modern chronicles, or to concoct a soup with roots from the underbrush and herbs from the ditches—all clearly testify to the difficulties of people whose daily lives were constantly threatened by the outbreak of catastrophe. But they also bear witness to the mental resources of a population capable of believing in the future even in times of great hardship, armed mainly with experience, ability, and imagination—or, in a word, with *culture*. In an account of the terrible famine that afflicted Italy in 1338, we read: "The poor were eating thistles cooked with salt and wild herbs. They would cut weeds and the roots of milk thistles and cook them with mint."[3] How can we deny that this qualifies as culinary art? It is unquestionably a kind of gastronomy based on hunger, one that is not devoid of rules and norms suggested by common knowledge and somehow codified by collective practices. The *Chronicon Parmense* informs us that not even during the famine of 1246, when bread was made from linseed and yet deemed "excellent," did the people of Parma choose to go without their beloved *torta*, a culinary genre then at the height of fashion. Still, they had to make do with cooking it almost devoid of filling, piling one scantily filled layer on top of the other, along with some roots and greens: "People would make their pies with a couple of crusts, or maybe four or five."[4]

The theme of hunger does not belong exclusively to the distant past, even if it appears today in a different guise. Observing the dietary behavior of Italians, one might assume that caloric deficiency was an episodic phenomenon, occurring on the margins of society and linked to shortages that cannot be ascribed to production or distribution. Nevertheless, the first half of the twentieth century was characterized by phases of obligatory food restrictions linked to war—including an especially severe period from 1940 to 1946—euphemistically described as "rationing." The greatest disparities between need and availability of goods, involving millions of people, are recent. Paradoxically, these shortages mainly affected urban areas, the very places purportedly protected by reserves of food administered by public officials. In wartime cooking we find all the classic ingredients of the culture of hunger: the substitution of other items for agricultural produce, the retrieval of elements usually discarded, the careful use of leftovers, the revision of recipes based on diminished resources, as well as the observance of formal rituals and rules of presentation. But we must add to these characteristics the constant presence of culinary concerns. In fact, the war years witnessed the continuous publication of recipe books or guides to the best use of ration books and of the few foodstuffs available in the marketplace. These publications were designed to make poverty bearable and to teach people how to transcend it with ingenuity. Lack of food, vitamin deficiencies, malnutrition, and chronic shortages are elements pertaining to a history that we unhesitatingly call contemporary, marked by severe economic recessions and the policies of war. All these elements have had an influence on the compensatory quality of the culinary models that have emerged over the past fifty years. The human stomach has a memory. We will therefore add some additional information pertinent to the construction of a history of the appetite.

The traces of a culinary tradition that came into being in the face of hunger are abundantly evident even in patterns of elite consumption and in recipe books of haute cuisine. They can be observed above all in techniques for the long-term preservation of foods, perhaps the primary culinary value discernible among the poor (where there the quest for security prevails). But more generally there are many products, recipes, and flavors in the culinary tradition that enable us to identify an aftertaste of the customs of ordinary people, despite the supposed ideological oppositions between the food of the rich and the food of the poor, a distinction that has been fundamental to the collective imagination down through the centuries. A slight adjustment in culinary forms, usages, and accompaniments suffices to reveal an insurmountable class difference: when garlic is mixed with costly oriental spices, its image as a peasant flavor will be profoundly modified. When the humble potato is enhanced by a prestigious butter sauce, who would recognize the original character of this tuber linked to dramatic tales of famine and regarded as animal fodder? And again when a dish essential to the caloric balance of the peasant diet—such as polenta or soup—shows up on a menu as an accessory, intended to enhance something more refined and costly (a dish of roast game, for example), who can deny that this is merely a whimsical, folkloristic allusion to something that belongs to a different culture? Yet all this points to a systematic exchange of information between the different social levels. Echoes reverberate in the opposite direction as well. The reformulation of recipes at the "upper" social level transmits, enriches, and modifies their basic components and in turn conditions the behavior of the so-called lower classes through a process of imitation.

These phenomena are not easy to examine, given the diversity of agents and languages involved, but perhaps we can recognize the cook as a key player or pivot in the dynamics of intercultural exchange. Often hailing from the lower social strata, cooks work in proximity with the upper classes. They bring their own culture with them, reshaping it in response to the needs of others. Thus modified, they bring it back to the social environment from which they came. In the cities not only household cooks but also those who ran cookshops and bakeries frequented by a large portion of the public constituted a kind of filter between different cultures, offering an environment that favored exchange. In all these cases, as Rebora writes, with particular reference to the Middle Ages: "Rather than an invention of the upper classes, cooking is a need of the elite that is met thanks to the skill of the common people."[5] At least until the eighteenth century, moreover, class differences did not prevent the daily intermingling of members of the nobility, the bourgeoisie, and the lower classes, who may have been rigidly divided in terms of rights, privileges, and prerogatives but who rubbed shoulders with each other in residential buildings, in neighborhoods, and on city streets.

This exchange among socially diverse cultures was not limited to urban environments. It had a special place in the dynamic juxtaposition of city and countryside already emphasized above and in equally important contexts such as the feudal castle and its holdings during the High Middle Ages, the monastic settlement, and the *masseria*, the farming compound in the southern countryside.

The culinary identities of the rural areas, cities, and regions of Italy emerged over the course of the centuries through the process of these vertical and horizontal exchanges. As the outcome of historical circumstances, these identities were continually changing and constantly reformulated and redefined on the basis of new experiences. Though temporally, spatially, and socially diverse, they referred to a common experience, a single image—also the fruit of a slow process of development, of perpetual modification and revision—that we have no choice but to call "Italian." This is precisely how it is named in various documents, reflecting perceptions that go back at least as far as the High Middle Ages.

The Italian image can hardly be taken for granted. In a culinary repertory favoring designations such as "risotto *alla milanese*," "Florentine steak," and "Neapolitan pizza," the adjective "Italian," like the expression *"all'italiana"* (Italian-style), is not typically applied to the name of a dish, whether a pasta, a pastry, or any other kind of food. We thus realize that adjectives evoking nationality belong to an *outsider's* perspective, and it would be more natural for a foreigner in a foreign country to use the expression *"spaghetti all'italiana"* (Italian spaghetti) than for an Italian to do so.

The effects of exchange are especially evident today, insofar as the territorial range of the Italian culinary model stretches well beyond the nation's political borders. A country exists through its products, and some of Italy's cheeses have been replicated in Argentina since the second half of the nineteenth century.[6] Recipes from Italy are known and copied in homes and restaurants all over the world. Italian cuisine, while still embodying all the rich diversity of its origins, no longer requires an arduous search for authentic or imported ingredients, as these have long been available in the markets of major cities everywhere. Pizzas and pastas, the dishes on which this tradition built its foundation, are among its most recognizable signs, and they contribute to the creation of a coherent, unified image of Italy that becomes more pronounced the farther away one goes from Italy. Thus Italy truly exists thousands of miles from home, where it has an unmistakable identity, especially at the dining table.

"What is the glory of Dante compared to spaghetti?" Prezzolini wondered in 1954, noting that pastas had "entered many American homes where the name of Dante is never pronounced."[7] Reformulating this question today, its prophetic import becomes strikingly clear, along with the relevance of the debate on the notion of culinary identity. There is no paradox underlying the juxtaposition of the two commodities—Dante's poetry and the creations of the cook—but rather a new way of finding a point of contact among the innumerable elements that make up a particular civilization. Spaghetti and pizza belong to a legacy that has spread throughout the world, just as books have, but unlike books these foods are immediately recognizable and accessible to all. They represent a culture of commerce and craftsmanship, based on taste and manual skill, that reconstitutes a body of knowledge through imitation and an element of reminiscence, despite the distance from the place where this knowledge originated. Cooking is perhaps an unlettered art, but it also survives thanks to remembered knowledge—the memory of what has not been lost as well as what will be recorded in writing—and it is thus a civilizing force. Literary writers have no precedence over cooks, and neither do their artistic visions have any particular usefulness in matters of cooking. Yet their role is no less important than the cooks.' Along with the exchange of food products, dishes, and flavors, there is also an exchange of documents and recipes. This lively traffic has been going on since ancient times and is vital for good taste. In fact, without realizing it, when we eat spaghetti we also ingest something of Dante.

CHAPTER ONE

Italy: A Physical and Mental Space

Mare Nostrum

Sausages from Lucania, ham from the Marsica, wild boar from Tuscany and Umbria. Eels from Lake Garda and the Strait of Messina, bass from the Tiber, golden bream from Lake Lucrino, moray eel from the Strait, turbot from Ravenna, sea bream from Brindisi. Sea urchins and shellfish from the sea of Misena, from Altio and Taranto. Cheeses from the Vestini hills, from Trebula in Sabina, the distinctively large cheeses from Luni, the pyramid-shaped variety from Sarsia, as well as cheese from Ceba in Liguria. Turnips from Norcia, and rutabaga from Amiterno. Radishes from the Alban Hills, onions from Marsi and Pompeii, and the smaller, sweeter sort from Tuscolo. Asparagus from Pozzuoli as well as the cultivated variety from Ravenna. Cardoons from Sicily, leeks from Taranto and Ostia, tight-leafed cabbages from Ariccia, and the big, sharp-tasting cabbages from Bruzia, Cuma, and Pompeii. Broad beans from Marsica, lentils from Gela. Stuffed olives from Piceco. Venafro oil. Semola wheat from Campania. Bread and sweets from Piceno. Salt from Ostia. Wines from Piceno and the Sabine Hills, Sorrento and Falerno. . . .

We can scarcely accuse the writers of Ancient Rome, such as Cato, Columella, Pliny, Varro, Martial, Horace, and Perseus, of neglecting to tell us about the food products and culinary specialties of regions we would categorize today as Italian. The items just listed are merely the most famous among the many examples found in Latin literature.[1] Yet we cannot claim that the mental geography underlying these references corresponds to an idea of Italy. Place names are one thing; the myths embodied in the gastronomic culture of ancient Rome and in its ideological conception of food are quite another. The first of these myths was the Arcadian dream of domestic self-sufficiency (a little garden providing simple, frugal food), and the second, the idea of Rome as the center of the world, the universal marketplace that drew products from gardens far and wide and where every culinary resource, whether invented by humans or found in nature, could be located, purchased, and consumed. The first, Arcadian image denotes attachment to a local culinary culture, barely in contact with neighboring regions, those nearby Italic territories to which Rome could trace its roots. In a kind of inverted reflection, the other image sharply contrasted with this, evoking a world economy largely coinciding with the area around the Mediterranean, then the undisputed center of the known universe. For Plato, the Greeks were "like toads around a pond."[2] This was more or less true for the entire population of the Mediterranean basin. Mistress of the world at large, Rome insisted on forging a link among all these people, effectively turning the sea—*mare nostrum* (our sea)—into a lake.

During the years of the Roman Empire, the Mediterranean was a formidable melting pot of different cultures and their diverse culinary traditions. It embraced all the diversity within reach and dispatched it onto a circuit of exchange that ultimately wound up in the capital, a gigantic commercial emporium and extraordinary center of consumption. Cultural and territorial identities did not disappear during the empire. Rome respected and absorbed them all, without bothering to construct new identities. The politically compact "Italy" of Roman times remained consistently outside the scope of this unifying principle. Indeed, Rome never identified itself with the land that had witnessed its birth but "preferred the empire to Italy."[3]

From the Mediterranean to Europe

Europe gradually came into being as a cultural and geographical concept in the High Middle Ages, thanks to the confluence of Roman and Germanic cultures, which had been diametrically opposed to each other up to that time. From the culinary viewpoint, these cultures were very different and may even have seemed incompatible. While the ideology of the Romans, based on the Greek model, continued to regard wheat, grapes, and the olive tree as instruments and symbols of an agricultural and urban civilization, the Germanic population maintained close links to the forests, on which they relied for most of their food, obtained through hunting, gathering, and raising livestock. The culture of bread, wine, and olive oil clashed with the culture of meat, milk (or beer, at best), and butter, which implied a different balance between humans and their environment, a different way of conceptualizing and using the land.[4]

For a long time, these dietary models were indicators of two different civilizations, one of which—the Roman—despised the other, considering it inferior and "barbaric." But when the "Barbarians" invaded the empire and gradually took it over, grasping the reins of power, their culture—culinary habits included—prevailed and finally became fashionable, as always happens with the customs of conquerors (exemplified by the triumph of the American way of life in the twentieth century). Hunting game and raising livestock were no longer considered uncivilized or undesirable activities. On the contrary, these now became the mainstay of the economy. At the same time, the Roman agricultural tradition spread among the so-called Barbarians, both by virtue of the prestige it still commanded and through the practice of the Christian faith,

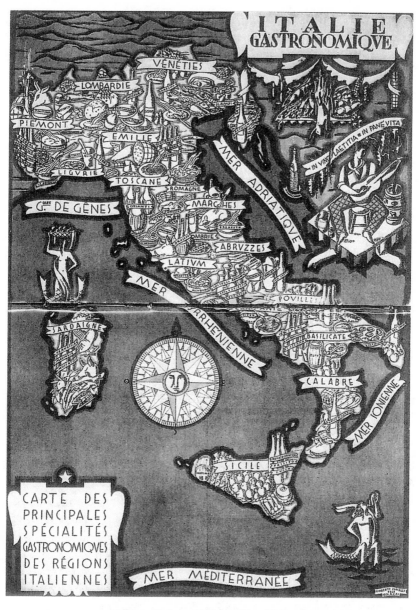

Culinary Italy by Umberto Zimelli (1931).

Source: L'albergo in Italia (Milan: Touring Club Italiano, 1932).

which was also gaining ground, having become fashionable during the early Middle Ages. It was not at all by chance that Christianity, which grew out of a Mediterranean culture, had adopted as its own alimentary symbols the bread, wine, and oil of the Greco-Roman tradition. (The first two became Eucharistic symbols and the third an instrument of sacramental anointing.)

During the Middle Ages, a new food culture was born from the encounter of these diverse influences. Now recognized as European, the new culture placed bread on the same level as meat and agriculture on a par with animal husbandry. The two dietary models no longer denoted opposing options but different components of the same value system. Bread, wine, and meat (especially pork, the primary player in the economy of the forest) were the main elements constituting this new identity. Liturgical obligations brought about the rest, requiring all Christians to rotate the consumption of "fat" and "lean" at different times of the year or days of the week, thus accelerating the fusion of the two culinary systems through the practice of alternating specific types of foods and flavors (meats, fish, and vegetables, lard, oil, and butter) on the dinner table at all latitudes of the continent.

The new alimentary culture did not emerge only through a process of accumulation that reflected the encounter of the Roman-Christian and Germanic cultures. It also defined itself through exclusion. By this time, on the southern shores of the Mediterranean, the non-Christian world constituted by Islam had developed a different dietary tradition. Muslims excluded wine and pork from their diet, regarding them as impure, but they allowed bread. In Islamic culture, however, bread was just one among many foods and was devoid of the special symbolic meanings it had accrued in Christian regions. As a result of these circumstances, a change occurred in culinary habits and patterns of consumption, and the cultural unity of the Mediterranean—which the Romans had constructed by sheer force—ultimately collapsed.

The *mare nostrum* thus became a maritime frontier, though traffic between one shore and the other did not completely cease.[5] Saracen pirates never blocked the transportation of merchandise from the Orient to Europe. Indeed, thanks in part to the Arabs, use of the eastern trade route increased during the High Middle Ages, as we will show in the following chapters, citing some important examples. After the Crusaders set sail for the Holy Land toward the end of the eleventh century, maritime access to the Orient increased to a greater degree than ever before. What occurred in fact was the expansion or strengthening of existing routes, facilitating European access to goods produced in distant lands. Venice, which had already become the principal gateway for trade with the Orient, functioned as a center of distribution from which precious Oriental merchandise—spices and all other products—were dispatched to the heart of the continent. Thus, while goods traveled *across* the Mediterranean, they were ultimately destined for points *beyond* its shores.

To be sure, the southern regions of Europe continued to manifest a specifically Mediterranean character. The age-old melting pot is vividly evoked in a twelfth-century account by John of Salisbury. Here, while attempting to characterize the ostentatious excesses of the wealthy classes of his time, the writer recalls a banquet he attended at the home of an Apulian merchant, where guests were offered "the finest products from Constantinople, Babylon, Alexandria, Palestine, Tripoli, Syria, and Phoenicia, as though the products of Sicily, Calabria, Apulia, and Campania were insufficient to adorn such a refined banquet."[6] Furthermore, southern tastes and cooking customs never fully adapted to the habits of the continent. What made the cuisines of the south special and diverse was in fact their proximity to the Arab world, which, following its expansion into Sicily and Spain during the Middle Ages, included significant portions of Europe. But these Arab influences soon penetrated all of continental Europe also, giving rise to a system of food preferences that eventually characterized the whole of Europe, including England and Germany. The dominant element in this system was the culinary tradition of the south, a tradition already mixed with northern influences (we have only to remember the presence of the Visigoths in Spain or the Lombards, and later the Normans, in Mediterranean Italy). In short, despite the stubborn persistence of older models, a new mental and economic balance was clearly beginning to take shape in the Middle Ages, a new cultural space that we have already described as European.

Naturally, this space coincides mainly with the culinary practices of the elite. The inevitably local character of rural consumption was juxtaposed with the cosmopolitan tendencies of the European gastronomic scene (and would continue to be for centuries), yielding a sort of culinary international Gothic style still in evidence, despite the changes occurring in the interval, in the recipe books that appeared more or less throughout the continent toward the end of the Middle Ages.

From Europe to Italy

Within Europe, *after* the emergence of Europe, diverse languages, cultures, and "nations"—including Italy—gradually emerged. Italy established its identity in a very clear and relatively rapid manner, despite many contradictions. The fact that the country was not entirely a new invention facilitated this process. At least in the geographical sense, some concept of Italy had existed from antiquity, and this was maintained or reinforced in the course of the Middle Ages, partly because of the disintegration of the numerous roads the Romans forged through the Alps—increasingly perceived as the natural boundary of a physical entity to the south, which was "naturally" cut off and protected by the mountains. Early medieval writers adopted the imperial concept of "Ytalia," a land divided into provinces, roughly corresponding to the model envisaged by the Romans. Elements linked to dietary and culinary heritage were certainly present in the delineation of this territory. In the sixth-century, when Narses, a Byzantine general, asked the Lombards to leave Pannonia for Italy, he enticed them with descriptions of a fertile land, sending his ambassadors with "samples of the types of fruit and other produce that Italy can offer in abundance."[7] Yet this Italy is essentially a geographical space, occasionally identified with political entities, such as the *Regnum Italiae*, which coincided only in part with the physical territory of the peninsula. It was not until the middle years of the medieval period, beginning around the eleventh or twelfth century, that the earliest signs of a real, consciously perceived identity began to emerge, an identity that was no longer determined merely by territorial belonging but by a common sentiment, a kind of solidarity based on culture and a way of life. As Le Goff puts it, "the political and mental realities of the Italian Middle Ages have to do with Italians and not simply Italy."[8] Salimbene of Parma, a monk and chronicler, had something similar in mind when he observed in the thirteenth century that "the red wines of Auxerre are not as good as our Italian wines."[9]

Even as late as the fourteenth century, recipe collections still seem driven more by a "European" than an "Italian" logic. The names used to describe dishes, in the few cases where names appear, refer to Teutonic or Hispanic usage or to France or England (not to mention dishes that are clearly of Arabic provenance) no less often that they invoke local customs from the Italian peninsula. Yet local references are certainly present (and are much more specific than other references), bringing to light regional and urban realities that imply a pattern of mutual familiarity and exchange. The oldest book on Italian cuisine, the *Liber de coquina*, which is thought to have been written in Naples at the end of the thirteenth century, offers a recipe for "Roman-style" cabbage (*ad usum romanorum*), a recipe for "small leaves" prepared in the "Campanian manner" (*ad usum campanie*)—probably another cabbage dish—and another for beans "in the style of the Marca di Treviso." In addition, we find an Apulian "*simula*," a Genoese "*tria*," a Parmesan pie or "*torta*" (a term to which we will return), and a "*compositum lonbardicum*," indicating the relish we know today as *mostarda di Cremona*.[10] Comparative allusions are plentiful, giving the references a striking authority. On one occasion, having described a German-style *compositum*, the author of the text notes that "according to the Lombards you can add *gambussi* to the mix," perhaps referring to *cappuccio* cabbages.[11] Other fourteenth-century recipe writers mention a Roman "*pastello*,"[12] a Lavagna pie, and salt from Sardinia or, alternatively, Chioggia.[13]

How much importance should we attribute to these designations? We must admit that in many cases we are dealing with names given to mark a special occasion or to honor an individual, with little significance on the culinary level. It is quite possible, for instance, that "Lavagna pie" does not refer to a culinary preparation originating in the Ligurian town of Lavagna but to a dish thus named to celebrate the ascent of Sinibaldo Fieschi, count of Lavagna, to the papal throne. Giovanni Rebora has argued this point persuasively, carefully noting the more or less explicit Guelph or Ghibelline allusions that can be discerned in the titles of medieval recipes.[14] In other cases, however, the geographical designation seems more closely related to the culinary context. Yet

Celebration by the people of Rome (Urbino faience, 1560–1565).

this is not the preeminent issue here; more important is the fact that such denominations (above and beyond their actual meaning) demonstrate that people generally believed in the existence of local specialties. As Flandrin notes, "leaving aside the question of the originality of national and regional cuisines, it is clear that people distinguished them from each other."[15] It is also clear that, within the broader European idiom, there was a special emphasis on the "Italian" dimension of gastronomic culture in its multiple local variants.

We can confirm that this local culture was in some sense widely shared and that this effectively meant the birth of an "Italian cuisine"—understood as a common framework of exchange among different realities—not simply by studying the names of the recipes but, more importantly, by observing that these texts *circulated* throughout the Italian peninsula, emanating from the two principal areas of influence: the Angevin kingdom of Naples and the city-states of Tuscany.

The *Liber de coquina*, capstone of Italian gastronomic literature, was almost certainly written in Naples toward the end of the thirteenth or the beginning of the fourteenth century. As was pointed out by Marianne Mulon,[16] who was the first to publish the manuscript, there should be no doubt regarding its "southern" character.[17] Mulon's claim is further supported by the careful research carried out by L. Sada and V. Valente, which is based on formal aspects of the text (such as the many linguistic elements that belong to the "basic dialect pattern common to southern Italy," with a particular prevalence of Neapolitan and Apulian examples) in addition to its contents (the recipes and ingredients that we will discuss in the following chapter).[18] This does not take away from the fact that the text is the expression of a syncretistic culture, international in character, of the kind that was emerging in Europe at the time and that in this case proved particularly sensitive to the Arabic influences of southern Italy. Derived from this work, with adjustments that generally take into account different regional realities, are the *Libro della cocina* of an anonymous Tuscan, which was compiled toward the end of the fourteenth century,[19] and numerous other variants that Bruno Laurioux patiently sought out in various European archives, arriving at the conclusion that "the *Liber de coquina* was used in its diverse incarnations from the end of the fifteenth century onward and achieved renown all over Italy and abroad, in France and Germany."[20] The success of this cookbook on a broad European level may also be attributed to the fact that it was written in the international language of Latin. With regard to Italy, the extent of its dissemination over time and space is the sign—and partly the channel—of a gastronomic culture that, though hardly uniform, was widely shared.

The same is true for the second family of thirteenth- and fourteenth-century recipe collections, the first example of which is a text compiled around 1338 or 1339, probably in Siena.[21] This book did not emerge in a courtly, aristocratic environment, as had occurred with the Neapolitan *Liber*, but was compiled in a city-state with a strong bourgeois character—though this adjective must be used with caution when applied to a social context such as that of the city-states of medieval Italy, where families of the traditional nobility shared the exercise of political power and cultural influence with members of the burgeoning middle classes involved in commerce, trades, and the professions. But it is very important to note that, unlike the recipes that originated at the Angevin court in Naples, which were aimed explicitly at an audience of aristocrats, or *signori*,[22] those of Tuscan derivation address a group of friends. These men, known as the "Twelve Gluttons" ("XII gentili homini giotissimi," "XII ricchi goditori") are frequently invoked in the recipes, where there is a special emphasis on the notion of wealth, an emphasis that does not seem characteristic of the traditional nobility but rather of the new, moneyed elite.[23] It is not the court but the private home that constitutes the reference point in this second group of texts. Equally significant is the precision (completely bourgeois in terms of quantity, costs, and previsions) with which the texts specify the amounts of ingredients in each recipe. The *Liber de coquina* and the recipe collections that derive from it by contrast never bother to mention particulars of this kind but offer sketchy instructions that presuppose the ability to consult professionals rather than domestic cooks or perhaps even individuals who are simply curious or interested in the subject (such characters, avid readers of culinary manuscripts, appear in other sources, such as short stories).[24] Unlike the recipe collections of the earlier compilers, those of the subsequent group were never disseminated outside Italy. Yet they remained in circulation over a longer period of time—until as late as the sixteenth century[25]—and reached all parts of the peninsula, from Tuscany to Bologna, from Liguria to the Veneto (if we include a version written in Venetian dialect), and even the southernmost regions of Italy.[26]

Le fait de la cuisine, an important recipe collection compiled by Maître Chiquart, a cook at the royal court of Savoy in the fifteenth century,[27] merits separate consideration. Even if it functioned as a bridge between the cultures of Italy and France, it belongs to the French circuit, and its dissemination was extraneous to the "Italian" pattern of distribution that characterized the other recipe books. We shall in fact see how long Piedmont was destined to remain marginal to the historical development of Italian cuisine.

The Fifteenth-Century Definition of the "Italian" Model

By the second half of the fifteenth century the Italy evoked in culinary texts was already clearly delineated. This was in fact the mental map on which Maestro Martino de Rossi worked. Martino—the earliest important signature in the history of Italian cooking—compiled Il libro de arte coquinaria, a recipe collection that marks a genuine, qualitative leap in content rather than form with respect to the preceding culinary literature. Born in the Blenio valley of Ticino, Martino's work gives voice to an interregional culture spanning the entire peninsula. Working first in Lombardy at the courts of Francesco Sforza and Lodovico Trevisani, he later moved to Rome, where he was employed by the Patriarch of Aquileia. Finally, toward the end of his career, he moved back to the north, where he worked for the condottiere Gian Giacomo Trivulzio. Maestro Martino may also have worked in Naples for a time. According to some writers, it was here that that he developed his professional skills,[28] which would explain the frequency of southern elements found in his cuisine and, particularly, a certain Catalan influence (which others explain simply as due to the "culinary cosmopolitanism" of the papal court).[29] In any case, Maestro Martino's Libro— probably written in Rome between 1464 and 1465 and updated in subsequent versions, the manuscripts of which have fortunately survived[30]—has a strong, interregional character, making a decisive contribution to the definition of an "Italian" model of cooking. The collection continued to circulate until the middle of the sixteenth century and then disappeared, or at least seemed to disappear, since in the meantime a "Frenchman" named Giovanni de' Roselli (iden-

tified by some as a person who really existed and by others as a publishers' invention)[31] took advantage of the recent invention of the printing press to plagiarize
Martino's text, publishing it with the new title *Opera nova chiamata Epulario*
(The new work called Epulario). This was an enormous commercial success: as
many as twenty-two editions had appeared in print by the middle of the seventeenth century.

Completely focused on elaborating a methodology of cooking by describing
strategies of selection and modes of preparation, Martino's text, however, makes
few explicit references to specific regional or urban traditions. He notes only a
small number of "Roman" recipes (*coppiette*, cabbages, *maccaroni*) and Florentine dishes (eggs), along with a "Bolognese *torta*," a "Sienese *torta*," and—in
just one of the surviving manuscripts—a group of specialties described as
Genoese (*piperata*, macaroni, squash, mushrooms, and a pie of spinach and
onions).[32]

In the work of the humanist writer Bartolomeo Sacchi, also known as "Il
Platina," we find a greater number of references to local recipes and still more
to local products. This writer knew Martino when he worked in Rome and probably collaborated with him in drafting the *Libro*. He later produced his own
treatise, *De honesta voluptate et valetudine* (On honest pleasure and good
health). On a strictly culinary level, this book makes direct, explicit reference to
Martino.[33] Platina's work is nonetheless of a different character, because it
places the recipes in a broader cultural and scientific context, emphasizing the
role that each food might occupy in the culinary "system" from the point of view
of diet as well as that of hospitality. His attention thus shifts toward the food
products, and he provides us with numerous, systematic references to local realities. It is here that his mentality seems unmistakably "Italian" in its cultural outlook, as it refers to personal experiences and circuits of commercial exchange
spanning the entire peninsula. His geographical references include in particular the areas that he knew directly: the Po Valley, his place of origin (he was born
in Cremona), and the area of central Italy where he worked, which included
Tuscany and the Papal States. But he also lists specialties from other areas such
as Liguria, Campania, Piceno, Apulia, and Sicily. He includes perch from Lake
Maggiore, sardines and the characteristic *carpione* from Lake Garda, grayling
from the Adda, Padua hens, olives from Bologna and Piceno, turbot from
Ravenna, rudd from Lake Trasimeno, carrots from Viterbo, bass from the Tiber,
roviglioni and shad from Lake Albano, Rieti snails, Tuscolo figs, grapes from
Narni, oil from Cassino, oranges from Naples, and moray from the Strait.
Among the grains mentioned are foxtail from Lombardy and millet from Cam-
pania. He also speaks of honey from Sicily and Taranto and of Sicilian sugar.
The wines he mentions include the classical Falerno variety and wines of the
Ligurian coast; Greco from Tuscany (San Gimignano) and San Severino
(Lucrini Hills); Trebbiano, also from Tuscany; and Piceno.

Sometimes his references are derived from classical authors—for a humanist such as Platina to omit these would be unthinkable—but even here the information is updated and embellished with comments revealing his direct knowledge and experience. When speaking of cabbage, for example, Platina alludes to Cato, who distinguishes three kinds, including one described as Appian, "which could be compared to the Zeviana variety that flourishes in the area around Verona, as well as the variety from Capranica."[34]

His use of comparisons is especially telling. On lampreys, he writes: "The lampreys caught in Cisalpine Italy are small, in Tuscany they are of medium size, and those caught in the Tiber in Rome are larger than the Tuscan variety" (p. 237). He claims that the value of particular cheeses depends on their place of origin and on the herds providing the milk. In Italy, "two kinds of cheese compete for first place: Marzolino, as it is named by Tuscans, and Parmesan from the Cisalpine regions." He asserts that salt must be "as white and as pure as the salt from Volterra in Tuscany" (p. 22), and, on the subject of chestnuts, he notes: "In the past, chestnuts from Taranto were regarded as preferable to others, but now the Milanese variety has become fashionable" (p. 247).

Platina's observations on specific local customs are also interesting. In describing how to prepare bread, he specifies that after the flour is placed on the pastry board, the cook should form a well in the center, "sealed off by a kind of bank surrounding it on all sides," and should pour hot, salted water into it, "as the people of Ferrara tend to do" (p. 23). On the subject of millet, he writes: "Polenta is made from millet, as is a variety of sweet bread prepared mainly in the Cisalpine region" (p. 147). In discussing the condiments used to flavor vegetables, he notes: "To counteract the chill of cucumber, some cooks sprinkle powdered spice on top. Tuscans, who are particularly fond of fruit and green vegetables, eagerly consume serpentine cucumber flavored with nothing more than a dash of salt" (pp. 27–28). There are also observations on local linguistic usage. Platina notes that the conger eel (*gronco*) is called "*bronco*" by the people of Anzio (p. 240), that "*bulbari*" is the term used for carp in the dialect of Mantua (p. 241), and so on.

"Lists of Things . . . Generally Used in Italy"

In the introduction to the fourth book of his monumental *Opera*, published in Venice in 1570, Bartolomeo Scappi explains that the volume is devoted to "lists of things that can be served from month to month, which are generally used in Italy, especially in the city of Rome." As the private cook of Pope Pius V, Scappi worked in Rome, which was not only the capital of Christianity but still, even at this juncture, the capital of the food market. No longer as universal as it had been during the years of the Roman Empire, the city's market was now solidly centered on the products of the Italian peninsula. Rome effectively meant Italy, and the gastronomic Italy that emerges from a careful reading of the several hundred pages of Scappi's densely packed recipe collection is an economic and cultural entity that is extraordinarily compact and homogeneous. Scappi's far-reaching vision is reflected not only in the detailed "lists" in the fourth volume but in the *Opera* as a whole. While emphasizing the comparative approach already proposed by Platina, he delineates an almost fully realized image of the "Italian" culinary heritage, which is consciously perceived as such and thus communicated to the reader. Scappi's identity was not established with certainty for many years. At various junctures during this period he was said to be from Venice, Bologna, and Lombardy; however, the recent discovery of a commemorative stone in the church of Runo di Dumuenza on Lake Maggiore seems to lend credibility to the last hypothesis.[35] The very fact that his identity could not be ascertained from his writings testifies to the pluralistic quality of his cultural formation, his ability to look in all directions and to absorb different traditions and customs, amalgamating and reshaping them all to a certain degree.

There are three Italies in Scappi's work: "Lombardy" (meaning the Po Valley), Italy of the Grand Duchies and the papacy, and, finally, "the Kingdom" (the south, along with Sicily). In accordance with a typically Italian perspective, three cities sum up the gastronomic culture of these different areas: Milan (many recipes described as "*alla lombarda*" are alternately named "*alla milanese*"), Rome, and Naples (in this case, the terms "Neapolitan" and "of the Kingdom" ("*del Regno*") are used interchangeably. But Venice also has a significant role, and Scappi shows that he is familiar with Venetian cuisine and knows the food market in Venice from personal experience. Other front-runners (Florence, Genoa, and some of the smaller cities) complete the picture of the territorially and culturally diversified Italy to which Scappi constantly refers, forcing himself to understand, and especially to compare and contrast, its diverse elements as well as to identify its points of communality. This is evident even at the linguistic level: "To make different kinds of *crostate* [pie dough], called *coppi* by the Neapolitans and *sfogliati* by the Lombards."[36] Bass, he writes, "is known by different names in different places. In Venice the term *varoli* is used, in Genoa *lupi*, in Rome *spigoli*, and in Pisa and Florence *ragni*" (chap. 112). But Scappi is mainly concerned with dietary and culinary usage. For example, in a paragraph devoted to the best ways to evaluate "the quality of cheeses, of both the fresh and aged varieties," he explains that the best varieties of fresh cheese come from Tuscany "and these are named *raviggioli*," although in Milan a "creamy cheese" imported from "Germanic areas" is "not unworthy of consideration." Among salted cheeses, "such as Parmesan, the cheese from the Riviera [Liguria], and the Marzolino varieties from Tuscany," he pronounces those produced from March to June to be the best. Less preferable in Scappi's opinion are the *casci cavalli* "brought to Rome from the Kingdom of Naples." These, he suggests, should be eaten fresh, "when they are as delicious as fresh Provatura." Scappi makes abundant use of fresh Provatura in his recipe collection, where it features among the ingredients for a large number of dishes. Among salted cheeses, he suggests using Parmesan with similar frequency. Finally, there is one mention of "the type of cheese that we call *sardesco*," which "should be firm, and white on the inside" (chaps. 5v–6r).

We find an important variation on Scappi's vertical perception of the peninsula in his opposition of east and west. This is especially important in his gastronomic commentary on fish, which often prompts him to compare the Adriatic and the Tyrrhenian, the two seas that flank the peninsula from north to south. In a discussion of cuttlefish, for example, Scappi asserts that "one can find a better type in the Adriatic than in the Tyrrhenian" (chap. 125v). Speaking of ray, he observes that "many are caught in the Adriatic and are better than those found in the sea near Rome" (chap. 121v). He also compares the oysters found in the Adriatic near Ancona and Chioggia with those from around the coast of Corsica (chap. 142r–v). Yet whenever freshwater fish is discussed the vertical model of comparison reappears. Scappi writes that the tench "brought to Milan from Lake Maggiore and Lake Como are very large in size, but those transported to Rome from Tagliacozzo and from the lakes of Vico and Santa Preseda are considered the best," with the exception of those caught in rivers, particularly the Tiber and the Po, which are deemed the very best of all (chap. 132).

Scappi claims that the trout "from Sora and Arpino are good but tend to have a blackish color, while those caught in the Tesino and the Tiber are white but really perfect, and those found in Lake Maggiore and Lake Como are very large" (chap. 127v). Still on the subject of trout he offers a comparison between the preparation favored by Milanese cooks and the method adopted "by ourselves, the cooks of Rome" (chaps. 127v–128r). With regard to freshwater crayfish, he tells us that "in some parts of Italy these are very big, in Milan extremely so and similarly in the countryside near Brescia and Verona. In the river Silo, which runs through Treviso and throughout that area, they are much bigger than anywhere else," and yet "those caught at the Salaria Bridge in Rome" are also very good (chap. 140v).

Scappi also provides information on the fish market (frequently comparing the markets of Venice, Milan, and Rome) and on the trade of cured or preserved foods: "various kinds of salted fish, preserved in leaves, either smoked, air-dried, or stored in brine." Among these are Lake Garda carp, which are fried, then marinated in salt and vinegar (a technique to which the term "*accarpionato*" is applied), and, "preserved in this manner for several days," they are "transported to different places throughout Italy." He adds that one may apply a similar preparation to the fish known as *temere*, "which are caught mainly in the Adda and the Lambro, as well as to shad caught in Lake Como and other locations," which "are transported all over Italy" after they have been preserved in salt (chap. 129r–v). He tells us that while shad are transported "preserved in barrels with rough salt," sardines "are caught in the sea around Genoa, salted in barrels of brine, and brought to different places in Italy" (chap. 149v). The same is true of Comacchio eels, since Comacchio "is surrounded by saltwater flats, and [the eels] caught there are very numerous and better than in any other part of Lombardy. These are preserved in salt and brought to all parts of Italy" (chap. 136r). Buca and arientino fish by contrast "are [fried, marinated in oil, and] transported from Genoa to several places in Italy" (chap. 146r). Other fish are simply preserved in oil, though this method seems mainly intended for local consumption: "In the Sabine countryside and around Aquila and Tagliacozzo, fish is often preserved in oil, and especially tench. These are kept in salt for about three days, depending on their size, then rinsed in wine and finally placed whole in oil-filled jars" (chap. 148v).

The list of products Scappi's recipes and menus name according to origin is quite extensive. In addition to fish,[37] it includes various kinds of fine fresh meats,[38] types of specialized cured meats,[39] cheeses,[40] vegetables,[41] fruit,[42] baked goods,[43] and even some grains.[44] In all cases, he is speaking of products that were destined to travel. This may involve the transportation of live animals from their place of origin, or the controlled ripening of fruit or vegetables, or the delivery of semifresh milk products or genuine preserves. In each case, the market constitutes the underlying structure of this gastronomic culture, ensuring the circulation of resources and the exchange of local identities.

Clearly, the existence of this market also facilitated the transmission and circulation of the recipes and culinary customs found in Scappi's work. Once again, it was not a question of inventing a cuisine that would be the same for everyone. Just as there are no "Italian" *products* (among the resources mentioned in the *Opera*, we find only one "Italian" reference: a type of barley found "in the Italian world" that is described as distinct in its culinary use from "German barley"), there is no "Italian" cuisine. What we see instead is the encounter of different traditions within a single circuit of exchange. Among the many hundreds of recipes furnished by Scappi, only one is defined as *all'italiana*: "pieces of grayling in broth, Italian style," suggested as a dish for the second cooked course in a summer dinner menu (chap. 225) Aside from this exception, it is clear that "Italy" was the sum of many local realities, the dominant *koiné* invoked in various dialects or languages (and cuisines): when a meal was followed by theatrical entertainment—as occurred on a late-February evening described by Scappi—performances were given in the languages "of France, Bergamo, Venice, and Spain" (chap. 304). Similarly, recipes representing various culinary "dialects" are presented in Scappi's *Opera*, one by one.

Most of Scappi's recipes reflect his Lombard origins, such as "Lombard soup," "Lombard rice," and "*tomacelle* sausages in broth, Milanese style." Other recipes described as "Lombard" or "Milanese" are a soup of *tortelletti* with herbs; a soup of turnip greens (to be served, however, "without the broth but covered with *agliata* sauce, as is done in Lombardy"); fried frogs, also topped with garlic sauce, and "*nosella*, Milanese style"; *offelle* (sweet scalloped pastries) made of puff pastry dough; *offelle* filled with almond paste; *torte* with herb filling; "stewed, stuffed *panciette* of veal"; stuffed *tortiglioni*; stuffed "pasta tubes"; ravioli soup; ravioli with a thin layer of dough; stuffed breast of suckling veal; large stuffed capons; large stuffed geese; "frittered" eggs; large pieces of trout in wine; and *nosetti* pies. What prevails here is the image of a type of Lombard cuisine where filled or stuffed dishes—meats, *torte*, or noodles—have a central role or at least are perceived as especially distinctive by the writer who identifies them, and this is an issue to which we will return.

Recipes "in the Venetian style" constitute another important group in Scappi's work. Here fish dishes dominate: grayling, bass, turbot "in pottage," and small stuffed squid in fish broth. We also find turnip soup, *brisavoli* made from veal cutlets, braised loin of beef (from the *seccaticcia* ox), fritters made of milk and eggs, marzipan *caliscioni*, and cinnamon cakes.

Genoese food is well represented. Indeed, given the quantity of references to the area around Genoa in the cookbooks of the sixteenth and seventeenth century, this city seems to have been much more important in Italian cultural history than scholars have traditionally assumed. In addition to *carpione* (fried fish marinated in oil, vinegar, and herbs), Scappi mentions Genoese macaroni, Genoese *gattafura*, and the quince-based confection known as *cotognata*.

The Emilian tradition is identified mainly with Bologna, the provincial capital. Recipes in the "Bolognese style" refer to tripe (from *seccaticcia* herds), pies filled with greens, and "*capi di latte*" (the dessert otherwise known as *panna cotta*). But Ferrara is also represented in recipes for tripe and *ginestrata* (a spiced egg soup), and Romagna is evoked in a recipe for *coppi*. Tuscany, which coincides with Florence and always implies the use of eggs, makes an appearance in recipes for omelets and "*ritortole* prepared with eggs." In addition to the egg dishes, there is a recipe for fried spinach "*alla fiorentina*." The Marche region appears in a recipe for "cooked ducks and ducklings," and Umbria in a recipe for "tench, Perugia style."

Rome, Scappi's adopted home, features in a broad array of culinary preparations: meat loaves, macaroni, "*cominata*," cabbage (imported from Milan or Bologna but cooked "in the Roman style"), pancakes of "stripped fish," meringues made with pine nuts, and *zeppole* (fritters made from chickpea flour). But the Neapolitan tradition is present as well, remembered for its "puff pastry shells filled with squab meat," "cabbage soup with mortadella," macaroni, and a dish of "dressed" broccoli. And these examples account only for the writer's *explicit* references to geographical origin.

Which Italy does Scappi have in mind? Clearly, he envisions an urban Italy, a country made up of large cities, extending from Milan and Venice to Genoa,

Bologna, Florence, Rome, and Naples. Each of these cities encapsulates the essence of an entire region. With some difficulty, this "Italy" has begun to include parts of the south and the larger islands, but it has not reached Piedmont, which was ruled by the House of Savoy and was still marginal, if not alien, to the culinary culture of the peninsula. It thus strikes us as unusual when we come across a reference to artichokes "cooked among the embers, Piedmontese style" in Giovan Battista Rossetti's *Dello scalco*, a treatise on household stewardship (the art of organizing the services associated with cooking and dining) written in 1584. Here we also find an asparagus dish described as "Piedmontese style, served on fried bread" and a mention of "savoy cheese."[45]

Itineraries

The interregional perception of Italian gastronomic culture is a common element in most of the texts that have come down to us from the Renaissance and is found even in sources that are not devoted mainly to culinary matters. Teofilo Folengo's *Baldus*, which describes a banquet celebrated by the king of France to mark the end of a joust (where all the food is Italian—and the author is quite emphatic about this), notes that "the land of Abruzzo had sent its hams. Naples has kindly provided headcheese, and Milan its golden *offelle* pastries and fresh sausages."[46] In writings addressed more specifically to cooks, stewards, and other supervisors, it would be easy, though tedious and pointless, to seek out the denominations of origin they provide with regard to products, recipes, and cooking customs. We will simply note that, while Scappi's work reveals a complex effort to evaluate and compare various regional traditions with each other (and for this reason we have emphasized the importance of his *Opera*), other authors seem more tied to a particular culture, to a particular vision and type of culinary practice that, though still interregional, regards a specific area as the main focus of its attention. This was the case with Cristoforo Messisbugo, who worked as an administrator and steward at the court of the Este family in Ferrara and whose *Banchetti* (Banquets), written in 1549, mainly refers to specialties and customs of the Po region (*torte*, *tortelli*, and *tortelletti* "in the Lombard style"; stuffed pigeons and capons; breast of veal or lamb or kid, also "in the Lombard style"; *ritortole* and *offelle* from Milan; "Venetian" cuttlefish soup and "sugared fruit"; herb-filled pies "in the style of Ferrara or Romagna"; trout in fish broth, Comacchio-style). Nevertheless, he also occasionally mentions "Florentine" recipes (with the usual eggs) or preparations described as *"alla romanesca"* (macaroni), "alla napoletana" (macaroni and "yellow dishes" of *nizzole* or almonds"), or "sicilian" (rice).

The same is true of Giovan Battista Rossetti's book on the professional duties of the steward, written in 1584, which we have already mentioned. Also from Ferrara, Rossetti was solidly rooted in a culinary perspective typical of the gen-

Harvest and sowing season (engravings).

Source: Antonio Tempesta, *I dodici mesi* (1599).

eral area of Lombardy and Emilia. This emerges in his writing not only in the usual references to Lombardy and its major cities but also in his striking familiarity with the region, demonstrated through references to less prominent locations. In addition to Milan and Venice, Bergamo, Lodi, Pavia, Vicenza, and Padua appear in Rossetti's work. Moving beyond the culinary crossroads of the Po region (Mantua, Cremona, Ferrara, Comacchio), he evokes all the cities of the Via Emilia, from Piacenza to Parma, from Reggio to Modena and Bologna. Specialties from other towns also appear: Sassuolo (for raisins), Scandiano (for bean cakes, red and white grapes), Carpi (for melons), Correggio (for citron dumplings, *mastelletti di brugnat*, and "citron, convent style"), and Mirandola (for mutton shoulder). Beyond Emilia, Rossetti's references become fewer and more sporadic, though all regions on both sides of the Apennines are represented, including the south of Italy and Sicily (remembered for snails cooked in their shells and served in bread, "covered" capon, and rice pasticcio). In their scope and richness of detail, Rossetti's itineraries through Italy (and not only peninsular Italy) are relatively comprehensive.

In 1548, before the treatises of Messisbugo, Scappi, and Rossetti saw the light of day, Ortensio Lando, an erudite and eccentric Milanese writer, published his *Commentario delle più notabili e mostruose cose d'Italia e d'altri luoghi* (Commentary on the most notable and outlandish things found in Italy and elsewhere). This is the fictional narrative of an improbable journey undertaken by an "Aramaic" traveler to Italy, which offers the pretext for a description of many strange, bizarre things. At a certain point in the protagonist's journey, Lando imagines that the owner of an inn where his traveler finds lodging serves him food and wine that are characteristic of the locality. The innkeeper becomes a sort of guide, offering to reveal Italy to the visitor though its different cuisines. In a certain sense, Lando reverses the procedure that was later adopted by Scappi and his colleagues. His idea is not to assemble different parts of Italy in the same dinner but to discover the country by traversing it from south to north, beginning with the "rich Island of Sicily." In Sicily, he tells us, one may eat macaroni that is "usually cooked with fat capons and fresh cheeses, dripping all over with butter and milk" and flavored with sugar and cinnamon. Taranto, the second stop in the journey, has an abundance of wonderful fish "cooked with vinegar and wine, with fragrant herbs and flavorings of walnut, garlic, and almonds" (it would be very pleasant to spend Lent there!). And then off to Naples to taste excellent breads and to Sorrento for veal, fresh caciocavallo cheese, and "*susameli, mostacciouli*, ravioli, fish, mushrooms, chestnuts, sugar, crushed almonds, almond paste, rosewater preserves, *biancomangiare*, thighs of capon and chicken, shoulder of mutton" and "peaches delicious enough to raise the dead." His itinerary continues with some uncertainty between Tuscany and Umbria, stopping off in Siena for its "wonderful marzipan, marvelous *bericoccoli*, and most flavorful *ravigioli* cheese," Foligno for its candied melon seeds and "other priceless confections," and Florence for its Marzolino cheese, peppery bread, and *berlingozzo* cakes, as well as its Trebian wine, which is not inferior to the "Greco from Somma" (invoking two wines also mentioned by Scappi). The journey proceeds to Pisa for biscotti (similarly recommended by Scappi) and to Val Calci, at some distance from Pisa, for the best ricotta in the world. In Lucca one can find good fresh sausage (also noted by Scappi) and "wonderful marzipan." The innkeeper continues: "I must not forget to mention that in Bologna they make the best sausages that man has ever tasted. They are eaten either cured or cooked and are always appetizing. Bless the one who invented this sausage; I kiss and worship his virtuous hands." Then comes the "magnificent city of Ferrara, which reigns supreme in the manufacture of cured sausages and in the preparation of greens, fruits, and root vegetables," where delicious light wines are consumed, "excellent shad, sturgeon, and *buratelli*," and where they make "the best *torte* in the world." Modena is next, noteworthy for its "good sausages and fine Trebiano." We then learn of the "perfect quince preserves" in Reggio, Mirandola, and Correggio, "though perfect only when accompanied by Piacenza cheese," which was praised by the poets and revered on the dining table. Piacenza also offers delicious apples, called *calte*, and a type of grape called *diola*, which is as satisfying to eat as "a most perfect pheasant." In the same city, a dish of gnocchi with garlic should not be missed. Moving beyond the Po, excellent meats are found in Lodi, and "tiny *pescagioni*" in Binasco. At the great emporium of Milan, one finds brain sausage from Brianza, "the royal dish among foods," which is accompanied by *offelle* pastries, sprinkled with a light vernaccia wine from the region, and special little game birds called "*verdorini*," grilled on a skewer. Monza follows, with its "*luganica sottile*" (thin sausage) and its "*tomacelle*" (pork liver sausages). Nor should the traveler neglect Como trout, shad from Lugano, or ortolans and mountain pheasants brought down to Chiavenna from the Grigioni hills. A stop in Chiavenna is also recommended for the chestnuts, and additional stops in the same area are advised for the cheese of Val Malenco and the trout caught in the Mera mountain stream. Turning back toward the southeast, one will find excellent bread in Padua, along with Marzemino wine, small pike, and "perfect frogs." Next comes Chioggia, for melons, and then Venice for its fish: "golden bream, oysters, scallops, and mullet," an excellent fish in aspic, as well as "little game birds from Cipri," *panna cotta*, and sharp, sweet malvasia wine. Going north again "you will find good wines in Frioli, though there are even better ones in Vicenza, where you will also eat most excellent kid." Nor does the "guide" fail to mention the carp, tripe, and prawns from the Sile that are served in Treviso or to note that one can drink Cellatica *vernaccia* and muscatel wines in Brescia which are "superior to those of Bergamo and Brianza." Above all Brescia's *fiadoni* pies should not be missed. These are "lovely to look at, excellent to taste, more fragrant than amber and musk, and soft to the touch." Equally noteworthy are the *gattare* from Genoa, which the traveler should certainly taste before leaving, along with muscatel pears, fine figs, peaches chopped with quince, muscatel, Razzese, and other light wines from the coast. And thus the journey ends.

Despite the predictable absence of Piedmont and the surprising omission of Rome, this traveler's itinerary envisioned by Ortensio Lando covers a broad swath of Italy and reveals a sense of gastronomic belonging, a clearly defined identity.

Toward Regionalization

In the seventeenth century, the era of "national" recipe collections seems to have come to an end. The project of creating a synthesis of Italian cuisine in comparative form—pursued by Scappi in particular but also by other individuals—gave way to a growing emphasis on regional diversity, which was to be the dominant theme in Italian culinary history for the next two hundred years or more. As we have already repeatedly noted, these differences were already a visible—perhaps even distinctive—element in the gastronomic landscape of the country. What was changing, however, was that the recipe compilers had begun to emphasize their geographical locations, positioning themselves on the map in a much more specific way than had occurred in medieval and Renaissance texts. This shift is especially noticeable in the treatises produced in Naples, where a complete picture of the culinary legacy of the south was articulated for the first time. Writers such as Giovan Battista Crisci, who published *Lucerna de corteggiani* (The courtiers' oil lamp)—a large collection of menus for different seasons of the year—in Naples in 1643, and Antonio Latini, who wrote the two-volume work *Lo scalco alla moderna, overo l'arte di ben disporre i conviti* (The modern steward; or, The art of organizing banquets), published in Naples between 1692 and 1694, are especially intent on communicating their sense of belonging to a particular place and cultural tradition.

Crisci's *Lucerna* is in fact the first extensive list of the food products and specialties of south-central Italy. Not only Naples—a symbolic point of reference even for northern writers—but also countless cities, towns, and agricultural centers dispersed throughout the area now emerge as crucial locations in a decidedly new culinary image, the novelty of which lay in the very fact of its becoming *explicit*. From Abruzzo to Apulia, from Campania to Basilicata and Calabria, and extending, as always, to Sicily, this geographical list of food products is focused mainly on cheese and fruit, though it also includes ham from Abruzzo, headcheese and sausage from Nola, "Giugliano fillet garnished with dormice," fillet of veal from Sorrento, macaroni—either from Sicily (or more precisely from Palermo) or from Apulia—and olives, either fresh or baked, from Gaeta and Maranola, Caserta and Cilento, Geraci and Messina. Lettuce comes from Avellino, and melons from Aversa. Among the locations associated with fruit are Amalfi for peaches; Arienzo for red cherries, apples, peaches, and apricots; Capodichino for red plums; Capodimonte for peaches and wild cherries; Giugliano for peaches; Marano for peaches and white apples; Moiano for apples; Posillipo for white apples, muscatel grapes, peaches, and apricots; Procida for apricots; San Giovanni and San Pietro for figs; Somma for wild cherries, pears, and azaroles; and Sorrento for plums, pears, and apples. There is a wide range of cheeses, both fresh and aged: mozzarellas from Aversa, Capua ("freshly prepared"), and Cerreto; caciocavallo from Basilicata (from Potenza or "Foio di Potenza") and Sicily; salted ricotta from Capua; goat's-milk ricotta from Pozzuoli and Vallo di Potenza; *ricotte di raschi* from Calabria (or more specifically from the Sila, Pollino, and San Lorenzo); provola from Garigliano, Capua, Eboli, Cerra, and Sessa; and other cheeses of an unspecified type from Abruzzi and Apulia.

The most striking aspect of Crisci's list is that the production and marketing of the foods mentioned are not for the most part associated with large cities. Instead, there are references to villages, townlands, and "shores." This, as we know, was the outcome of a historical pattern that began to manifest itself in the middle centuries of the medieval period, when the autonomy of the towns was sacrificed to the might of the barons and the ruling power. For this reason, the south developed in a way that was structurally very different from the pattern established in north-central Italy, with its communes and city-states. Hence the place names that synthesize the gastronomic culture of the Kingdom of Naples do not evoke a network of cities. We find by contrast examples such as "fresh Provola cheese from the Evoli countryside" and numerous types of fruit "from the Posillipo coast." The only city that dominates is Naples, the kingdom's splendid capital, but this is clearly not the same thing. City names reemerge in Crisci's work when the writer discusses products and recipes from north-central Italy, and his points of reference then become Rome, Florence, Bologna, Milan, and Genoa.

Another catalog of southern specialties can be found in the work of Antonio Latini. Here, however, the foods are not listed as options among a wide array of suggestions for the creation of a menu (as occurs in Crisci's treatise) but organized into a systematic list. The first volume of Latini's work presents a "brief description of the Kingdom of Naples." Though it contains references from "various authors," it is based above all on "custom and experience" and aims at illustrating the "edible fruits and other things of special and rare quality that are produced in different parts of the same kingdom." One by one, the twelve provinces that constitute the kingdom are named and discussed, beginning with "Happy Campania, known today as Terra di Lavoro," which supplies Naples with all manner of God's bounty: "exquisite fruit" and "renowned fennel" from Poggio Reale; "all kinds of greens and vegetables" from Padule; "famous peas, cardoons, artichokes, radishes, and horseradish" and "lovely cauliflower" from

Chiaia; "delicious salads" and "all kinds of fruit" from Posillipo. Excellent meats come from Ischia and Capri—"quantities of pheasants," "fine veal, marvelous quail, and all kinds of game"—as well as from Sorrento and Vico. Freshwater and saltwater fish are so plentiful that "Naples has an abundance of different kinds of fish at good prices all year round." Latini goes on to mention cucumbers from Orte and headcheese from Nola, *torrone* (nougat) from Aversa and melons from Cardito, olives from Gaeta and cardoons from Giugliano. The other eleven provinces follow: Principato Citra is mentioned for the dried figs from Agropoli, San Severino trout, and tender capons from Nocera. Principato Ultra is remembered for its brain sausages (*cervellate*), onions, and *torrone* from Benedetto and hazelnuts and freshwater fish from Avellino. Basilicata is invoked for caciocavallo cheese and "excellent game" from Laterza. Calabria Citra is cited for its "good cheeses, ricottas, *rasche*, sugars, apples, and many other things," such as oil and capers from Rossano, raisins from Belvedere "that travel all over the world," and cheeses from Cassano, Foio, and Pollino. Calabria Ultra is invoked for its "great quantity of superlative oil," and Terra d'Otranto for its "abundance of meat and dried figs," the oil, wine, and cheese from Gallipoli, the oysters "and all kinds of sea food" from Taranto, and the "wild game" of Ostuni. Terra di Bari is mentioned mainly for its renowned lamb (excellent mutton and, in Bitonto, kid), almonds, cheese, oil, and citrus fruit. Abruzzo Citra is especially famous for the "sweet confections" of Sulmona; Abruzzo Ultra for L'Aquila saffron and Cicoli hams; and Contado di Molise is mentioned for the hams of Campobasso and for an abundance of mushrooms and truffles. Finally, Capitanata is invoked for the fish caught in Lake Varano: large eels, tench, and mullet, from which roe was harvested to make *bottarga* (cured, pressed roe). Latini concludes: "Naturally, for the sake of brevity, I have listed only the best-known items, since each of the twelve provinces contains as much goodness as you would find in the whole wide world."

The "regionalization" of the recipe collections in the north of Italy is less striking and was undertaken less self-consciously. Yet by the seventeenth century we can see that here too the outlook reflected in the treatises is less ambitious, more limited in scope than in the earlier collections, though perhaps closer to the daily practices of the kitchen. We witness a geographical horizon that is clearly limited to the Po Valley in the work of personalities such as Francesco Vasselli of Bologna, a steward at the Pico Court of Emilia, who published *L'Apicio overo il maestro de' conviti* (Apicius; or, The banquet master) in 1647, and Bartolomeo Stefani, also from Bologna, who worked as the principal cook at the Gonzaga Court in Mantua (and before that in other households), where he published *L'arte di ben cucinare, et instruire i men periti in questa lodevole professione* (The art of fine cooking, and for the instruction of those less expert in this worthy profession) in 1662. Although Stefani, when given the opportunity, decided not to limit himself "to the bread of [his] native city" but to travel beyond "the river that runs through the countryside of [his] birth" searching for fine foods for his banquet table, his work invokes a system of exchange based on "gastronomic districts" that are quite distinct from each other. Naples and Sicily, he states, produce citron, oranges, artichokes, asparagus, cauliflower, fresh broad beans, and lettuces that supply "the entire kingdom" during "the cold season" when it is impossible to find such produce elsewhere. Similarly, the Gaeta coast "supplies Rome with fruit." The coast of Genoa "has an abundance of the same products," which it provides to Milan, Florence, Bologna, Turin, Piacenza, and "neighboring towns, along with the greater part of Lombardy." The lakeshore of Salò and the orchards of the Veneto are additional sources of winter vegetables. Bologna produces excellent fennel, grapes, and large olives "and shares these with Lombardy, Romagna, Florence, and its neighboring provinces, even Rome."[47] Even Rome. Stefani's three Italies seem much farther apart than Scappi's were.

As Italy's gastronomic culture became regionalized, a space opened up for Piedmont. As we have already noted, Turin finally shows up in Stefani's recipe book, and "savoy *biscotti*" (ladyfingers) seem almost fashionable.

From the end of the 1600s through the entire first half of the following century, there was a lull in Italy's gastronomic literature. This silence reflected the sense of cultural inferiority experienced by Italians when French cuisine began to dominate throughout Europe, and it proved to be long lasting. It also coincided with a return to local tradition and to oral transmission, which is the primary instrument of local heritage. Yet the return to the local also produced some positive effects, consolidating the links between gastronomy and the land and reinforcing the idea of origins that is characteristic of Italian cooking. This proved to be a sound investment in the long term.

Municipal Recipe Collections

The growing influence of French cuisine reached Italy's major cities by way of Piedmont, unifying practices of food preparation and presentation. This became clear with the publication of *Il cuoco piemontese perfezionato a Parigi* (The Piedmontese cook trained in Paris) in 1766, a collection that was reprinted in Venice in 1789 and in Milan in 1791, in the general area south of the Alps and close to the Po that was already receptive to French culture. The influence of the collection spread from there to other cities and eventually to Rome and Naples, where it encountered and collided with older, stubbornly rooted traditions. The French model was reformulated with native ingredients and coexisted with a substratum that varied from state to state, evidenced in the selection of ingredients as well as in the names and methods of food preparation. Thus, for example, *Il cuoco piemontese* recommends the onions of Ivrea, Piedmontese truffles, and Aosta cheeses.[48] These adjustments were to become increasingly prevalent. In *La cuciniera piemontese* (Piedmontese cooking). published in Vercelli in 1771, we find a flat bread in the style of Monferrato, as well as "Vercelli-style soup," "wings, Venetian style," and "cabbages, Roman style."[49] Cultural or political pressure did not necessarily translate into an adjustment to Parisian taste. Rather, it reinforced the split between the public and private levels on which dishes circulate. The books written in private households are particularly revealing in this regard, recording not only some spontaneous borrowings but also the usual daily fare served at a gentleman's table. The cook employed by the bishop of Imola between 1785 and 1800 documented a type of cuisine that had developed in the area between Bologna and Romagna (which stretched just about as far as the bishop's own diocese), with a profusion of *cappelletti alla bolognese* as well as the spiced sausages of Ferrara. In his discussion of fritters and stews, the flavors of France are marginalized, though there is one allusion to béchamel, a sauce that was already half a century old.[50] The Cassoli household in Reggio Emilia was similarly inattentive to dishes from France. Here domestic records mention *cappelletti di grasso*, sausages prepared in the style of Modena, *spongate* (marzipan with honey), and *mestocchine di formentone* (sweet flatcakes baked in the oven),[51] demonstrating a staunchly provincial image with little concern for changing fashions. An investigation into the codes of aristocratic behavior reveals not only their relative impermeability to outside influences but also the existence of firmly rooted customs and the striking presence of refined, representative foods.

The correlation between wealth and the acceptance of international cuisine is far from evident. In the case of gourmets of the caliber of Vicenzo Corrado, author of *Il cuoco galante* (The gallant cook), published in Naples in 1786, even the refined (or "gallant") table has its own distinctive makeup, adopting a creative approach to the aristocratic tradition of favoring products from the local countryside as well as to the preferences of French visitors. One of the most fundamental characteristics of the new cuisine is in fact that it makes exclusive use of local foods, and the new methods are applied even to products such as fresh tomatoes and freshly caught anchovies, which are absent from the Parisian marketplace. To reemphasize the value of the fish hatchery, the art of fishing, and the cultivation of fruit and vegetables takes cooking styles and dishes in a direction where the adoption of complex techniques seems difficult or useless. Squid "when small, are fried and eaten with salt, pepper, and lemon juice." As for whitebait, "these are so tender that they are cooked as soon as they are put on the fire."[52] There are sauces such as *"Roberta"* (*sauce Robert*), *"Ramolata"* (*remoulade*), and *"alla francese"* (in the French style), but these are confined to the end of the book, which is planned and constructed around food products rather than their transformation. It is difficult to imagine a procedure more contrary to Parisian practice.

The rebirth of Italian cuisine in the last three decades of the 1700s developed from these premises, among which we must not overlook an important dimension: the existence of a gastronomic culture spanning the boundaries of Italy's diverse political states. The use of the term "Italian" was, and continued to be, anything but characteristic, but some food products and several dishes were already circulating outside their areas of origin. Francesco Leonardi, with a career in the service of the most important households of Europe, after having drafted his *Apicio moderno* (1790), an account of French ways of preparing pork, begins an appendix on mortadellas, salami, cotechino sausages, pork feet, brain sausages, and Milanese liver sausage, revealing the use of these items in the area from Rome to Naples.[53] These indications suggest a sense of local culinary identity, of belonging to a state, that is indirectly Italian. This sense of identity was consolidated in the municipal recipe collections in the course of the nineteenth century.

The publishing houses of some of the great urban centers produced a growing number of instructional volumes intended for a limited range of consumption at variable cost and reflecting the traditions of specific areas that often coincided with the use of a particular dialect. In large cities such as Naples, high-profile books like Ippolito Cavalcanti's *Cucina teorico-practica* (Theoretical and practical cuisine) of 1837 that were conceived for the aristocracy and therefore philo-French and philo-Neapolitan in outlook were juxtaposed with less imposing works available at lower prices and in smaller formats, such as *La cucina casereccia* (Home cooking), published in 1828, that were aimed at more modest households. Both types of publications cover the gastronomic usages of the same locality and mention dishes from other states. In a municipality of modest dimensions, such as Como, a single recipe collection, *Il cuoco senza pretese* (The cook without pretensions), published in 1834 by a writer named Odescalchi (from a well-regarded family), proposes a culinary model that includes a number of local dishes from the Alpine foothills and the lake region while maintaining an openness toward the customs of the Milanese area and the practices of elegant cuisine. Mentioned are *Pasticci di maccheroni* (macaroni pies) and *vitello tonné* (veal with tuna sauce), which are obviously not native to the area.[54] Considerations of an ethnological or purist character are not part of this municipal mindset. What is evident instead is a self-conscious mirroring of the dining habits of the upper classes.

A map visualizing the distribution of these small recipe collections would show that they extended from Naples to the entire north-central part of Italy, although they were most evident in the publishing and gastronomic capitals Milan, Naples, and Turin. Tuscany had its own lively publishing market, with editing houses in Lucca, Livorno, Florence, and Siena.[55] During the first half of the nineteenth century, there was some similarity among the titles of these collections. Thus we find "Milanese cooks," "Bolognese cooks," even "Italian cooks." These works were often anonymous. Local preparations or dishes from other parts of the peninsula alternate with instruction on the French culinary tradition, which often provides a continuous and conspicuous thread that is woven in along with the provincial elements. The professional qualifications and geographical provenance of those employed in these projects reflects a cross-section of cultures, each delegated to perfecting an art. *Il nuovo economico cuoco piemontese e credenziere napoletano* (The new economical Piedmontese cook and the Neapolitan butler), which appeared in Milan in 1822, gives a sense of interregional collaboration with its three different place names: the two mentioned in the title and the city of its publication. This impression is confirmed in an illustration showing a cook in an apron and white hat cutting some meat, while a pastry cook in a formal evening coat rolls out the dough. The men are working at different tables, with their backs turned to each other. Here the hypothesis of associating distinct cultures and skills prevails over the idea of creating a unified body of professionals.

The publication of culinary texts intensified after the unification of Italy, clearly showing how the interaction of the three models (local, state-based, and international) constituted a deeply rooted cultural pattern and made possible the description of a socially stratified and geographically specific cuisine. The process of municipalization brought about the documentation and development of local markets and stimulated a connection, through recipes, among small centers that could not have their own publishing companies, by modifying dishes made for peasant festivals with the use of ingredients available at the local market. The rural, urban, and regional recipe collections not only provide a picture of the situation before and after Italian unification, but they also had a long-lasting influence, multiplying in the very tradition that is known as Italian in our own time.

Through these books, the culinary customs of the countryside and coastal areas, lakeshores and hills, were ultimately represented by the city, since this was both the market center and site of publication, as well as a hub for migrating peasants and servants. This phenomenon would be of decisive importance in the process of culinary regionalization, which was barely noticeable at the beginning of the nineteenth century, despite the use of adjectives such as "Piedmontese" or "Milanese" to describe the cooks. After national unification, each regional capital constructed the region according to its own administrative image, planning transportation, overseeing production, and defining a culinary identity in competition with the identity of other regions. This was the basis for the creation of Artusi's code.

Artusi and National-Regional Cuisine

Artusi was born in Forlimpopoli in 1821 and lived in Florence for over half a century. Inscribed in his life story is the culture common to the part of Italy that includes Tuscany and Romagna, which is the basic axis of his cuisine.[56] As a youth he accompanied his father to various markets from Senigallia to Rovigo, moving about in a horse-drawn carriage. He then crossed the Apennines by coach, going as far as Livorno. He traveled by mail train to Italy's principal cities: Naples, Rome, Padua, Milan, and Turin. He visited Bologna, with its many opportunities for dining well, more often than anywhere else. In 1891 he constructed a gastronomic map based on these experiences. He was intimately familiar with the entire area: the roads, villages, mountains, and seaside towns in the Grand Duchy and the Papal States, from as far north as Polesine to as far south as the Marches. His familiarity with this part of Italy was translated into recipes that were derived mainly from the rich province of Tuscany, in the greater proportion from Romagna and hence from Bologna, a city where he felt at home.

Apart from this broad swath of territory divided up by mountains, Artusi was best acquainted with the cities of Italy, from Trieste to Turin in the north to Naples in the south. There is no mention of the Marches, Abruzzo, Apulia, Basilicata, or Calabria in any of the recipes. Even when his *Scienza in cucina* was expanded in its later editions to incorporate information provided to him in letters from women readers, Artusi did not take on the south, with the exception of Sicily, from which just three recipes are featured. Sardinia is an unknown island. This is the country that Artusi knew and presented to his readers. His Italy is incomplete and is divided longitudinally by the Apennine mountains, with different denominations used for the fish caught in the Adriatic and the same fish caught in the Tyrrhenian. We find the richness of Tuscany on the one hand and on the other Romagna, the poorest and most depressed region. The north-central model of cuisine is also evident in his seasonings (from which hot pepper is excluded) and in his use of three types of fat: oil in Tuscany, lard in Bologna, and butter in Lombardy. How did it happen that this interregional recipe collection, with its gaps and lack of balance, became the symbol of Italian cuisine?

A similar image of the country was shared by many gastronomic experts and members of the general public. *Il viaggio per l'Italia di Giannettino* (Giannettino's journey through Italy), a pedagogical text by Collodi, was complied with the Baedecker Guide insofar as the regions named were concerned. Far from fascinating the author of Pinocchio, the south incited his distrust, and his description of a pizza seen in Naples became famous: "The blackened aspect of the toasted crust, the whitish sheen of garlic and anchovy, the greenish-yellow tint of the oil and fried herbs, and those red bits of tomato here and there give pizza the appearance of complicated filth that matches the dirt of the vendor."[57] A similarly pejorative description of macaroni flavored with a great deal of pepper and cheese and offered on the streets of the same city is found in Artusi's autobiography.

This does not mean that local cooking, the food of the common people, is absent from Artusi's *La scienza in cucina*. But to understand how it was assimilated into the style of the bourgeois household, it is helpful to complete the culinary map already sketched out. Only two dishes described by Artusi carry the description "Italian," namely, tortellini and *lesso rifatto* (twice-cooked meat). The others by contrast refer to regions, cities, or villages. The villages are relatively few, as are the areas, such as the Maremma or the Comacchio Marshes, that today are considered wild-life parks. Artusi constructs his geogastronomic model on the cities, which have a representative quality because of the presence of markets and shops and their relationship to outlying areas, provinces, and regions. It is an open model and as flexible as could be desired. Foods such as eels and aniseed, produced in Artusi's Bologna, travel to Florence, where they are transformed in the Piazza D'Azeglio by a cook from Massa and a cook from Bologna. In Artusi's home too this spatial triangle is reestablished, reformulating recipes, dishes, and preserves in an urban and hence "refined" key. The adjective *raffinato* (refined) is often used, along with *delicato* (delicate) and *signorile* (elegant), to designate the style of the dishes, the choice of seasonings, and the distinctiveness of the flavors.

With this transference of resources from country to city, and with the urbanization of culinary practice, the model of Italian cuisine was potentially established, to the extent that new centers and marketplaces were now linked up to the national rail network on which ingredients, tourists, and hence new foods could circulate. Both attentive to territorial and human divisions and confident in the unified articulation of the country, this method was widely accepted, as can be seen in the recipe collections that carry forward Artusi's project in the geographical sense. Agnetti, one of the most careful compilers at the end of the nineteenth century, showed how expandable the geography of the culinary areas was in his *Nuova cucina delle specialità regionali* (New cuisine of regional specialties) and *Cucina nazionale* (National cooking), published in 1909 and 1910, respectively, when Artusi was still alive. These collections gave increased representation to the Veneto, accorded greater importance to Rome, and added Sardinia as the source of six recipes.[58] A comparison between the two volumes shows that twenty-seven out of one hundred and one savory dishes in the regional volume are also found in the national volume, and of the twenty-seven sixteen are pastas and soups. The national-regional dishes include agnolotti, cappelletti, Roman gnocchi, macaroni with sauce, macaroni with tomato, minestrone, Milanese risotto, macaroni pie, ravioli, Genoese ravioli, risotto with wedge shells, Bolognese tagliatelle, tagliatelle pasticciate, tortellini, and Pavese soup. The regions represented are Liguria, Lombardy, Venice, Emilia and Romagna, Tuscany, Rome, Naples, and Sicily. Leaving aside the utility of the typologies used for pasta, this is a common denominator for future recipe collections.

Views of Capua, Bologna, and Pisa engraved on
drawings by the Rouargue Brothers.

Source: Paul de Musset, *Voyage pittoresque en Italie* (Paris, 1855).

In the configuration of an *Italian* space, the regions selected are not administrative/political units but "compartments,"[59] each with a physical and historical identity. These identities are particularly important from the cultural point of view because they encapsulate some general characteristics that are intelligible to all. Foods function similarly to dialects, since they express a particular taste that can be understood and translated into Italian. Interregional exchange thus seems to have been crucial to the progressive attainment of national consciousness, without requiring that the past be sacrificed or that particular identities be abandoned. Pellegrino Artusi benefited from this compromise, becoming the father of Italian cooking from the perspective of future housewives.

The Mediterranean Again

During the two decades of Fascist rule, the exploration of gastronomy was completed by obtaining a complete map of the regions, by sketching out a preliminary inventory of typical products, and by promoting the awareness of local cuisines with books, advertising campaigns, shows, and festivals. The artist Umberto Zimelli was commissioned by ENIT (the Italian national tourist board) to create "La carta delle principali specialità gastronomiche delle regioni italiane" (Map of the principal culinary specializations of the Italian regions). This was a map with which foreigners could identify the best products available in the cheese or dessert industry, the best wines and preserved foods, and contemplate steaming bowls of pasta placed between bottles of wine and molds of cheese.[60] Maps of the *"bel paese"* (beautiful country) increased and multiplied, and those showing the location of the Cirio factories and warehouses demonstrate how closely the canning and preserves sector was linked to educational propaganda and tourist promotion.[61] *La guida gastronomica d'Italia* (Gastronomical guide to Italy), published by the Touring Club Italiano in 1931, completed the shift from the representation of the entire country through food symbols to a topographical survey of its culinary heritage. In this guidebook we find culinary definitions rather than recipes, descriptions of local products available from midsize or small-scale producers, and all the ingredients necessary to cook in style. Traveling along the Adriatic Coast from Manfredonia toward Bari, we find the white onions of Barletta, black *laganelle di Bisceglie* (fettuccine in *vin cotto*), and Molfetta oil. The landscape is certainly different from the terrain glimpsed in the recipe collections of Artusi and Agnetti, since each region is now pulverized into the hitherto unknown, rarely discussed, but infinite riches of its soil. Learning to eat Italian style was one of the projects of the Fascist regime. It was implemented with the help of regional exhibitions, fairs, festivals, autarchic campaigns and a great deal of folklore.

One of the most noteworthy consequences of these initiatives was the reappearance of the south on the gastronomic map of Italy. Calabria and Basilicata, regions that were vaguely known for dried figs and a few wines of Greek origin, are now given a more flattering image, thanks to the members of the Touring Club, with pastas and soups with amusing names, such as "*schiaffettoni*" (big slaps), which are described as "large tubes of pasta filled with mixed ground meat, salami, and fresh sausage, sealed at both ends, boiled, and served with sauce and cheese."[62] This appraisal was accepted, repeated, and imitated. Imagining a journey through Italy by train, Umberto Notari, the founder of the monthly magazine *La cucina italiana*, reproduced entire chapters of *La guida gastronomica*.[63] Those who recorded such excursions around Italy were numerous, eager, and curious. Among them Paolo Monelli became the most famous by virtue of his wit and literary style. All these writers traveled from north to south, and no one stopped off at Naples, as Pellegrino Artusi had done; instead, they branched out, toward either Abruzzi and Apulia or the Tyrrhenian coast. The center of gravity shifted toward Rome, thus bringing the south closer.

The territorial ambitions of the Fascist era can be observed in the culinary maps such as Zimelli's, where a few gastronomic symbols are placed outside Italy's borders, as though allowing for future occupations. A bottle of maraschino liqueur is thus placed over Zadar (then called Zara), and *boiabessa* (a fish soup) appears over Nice. In presenting Italy as a bridge between Africa and Europe, the Mediterranean becomes the center of gravity of Western civilization. This was not, however, an exclusively Italian ambition. Even French cooks (the best of whom were born, like Prosper Montagné, somewhere between Nice and Carcassonne) published collections of recipes from Provence, the Riviera, and North Africa. But between 1935 and 1940 the Italian Fascists had begun to highlight their political role in relation to the Germans, almost is if to foreshadow the division of Europe into two productive and gastronomic areas organized along the lines of their reciprocal interests. Following the signing of the Pact of Steel, the flow of fruits and vegetables increased, as these began to be transported north to the colder regions during the spring.

The shift toward a southern orientation in culinary matters was not limited to Italy or to the Fascist period. Rather, it began at the turn of the century with the emergence of tourism to seaside resorts. Southbound tourism (to the Riviera or the islands off the Neapolitan coast) resulted in a growing taste for shellfish, fresh vegetables, oil, sharp flavors, and colorful food, which in turn stimulated an increase in the availability of pastas, spring produce from gardens and orchards, and anchovies in the north of Italy and abroad. Availability of these foods was guaranteed all year round by the canning and bottling industry, which sold sunshine and orchards in a can. Even though a large part of the tomato-canning industry was concentrated in the area around Parma and Piacenza, it was the San Marzano tomato—the Neapolitan pear-shaped variety—that became the exclusive symbol of the Cirio Company. Cheeses such as caciocavallo, provolone, and *provolette* were produced in Lombardy beginning in the 1930s, without losing their claim to southern provenance (which corroborates other evidence suggesting that southern origins are held in high esteem). Italy, the needle in the Mediterranean compass, had found its bearings and was pointing southward, toward Africa, another source of imagined riches.

If the war put paid to fantasies of colonial expansion and turned the "garden of the empire" into a desert, the culinary tendencies that emerged under Fascism continued to prevail and proved to have some value. While on the one hand underdevelopment and malnutrition were the underside of an agricultural policy that believed in its own propaganda, on the other some attempt was made to revitalize the south of Italy. Booklets such as Cavazza's *Itinerario gastronomico ed enologico d'Italia* (The Italian itinerary of food and wine) echoed an approach that was no longer politically fashionable with the same arguments, comparing Abruzzo with its *maccheroni alla chitarra* to Apulia with its *panzerotti*, before moving on to a discussion of the vineyards of Aglianico and Cirò (in Calabria). It was only in 1957, however, that Guido Piovene's *Viaggio in Italia* (Journey through Italy), which was made available to Italians both on the radio and in print, provided a sharply focused image of the imbalance between north and south, an image that in no way excluded a policy of cultural investment in the gastronomy of the depressed regions and particularly the revival of the style of cooking invented in the midst of poverty. From Piovene's perspective and that of his audience, no culinary miracle had yet occurred in the south, but it might well be on the way. This is perfectly encapsulated in an account of his visit to Naples, where he writes, "What remains imprinted in my memory is the image of a vendor who was running around with a basket of piping hot fritters and yelling: 'How did I manage to make these? How did I manage?' He too was astonished at his own ingenuity."[64]

The myth of the south as a miraculous, therapeutic place, as a major resource of vitamins and polyunsaturated fats, was destined to become more widespread over the subsequent decades, because of increased efforts by the National Institute of Nutrition and a heightened awareness on the part of those employed in the agricultural and food industries within the expanding markets of the Western world. In the continuum that stretched from the politics of the Fascist era to those of the postwar Republic of Italy, despite the fact that fats and proteins remained exclusive to northern Italy, a general pattern took root that would be described by Italians twenty years later as the Mediterranean diet. The illusion that the *mare nostrum* of Roman antiquity could be revived had by now evaporated. Yet thanks to the efforts of American researcher Ancel Keys and his collaborators the myth of the Mediterranean diet resurfaced at this juncture. This myth was based on the discovery of isolated areas where poverty and good health existed side by side. Here small, self-contained communities were rigorously dedicated to a way of eating that rendered them resistant to heart disease. Extrapolating from the dietary principles of the Mediterranean people, Ancel and Margaret Keys published their findings in *How to Eat Well and Stay Well the Mediterranean Way*, which appeared in Italian translation as *Mangiar bene e stare bene* in 1962. The volume presented Italian cooking—and not only the cuisine of the south of Italy—as a valuable tool in combating cholesterol, heart problems, and obesity. Substituting oil for butter, most of the recipes offer lighter versions of traditional dishes, among which are found Artusi's *vitello tonnato*. This message was intended mainly for Anglo-Saxon audiences, as can be seen in its peculiar, if not downright contradictory chapter headings, such as "Cocktail Snacks." In promoting the book Italian publishers and newspapers brushed over these details by favoring a purist, "philo-southern" interpretation of the cuisine outlined by the authors. The saying "It's a mistake to think spaghetti will make you fat" was taken out of context and reiterated and applied in reference to all kinds of sauces.[65]

The image of islands and beaches, as exemplary origins of the modern diet, proved to be a successful concept in the United States, where the Mediterranean seemed like an ancient patch of blue, and the same idea was adopted in Europe (including Italy) in the late 1960s. This increasingly polluted and almost completely landlocked sea had in the meantime seen the development of mass tourism, characterized by the seasonal migration of travelers from wealthy countries. Tourists have an interest in food and food festivals. Sun, spaghetti, pizza, and vegetables have by now become part of the myth of good health. Italy is the central focus of this interest because of its diversified cuisine and its food industries, which had been living off the Mediterranean myth for centuries. Thus while Italy does not strive to expand its confines, it exports products and messages in every direction, aiming at distant markets and replicating a particular gastronomic image, thanks to the solid reference points offered by pizzerias abroad—restaurants with the traditional bottle of wine and mortadella in the window—and tourists from all over the world. As happened in the 1930s, the south of France, the Riviera, the Costa Brava, and Andalusia in Spain are collaborating with each other in today's Mediterranean with its distressingly endless chain of tourist resorts. But unlike France, where Parisian cuisine competes with Provençal cooking, Italy, though gastronomically divided by regions, gains from its decentralized character and manages to sell pizza with tomatoes everywhere, popularized by emigrants of southern Italian origin.

Along with the improvement in living standards there has been a general decline in traditional gastronomic patterns, such as the prevalence of meat in the area around Paris, the cult of ham in Emilia, and the preference for fresh stuffed pastas flavored with butter and cream. The cook influenced by southern, or philo-southern, customs replaces animal protein with vegetables, emphasizes the importance of fresh foods and oil, and places a bowl of fruit on the dinner table. Much of the success of the best-known dishes, pizza and spaghetti, is due to the variations in flavor and color that can be obtained through improvisation. One of the characteristics of this model of cooking is that, despite its association with a limited geographical area, it can be replicated everywhere by using either the original ingredients or substitutes. The Mediterranean is a metaphor expressed through synonyms. Increasingly dependent on the industries that manufacture partially prepared foods, Italian cuisine is experiencing an internal identity crisis. Without abandoning its polycentrism, its regional traditions, local dishes, and age-old rivalries, it is in the process of resurrecting itself from the ashes, demonstrating paradoxically how a country composed of diverse fragments and an excess of different identities can convey the impression of a consistent, homogeneous beacon of gastronomic culture when viewed from a distance.

CHAPTER TWO

The Italian Way of Eating

Flavors and Fragrances from the Vegetable Garden

Written at the end of the thirteenth or the beginning of the fourteenth century, the *Liber de coquina*, Italy's oldest recipe collection, begins quite deliberately and intentionally with vegetables. "Since we wish to discuss cooking and different kinds of food in this work, we will start with vegetables as the first group of foods." The book thus begins with cabbages, "white, green, Lenten-style, Roman-style, English, French," and other varieties. Ten different cabbage recipes are offered in succession, followed by recipes for spinach, fennel, and "small leafy greens" and ultimately by several others for legumes: chickpeas, peas, broad beans, lentils, and string beans. To organize the collection in this manner was certainly not the most obvious way to proceed, for the simple reason that vegetables had never been fashionable on the dinner tables of the powerful in the Middle Ages, when the culinary symbol of power was meat.[1] Hence the writer carefully justifies his approach with the pretext of beginning with "the easiest things."

Are we dealing with a book of popular cooking? Certainly not. The kind of cuisine described in the *Liber de coquina*, created in the environment of the Angevin court of Naples, was destined for the upper classes: "Prepare some delicate cabbages, of the sort to which gentlemen are accustomed." Or, "these fragrant leafy greens may be served to persons of distinction."

Are we dealing then with a regional phenomenon? With the suggestion of a Mediterranean peculiarity? Even if this were the case at the outset, the basic model presented in the book was subsequently adopted all over the Italian peninsula. The Tuscan version of the *Liber* not only imitates the structure of the original work (by beginning with cabbages) but also adds many new vegetable dishes, expanding the selection of greens and root vegetables. Here, along with cabbage, fennel, spinach, chard, and turnips, we also find leeks and scallions, squash, asparagus, borage, lettuce, and rutabaga. These modifications reflect local customs, proving the concrete, representative quality of these "written" cuisines. Cabbage, the preeminent presence in the *Liber,* is less dominant in the Tuscan collection, where more space is devoted to turnips—for which many more recipes are offered—and leeks: "Take some white leeks, as is the custom in Tuscany."[2]

Medieval culture was finely attuned to class differences communicated through behavioral codes, among which eating habits were of primary importance. Within this scheme of things vegetables were clearly identified as the food of peasants and impoverished people. When a monk named Giovanni drew close to an elderly pilgrim returning from Rome, he was sickened by the stench of the garlic, onions, and leeks the old man carried in his sack along with a loaf of bread, an odor that simultaneously revealed the man's inferior social standing. This episode, reported in a tenth-century monastic text,[3] is just one among many similar indications of the lowly status of garlic. We find another in a short story by Sabadino degli Arienti (who lived in the fifteenth and sixteenth centuries), describing a trick played by Ercole d'Este, duke of Ferrara, on a peasant named Bondeno who had the audacity to seek induction to knighthood. Preparations for the ceremony were duly carried out. However, when the moment came to display the shield bearing the coat of arms of the new "nobleman," what emerged into view, as trumpets blared and the crowd roared with laughter, was an emblem that signified the impossibility of his social advancement: a head of garlic against a blue background. Sabadino explains that garlic is "always a rustic food, although it is sometimes artificially ennobled, as when it is inserted into the meat of roast goslings."[4] This observation gives us a sense of the conflict between ideology and actual practice, between the theoretical alimentary code that relegated garlic to the peasants and everyday experience, which allowed its use even in the cuisine of the courts. The conflict between the two levels is a powerful one, requiring equally strong signs for its resolution.

Sabadino himself alludes to one of these signs: the social destination of a particular dish is identified by the elements that accompany it and the way in which it is served. When a humble food appears as a simple ingredient (though not the main element) in a prestigious dish, it is "ennobled" by becoming part of a different gastronomic and symbolic system. As soon as garlic is added to the meat of roast goslings, its rustic nature is artificially modified. For this reason, *agliata*, a sauce based on crushed garlic, typical of peasant cooking,[5] can be found even in the recipe collections of the upper classes. The Venetian cookbook produced in the fourteenth century, for example, suggests that it be served "with all kinds of meat."[6] Similarly, a recipe for "delicate cabbages of the sort served to gentlemen" that appears in the *Liber de coquina*, indicates that *agliata* may be used as an accompaniment to any kind of meat ("*cum omnibus carnibus*").[7]

The gastronomic and alimentary division between the social classes, harshly asserted in literary texts and treatises, does not, then, exclude the presence of rustic flavors and food products in upper-class cooking, strongly marked by an aftertaste of the culture of the masses. These elements, though perhaps predictable to some extent, are surprisingly prevalent. In the courtly recipe collections of the fourteenth century we note the surprising quantity of dishes with a vegetable base and the regular use of garlic and onions in condiments and *soffritti*. The simplicity of many of the preparations is equally striking, and we could easily imagine these dishes eaten at a peasant's table, were it not for the presence of a few precious ingredients or a distinctive finishing touch, such as the addition of spices, that immediately brings us back to a world of social and economic privilege. The presence of refined details is in fact another important indicator of the process of "ennobling" humble food, in addition to the juxtaposition of contrasting elements. Hence we find the following instruction: "Take some turnips that have been well boiled in water, and fry them in a pan with oil, onion, and salt, and, when they are cooked and ready to be sent to the table, add some spices to the serving bowls."[8] A Tuscan recipe for "onion salad" makes a similar suggestion: "Take some onions, cook them in the embers, then peel and cut them into long thin strips. Add some vinegar, salt, oil, and spices, and serve."[9] Here only the addition of spices signals the difference in class. We find another example in a recipe for "garlic *torta*" in the Venetian cookbook: "Take a few cloves of garlic, peel them, and place them on the boil. When they are cooked, steep them in cold water, and then pound them into a paste," moistening the mixture with eggs. Finally, the recipe proposes adding some saffron, fresh cheese, whipped lard, strong, sweet spices, and raisins.[10]

All this implies the existence of a shared base of culinary culture, a pattern of food practices and customs that cuts across all social classes, transcending symbolic differences. The mixing of "common things with precious things" or the possibility of choosing either option is already present in the Tuscan recipe collection at the end of the fourteenth century, which leaves all decisions to the discretion of the gentleman: "In every sauce, condiment, or broth, one can put precious things, which is to say, gold, precious stones, rare spices, cardamom, aromatic herbs or common greens, onions, and leeks, as you may desire."[11]

Not everyone shared this perspective, however. At the end of the fourteenth century, a northern version of the *Liber de coquina* eliminated the entire section devoted to vegetables.[12] Still, as Rebora has pointed out, it is remarkable how many elements from the cuisine of the poor were unhesitatingly assimilated into the cuisine of the court, as we see in the *Liber de coquina* and the majority of its Italian offshoots, a pattern that stands in sharp contrast with the bourgeois recipe collections, which tend to exclude these elements. This may be due to the fact that there was greater social proximity between the bourgeoisie and the lower classes, stimulating the desire of the middle classes to distinguish themselves from the poor.[13] Yet, as we have taken pains to emphasize, the quantity of foods and flavors shared across class lines was generally considerable, a phenomenon that was typically, if not exclusively, *Italian*.

From medieval times onward, Italian cooking distinguished itself within the European culinary context by virtue of its abundant use of garden products, not only vegetables (cultivated, or wild if the garden variety was unavailable)[14] but also aromatic herbs—often used with precious spices—such as marjoram and mint (two flavors characteristic of Italian cooking during the Middle Ages and the Renaissance and frequently recommended by Scappi in his sixteenth-century recipes), as well as rosemary, parsley, sage, and dill. Other flavors mentioned, somewhat less often, are basil, bay leaf, catnip, and, in Scappi's work, pimpernel and wild thyme. Italian recipe collections reveal an acceptance of nature that was unparalleled elsewhere, since they feature even ingredients such as mushrooms and truffles, the sign of an intense exchange of knowledge between the world of the peasants and urban and aristocratic environments.

The great recipe collections of the fifteenth and sixteenth centuries adopted and expanded this tradition. Cabbages, turnips, fennel, mushrooms, squash, lettuce, parsley, and all sorts of herbs and legumes—such as broad beans and peas—are the basis of many preparations proposed by Maestro Martino (soups, torte, and fritters). Platina carefully offers detailed instructions on how to flavor lettuce, endives, oxtongue, moss rose, mallow, radishes, sassafras, pimpernel, and sorrel, as well as mixed salad:

> A mixed salad is prepared with lettuce, oxtongue, mint, catnip, fennel, parsley, watercress, oregano, chervil, chicory, and dandelion greens (described by doctors as *taraxacum* and *arnoglossa*), wonderberry, fennel flowers, and various other aromatic herbs, well washed and drained. These are placed in a large dish and flavored with abundant salt. Oil is added, and vinegar sprinkled on top. The salad is then left to macerate for a short while. Because of the wild coarseness of the ingredients, one must be careful to chew thoroughly when eating.[15]

In 1569 Costanzo Felici wrote: "Salad foods, according to those who live beyond the Alps, are almost exclusive to greedy Italians, who have appropriated the food of those base animals that eat raw greens." His statement appears in a long letter to Ulisse Aldrovandi, titled *De' insalata e piante che in qualunque modo vengono per cibo del'homo* (On salads and plants that in some way become the food of men), which constitutes a genuine treatise on gastronomic botany.[16] We find many other famous examples of this type of document—part scientific treatise and part cookbook—in Italy. We must also mention *Archidipno, ovvero dell'insalata e dell'uso di essa* (Archidipno; or, On salad and its uses), a monumental work of erudition published in 1627 by Salvatore Massonio from L'Acquila. Massonio, a physician, applies the scholarly touch of the humanist to the selection and harvesting of greens, co-opting the Greek term "*archidipno*" to describe the initial part of the meal where salads composed of greens, flowers, and fruits, all mixed together, constitute the central principle and the major appeal.

An especially important work from our perspective is the *Brieve racconto di tutte le radici, di tutte l'erbe e di tutti i frutti che crudi o cotti in Italia si mangiano* (Brief account of all roots, greens, and fruits that are eaten in Italy, raw or

Woman milking, woman carrying eggs, man toasting,
man carrying a main dish (woodcuts).

Source: Hortus Sanitatis (1491).

cooked), by Giacomo Castelvetro, who lived in exile from Italy because of his Protestant convictions. Written in 1614 and remaining unpublished during the author's lifetime, this document offers a kind of overview of Italian gastronomy, highlighting one of its most original and distinctive aspects: the use of vegetables and salads, foods that Castelvetro misses in "carnivorous" England. With what we can best describe as a profound sense of homesickness, he extols and yearns for a gastronomic identity that he believes to be his own. This is especially interesting when we take into account the fact that Castelvetro was born in Modena in the Po Valley and adopted Venice as his home after a long period of travel around Europe. If we tend to think of vegetarian cooking as confined to Mediterranean interests, this example suggests otherwise.

A Neapolitan writer reflects a feeling for vegetables that is no different from Castelvetro's. In a short story by Giambattista Basile, we find the grief-stricken farewell of a rich merchant's son, exiled from his beloved Naples: "Goodbye to parsnips and dead leaves; goodbye to *zeppoli* and puddings; to cabbages and *tarantello* [tuna sausage]. . . . Goodbye Naples, city beyond compare. Bereft of your hearty soups, I must go, for I have been evicted from this fine home. My broccoli, I must leave you behind!"[17]

Castelvetro takes care to explain why "Italians eat more greens and fruit than meat": "The main reason is that our lovely Italy is not as attached to meats as is France or this island [England]. For we must make great efforts to find new foods to nourish the large number of people found in such a small area of the earth. The other motive, no less compelling than the one already given, is the great heat experienced there nine months of the year, which makes us grow tired of meat."[18] He thus explains the consumption of vegetables in terms of poverty and climate, motivations that are soon transformed into customs, skills, and *culture*. Castelvetro writes that, "in order to prepare an excellent salad, it is not enough to be able to procure many fine greens," since the cook also needs to know how to treat the ingredients appropriately. He finds this skill lacking in many foreign cooks, both women and men, and he addresses his lengthy instructions to this audience, describing all the necessary phases in the preparation of salads: one must clean, wash, and dry the leaves, add salt and then oil, toss the salad, add vinegar, and toss again. This is in keeping with the "salad law," which requires that "salad must be well salted, with little vinegar and lots of oil." His conclusion is that those who sin "against this worthy commandment" deserve "never to eat a good salad again."[19] Obviously, his directive is intended for those who can afford to use abundant quantities of oil. The dinner table of Berto Panada, the peasant described in Folengo's *Baldus*, offers only "a little salad of various greens," dressed with "salt, vinegar, and a few carefully counted drops of oil."[20]

The range of vegetables and fruits consumed, which had not changed substantially in the thousand years since the end of the Roman era, was in the process of expansion. From the fourteenth to the fifteenth century, spinach, which came to Italy from Persia by way of the Arabs, had spread throughout the land.[21] At the beginning of the fourteenth century Bonvesin de la Riva already included it among the specialties of the Lombard countryside.[22]

Then came the artichoke. It was derived from the wild cardoon or thistle through a process of cross-fertilization, already long practiced in the Middle East, though various authors have attributed it to the talent of Italian horticulturists in the fifteenth century.[23] "In Italy today you can find artichokes of different kinds, the prickly variety, open and closed, or the smooth variety, round, broad, open, and closed," according to Andrea Mattioli in 1557.[24] In the letter of 1569 cited above, Costanzo Felici notes the widespread availability and consumption of artichokes, especially in elevated social environments. "They are the fruit of prickly plants or grasses that are known by now to everyone. The craze for them has grown so much that they have become very familiar to all, and they enjoy an excellent reputation among the great," who eat them both raw and cooked, "in different ways, with oil or fat or butter, with salt and pepper, cooked on the grill, on the fire, or in rich broth, and in many other ways, depending on which gives most pleasure."[25]

The first mention of artichokes in a culinary text is found in an anonymous work produced in Naples at the end of the fifteenth century.[26] In the sixteenth century, culinary writers (Messisbugo, Romoli, and Scappi) make abundant use of them, in one case going as far as to provide instructions on how an artichoke should be correctly "carved."[27] As the craze for artichokes spread, what seemed especially striking to foreigners was that the Italian enthusiasm for raw food could extend even to artichokes. In 1581 Montaigne notes in his *Travel Journal*: "Throughout Italy they serve beans raw, and also peas and green almonds, and they seldom cook artichokes." It is possible to serve them like this mainly "at the beginning of the [artichoke] season," which is to say, "in the time of Lent," when, not surprisingly, they are "very sought after."[28] In 1636 Paolo Zacchia, though finding that the artichoke tastes best when cooked in one way or another, notes in his *Il vitto quaresimale* (Food for Lent), "It goes down more smoothly when boiled; when roasted, it is easier on the stomach, and when truffled (as cooks describe it when it is flavored with wild mint, a small quantity of finely chopped garlic, pepper, oil, and salt), it reawakens the appetite. And, in any case, it can make a good drink, for it is appetizing."[29]

The artichoke's success was quite different from the fate of the eggplant, imported by the Arabs to Spain and Sicily. Although it already appears in the thirteenth-century *Novellino*,[30] and it returns in the fourteenth-century *Tacuina sanitatis*, the eggplant was viewed with suspicion for a very long time. In fact, its Italian name, *melanzana*, derived from *mela insana* (unsound apple), and Scappi's preference for the term *pomo sdegnoso* (lowly apple) already give us some idea of its humble status. Mattioli calls it a "vulgar plant," since it was customarily eaten by the common people: "Fried in oil with salt and pepper, it is eaten by the masses, in the way that mushrooms are eaten."[31] Costanzo Felici is similarly suspicious of the eggplant, disdaining the widespread enthusiasm of those who consume it greedily, "usually cooked on the coals, on the grill, or fried."[32] Despite the eventual, though still infrequent, presence of the eggplant in the most important recipe collections, it continued to retain an image of social and cultural marginality, which was accentuated by its special place in Jewish cooking. In the seventeenth century Frugoli wrote that "eggplants should be eaten only by people of lowly station or by Jews."[33] Vincenzo Tanara echoes the same association: "[eggplants are] for the consumption of people from the countryside and especially for families, since they are a customary food of the Jews."[34] We find it again in the middle of the nineteenth century, but at this juncture Pellegrino Artusi reverses the terms of the earlier appraisal, noting that if the eggplant "was regarded as an inferior food because it was eaten by the Jews," this would only confirm that "in this matter and in other issues of greater importance, Jews have more discernment than Christians."[35]

Green beans, mentioned in Messisbugo's *Banchetti* (Banquets), and cauliflower, in Scappi's *Opera*, made their earliest appearance in the recipe collections of the sixteenth century. The cultivation of sweet fennel began in the course of the same century. This was a new variety, which is still used today, different from the smaller, aromatic fennel that appears as a condiment in medieval cooking. According to the agronomist Tanara, fennel was "the glory of Bolognese cultivators,"[36] and it enjoyed enormous success on the dinner tables of the Renaissance. "Sweet, fresh fennel" (or more precisely, "sweet green fennel, peeled") appears in practically all of Scappi's lists of foods. It is always served at the end of the meal, as is the custom in the south of Italy even in our own time.

Next comes the great historical chapter on the foods of the Americas. Scappi's work contrasts "Turkish" squash (still widely used today) with the native variety (*lagenaria*), well known since ancient times and used regularly in medieval cooking. In 1584 Giovan Battista Rossetti makes an allusion to "eyeless beans" that were brought from America,[37] since the only bean known in Italy and Europe in ancient and medieval times was the smaller *dolico*, with its characteristic "eye."[38]

The tomato, initially regarded as an ornamental fruit and later adopted as a food, was an exotic curiosity that first appears in the writings of P. A. Mattioli and José de Acosta, travelers and naturalists.[39] Apart from these sources, allusions to its consumption are very rare. Costanzo Felici tells us, however, that the usual "gluttons and people greedy for new things" did not realize that they could eat the tomato as they would eat mushrooms or eggplants, fried in oil and flavored with salt and pepper.[40] Although we must not exclude the possibility that tomatoes were consumed at an earlier date by the common people, it is only at the end of the seventeenth century that we observe their inclusion in elite cuisine, thanks to the Neapolitan recipe collection of Antonio Latini. Iberian influences may be detected in their adoption for culinary purposes, since various recipes that call for tomatoes are designated as "in the Spanish style." Among these is a recipe for "tomato sauce,"[41] which is flavored with onions and wild thyme "or *piperna*" and subsequently adjusted to taste by adding salt, oil, and vinegar. With a few modifications, this preparation was to enjoy a remarkable future in Italian cuisine and in the industry of preserved foods. The custom observed in ancient and medieval times, as well as during the Renaissance, of serving sauces as an accompaniment to "boiled foods or other dishes"—as Latini expresses it in this instance—facilitated the acceptance of the tomato by integrating it into an established gastronomic tradition. For the same reason, it gained widespread currency in Italian cooking in the eighteenth and nineteenth centuries. Panunto in Tuscany, Vincenzo Corrado in Naples, and Francesco Leonardi in Rome all include it in their recipe books.

The "social success" of the pepper, another vegetable that originated in the Americas, was more complicated, as it was not integrated into Italian cuisine for a long time. We find a few references to peppers in the gastronomic literature of the seventeenth century. Carlo Nascia suggests it the preparation of turkey, and Antonio Latini proposes it as flavoring in some sauces.[42] *Il cuoco galante* (The gallant cook), written by Corrado a century later, echoes the same lukewarm attitude toward the pepper. Here it is described as a "vulgar, rustic food," though the writer admits that it already appeals to "many people." We can thus imagine a history rather similar to that of the tomato. In the nineteenth century peppers preserved in vinegar by an innkeeper in Verona ended up on the table of Napoleon, the emperor of Austria, and the king of Naples.[43] Such accounts seem to contradict the myth of an unchanging cuisine practiced by the common people, extremely resistant to innovation. Although it is often thought that innovation occurs only among the aristocracy and the bourgeoisie, who are less conditioned by the pangs of hunger,[44] in some cases the exact opposite appears to be the case.

The potato on the other hand was treated with enduring suspicion. Italian navigators who encountered it for the first time in the Americas in the sixteenth century found that it tasted like chestnuts.[45] Yet it took another two hundred years before potatoes became a regular part of the Italian diet. With the onset of various famines in the eighteenth century, the public authorities launched an intense propaganda campaign that finally convinced the peasants to accept this strange "white truffle" (as the potato was often called), both as an everyday food item and as a crop for cultivation, even if common sense seemed to suggest to them that it might be more appropriately used as pig feed. It is interesting to note that, as in the case of the tomato, the integration of the potato into traditional cooking went through a process of acclimatization, though the process occurred here in a rather erratic fashion. The potato was recommended to the peasants as a replacement for wheat flour in baking. Italian agronomists of the 1700s, such as Giovanni Battarra, were particularly insistent on this point, as was

Parmentier in France.[46] It was also assimilated into the traditional way of preparing turnips. According to Battarra: "Boiled and cut into slices, dress with garlic, pepper, petrosellino, and oil in a pan, they make a tasty treat. [Potatoes] can also be boiled and dressed with oil, salt, and vinegar, in a manner similar to that used for preparing turnips."[47] In addition, potatoes were used in preparing dumplings, a dish favored by the common people since the Middle Ages, when they were first prepared with flour or grated bread.[48] This experience soon showed the variety of refined preparations to which this new import could lend itself. Recipe books written in the early nineteenth century already indicate the level of attention paid by "high" culture to the use of the potato in cooking. The Neapolitan writer Vincenzo Corrado includes a "Treatise on Potatoes" (*Trattato sulle patate o pomi di terra*) in his work *Il cuoco galante*. Bearing in mind the lesson taught by the eighteenth-century agronomists, he too recommends that potato meal be used in baking bread, suggesting that it be mixed with an equal amount of wheat flour. In addition, he "reveals" over fifty different culinary uses for potatoes.[49]

Polenta, Soup, and Dumplings

We dedicated the opening section of this chapter to vegetables in order to acknowledge their centrality in Italian cuisine. Nevertheless, in tracing the history of Italy's resources and gastronomic products, we must not overlook the fact that throughout much of this history grains played a consistent role in the nourishment of the poor, offering them an essential weapon in their daily struggle for survival. In this sense, we must point out that the use of polenta, more than any other food, reveals the continuity of Italian cooking, going back to long before the Middle Ages, to the customs of the ancient Italic people who inhabited the peninsula in antiquity. This was an important dish in the diet of the peasants since Roman times, when it was called *puls* and prepared with spelt flour. Over time, spelt was used side by side with wheat flour, from which bread was eventually made, and with various other, less valuable grains and seeds, such as barley, millet, foxtail, and sorghum, some of which were native plants and some of which had been imported from other parts of the Mediterranean shore. Given their lack of suitability for bread making, these grains functioned mainly to transmit and diversify the primordial culture of polenta.

Although the ancients had regarded rye as a weed, between the late Roman period and the early Middle Ages it began to be cultivated for food, first in the Alps and then throughout a wider area, as it was found to be extremely hardy and reliable. During medieval times, rye flour became one of the main ingredients for making bread in the northern part of the peninsula. This bread had a dark color that contrasted visually and symbolically with the whiteness of wheat bread, a luxury food reserved for the nobility. In the south, barley, not rye, was used along with wheat (and, on the social level, in contrast to it).

Legumes were normally associated with the inferior grains, partly because they were cultivated alongside them in the fields, and partly because they had similar nutritional uses. After legumes had been set aside to dry for a period of time, their floury substance could be mixed with grains to bake bread or more often to make polenta or soup.[50] A *pulmentario*, or gruel, of broad beans and fox-tail millet (*faba et panico mixto*) appears in a document issued in Lucca in the year 765, referring to the food distributed three times a week as alms to the poor.[51] Similar use was made of chestnuts, which, from the High Middle Ages onward, were an important resource for people living in mountainous regions, particularly in the Apennines, as well as for those living farther afield. "Many are nourished by an abundance of chestnuts, foxtail, and beans, instead of bread," wrote Bonvesin da la Riva at the end of the thirteenth century, referring to the inhabitants of Milan.[52] *Panicium*, a dish also mentioned by Bonvesin, in *De magnalibus Mediolani*, derived its name from *panico*, or foxtail, which had become widespread mainly in the north-central part of Italy. A trace of this name survives today in the term *panizza*, used in Piedmont to designate a rice soup and in Genoa to indicate a dish made with chickpea flour.[53] At the turn of the thirteenth century the Bolognese agronomist Piero de' Crescenzi informs us that foxtail could be cooked in water or milk, "either whole, or broken up and ground." Showing a preference for foxtail, he notes that, "regardless of how it is prepared, it is superior to millet."[54] Yet millet was to be more widely cultivated, spreading from the north to the south-central part of Italy, and it probably constituted the main ingredient used in polenta until the emergence of maize in modern times. In an agricultural treatise written in the middle of the sixteenth century, Agostino Gallo from Brescia offers a recipe for millet polenta in the voice of the shepherd Scaltrito.[55]

Polenta and soup are foods of the poor. Yet even these "poor" dishes, intended mainly to appease the pangs of hunger and guarantee basic survival, left significant traces in the cooking manuals addressed to the upper classes. The dish of "broken broad beans" recommended by the Neapolitan writer of the *Liber de coquina* at the beginning of the fourteenth century is really a type of polenta made with beans, similar to the dish known as *macco*, widely documented as typical of the diet of the peasants.[56] The initial recipe is quite basic and straightforward (though a subsequent, more elaborate version, calls for the addition of spices and sugar): "Carefully select some broken broad beans, and boil them in water. When they are ready, remove them, and rinse thoroughly. Then place the beans back in the pot with some lukewarm water and salt, making sure that there is enough water to cover them completely. Stir frequently with a spoon. When they are ready, take the beans off the fire, and mash them firmly with a spoon. Let them stand for a while. After they are drained, add some honey or onion-flavored oil, and eat."[57]

The "*paniccia* with milk" that appears in the Tuscan recipe collection from

Selling Parmesan Cheese; facing page: *Grocer, Doughnut Maker, Baker, Tripe Vendor* (engravings).

Source: *Le arti di Bologna disegnate da Annibale Carracci* (Rome, 1646).

45. Pizzicarolo.

4. Tripparolo.

the same century is equally telling. A simple "legume" (thus defined by the writer, who perhaps mistook foxtail for a legume) is carefully washed and pounded, boiled, and then mixed with milk and lard. This would be a genuine peasant recipe were it not for the fact that here, rather than constituting the main part of the meal (as occurred in the case of the stew offered to the poor of Lucca a few centuries earlier), the "*paniccia*" is destined to accompany something more substantial: "This item may be eaten with roast kid."[58]

The medieval recipe collections also include polentas made from oatmeal, barley, or millet that are sometimes proposed as dishes "for the sick,"[59] meaning that they are simple, straightforward, and without added elements. Yet for this very reason they are close to the version consumed by the common people. Spelt, millet, and legumes appear in the recipe collections of Maestro Martino and Platina. Numerous soups based on the use of the minor grains (barley, foxtail, and millet), as well as chestnuts and legumes (peas, chickpeas, chiclings, broad beans, lentils, and split beans), appear in Scappi's work,[60] where they are embellished with the addition of spices, sugar, and choice meats and are nonetheless still reminiscent of a cooking style rooted in peasant custom. Scappi seems perfectly aware of this, when, for example, he notes in his recipe for a soup of dried split beans that the dish "is called *macco* in Lombardy."[61]

The word macaroni (*maccheroni* in Italian), which was used in earlier times to denote dumplings (*gnocchi*), is also derived from *macco*.[62] Dumplings were a cherished dish among peasants (typically in northern Italy), unlike pasta, which we will discuss shortly. They are really a variant of the *pulmentum* and are defined as such by Folengo,[63] whose fourteenth- and fifteenth-century recipe collections provide us with the earliest recipes, written with absolute simplicity: flour or grated bread is mixed with cheese or egg yolk, forming dumplings that can be cooked in boiling water.[64]

These are the famous "macaroni" that are seen sliding down a mountain of grated cheese along with ravioli in one of Boccaccio's tales. The mountain is located at the center of Bengodi, whose marvels are celebrated by the simple-minded Calandrino.[65] A comparable image of the "Land of the Good Life" is evoked in a story by an anonymous sixteenth-century writer, who transfers the traditional, utopian land of abundance (*La Cuccagna*) to the other side of the Atlantic Ocean, recently traversed by European explorers. Rather than offering exotic food, this faraway place features a freestanding mountain of grated cheese that looms over the plain. At the top stands a huge, ever-boiling cauldron full of macaroni that, when cooked, will be sent off to supply the whole world.[66] By the sixteenth century (despite the fact that other kinds of macaroni had appeared in the meantime, including the variety we recognize as such today), not even the cooks employed at court, including those of the caliber of Scappi or Messisbugo,[67] omitted the preparation of "*maccheroni* called *gnocchi*," which is "made with the best flour breadcrumbs and boiling water, cooked on the grate, and covered with *agliata* [garlic sauce] when boiled." Such dishes now appear alongside the most prestigious and refined recipes.[68]

Buckwheat was first introduced into northern Italy between the end of the fifteenth and beginning of the sixteenth century. With this grain the peasants of Lombardy and the Alpine regions began to make a type of polenta that had a sharper taste and a different color. Who indeed could forget the "little gray polenta made of buckwheat" that the nineteenth-century novelist Alessandro Manzoni places on the table of Tonio and his impoverished family in *I promessi sposi* (set in seventeenth-century Lombardy)?[69] In contrast to this gray polenta, the new yet ancient dish the peasants of the Po Valley began to make from maize (which had been discovered in America) was yellow, the same color as the polenta traditionally made from millet.

By the second half of the sixteenth century, maize was widely cultivated and consumed by the peasant population.[70] Though its use was first limited to the Veneto, it was soon adapted and modified according to the customs of traditional cuisine. In a document written at the time, the physician Castore Durante of Gualdo reported that "the peasants make polenta with [maize] flour."[71] The special use that Italians made of maize, which became part of their national history, was unknown to the populations of the Americas, who, as Francesco Carletti noted in his travel journal, consumed maize in many different ways, boiled or roasted, whole, grated, or mashed, but not in the form of polenta.[72] As often happens in cultural history, and hence in culinary history, an element that was perceived as different was transformed or adapted in such a way that it became recognizable as part of a familiar value system. We have already seen how this mechanism worked in the case of the potato (which was used to prepare dumplings and often to make bread) and the tomato (which was transformed into a sauce).

In the case of maize, however, the process of adaptation had drastic consequences. Around the turn of the eighteenth century, epidemics of pellagra spread across the Italian countryside. This illness, which is caused by a vitamin deficiency, was activated by the limitations of a diet consisting almost exclusively of maize in the form of polenta. The special way in which maize is treated in order to make polenta destroys some of the vitamins that are essential to the human body, and for this reason a phenomenon of this type had never occurred in America.[73]

Though initially used alongside traditional grains, maize gradually swept away everything else in its path. Because of the unrelenting food shortages of the eighteenth century, peasants were obliged to choose the most productive crop at the expense of all others. "Since flour is scarce in a time of famine, they must turn to sweet polenta," the agronomist Vincenzo Tanara wrote in the middle of the seventeenth century, referring to the habits of the peasants of Emilia.[74] A century later, Giovanni Battarra, another agronomist, reported that after 1715, "which the elders always call the year of famine," maize (along with potatoes) helped many people to survive.[75] Faced with images like these, we can understand the almost total absence of maize in the cuisine of the upper classes. This absence is perhaps essential in both symbolic and gastronomic terms. A soup of "coarse wheat," meaning maize, appears in Scappi's *Opera*,[76] but the cooking treatises of the seventeenth century by Bartolomeo Stefani and Antonio Latini refer to the new grain product only as animal fodder.[77] By contrast, in one of Carlo Goldoni's plays, *La donna di garbo*, which features the perpetually hungry Harlequin as its protagonist, the beloved Rosaura sings the praises of "golden" polenta.[78]

During the modern era, rice too became a food of the common people. This has a more complex history and also involves the cuisine of the upper classes. Almost unknown to Greek and Roman writers, rice was introduced into the West by the Arabs, who began cultivating it in Sicily and Spain. Outside the areas where rice was rapidly introduced into cooking traditions, its availability was for a long time limited to the spice shop. In north-central Italy, in fact, rice was sold by spice vendors along with medicines and exotic items from abroad. In the Middle Ages it was used mainly in the form of flour, either for medicinal purposes (the sixth-century treatise on dietetics by Anthimus, for example, recommends it as a remedy for dysentery)[79] or to thicken soups. Thus the fourteenth-century *Liber de coquina* uses it in the preparation of *biancomangiare* with the specific purpose of providing a thicker consistency (*sit spissum sicut risus solet esse*).[80] The cultivation and consumption of rice in the human diet became widespread only in the fifteenth century. Written sometime around midcentury, Martino's cookbook offers a recipe that had already been foreshadowed as a variant in many earlier recipe collections and is in some ways the missing link between the medieval use of rice in the form of flour and its modern use as a dish unto itself.[81] This recipe, for rice with almond milk, is an "autonomous" dish, but it is unmistakably reminiscent of *biancomangiare* in its exclusive use of white ingredients such as rice, milk, and sugar.[82]

Rice took hold in the north of Italy in the fifteenth century. In 1475 Galeazzo Maria Sforza, lord of Milan, wrote two letters agreeing to export some bags of rice for cultivation to the countryside of Ferrara. This suggests that it had already been cultivated in Lombardy for some time. In the sixteenth century rice, like maize, joined the list of the "new foods" used by official food agencies in their attempt to resolve nutritional shortages among the peasant class. The fact that it is destined for the common people is verified in the chronicle of Pompeo Vizani of Bologna in an account of the dramatic consequences of the famine of 1590. Vizani describes how a large number of poor people from the countryside poured into the city seeking food but were immediately forced back outside the walls so that they would not upset the precarious balance of provisions stored in town. To keep the peasants quiet until the next harvest, an order was issued that "each day in different parts of the county, four ounces of rice should be distributed to each person among them."[83] Probably as a result of this revised image of rice as a "poor" food suitable for filling the bellies of the starving masses, it did not command special attention in the recipe collections used at court in the sixteenth century. In fact, following the boom of the fifteenth and sixteenth centuries, rice seems to vanish from sight in the seventeenth century, especially because of the controversy over environmental hygiene that convinced the authorities almost everywhere to limit or prohibit the cultivation of rice as "unhealthy and pestilence-ridden." This was due to the fact that in the north there was a widespread custom of flooding the rice fields to accelerate the growth of the crop. Rice came back into its own in the eighteenth century in answer to particularly severe food shortages, in much the same way as maize and potatoes did. It was now introduced into some areas for the first time, and its consumption was resumed in others. The reputation of rice as a "poor food" was thus confirmed, though more refined uses were springing up side by side with this image thanks to the introduction of different kinds of risotto in the north and the creation of complex dishes such as molds and *sartù* in the south.

The Invention of Pasta

Like other communities around the Mediterranean and elsewhere in the world, the Romans had already adopted the custom of preparing dough from flour and water and flattening it into a wide sheet called a *lagana* —known today as lasagna— that was then cut into broad strips and cooked. But it was only in the Middle Ages that some of the distinctive elements emerged that make pasta the culinary category we know today.[84] These elements include above all a great variety of shapes and sizes, broad or narrow, elongated or short, hollow or filled. Another aspect of pasta is its enormous range of preparation. In contrast to the Roman custom of cooking the *lagana* in the oven along with the sauce that functioned partly as a cooking liquid,[85] a new custom emerged in the Middle Ages that was destined to last down through the centuries: the practice of boiling the dough in water, broth, or occasionally milk.

Dried pasta, designed to last over time, eventually came into use. Its invention marked the transformation of a handmade product into an industrial one, suitable for transportation and commercialization. The origin of this fundamental aspect of the history of pasta is usually attributed to the Arabs,[86] who introduced the technique of drying dough in order to guarantee food supplies for their long journeys through the desert. Dried pasta appears in Arabic recipe collections in the ninth century. Hence the presence of pasta manufacturers in Sicily, specifically in western Sicily, where Arab culture dominated, can be plausibly linked to this tradition. The phenomenon is documented from the twelfth century onward. The geographer Edrisis informs us of the existence of a

genuine industry of dried pasta (*itrija*) during this period in Trabian territory,
thirty kilometers from Palermo. He notes that so much pasta was being manufactured in the area that it could be exported to many different places, "to Calabria and to other Muslim and Christian countries, and many shiploads are dispatched by sea."[87]

The use of elongated pasta was also probably introduced by the Arabs, and
this is corroborated visually in the illustrations accompanying the fourteenth-
century *Tacuina sanitatis*. Italy was in fact the meeting point of two diverse and
converging gastronomic traditions, the Roman and the Arabic, that were probably linked in turn to other traditions and cultures. Some writers maintain that
pasta originated in Persia, spreading from there to the west with the help of the
Arabs and to the east, where it ultimately became part of Chinese cuisine. A
series of circumstances, not least of which was the decisive role of Italy's maritime cities in the commercial system of the Middle Ages, favored the adoption
of these different traditions by those who lived on the Italian peninsula, as well
as their progressive transformation and extraordinary variety. An increase in the
varieties of pasta accompanied the diffusion of their culinary use, both in the
guise of food freshly prepared for domestic use (in urban as well as rural areas)
and in the form of industrial products shipped along the coast of the peninsula
or transported deep into the European continent. In the twelfth century
Genoese merchants were mainly responsible for the spread of Sicilian pasta in
the regions to the north. Shortly thereafter Liguria established itself as the primary location for the production of vermicelli and other types of pasta, as well
as the site of its heaviest consumption. It is no accident that the recipes for *tria*
presented in the fourteenth century cookbooks are designated as "Genoese."[88]
In subsequent centuries, even down to the modern period, recipe collections
attach the label "Genoese pastas" to this product. In the course of the fifteenth
century other areas of production developed beyond Liguria and Sicily, especially in Apulia, while the Po region (Emilia, Lombardy, and the Veneto)
remained more committed to the domestic use of fresh pasta, a trait that still
endures.

In the meantime, documents mention fresh pasta with increasing frequency.
In the twelfth century lasagne, *tortelli*, and a pasta of "*granelli*"[89] appear on the
table of the hermits of Camaldoli in the Apennine region between Tuscany and
Umbria. These dishes are served on specific occasions and on special feast days,
according to a calendar specifically attuned to the customs of the religious community.[90]

Among fourteenth-century recipe collections, only one, the Neapolitan
Liber de coquina, offers a step-by-step description of the preparation and serving
of lasagna. Here *fermented* dough (we do not know if this is an exception or the
rule) is flattened into a thin sheet and cut into rectangles three inches long.
These are boiled in water and then seasoned, layer by layer, with grated cheese

(*caseum gratatum*) and, if desired, pulverized spice.[91] The recipe concludes with the stipulation that the dish should be eaten with a pointed wooden utensil (*uno punctorio ligneo*). This detail suggests that the precocious use of the fork in Italy was prompted at least in part by the introduction of a dish as difficult to handle as pasta, which is slippery and dangerously hot.[92] In fact, while Italians regularly dined with forks from the fourteenth century onward, other Europeans resisted this innovation, continuing to use their hands right up to seventeenth and eighteenth centuries.

The *Liber* also tells us that "*croseti*" are prepared in a manner similar to lasagne. These are round or oblong in shape, and the cook must press the dough firmly with his finger in order to create a hollow in the center. This is obviously a description of *corzetti*, used in Genoa and Provence, which are not unlike Apulian *cavatelli*.[93]

Elongated pasta is perhaps what is meant by the term "*ancia alexandrina*" that appears in the *Liber*; it is a dish prepared with "Apulian semola" that is supposed to be cooked in almond milk. It is thought that this name derives from the word *ancia*, meaning tube, straw, or "little worm" (*vermicello*).[94] Certainly this is what is indicated by the term *tria*, which appears in a number of written texts and illustrated documents. The earliest technical instructions for the creation of vermicelli are found in Maestro Martino's fifteenth-century recipe collection: "Moisten the dough . . . and spread it out into a thin sheet. Using your hands, break it into little pieces that look more or less like worms, and place these in the sun to dry." Martino also gives us a recipe for "Sicilian macaroni" in which the term "macaroni" clearly indicates the product as we know it today—as short, tubular pieces of pasta (*pasta pertusata*): "Take some flour of very fine quality, and mix it with egg white and rosewater, or even with common water . . . and make dough of a firm consistency. Then break off pieces of dough the length of your palm and as thin as a straw. And take a rod of iron the length of your palm, or longer, and as thin as a piece of string. Place this over the said piece of dough, and, using both hands, roll it over on the table. Then remove the iron and the macaroni will have a hollow space down the middle."[95]

The dish described as "Roman macaroni" is prepared differently, since it does not really involve macaroni (unless the term is used to designate a pasta dish in the broadest sense) but rather *fettuccine* or *tagliatelle*: "Take some fine quality flour, moisten it, and make a sheet of dough a little thicker than that used for lasagne," and fold it across a stick.[96] (This strategy does not create a tubular piece of pasta but allows the *fettuccine* to maintain the same width along the length of each piece).[97] "Then remove the stick and cut the pasta into pieces a scant inch wide, and it will take on the look of ribbons or strings."[98] The same procedure is described with some variations by Messisbugo and Scappi.[99]

Although the pasta products described in texts from the Middle Ages and the Renaissance seem very familiar to us, the rules for cooking them are quite different, as are the condiments that accompany them and the ways in which they are served. In comparison to the contemporary preference of Italians for *pasta al dente* (the consistency of which becomes less firm, however, as one travels from the south to the north of Italy), involving a very brief cooking time, the pasta eaten five or six centuries ago seems decisively overcooked. "The macaroni must be boiled for a period of two hours," writes Maestro Martino in his instructions for "Sicilian macaroni."[100] It is difficult to ascertain when the preference for *pasta al dente* began to prevail. In Scappi's recipes, produced in 1570, it seems to lie in the future, but by the beginning of the 1600s Giovanni Del Turco states that the "appropriate" period for cooking macaroni should not be too long. He also suggests pouring cold water over the pasta immediately after cooking in order to make it "firmer and harder."[101] Nevertheless, the taste for well-cooked pasta persisted for a long time. It can still be found today outside Italy, especially in Germany, where another important trace of the more archaic models of pasta can be observed in the custom of serving it as an accompaniment to other foods, particularly meat. The fourteenth-century *Liber de coquina* suggests that "Genoese pasta" (*tria ianuensi*) should be served "with capons, eggs, and meat of any kind."[102] This rule prevails even two centuries later, as seen in Scappi's suggestions for "capons in dough, boiled and wrapped in lasagne," "boiled domestic ducks, covered with macaroni, Roman style," "fowl boiled and covered with Neapolitan macaroni," "fat geese, boiled and stuffed, covered with *annolini*," and so on.[103] Yet this did not exclude simpler ways of eating pasta. From the thirteenth century onward we find many literary portraits of diners greedily anticipating plates of steaming pasta, including that of Fra Giovanni of Ravenna, about whom Salimbene da Parma wrote: "I never saw a man so eager to eat lasagne with cheese."[104] There is also the figure of Noddo d'Andrea in a story written by Franco Sacchetti; this individual is supposedly famous for his ability to devour "boiling macaroni" with great speed, much to the dismay of those who dine with him, since they often find themselves with nothing left to eat.[105] One might in fact distinguish two different types of consumption split along social lines: pasta as a side dish, which appears in the cuisine of the aristocrats, and pasta as a dish unto itself, which belongs to the customs of the masses and the bourgeoisie.

Cheese—possibly enriched with spices—was the obligatory flavoring for pasta from the outset. This custom lasted at least until the eighteenth century. "It must be known"—says the *Liber de coquina*—"that one should use a large quantity of cheese with both lasagne and corzetti."[106] The cheese could be sliced rather than grated, which is the alternative suggested for Genoese *tria* in the same recipe collection.[107] It is clear, however, that grated cheese was the preferred choice, signifying from the start a successful union between pasta and cheese, the foremost variety of which is Parmesan (or Piacentino, or Lodigiano, as cheese of this type was also known for centuries).[108] All cookbooks confirm this, and not even the new and successful combination of pasta with tomato sauce, which was first introduced around the end of the eighteenth century and fully established by the 1820s,[109] would really change things. Cheese and tomatoes, together or separately, are the most popular and most accessible flavorings for pasta, in contrast to meat sauce and *ragù*, the prevailing choice in Parisian and Neapolitan cooking.

Butter rather than lard, which had appeared from time to time in fourteenth-century recipes, was added to sweeten the cheese from the fifteenth century onward.[110] The spices that were pulverized and sprinkled on top of the pasta are also described as "sweet": "Add fresh butter and sweet spices to the dish along with grated cheese in a goodly quantity," wrote Maestro Martino in his recipe for "Sicilian macaroni." Throughout the modern era, sugar and cinnamon were considered as indispensable as cheese. Practically all the pasta dishes in Scappi's recipe collection are served with the addition of "cheese, sugar, and cinnamon on top."

The extraordinarily long shelf life of pasta (macaroni and vermicelli dried in the sun can last "two or three years," according to Maestro Martino) led to its growing commercial and gastronomic success, above all in areas served by urban markets. We do not know a great deal about pasta consumption in rural areas, but it is significant that Teofilo Folengo's *Maccheronee* associates all kinds of pastas—macaroni, lasagne, *tagliatelle*, and *tortelli*—with peasant cooking.[111] Normally, this would have meant fresh pasta, made as needed. The pasta industry did not extend to the countryside, and in fact the climate in many parts of Italy would not have facilitated the domestic production of dried noodles. Nevertheless, for peasants, to serve a dish of pasta meant a feast. In 1694 Girolamo Cirelli notes, with the kind of condescension typical of a city dweller, that "[peasants] imagine they are putting on a big show when they invite a friend to eat and serve him lasagne or macaroni."[112]

The recipe books often describe pasta as a "lean" dish, referring to the observance of liturgical requirements.[113] It is hardly surprising, therefore, to find one of the most complete inventories of "pasta soups" in Paolo Zacchia's *Vitto quaresimale* (Lenten food) in 1636:

> They are very varied, depending on whether the pastas are dried or fresh, broad or narrow, or made with wheat flour or other ingredients. They have many different shapes, since some are round, like those that we call vermicelli or macaroni, and among these some are hollow and others are not. Some pastas are broad and flat, like lasagne, and others are little and round, like the type we call *millefanti*. There are also pastas that are flat but narrow, like *fettucce*, which are usually called *tagliolini*, and others that are short and thick, and we call these *agnolini*. Others are longer and plumper and are called *gnocchi*. And they exist in a thousand other guises, none of them being any better or worse than the other.[114]

Contrast between Carnival and Lent (woodcuts, Florence, ca. 1495).

For a long time, pasta was only one food among many. Even in the sixteenth century it was perceived as a delicacy that could be, or should be, abandoned in times of difficulty. In Naples (where pasta began to be imported from Sicily only toward the end of the fifteenth century), an ordinance issued in 1509 forbade the making of "*taralli, susamelli, ceppule, maccarune, trii vermicelli,*" and all other "things made with dough" during times in which the cost of flour increased "as the result of war, famine, or a bad season."[115] This is evidently not the main dish of the population, nourished on a diet of bread, soup, vegetables, and meat. Even in Sicily pasta was a costly product. Only in 1501 was it included among the basic foods subject to price control, and in the middle of the same century macaroni and lasagne still cost three times as much as bread.

It was during the course of the seventeenth century that pasta began to take on a different role in the Italian diet. The shift was first observed in Naples, where by midcentury overcrowding and a political and economic crisis had led to problems in the availability and distribution of food, particularly meat. In the meantime, a minor technological revolution (brought about by the greater accessibility of the kneading trough and the introduction of the mechanical press) enabled macaroni and other types of pasta to be produced at a considerably more moderate cost than in the past. For this reason, pasta gained a position of great importance in the diet of the city's poorer classes. Thus in the eighteenth century Neapolitans became known as "the macaroni eaters," a term previously reserved for Sicilians.[116] When Goethe visited Naples in 1789 he observed that "macaroni of all kinds . . . are found everywhere at a low price." The method of preparing pasta, however, was still medieval: "Macaroni is cooked in water, and the grated cheese serves both as fat and as flavoring."[117]

The stereotype of the Neapolitan as a devourer of macaroni—further reinforced through visual images—would soon become widespread. In 1860, as the process of Italian unification drew to its conclusion, we find the annexation of Naples by Piedmont evoked symbolically as a pasta feast: "The macaroni is ready, and we will eat it," Cavour wrote to Costantino Nigro, the Piedmontese ambassador to Paris, referring to Garibaldi's entrance into the capital of the erstwhile kingdom.[118] Since this national revolution meant the takeover of the south by the north, it also entailed a revolution in Italy's culinary image. As Franco La Cecla has put it, "the Mediterranean blanket, of which macaroni constitutes an essential part, is drawn further toward the north."[119]

Outside Italy, the stereotype of the macaroni eater was already perceived as part of the Italian character in the broadest sense. At the end of the eighteenth century, Carlo Goldoni, who was invited to dine at the home of "a very agreeable lady" in Paris, was surprised to hear a man named La Cloche reproach his hostess with the words: "Are you serving soup to an Italian? But Italians eat nothing but macaroni, macaroni, and macaroni."[120]

Torte and Tortelli

Stuffed noodles have a special place among the gastronomic innovations of the Middle Ages. They have an interesting history, which would be difficult to comprehend outside the cultural context that saw the emergence of this type of food that was as simple as it was ingenious. Perhaps inspired by an ancient custom

but presented in a substantially new guise, the food of which we speak is the
torta or *pasticcio*, also known as the *pastello* or *coppo*, terms that are used interchangeably in various documents to indicate a container made of dough, with
the dual purpose of containing and cooking a filling, that is placed in a heated
oven or left to cook among red-hot bricks of terracotta or stone.[121] Preparations
of this type were not unknown in the cuisine of ancient Rome, where they were
accorded little importance. We find a few references in Apicius,[122] and the *moretum* in the famous pseudo-Virgilian text simply involves *bringing together* a
piece of flatbread and a mixture of herbs.[123] European cookbooks of the late
Middle Ages, however, include a virtual feast of *torte* or pies, which had apparently originated in Italy. The *Liber de coquina*, written at the beginning of the
fourteenth century (or perhaps at the end of the thirteenth), already reveals a
clear knowledge of this culinary preparation, while beyond the Alps the "*torta*"
would emerge somewhat later, in recipe collections that were probably of Italian influence.[124] In addition, literary and other kinds of textual references allow
us to backdate the product by at least two hundred years. For example, we find
torte in the weekly menu of the hermits of Camaldoli in the twelfth century.[125]

Little is known about the origin of these dishes. It has recently been suggested
that the Parmesan *torta* derives from the ancient cooking tradition of
Mesopotamia, in which we find a preparation quite similar to one described in
Italian and other European recipe collections in the Middle Ages.[126] The recipe
for this extremely complex creation, which appears in the *Liber de coquina* and
was later imitated and adapted, calls for at least six different layers of filling to be
placed in the dough container—pieces of fried chicken with onion and spices,
white and green ravioli with cheese, sausages of meat and ham, slices of pork with
cheese and eggs, sausages made from organ meats, ravioli flavored with almonds
and sugar, and so on—with more layers "if there are sufficient ingredients available." Dates and spices are added to each layer. The entire creation is covered
with a final layer of dough decorated with plums and is left to cook between two
red-hot earthen bricks. The cook must open the top from time to time during the
cooking in order to add lard. Finally, the finished product "is served to the gentle
lord with great pomp and ceremony."[127] The spectacular manner in which this
dish is presented has led to the reasonable supposition that the term "Parmesan"
is not derived from Parma but from the word "*parma*," meaning "shield" or "a
tower-shaped *torta*." The timing and pattern of the arrival of this concept in
Italy—perhaps directly from Egypt, skipping both Greece and Rome—may lead
us to hypothesize the mediation of the Arabs in the High Middle Ages. In any
case, apart from pointing out the strong possibility of its Middle Eastern origin,
we are mainly interested in emphasizing the place (Italy) and the time (the Middle Ages) in which this archetypal idea—if we can call it this—gave rise to an original culinary culture that was shared at the social level, a point of departure for
subsequent important developments. As happens in the case of every invention,

gastronomic or not, it is not so much the origin of the product that captures the interest of the historian but rather the timing and manner of its diffusion.

The *torta* is a food that could have been created expressly to meet the needs of all social classes. Extremely practical and easily prepared and preserved, it was apparently within everyone's reach and could thus be said to connote, in a general way, the existence of a gastronomic culture. From the outset, there was great diversity in its preparation (the filling could be simple or complex, humble or sophisticated) and in the ways used to cook it (not everyone possessed an oven, an attribute of wealthy homes and urban cookhouses). In this sense, it could be described as a typically urban invention.[128] Could it be an accident that the *torta* in its various forms is most conspicuous in recipe collections of bourgeois origin? Yet it was also a dish that was adopted by the poor, and we have already mentioned how the citizens of Parma had to make do with pies prepared without filling during the famine of 1246.[129] Furthermore, how does one account for the agrarian contracts requiring a tribute from peasants to their landlord in the form of a "*turta munda*," or "round pie"? Could this mean that the peasants were supposed to provide *empty* receptacles made of dough? At the very least, it certainly testifies to the sharing of culinary knowledge between the city and the countryside. The *torta* may also have been used as a practical container in the transportation of food. In the thirteenth century Salimbene's chronicle describes pilgrims accompanied by "donkeys laden with bread, wine, and *torte*."[130]

Generally speaking, medieval culture associated the *torta* with vegetables. According to Platina, "the dish that we generally call *torta* probably takes its name from the fact that the vegetables generally used in its preparation are cut up and crushed [*tòrte, cioè strizzate*]." He notes, however, that the greedy appetite characteristic of his own century no longer limits itself to vegetable fillings but demands that "pies be made from the meat of fowl and other farmyard animals." For this reason, he claims, people no longer recognize the (presumed) etymology of *torta*, and the term now designates both the "Pythagorean" variety (made of greens) and the "Gallic" type (made of meats).[131] In the recipes that follow, Platina proposes additional ingredients: fish, grains, fruit, and everything that could be placed in a pie, with eggs and cheese used as binding agents. Cheese, however, was the main ingredient in *fladones*, a type of pie already described in documents dating from the eleventh century.[132]

From what we observe in the medieval recipe collections, the dough container destined to hold the filling does not seem to be made for eating. These recipes emphasize above all that the container must be hard and consistent enough to withstand the cooking process: "Use very hard white dough (*valde durum*) and mold it into the shape of a *coppo*."[133] It can be made with flour and water only, or some egg may be added, as is done in preparing dough for lasagne: "Using the same mixture [as for lasagne] but adding more flour so that the dough becomes firmer and stronger (*durior et forcior*), you shape the hollow crust."[134] Making this crust edible was an important innovation of Renaissance cooking.

"Infinite varieties of *torta*" are evoked by Tommaso Garzoni in 1585 in his *Piazza universale di tutte le professioni del mondo* (Universal marketplace of all the professions in the world), describing the skill and creativity of the cooks: "the common pie, made in the garden, the *tartera*, the *tartaretta*, the sage pie, the *gattafura*, the *migliaccia*, the Lombard pie, the Romagna pie, or the German pie, the 'mad' pie, the Marchesana pie, the containerless pie, the white or black or green pie, and pies made with any other filling."[135] But if we wish to enter the kitchen and see how such dishes are prepared, we must, as usual, consult Scappi. The fifth volume of his *Opera*, entirely dedicated to pastas, reveals that this skill was already fully codified in all its possible alternatives and variations.

There are three basic typologies of pie dishes: the *pasticcio*, the *crostata*, and the *torta*. By *pasticcio*, Scappi means a container made of hard dough, not necessarily intended to be eaten, according to strict medieval tradition. An example of this type is the *fiadone* (thus named "by the common people"), in which "various grains" are cooked, including flour, barley, rice, spelt, millet, and foxtail.[136] The rules for preparing the dough are very precise: it must be made from flour and cold water, without salt, "because when made with warm water and with salt, it rises and then easily collapses and is not very good" (but one should be careful in wintertime that the water does not get too cold, which would affect the result at least as much as using water that is too hot). "It should be allowed to rest on the table for half an hour" to make it firm and dense, and it is then worked into "a round sheet of dough, half an inch thick." Next, the filling is placed on the dough, and it is then topped up and placed in an oven that is "hot enough for baking bread (chap. 335r–v). If no oven is available, the *pasticcio* can be cooked between two terracotta bricks.

When making a *crostata* or a *torta*, however—and here lies the novelty—one must use layers of dough, flavored with clarified fat and butter, that are friable and suitable for eating. Scappi's recipe requires a multilayered base (usually consisting of three layers) sealed around a "*tortiglione*," also made of flaky dough, and topped with two more layers of dough (except in the case of *crostate*, or open pies, which are "without a top layer" [c. 359v]). The difference between the *crostata* and the *torta*[137] lies in the preparation of the filling: large pieces of meat, fish, vegetables, or fruit are placed in the open pie and a blended mixture in the *torta*. "If you want to make a *torta*, mix the ingredients in it," he writes, following his description of a *crostata* made with plums and sour cherries (chap. 386v). And again, at the conclusion of a recipe for a *crostata* of crabmeat and shrimp, he notes: "If you want to make a *torta*, crush the crabmeat or the shrimp" (chap. 384v). This is a frequently suggested variation.

Several different terms can designate the same kinds of preparation, depending on local custom. We learn that open pies (*crostate*) "are called *coppi* by

Neapolitans and *sfogliate* by the people of Lombardy" (chap. 350r), whereas the *torta* is called a *pizza* in Naples—and here the writer explains that what is meant by "*pizza*" is a basic layer of dough "no more than an inch thick, without a top crust" (chaps. 355v, 365r). This item, along with its name, was to achieve the fame and fortune that we all acknowledge.

Scappi does not fail to explain the difference between a vegetable *torta* prepared in the Lombard style (chap. 360r) and the Bolognese variety (chap. 360v), the version most often mentioned in the menus. Both are closed pies, but the Lombard version is deep, and the Bolognese is shallower—"no more than half an inch in height—"and perforated with holes that allow the crust to "deflate." In addition, the dough used for the Lombard *torta* contains eggs, whereas the other dough does not. Otherwise the ingredients are more or less the same (Swiss chard is the basic vegetable, combined with cheese and spices), with a few variations.[138] A third model is the *gattafura*, the Genoese *torta* (chap. 361), whose principal characteristics are the absence of all spices except for pepper, the addition of mint, and most notably the use of "sweet oil" instead of butter.

It is difficult to name a product that Scappi does not manage to translate into an ingredient for a *torta*. He goes as far as to propose an "acorn *torta*" as a variation on the chestnut pie, noting that the flavor of "acorns from the Turkey oak is better than any other kind in producing the desired effect" (chap. 365). The acorns should be cleaned carefully, left to steep, and then boiled in a good broth. When ready, they are pounded through a sieve, and the pulp is added to a mixture of butter; milk; dry, fresh cheese; ricotta or fresh provatura cheese; sugar; cinnamon; pepper; and egg yolks. The mixture is finally placed in a sheet of dough and baked in an oven or between red-hot terracotta bricks. What we have here is an example of how the culture of hunger can be transformed into culinary pleasure.

Along with the *torta* and obviously derived from it both etymologically and as a culinary concept, we find the *tortello*, which was created in medieval times. Margutte, the sly, greedy "half giant" who features as the protagonist of Luigi Pulci's *Il morgante*, has no doubt about the relationship between the two: "I believe in the *torta* and in the *tortello*: one is the mother and the other is her son." More accurately and equally enlightening is Scappi's instruction: "One can make *tortelletti* of the same composition as all kinds of pies and like the *torte* described above" (chap. 389v).

One could easily imagine that this custom originated in the mists of time. Yet it was invented in the Middle Ages, when the art of pasta making and the art of *torta* making developed side by side. The *tortello* involves a kind of synthesis between the two skills. The cook prepares a thin layer of dough, similar to that used for lasagna, which is then cut into little pieces on which some filling is placed. The pieces are then folded over, and the filling is sealed inside, to form little pies (*piccole torte*). They may be cooked in two different ways: boiled in water or broth (and served, like pasta, with cheese and spices) or, alternatively, fried and sweetened with sugar and honey.[139]

The author of the *Liber de coquina* calls for eggs and flour in his recipe for very thin *tortelli* ("*tortella que alio nomine dicuntur crispella vel lagana*").[140] His Tuscan emulator specifies that the *tortelli* may be sealed in different ways, creating all kinds of shapes: "About *tortelli*: You can shape the dough into any instrument you want. You can cut it into the form of a horseshoe, or brooches, rings, letters of the alphabet, or any kind of animal you can imagine. And you can fill these if you wish and cook them in a pan with lard and with oil."[141] The statement "you can fill these *if you wish*" enables us to understand that the *tortello* is designed as the wrapper or container of a possible filling.

But the opposite is also true: the "filling" is not necessarily wrapped or contained in dough. Gastronomically, it also has an independent existence as a kind of blended mixture or rissole that is boiled in broth or fried in fat. This is what the texts call a "*raviolo*," though the term is used with some degree of inconsistency and ambiguity. "*Raviolo*" can also be used as a synonym of "*tortello*," and each of these terms may indicate the finished product, that is, the container along with its filling. Generally speaking, however, *raviolo* designates the filling, and *tortello*, the wrapping or container.[142]

The distinction is absolutely clear in the *Liber de coquina*, which proposes the preparation of egg-sized "*raviolos*" using pork belly that is thoroughly minced and pounded, to which egg, cheese, milk, and spices are added. The cook wraps each meatball in *tortello* dough before cooking them in a pan with plenty of fat. As an alternative to dough, the writer suggests that the filmy substance surrounding the stomach of a kid goat, or something of the same texture, may be used as wrapping.[143] There is a similar recipe, with a different order of preparation, for another ravioli dish, also made of pork belly but additionally enriched with pork liver or lamb's giblets, or with the organs of any other animal desired. The meat is first finely chopped on the cutting board, and aromatic herbs and spices (including saffron) are added. The cook pounds this mixture in the mortar and adds some beaten eggs, blending all the ingredients to create a thick filling. Egg-sized meatballs are carved out of this mixture and then wrapped either in the membrane that surrounds the pig's heart or in a thin layer of pasta ("*loco illius pellis fac alios de pasta*"). These are fried in a pan with oil or other fat, and they may be dipped in honey before serving, if desired.[144] Clearly, the *ravioli* of various colors that are placed in a Parmesan *torta* are also meatballs.[145]

In short, although a *raviolo* may be wrapped in pasta, this is not mandatory. Even Maestro Martino is explicit on this issue. When discussing "white ravioli," he states that these "can be made without dough." But a gloss in the margins adds, "but if you want to make them with dough, you may do so."[146] This was already a time-worn alternative, as we discover in the chronicle written of Salimbene da Parma in 1284. Here the writer notes that on the Feast of Saint Clare he "ate ravioli without a covering of dough for the first time."[147] Similarly, Scappi's recipe collection calls for both "wrapped" and "unwrapped" ravioli.[148] Del Turco's *Epulario* (written at the beginning of the seventeenth century) makes a sharper distinction between *tortelli* and *ravioli*. For the latter "you must use the same filling as for the *tortelli* mentioned above and omit the shell," molding the ravioli into shapes that look rather like long, thick strips of pork liver and then sprinkling them with a little flour "so that they do not stick to each other."[149] Although there was some confusion and variation in the terminology used from one location to another, the same concept prevailed right up to the time of Pellegrino Artusi, whose "Romagna-style ravioli" are simply small flour dumplings made with ricotta, cheese, and eggs and then boiled and flavored with cheese and meat sauce or "served as a side dish with a stew or a *fricandò*" (in much the same way as suggested by Scappi).[150] Artusi then introduces "Genoese-style ravioli," noting that "these really should not be called ravioli, as true ravioli are not made with meat and are not wrapped in pastry shells."[151]

Although they are the outcome of a refined culinary preparation, *tortelli* and *ravioli* also bring to mind the popular art of recycling leftover food, which is implicit by nature in all meat loaves or meatballs.[152] The existing culinary texts reveal almost nothing about this, but it is interesting to note that Ortensio Lando's imaginative work *Catalogo de gli inventori delle cose che si mangiano* (Catalog of inventors of things that may be eaten) attributes the invention of such dishes to a peasant woman from Lombardy rather than announcing a more predictable yet more improbable attribution to an illustrious personage of classical antiquity, of the type frequently invoked in discussing all kinds of food practices, from the simplest to the most abstruse. According to Lando, "Libista, a peasant woman from Cernuschio, was the inventor of ravioli wrapped in dough."[153] In the *Baldus*, Teofilo Folengo also makes an agreeable connection between the common people and *torte* or *tortelli* by including these dishes— along with gnocchi and a polenta of broad beans—in the list of treats the late wife of the peasant Tognazzo was apt to prepare for her husband.[154] It is also significant that preparations of this kind are more common in recipe collections of domestic cooking, such as the "notebook" complied by Sister Maria Vittoria della Verde between 1583 and 1606 in the Convent of Saint Thomas in Perugia, than in treatises written by professional cooks.[155]

The Pleasure of Meat

"This nation is not in the habit of eating much meat," Montaigne observed in his *Travel Journal* on describing his visit to Italy.[156] This was not a false impression, as the Italians themselves—including Castelvetro and others—perceived their own nutritional identity above all in terms of grains, vegetables, and

Making *biancomangiare*, working pasta dough, preparing
sauces and seasonings (engraving).

Source: Bartolomeo Scappi, *Opera dell'arte del cucinare* (Venice: Tramezzino, 1570).

legumes. The perspective offered by these contrasts, however, is a comparative
one. In nations such as France, Germany, and England, the culinary system
gives absolute preeminence to meat. Other countries, such as Italy, allow different foods to share the limelight. Even so, having made the necessary adjustments, meat is still regarded as the central value around which the meal is
organized and against which the significance of all other foods is defined. This
is true even when meat is replaced by something else, as is required on days of
abstinence and in the monastic diet, where fish, milk products, and vegetables
play the dominant role, since the concept of substitution seems to imply the
acknowledgment of a superior hierarchical status.

It was during the Middle Ages that the culinary preference for meat began to
assert itself with particular force. As we have already pointed out, this occurred
as new cultural models and new forms of production abolished ancient prejudices (the Romans had for a long time perceived the exploitation of unculti-
vated land as a sign of barbarianism), placing a high value on the activities associated with exploiting the woodlands, such as hunting and grazing, which now
became an integral part of the economic system. It is sufficient to say that in Italian texts of the High Middle Ages the forest was measured in pigs: the number
of pigs it was capable of fattening, or how far it extended.[157] The pig was for a

THE ITALIAN WAY OF EATING

long time a culinary value of primary importance and the principal source of meat at all levels of society (sheep farming, by contrast, was carried out in order to provide milk products, and the sheep was used mainly while it was alive). Game, the other great resource of the forest, was closely linked to the identity of aristocratic cuisine. From different points of view (technical as well as symbolic) hunting evoked an image of war, the true "calling" of aristocrats.[158] The princely table of the High Middle Ages thus involved a triumphant display of large game: stag, wild boar, and bear. Even a wild ox that had been hunted down as prey appeared in a banquet offered by Charlemagne in Pavia to celebrate his conquest of the kingdom of Lombardy.[159]

As time passed, styles of living changed, and culinary preferences and tastes were duly transformed. In courtly society of the thirteenth and fourteenth centuries and in urban circles quick to imitate the style of the elite, preferences shifted toward the consumption of fowl, both game (pheasant, partridge, and quail) and farmyard birds (capons and geese) but generally involving the more delicate meats the doctors considered "light." These meats are not closely associated with images or symbols of war, like those evoked in the hunt for large prey and the duel fought out in physical contact with the hunted beast, images that were preserved for a long time by aristocratic culture, though in a gradually less forceful way. The shift in tastes thus reveals a shift in the process of understanding the exercise of power and the importance of class. Courtly society no longer identified itself (or at least did not do so exclusively) as a class of warriors bearing weapons but upheld refinement of manners and the art of living well as the mark of social difference. The earliest manuals of good manners came into existence at this time.[160]

The discussion of meat in the late-thirteenth-century *Liber de coquina* begins with fowl, particularly the domestic variety ("*de carnibus volatilium et primo de domesticis*"). This is a sign of changing times, since a couple of centuries earlier no one would have singled out poultry as the worthiest class of meat for aristocratic dining. If such items had appeared anywhere, it would have been in monastic menus, where they would have been associated with the ideology of "light food."[161] Fatter, more filling meats, richer in sanguine properties, considered the height of culinary pleasure in the High Middle Ages, were now willingly relegated to the peasant class. Even the pig, despite the importance it maintained both in cooking and in the practice of food preservation, lost its preeminence and was confined to more limited social and environmental settings than before. The gradual shrinking of the forests and the development of cattle raising, which had begun in the early Middle Ages, began to confer a more clearly rural and familiar connotation on the consumption of pork meats. Even if the city shops still offered pork cuts and dried sausages of all types, different customs were already taking hold, customs that were often perceived as a sign of liberation from the nutritional models of the countryside. Already in the late Middle Ages, the urban population seemed to prefer other meats available on the market, such as beef and mutton, in order to affirm a separate identity and a different way of life.[162] The taste for beef, and for veal in particular, began to assert itself in Italy earlier and with greater intensity than in other European countries. Veal was perceived as a delicate meat with a light taste, in accordance with the line of thinking described above. At the beginning of the fifteenth century, the physician Lorenzo Sassoli, in the course of advising his distinguished patient Francesco Datini, a merchant from Prato, makes two recommendations that strike us as particularly noteworthy. First he suggests: "Eat as many turtle doves as you can, since, of all meats, the nature of this creature has a special ability to comfort the memory and the emotions." (This comment, which follows his praise for chicken, gray partridge, and pigeon, confirms the emerging interest in fowl.) Sassoli then observes: "My other recommendation is to put veal into your body in any way you can, since, with all its good properties, you will find no healthier form of food."[163] This recommendation to consume as much veal as possible, because it is regarded as the perfect food, is offered in the name of health and nutrition, and it confirms and reinforces the development of taste.

The biographer of Filippo Maria Visconti writes: "Among meats, he liked veal best," with kid and chicken next in his line of preference, and when he wished to indulge his appetite, he ate pheasant, gray partridge, and rock partridge.[164] Whereas the enthusiasm for fowl was prevalent in the contemporary European diet (underpinned by a belief system that associated winged creatures with the nobility, linking the "higher" levels of the animal world and of human society),[165] the passion for veal—and preferably meat from the female calf—was uniquely Italian. "A few cuts of veal or one or two brace of chicken" form the basis of Italian banquets, according to Montaigne, who, as we have already noted, otherwise complains of the scarcity of meat on Italian dinner tables.[166]

The shift in custom seems to have taken place between the end of the fourteenth and beginning of the fifteenth centuries. In the middle of the fifteenth century, the writings of Maestro Martino and Platina still seem to reflect the preference for fowl, from which "the most delicate dishes are made and which is much more suited to the tables of kings and princes than to those of humble men and people of modest means."[167] Platina also tells us, however, that "the meat of the female calf is perhaps the most temperate dish, and it is not surprising that it is frequently found on the tables of the nobility."[168] In the following century this choice becomes clearer. "All kinds of meat from the ox, the cow, and the calf" are at the top of the list of meats that Messisbugo suggests be stocked in the pantry, ready to supply the banquets of the prince. We should note, however, that other meats are also listed. The splendor of the princely table demands that the following items be kept available, in addition to preserved meats: "Wild and domestic boar, stag, deer, roe buck, lamb, kid, wether, suckling pig, hares, rabbits, dormice, peacocks, wild and domestic pheasants. Partridge, rock partridge, francolin, thrush, gray partridge, woodcock, ortolans, garden warblers, quails, crake, turtle doves, ducklings, cranes, geese, bittern, herons, snipe, wild and domestic duck, large, medium, and small-sized teal, plover and other fowl. Fat, fleshy capons, and hens of a similar kind, chickens male and female, domestic doves, and wood pigeons."[169] In this long list, the order in which the items are placed is certainly of some importance.

The introduction of the American turkey (soon assimilated with the peacock and gradually destined to replace it on patrician dinner tables)[170] was not enough to overturn these evaluative criteria. On the issue of meat, Bartolomeo Scappi expresses no doubt with regard to what deserves priority in his recipe collection written in 1570: "Second Book, dealing with different dishes using the meat of quadrupeds or fowl, beginning with *Beef*."[171] He dedicates about twenty recipes to beef or "ox meat." Veal appears in no less than thirty-six recipes, with the animal divided up from head to foot. Six recipes are for the calf's head, four for the tongue, four for breast meat, and others for the shoulder, the back, the neck, loin, kidney, haunch, liver, feet, sweetbread, brain, eyes, heart, tripe, and blood—plus the inevitable panoply of meatballs, meat loaves, *brisavoli*, and brain or blood sausages. The meat of the male calf is mentioned, for obvious reasons, in the chapter on testicles.[172] This great diversity of culinary suggestions is based on a superlative knowledge of anatomy. No part of the animal is wasted, and every cut involves a specific preparation. The writer's knowledge of the edible object is total, exhaustive, almost intimate. Nor is this kind of knowledge exclusive to Scappi and his cuisine. Rather, it indicates a broad-based learning shared by cooks and stewards of the court as well as their buyers and, just as surely, by the peasants who carved up, cooked, and salted the meat of a slaughtered pig. "No part of the pig should be thrown away" ("Del maiale non si getta nulla") is an ancient adage associated with the countryside, which expresses faith and confidence in a deeply rooted cultural legacy, in the kind of skill that arises from the struggle for daily survival, but it should be added that *no one threw away a part of any resource*. The special enthusiasm for organ meats and giblets is linked to this practice, but we would be mistaken to consider it the hallmark of poor cuisine. As Scappi's *Opera* and every other recipe collection from the Middle Ages onward reveal, the use of such meats was a widespread phenomenon, witnessed across the social spectrum, including the highest levels. Necessity was not the main motive underlying their consumption but rather an appreciation for all parts of the animal, arising out of a kind of respect for the sacrificed victims.

In the seventeenth century Stefani, having asserted the excellence of cow's meat (his first "discourse" is on veal, "because, among four-legged animals, the calf is of primary importance, and one can make a great many different dishes from its meat"), launches into a discussion that begins with the liver, head, brains, tongue, sweetbreads, and tripe, moves on to the shoulder, breast, spine, and belly, and ends with the hooves.[173]

Perhaps, on the social level, differences were not reflected to an important degree in the cuts of meat, which are so important today in defining the cost of meat and the distribution of various parts. In premodern Italy, the "fifth quarter" was appreciated by everyone at least as much as the other parts of the animal (in fact it was something of a challenge to the cook to determine how to make the most of even the most difficult parts of the animal, those that we would consider "less noble"). When Vincenzo Tanara refers to "the honor of invited guests, the delight of those who enjoy eating, and a tonic for those who are ill," he is not discussing—as we might expect—the flesh of the animal, the breast and the thighs, but the sweetbreads, "commonly called *latticini*."[174]

Social difference was more accurately reflected in the kinds of animal consumed. Throughout the modern era beef and veal have been the meat of the elite, only rarely appearing on the tables of the peasants. "The food [of the people] consists for the greater part of pork or mutton, except during important feasts, when beef is eaten," Girolamo Cirelli wrote in 1694.[175] The pig continued to be the main point of reference for all classes only in a small number of regions, especially those where the single-family farm survived as the model of agricultural production, along with sharecropping. Since Emilia was among the regions with the strongest sharecropping tradition, along with Tuscany and the Marches, it is hardly surprising that, among those who produced agronomic treatises in the modern period, the writer who held pork in the highest esteem was from the "nation" of Bologna. In his *Economia del cittadino in villa* (The economics of the city dweller in the country), written in 1644, Tanara pays careful attention to illustrating the different qualities of pork meat and "the hundred and twenty ways of preparing dishes from it."[176]

Knowledge of these products also involved paying careful attention to the natural maturation of the meat of the slaughtered animals. Scappi gives precise instructions on the right moment to bring the meat to the kitchen for cooking. Generally speaking, he does not like to delay the process: "I find that all kinds of fowl have the same quality as four-legged animals, that is, they are always flavorful when placed on the spit as soon as they are dead, and the longer this is delayed the more juice they lose. It is true that the meat may be a little tougher, but they will be more flavorful than those that have been dead for longer."[177] Only the meat of an older animal should be allowed to mature for a few days in order to acquire a better flavor (chap. 12). Alternatively, it could be parboiled.[178] Young meat, by contrast, "can be cooked immediately" (chap. 34v).[179] In all cases, the waiting period is brief, involving only one or two days at the most. There was thus a marked preference for fresh meats, cooked almost immediately after slaughter. This practice, which was already observed in the Middle Ages, goes against the grain of many commonly held beliefs about our forebears.

This approach to determining the quality of meat and the best moment to cook it was fundamental to the tradition of consumption for hundreds of years, or at least until the practice of preserving meats at low temperatures was introduced into Italian butcher shops after World War I. The introduction of chilled storage lockers and refrigerators brought an end to the practice of keeping animals alive and butchering them in different quantities according to the season, which had meant that in the warmer months, when the meat had to be sold more quickly, its availability was more limited. In Florence during Artusi's lifetime, the quantity and type of meat available at the butcher's depended on the relationship between demand and perishability. Just a few years later, however, poultry and sides of beef could be transported from a great distance and thus made available at all times of the year. One must also realize that the transportation of beef across the ocean from Argentina to Europe greatly intensified during the twentieth century, with shipments of meat arriving in Italy through the port of Genoa.[180] This phenomenon did not merely affect cost and supply. Left to hang in a chilled, ventilated space at a constant temperature, meat was no longer affected by atmospheric conditions and thus gave the consumer the sense of perpetual availability.[181] Wild game, which can be killed only during the short hunting season and is off limits during the reproductive months, revealed the culinary implications of this innovation in an especially striking way. As soon as it could be transported at a low temperature from distant locations or simply processed on site after slaughter, game became available even out of season in the best hotel kitchens too. This occurred to a far greater extent than would have been possible under normal environmental conditions, given the size of the animal population both in the wild and in designated parklands. Altered circumstances gave rise to a kind of cooking that was increasingly indifferent to the calendar, to the natural maturation of food products, and to the normally restricted season for obtaining prime, fattened fowl. Thus refrigerated meat and—deceptively—frozen meat, which really betrays a modification in taste, both became "fresh" products, while only canned meats were considered "preserved" foods.

Eating "Lean" Food: The Liturgical Calendar and the Cooking of Fish

In the history of culinary models and cooking customs, there are parts, like the chapter dedicated to fish, that cannot be written without introducing the issue of the liturgical calendar and the rules of behavior imposed by the ecclesiastical hierarchy on the members of the faithful. Beginning in the fourth century the seasons of the church strongly conditioned the relationship between humans and food, influencing the criteria governing the choice of food products and cooking practices. In effect, the liturgical calendar called for a fundamental distinction between "fat" days and "lean" days. On lean days, members of the faithful were obliged, with varying degrees of severity and a progressive scale of restrictions, to abstain from animal meat, which could involve foods derived from animals as well as meat itself. Up to the fourteenth century the Lenten diet in the strict sense excluded milk products and eggs, which were allowed only on the lean days of midweek or on the eve of feast days. Then these products were permitted even during Lent, with special dispensations granted first on a temporary basis and gradually transformed into a general rule.[182]

We will not dwell on the complex motivations of this prescriptive system.[183] It is enough to note that its superimposition on the seasonal calendar brought with it a rather demanding system of substitution and adaptation, given the total number of penitential days, which ranged from one to two hundred a year, depending on the time and place (two or three days a week, on the eve of the main holy days, during "greater" Lent and other minor penitential periods distributed throughout the year). The obligation to alternate periods of fat and lean, common to the entire Christian world, contributed in no small way to dietary customs in areas that were naturally diverse: meat and fish, oil and lard *had* to appear on everyone's table.[184] It also served conversely to distinguish, or to separate, lean and fat food products in cooking practices and menus: fish and meat tended to be mutually exclusive, for they could not (and should not) appear together in the preparation of dishes and the composition of menus. A sauce with a meat and fish base, like the *minutal* featured in ancient Roman cooking,[185] was inconceivable in the Middle Ages, as was the custom of serving meat and fish dishes at the same meal. These contaminations were certainly not prohibited, but they would have seemed inappropriate in a cultural climate that attached important symbolic value to various foods, placing them in opposition to each other as bearers of different meanings. Fish soon became the symbol of Lenten food (as well as the symbol of the monastic diet, which was perpetually penitential, at least in its intentions), and it was paradoxically mainly because of this association that its image suffered a decline in status in the course of the Middle Ages. In short, it took on penitential values, becoming a symbol of lightness—in both the physiological and the metaphorical senses—that was too removed from the dietary desires of most people. The division of roles was quite clear, and in fact the battle between Carnival and Lent, to which various literary works were dedicated from the thirteenth century onward, was really a false conflict, since the territorial struggle had already been preventively (and peacefully) resolved between the two contenders. The image of the battle is merely a rhetorical gesture concealing the profound integration between the two groups of foods, which were opposite but complementary and alternated with each other in chivalrous fashion over the course of the weeks, months, and years. It is therefore hardly surprising to find that in some Italian cities a single guild or corporation oversaw the sale of both meat and fish.[186]

For a long time the alternation of lean and fat foods took precedence over all other distinctions articulated in cookbooks, determining the selection of recipes and the general organization of the material. The third book of Bartolomeo Scappi's *Opera*, which is dedicated to fish and other lean foods, begins as follows: "Having treated different kinds of foods for fat days, I will now move on to discuss foods belonging to lean days and to Lent."[187] Clearly, the cook's complete familiarity with the products available in his area in any given season was absolutely crucial, so that "when lacking certain things not found there, or unavailable in the season, and being unable to make a dish out of these things, he would be able to use something else offered in that place and season."[188] But it was equally important that he should learn to make best use of the products while respecting the rules of Christian behavior. Oil and butter had to replace lard as the basis for cooking on lean days,[189] and fish was the necessary substitute for meat. The cook had to take this into account in planning the combination of dishes to be served and in selecting the appropriate flavors, thus balancing the needs of the palate with the possibilities of the season and the restrictions imposed by liturgical obligations.

Because of a system of economic and cultural exchange that was Mediterranean in character, the type of fish used in the cuisine of ancient Rome was generally the saltwater variety. In the Middle Ages, however, this tendency changed. Now even the culture of fish became continentalized, as had happened with the culture of meat. The preferred varieties were now for the most part local, which is to say, the fish found in rivers, lakes, and marshes. Freshwater fish thus gained prominence in recipe collections, though not uniformly in all regions. Whereas the Neapolitan *Liber de coquina* offers many recipes for saltwater fish, its Tuscan adaptation largely eliminates them.[190] The preference for freshwater fish was nonetheless a general tendency, even in coastal areas, where fishermen preferred to work by lakes and rivers,[191] and it constitutes the most important difference between the taste of the Middle Ages and that of both the ancient and modern eras. Of all fish, sturgeon was by far the most highly prized (and remained so for a long time), as it was considered particularly refined and very suitable for aristocratic cuisine. The twenty-three recipes for sturgeon in Scappi's *Opera* and the banquet he suggests for fast days in any month of the year, which is based exclusively on this fish, are not only an exercise in breathtaking virtuosity but also indicate a substantial continuity in the symbolic and gastronomic value attributed to the sturgeon from the Middle Ages to the modern period.[192] The eel was also widely appreciated, especially because eels could be transported over relatively large distances in grass-filled baskets where they could survive outside water for many days.[193] Trout, dentex, eels, tench, grayling, and lamprey were, according to Bonvesin de la Riva, the main types of fish found in Lombardy at the beginning of the fourteenth century,[194] and the recipes that appear in medieval cookbooks refer primarily to these varieties.

In the fifteenth century Maestro Martino expanded the repertory of fish dishes by offering a good number of recipes for saltwater fish along with the usual recipes for freshwater varieties. He thus includes sea bass and golden bream, turbot and sole, red mullet, scorpion fish, octopus, squid, and sea shrimp (along with crayfish, which was present everywhere on the medieval dinner table). Yet the most detailed recipes in the collection are still for sturgeon, trout, pike, tench, and lamprey.[195] Echoing Martino, Platina reaffirms medieval tastes: "Regardless of the method of cooking, saltwater fish should not be considered healthy. It is not in fact good food, and it creates a great thirst."[196]

The panorama of fish that Scappi offers in his *Opera* in 1570 is much broader, more authoritative and convincing, as he traces an itinerary that stretches from north to south, from east to west of the peninsula, proposing many different varieties of fish—available either fresh or preserved—from Italy's lakes, rivers, and surrounding seas to please the appetites of princes and cardinals.[197] Scappi's great expertise on the subject, his accurate information on the markets of Milan and Rome, and the precision with which he records the various local names for particular varieties of fish stand in sharp contrast with the perplexity expressed by Platina a century earlier as he began his chapter on fish: "It was my intention to speak of the nature and qualities of all fish, but the confusing, unreliable ways in which they are named makes me embarrassed to deal with them."[198]

Knowledge about fish and its culinary preparation is one of those magical areas where the learning of the professional, cosmopolitan cook intersects and enters into dialogue with the customs of ordinary people and with the culture of the locality. On more than one occasion, Scappi records the simple recipes of fishermen, observing that he has nothing further to add to them. "[The *gho* fish] should be cooked when freshly caught, since it decays quickly. Fishermen from Chiozza and Venice cook the fish over the coals or cook it in a broth of malvagia wine and water, along with some vinegar and Venetian spices. Or it can be fried in oil like other fish and served hot with a bitter orange sauce."[199] In the same way, "fishermen on the Po river make a soup from barbel fish, or fry it, or cook it on the grate" (chap. 130v). And after providing a recipe for turbot cooked in broth, Scappi goes on to say: "During the time I spent in Venice and Ravenna I learned from the fishermen of Chiozza and Venice, who make the best soups, that along the entire seashore they have no other method of preparing [turbot] than the one I mentioned above." He then adds, however: "I think that fishermen are more successful at this than cooks, since they prepare it as soon as the fish is caught" (chap. 120). This statement does not reflect a populist cliché but merely alludes to the question of timing: fish cooked by fishermen is better than that prepared by "cooks" simply because it is fresher.

The penitential image ascribed to fish proved to be long lasting, and it has not disappeared even today, although one could not say that it had much influ-

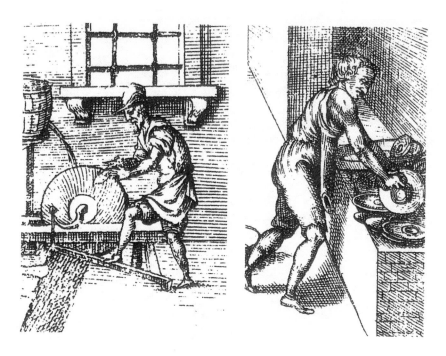

Knife sharpener, dishwasher, and broiler (engravings).

Source: Bartolomeo Scappi, *Opera dell'arte del cucinare* (Venice: Tramezzino, 1570).

ence on the type of cuisine that was increasingly concerned with obtaining the greatest possible pleasure from available — and permitted — resources. Medieval recipe collections already showed evidence of this tendency, which asserted itself with greater force in the fifteenth and sixteenth centuries. The growing interest in "delicate" foods, which were increasingly compatible with the image projected by an aristocratic cuisine newly dedicated to refinement and lightness, would increase the value placed on fish over time. Still, at the end of the seventeenth century, Antonio Latini organized his book *Scalco alla moderna* (The modern steward) into two volumes, dedicated to fat and lean dishes, respectively. At this point, however, the importance of taste prevails over liturgical concerns. Thus the introduction to the second volume proclaims the gastronomic excellence of the "swarms of food" provided by the rivers and seas: "For fish is not inferior to the kinds of meat most often chosen to satisfy the palate. Indeed fish is the tastiest, most delicious food that Nature has provided. Of the foods supplied by water, it is the most apt to satisfy the needs of variety, taste, and appetite." Latini mentions the issue of the liturgical calendar only at a later moment, when he notes that "great praise for fish" has become widespread, thanks to the fact that "the Holy Church has designated fish as a Lenten food, knowing its ability to repress the pangs of human weakness."[200] Fish is therefore good for the health of the spirit as well as the health of the body.

Has the weakening of penitential rules damaged or enhanced our taste for fish? Has it altered its basic values? Fish consumption today is not associated with the fulfillment of religious obligations and is more dependent on issues linked to fish farming and pollution, transportation and refrigeration. The pollution of European rivers has been countered by efforts to salvage various species with modern reproductive techniques and new methods of fish farming. This has resulted in the reappearance of sturgeon and crayfish in contemporary cuisine, where they are regarded with almost as much esteem as they enjoyed in antiquity. The capacity to process and store the fresh catch at low temperatures on fishing trawlers has eliminated the risks involved in transportation, delaying the perishability of the fish until the moment of sale, when it is placed in the hands of the consumer. Paradoxically, this has not eliminated most of the traditional values associated with fish, which continues to enjoy an excellent nutritional profile, a reputation for ideal lightness, and an elevated gastronomic status, lacking only the extraordinary prestige that was reserved in the past for the large food item that was presented conspicuously at the center of the dining table.

Milk Products

Until the close of the Middle Ages, the animals whose milk was most highly prized were the ewe and the she-goat. Cattle raising, which was marginal to the system of production for a long time, functioned primarily to provide beasts of burden (the oxen used to draw carts and plows), secondarily to provide meat, and only occasionally to provide milk. The attribution of nutritional value faithfully mirrors these customs. Platina wrote that "milk has the same properties as the animal that produces it. Goat's milk is considered excellent . . . ewe's milk is next, with cow's milk is in third place."[201] Yet milk was almost never used as a drink. The most usual way of consuming and preserving it was in the form of cheese.

For a long time, medical culture viewed cheese with a great deal of perplexity. The mysterious mechanisms of coagulation and fermentation were a source of suspicion for medical scientists,[202] and dietary treatises placed severe restrictions on the consumption of cheese, if they did not discourage it outright. The saying "Only when eaten sparingly is cheese a healthy thing" (*caseus est sanus quem dat avara manus*), which is attributed to the Salerno school, became something of a cliché in medieval literature.[203]

Cheese was also long associated with the cooking of the poor and with the world of peasants and shepherds. It featured almost always in the fare of ordinary people, or at least in the menus recorded in literature or documented in accounts of the type of food served in hostelries.[204] Still, from the Middle Ages onward, the status of cheese began to undergo a process of ennoblement—though this was not without ambivalence—that was also linked to the image of cheese as a lean food (a true nutritional paradox). Cheese was allowed as a substitute for meat on weekdays that were designated as days of abstinence, on the vigils of church holidays, and, from the fourteenth and fifteenth century onward, during Lent also. While this confirmed the status of cheese as a "poor food," that is, as the substitute for another food—meat—that was regarded as prestigious and desirable, it nonetheless granted it an important role in the dietary system, analogous to the status attained by fish. In the long run, the culture of renunciation prompted a sense of curiosity and creativity, from which many innovations in taste arose. "Can we think of any highly valued cheeses that were not in their distant origins the product of a monastic setting?" asks Léo Moulin.[205] He is certainly exaggerating, since origin stories are often nothing more than myths. But myths reflect a common feeling, and for a long time monastic centers were identified as places where a type of culinary culture came into being. Yet even when we speak of monastic gastronomy, we cannot ignore the primary importance of the peasant world in the development and transmission of that culture.

The fact remains that the Middle Ages renovated the image of cheese, despite the warnings of physicians. Cheese roasted on the spit, according to the fourteenth-century *Libro della cucina*, should be served to "his lordship" on a slice of thin bread.[206] Pantaleone da Confienza, the author of the oldest-known treatise on milk products (*Summa lacticiniorum*, written in 1469), writes that he knew "kings, dukes, counts, marquises, barons, soldiers, nobles, and merchants" who frequently and willingly nourished themselves on cheese.[207] This process also emerges in more modern times, when cheese had enthusiastic admirers and won the praise of individuals such as Ercole Bentivoglio, from Ferrara, the sixteenth-century author of a long poem (in *terzina* form) praising the milk product: "Cheese is the principal human nourishment," he begins, proclaiming the nobility of cheese, which only fools could describe as vulgar and plebeian: "People who are coarse and of little discernment say that it is the food of country folk." It gives strength to the body ("nor do I believe that a man can be vigorous without eating plenty of it") and adds flavor to many dishes ("Without it, soup, *tortelli*, and *torte* cannot be perfect dishes but are insipid, silly, inert, and dead"). He praises instead a custom practiced in Lombardy, where "the first thing placed on the table is cheese," and "those people, so intelligent and blessed, never allow it to be removed until all the dishes are taken away from the table, and the supper is ended."[208]

The presence of cheese among the dishes that constitute an aristocratic banquet is almost always taken for granted in texts on cooking and stewardship. Among the provisions considered indispensable to the pantry of the court, Messisbugo includes "hard, fatty cheese: tomino, pecorino, sardesco, marzolino, and provatura cheese, as well as *ravogliuoli*."[209] Bartolomeo Scappi's already cited recipes for the Papal Court regularly include "*casci, marzolini, spaccati*," "Florentine *raviggioli*," "sliced Parmesan cheese," "cheese from the Riviera," "*romagnolo*," "*romanesco*," along with caciocavallo, *provatura*, and mozzarella.[210] An infinite number of similar citations can be found in other texts.

The preeminence enjoyed by cheese made from ewe's milk in the Middle Ages was now on the wane. In the middle of the fifteenth century Platina already notes that two cheeses are "vying for first place" in Italy: "marzolino, which is made in Tuscany in the month of March, and Parmesan cheese, which comes from the Cisalpine regions and may also be known as *maggengo*, from the month of May."[211] The differences in season really conceal a much deeper opposition—which oddly enough is not underlined by the author—between ewe's milk cheese and cow's milk cheese. The growing success of Parmesan, whose gastronomic traits have already been acknowledged in relation to the growing success of pasta,[212] is the expression of a culture that was becoming more diversified and of a type of production that had attained such importance in the Cisalpine regions that it was already able to compete with the traditional ewe's milk cheese. Notably, from the beginning of the fifteenth century onward, this kind of diversification in production began to mark the history of Italian gastronomy.

Pantaleone da Confienza also singled out marzolino as the best Italian cheese (it was also called *Fiorentino*, or Florentine, "since it is made in areas dominated by Florence, in both Tuscany and Romagna"), along with *Pia-*

centino, or Parmesan cheese (as it was identified by Platina), also produced in the areas of Milan, Pavia, Novara, and Vercelli. To these two models of cheese, whose excellence is universally acknowledged, Pantaleone, in parochial fashion, adds a third, the *robiola* of the Langhe and Lomellina regions, a minor cheese usually made with ewe's milk but in some cases with the addition of cow's milk.[213] The custom of mixing both types of milk, regarded by Platina as a recent practice, was treated with suspicion for some time: "Gourmands claim that mixing cow's with ewe's milk results in more excellent cheese," wrote Domenico Romoli in the fourteenth century. But ewe's milk cheese continued to be esteemed as having "better odor and flavor and more proportionate taste, being made of a type of milk that has a better complexion."[214]

Eggs

"There is so much known about fried, roasted, and scrambled eggs that it is not necessary to speak about them" (from the fourteenth-century *Libro della cucina*).[215]

Cooked Food and Preserved Food

"I will not speak about mortadellas and other sausages that are made of the said meat, because this has never been my profession."[216] By declaring himself a cook rather than a preserver of foods, Scappi seems to make a clear distinction between the two "arts." This is, however, a difference of skills, not of principle. In fact, for a long time sausage making was an essential part of cuisine. Fresh sausages as well as "fat sausages" were methods of treating meat, and they were primarily food preparations or *dishes* before they were preserves. It is not by chance that many old terms that now indicate special forms of cured meats, such as mortadelle and *tomacelle,* initially indicated meat loaves contained in gut or pork net.[217] Recipe collections from medieval times and the Renaissance (today historical relics) make ample use of cooked salami, while sliced cold cuts barely feature in the menus of the time. Scappi offers the following directions:

> To cook all kinds of meat or pork salami: Large salami and hams can be cooked with water and with wine. It is true that hams are often cooked with fresh hay and water and are best in the month of May. This is done so that the meat can take on a grassy fragrance, but before cooking they should be steeped in lukewarm water. . . . The salamis are stripped of their skin and are served as hot or as cold as desired. Sometimes hams made from the meat of piglets are cooked in cow's or goat's milk, after they are first steeped in the manner described above. And having been boiled in two rounds of plain water, they are placed in a jar and covered in milk with three inches to spare with two pounds of sugar for each eight pounds

of ham, and they should be cooked like this until ready. One can also cook the entire animal like this, although it is sometimes roasted on the spit after it has been desalted. Mortadellas, pork tongues in gut, *barbaglia*, and pork belly are cooked with legumes and greens and are served hot. Sausages that are not too huge in size are sometimes cut into slices, heated on the grate, and served with bitter orange sauce.[218]

Though closely related to cooking customs, the preparation of sausages and cured meats is framed by the culture and economics of food preservation. It is in fact one of the crucial features in the construction of a culinary model, since it enables the diffusion of specialties based on local products—thus introducing them into the context of a common culinary heritage—along with techniques and skills found in different parts of the country. We have already discussed this at length, pointing out that in these exchanges one can distinguish the real sense of an *Italian* culinary identity.

Certainly, the logic of exchange does not exclude fresh products. On the contrary, it gives preeminence to these. The prestige of a well-adorned table is also measured in terms of ingredients that come from afar, which challenge the laws of the seasons, crossing the length and breadth of the peninsula. Bartolomeo Stefani reflects on this with particular astuteness. By serving fruit and vegetables out of season, Stefani, the chief cook at the court of Mantua, enjoyed the astonished reaction of the banquet guests. Thus, for example, the first item he served at a banquet held on November 27, 1655, in honor of Queen Christina of Sweden was a cup of strawberries in white wine. At the conclusion of Stefani's recipe collection, which brings together the results of his long professional experience, he adds some "suggestions to the noble readers," where he notes, "in my discussion on some occasions I call for certain things, such as asparagus, artichokes, *roviglia*, or peas, and similar things in the months of January and February, which at first glance seem contrary to the season." But this, he observes, will seem to be the case only to those "who have not traveled beyond the river of their native land" because they are too attached to "the bread of their own city." Let those people who are unable to look beyond the threshold of their home know that "those who have fine steeds and a good purse can find all these things in every season—the things that I propose to them and at the same time describe."[219] "Fine steeds and a good purse" indicate rapid transportation and sufficient financial resources. Under these conditions, nothing is really impossible.

But cured meats really guarantee a continuity of exchange, the establishment of daily habits, practices, and common tastes. Having praised an interregional market that supplied fresh products in all seasons, Stefani does not hesitate to open his chapter on preserved foods, salted preserves, and commercially successful cheese of great renown that is enjoyed "beyond Italian borders." Repertories on the subject are not lacking in the recipe collections, in the texts on stewardship,

Milk-based Preparations (engravings).

Source: Bartolomeo Scappi, *Opera dell'arte del cucinare* (Venice: Tramezzino, 1570).

and literary works. We have already given some examples and will not repeat them here.[220] Other examples can be found in encomiastic and satirical poetry, which links a commercial inventory of cured meats with the sensory properties and literary notoriety of each. An illustration printed alongside the frontispiece of Antonio Frizzi's *La salameide*, published in 1772, proclaims the ability of such poems to convey the taste of the plump, spicy, and fragrant sausage. Here we see a gentleman standing in a shop with a salami in his left hand, which he has just raised to his nose to sniff, while the proprietor looks on, awaiting his judgment. What follows is a poem in *ottava rima* — in mock imitation of Ariosto — giving an account of the origin of pork sausage, expressing praise for "the animal loved by St. Anthony the Abbot," and offering a long and well-organized catalog of specialties from various Italian cities: pork sausage from Ferrara, salami with garlic from Verona, cured trotters from Modena, Bolognese mortadella, Lombard *bondiola*, and sausages from Florence, the Lucchesia, and the Mincio.[221]

The importance of cured or preserved foods in culinary history is also due to the fact that these constitute a fundamental point of encounter between the culture of ordinary people and that of the elite. Cured food is in fact the most important concern of those living on a subsistence diet, who do not have the luxury of trusting the daily market or the whims of the seasons. Preserving or storing food products has always been a crucial strategy for warding off hunger. But the surplus of effort and culture directed toward natural products then becomes a valuable opportunity to give pleasure to the palate. Cured food thus abandons the field of necessity and takes its place in the field of pleasure, as significant resemblances can be observed between the food of the poor and that of the ruling classes. One example will suffice: *scapece*, fried (or boiled) fish that is marinated in salt and vinegar in preparation for preservation and possible transportation. Already foreshadowed in a recipe by Apicius,[222] it reappears during the Middle Ages on the table of Emperor Frederick the Second,[223] as well as in the recipe collections of the fourteenth century. The particular name given to it here (*schibezia a tavernaio*)[224] reminds us, however, of another social class, recalling the tavern and the simple foods that are always available for occasional consumption or as needed by travelers. One of its variants is *carpione*, which was prepared with a contrasting procedure: the fish is marinated in brine and vinegar and then fried. The recipe appears in these terms in Maestro Martino's recipe collection in the fifteenth century.[225] Scappi, however, uses the term *accarpionare* to describe his procedure for making *scapece* and gives precise information on the marketing of fish that "is stored for several days and transported to different places throughout Italy."[226] The custom continued to be practiced on different social levels. While Scappi offers it at the pontiff's table, Montaigne finds it at an inn in Foligno, commenting that in these regions, "they serve fish marinated, and have little of it fresh."[227] The difference is still the same. While elite cuisine uses preserved fish (or meats) along with other types, the cuisine of the poor uses preserved food exclusively, or almost exclusively. This tradition, like many others, continued unchanged for centuries. A recipe for eel that is first fried and then boiled in vinegar, reminiscent of the fourteenth-century *schibezia a tavernaio*, is included in the diary of a Tuscan innkeeper in the middle of the nineteenth century.[228]

A New Sense of Typicality

If we try to update, from the historical and commercial perspective, the panorama we have just traced of meats and fish, cured meats and milk products, fruits and vegetables, whether fresh or preserved, both the lines of continuity and the breaks imposed by modernization become evident. While the legacy passed down from the Middle Ages to the modern period serves as the basis for an understanding of the contemporary period, our own age has witnessed a technological manipulation of natural products and human skill that cannot be found in a study of food origins. It is difficult to describe the gastronomic model that characterizes the twentieth century after the end of World War I by keeping the past as a point of reference. The contrast between edible goods from before and after reveals a complex balance between the survival and the extinction of a long heritage, between approaches to taste and their cultural variability, between effective resources and the transmission of recipes. Many foods used during the modern period had different functions in the past. Today's preserved foods have not completely wiped out their historical antecedents, allowing the processes of salting cheeses and drying sausages to coexist with modern food technologies. These technologies in turn have affected craftsmanship and techniques, bringing about major improvements from the purely sanitary and profit-making point of view. More changeable than the foods themselves is the aspect of taste. Today's salami and ewe's milk cheese do not seem outdated, unlike the ways in which these products used to be kept cool in the past, relying on very questionable techniques from the hygienic or organic point of view. Like Antonio Frizzi's master, we have not lost the habit and the pleasure of sniffing salami, although some levels of ripeness or gaminess in meats now seem unpalatable to us.

The most obvious transformations can be seen today in the definition of products and their relationship with local raw materials. In the 1500s names reflecting cities of origin—marzolino cheeses from Florence or mortadella sausages from Bologna—represented circumscribed areas of the county and a single market center from which the foods were sent to distant parts. Even less prestigious forms of cured pork meat and cheeses, the substance of local commerce, enjoyed a territorial reputation that made them recognizable. Thanks to the industrial transformation of pork meats, these historical denominations persist in our own time, as we see in the case of Verona salami and Bolognese mortadella. Some blood sausages of great renown also survive, such as Sienese *buristo*, but similar foods produced on a smaller scale have begun to fade out and disappear. In the Hoepli manuals dedicated to pork, sausages have lost the place names that once made them appetizing and sought after, while many foreign names have begun to enter Italian delicatessens: hams from Magonza, Westphalia, Sutland, York, and Bayonne and French and Hungarian salami.[229] Several products have thus begun to arrive from afar, and imitations of foreign specialties are produced in Italy, while the names of small villages such as Felino are still used as brand names or product types. A comparison of the three culinary guides to Italy published by the Touring Club Italiano in 1931, 1969, and 1984 reveals the full extent of the change in this sector. In the thirty-eight years between 1931 and 1969, 30 percent of Italian cured meats disappear, and three species (*zucco* from Reggio Emilia, donkey-meat salami from Pavia, and Viterbo mortadella) are pronounced extinct. The list grew in the subsequent fifteen years with the disappearance of another thirteen types of cured meats, a situation brought on "by the increasing difficulty of obtaining many raw materials, altered methods of farming, and weather changes that make some methods of preservation unreliable." A comparative analysis reveals an equally conspicuous number of products that are either new or were overlooked by earlier surveys.[230] The industry does its part in inventing or reinventing tradition, and there is often an absence of documentation available for analysis or retrospective study.

This balance sheet showing a disparity between profits and losses raises the issue of what is considered *typical*. Indeed, typicality increasingly indicates techniques of production rather than the geographical origins of the raw materials. A shift in the conditions of production has begun to emerge even in protected, homogeneous areas. Italian valleys traditionally associated with cured meats and cheeses have relinquished the practice of agriculture without losing the industries associated with it. A local economy based on the cultivation of beef and buckwheat is now a mere memory in the mountainous landscape of Valtellina, but this has not brought about the extinction of the *bresaola* produced there or of the fresh and dried tagliatelle called *"pizzoccheri"* that are flavored with fried butter and *bitto* cheese. Within the valley, but more often outside, we observe the continuing production of the raw materials and foods necessary to assure the sense of enduring identity that is particularly vital to tourism. The phenomenon is still more pronounced on a global scale, since the process of displacement is driven by economic principles. Countries such as Argentina, which has a large population of Italian immigrants, have become involved in producing imitations of Italian specialties in more financially and climatically favorable circumstances. The wines, cheeses, and cured meats produced there have names that hark back to their Italian origins and with the availability of new raw materials hybrids have been created, such as a combination of gorgonzola and Roquefort cheese.[231] New lands of plenty, no longer mere fantasy, now flourish in the Southern Hemisphere, offering food in great abundance at incredibly low prices.

The standardization of raw materials has also homogenized food products and their methods of cultivation, without bringing an end to the diversity of culinary preparations. Gone are the local markets of the past, abundantly or sparsely stocked, changing with the season and shifts in weather, and diverse from one town to the next. What we find today is an ever-expanding yet one-dimensional system of distribution offering fresh products that, because of issues of cost, preservation, and recognizability, are limited to a small number of recurrent typologies. Some of these, such as salads, valerian, or rocket, are part of a legacy but have no particular history. They have names that are devoid of clear horticultural traditions and are cultivated in greenhouses from one end of the Mediterranean to the other, motivated simply by the logic of opportunism and profit. The flavor of these greens is monotonous and ephemeral, like their color, appearance, and the consistency that serves to convey their formal identity to the consumer. The appraisal of such phenomena over the past fifty years is unsystematic and does not allow us to draw conclusions, especially in the absence of a historical atlas of Italy's typical products. If every vegetable has a pedigree, to reconstruct it would be difficult at present. At the same time we cannot be sure if the characteristics of today's cuisine, which draws on a large urban market, are traditional or innovative.

The pressure to standardize varies according to food types and is particularly strong in the case of fresh food. This has led to a decrease in some types of products, such as apples and pears, that in the past were the pride of the orchard and symbols of the inexhaustible richness and whimsicality of nature. The pressure is less marked in the case of preserved foods, since we see the ongoing survival of small establishments dedicated to creating products of high quality that do not require anything other than specific environmental conditions and are not threatened by the fluctuations of traditional rural economies. Shifts in climate and environment, the revaluation of craftsmanship and industrial labor, the selective revival of some specialties and the simultaneous loss of many others have brought about many tensions in the field of culinary resources. This is accompanied by the difficulty of discerning a future pattern in the Italian heritage as a whole. "Tradition," "specialization," and "typicality" are terms that belong to different languages, those of industry and community law, cooking and commerce, and their meanings shift significantly when applied by each of these sectors. The problem of their redefinition is not linguistic but mainly historical. Faced with a shrinking or expanding market, alternating from Northern to Southern Hemisphere, culinary models that reflect longstanding customs and deeply rooted values (and also an ancient system of knowledge and the language to express it, as we have shown) struggle to adapt to current conditions. These models shift, are transformed, and die out. If the future of a culinary tradition such as Italy's is tied to a specific territory and to specific products necessary for its elaboration, then its mutation is already under way.

CHAPTER THREE

The Formation of Taste

Flavor and Taste

Like all other aspects of culture, taste is a product of history and changes with time and location. In culinary matters, as in other human activities, the choices, exclusions, and preferences that distinguish individuals, populations, and regions of the world have changed over the centuries. How do we know this? How can we presume to reconstruct the food preferences of people who lived and died in times long past?

This problem presents itself on two different levels. The first concerns taste as *flavor*, an individually felt sensation of the tongue and the palate, an experience that is by definition subjective, fleeting, and incommunicable. In this sense, the historical experience of food is irrevocably lost to us. But taste also involves *knowledge*, the ability to determine what is good or bad, pleasant or unpleasant. This ability comes from the mind and not the tongue (and in fact the organ of gastronomic pleasure is also the mind and not the tongue), because someone has to have taught us how to recognize and classify flavors as good and bad, pleasant and unpleasant. From this perspective taste is not a subjective, incommunicable reality but one shared at the collective level. It is a cultural experience, the fruit of a tradition or system of aesthetic values (cooking as the *art* of eating) that the society we inhabit transmits to us from birth. This dimension, which is not the same as individual taste but conditions it to a large degree, can be examined historically by studying recipe collections and other kinds of texts. Taste is part of who we are. It can be discerned in every circumstance where previous generations have left a trace of their experiences, plans, and desires. But when we wish to discuss models of taste and how these are shaped and modified over time, we must first ask another basic question: with whose taste are we concerned here? We ask this since it is quite clear that the world is divided into at least two parts, and to say that the rich are rich and the poor are poor is to assert something that is all too obvious. Yet it is simply a fact that abundance and hunger are unlikely to lead to the same choices, and if everyone has the right to transform the need for daily sustenance into pleasure, the ways in which this is manifest are very varied indeed.

The anthropologist Marvin Harris claims that food choices are always determined by a more or less conscious calculation of positive and negative outcomes. This ultimately implies that the various dietary and culinary systems—including those that permit cannibalism—are the most economical and practical solutions historically possible under the given circumstances. According to this logic, the calculation of advantages and disadvantages leads to the creation of dietary customs, and these in turn give rise to taste, which is the appraisal of certain foods as good and others as bad.[1] But if this argument holds up, it does so only when discussing the poor and the hunger experienced by the poor. Clearly, the customs of the poor are determined by the availability of food, its adaptability to preservation and cooking, and its capacity to fill the stomach. This is how we explain the taste of the masses for starchy foods: grains, root vegetables, and chestnuts. It is also how we explain their "taste" for salt (to be discussed below), which not only provides flavor but, more important, can be used in food preservation.

In the first place, habits do not necessarily correspond to taste. As Flandrin has pointed out, it is one thing to eat a particular food but another to enjoy it. In many cases, it is the element of necessity that explains the failure of these two experiences to coincide with each other.[2] To be sure, peasants who had eaten dark rye bread, spelt soups, flatbread made of barley, and polenta made of millet down through the centuries became physically accustomed to such foods (at one point, physicians expounded this in theoretical terms, thus supporting the inevitability of social privilege in the name of science).[3] Yet this does not contradict the fact that people have always preferred white bread made of wheat flour, which was for a long time unavailable to all but the upper classes and urban residents. Nonetheless, with a kind of historical irony the privileged classes eventually began to imagine that they recognized in these poor foods of the past a long-lost treasure of inestimable culinary worth and transformed them, according to the image and values of the marketplace, into objects of desire and symbols of a happy, innocent, rural way of life that peasants have never experienced. In reality, these objects became desirable when (and to the extent that) they seemed to be dying out, in other words, when they started to become *rare*.

If we reverse the terms of social reference and focus on the rich rather than the poor, we find rarity, not abundance, at the root of the taste-forming mechanism. Here the object of desire is not food that is easily and abundantly available but the rare, precious variety. It is certainly not the type of food that fills the stomach and dispels the pangs of hunger but the kind that stimulates the appetite for more. This explains the craze for spices in the kitchens of the upper classes in the Middle Ages and the Renaissance, as well as their fall from favor as soon as they became plentiful in the marketplace.[4] It also explains the advice offered by some hedonists (immediately condemned by the moralists) to eat salads halfway through a meal, with the aim of rekindling the appetite.[5] "These foods are suitable when one no longer feels hungry," wrote Costanzo Felici, a sixteenth-century botanist and food expert.[6] The *uneconomical* aspect of certain foods seems to have been an important factor in the formation of taste among the upper classes for the simple reason that "everything that is plentiful is lowly," as Isidore of Seville observed in the seventh century, in reference to beans.[7]

There were nonetheless significant points of connection between elite cuisine and the cooking of the poor, both with respect to the foods consumed and the condiments used to flavor them, for the simple reason that the poor tend to imitate the rich whenever possible. And the rich in turn readily adopt "poor" foods and flavors when they desire to do so (as we see in the current success of coarse grains, a phenomenon not without precedent in the history of cooking). For this reason, it will be useful to our discussion to look carefully at the tastes of the upper classes, about which we can learn a great deal, given the availability of documentary evidence.

The Culture of Artifice

It seems quite obvious that our concept of cuisine, the system of flavors that we "naturally" prefer, is very different from what people looked for and considered good in foods for a long period of time (which lasted until a couple of centuries ago). Although there are many differences in the details, these disparities can be linked to a few basic notions that we no longer hold today. Contemporary Italian or European food has a predominantly analytical character, which means that it tends to *distinguish between* flavors (sweet, salty, tart, sour, or spicy), reserving a separate place for each, both in individual dishes and in the order of courses served at a meal. Linked to this practice is the notion that the cook should respect as much as possible the *natural* flavor of each food: a flavor that is distinct and different and should be kept separate from other flavors. But these simple rules do not amount to a universal archetype of cooking that has existed unchanged since the beginning of time. Rather, they are the outcome of a minor revolution that occurred in France around the turn of the eighteenth century.

"Cabbage soup should taste of cabbages, leeks of leeks, turnips of turnips" was the advice given in a "letter to household stewards" written by Nicolas de Bonnefons in the middle of the seventeenth century.[8] This apparently innocent declaration ran counter to a very different way of thinking that had consolidated over the centuries. Renaissance cuisine, like that of the Middle Ages or—to go back further—the cuisine of ancient Rome, had developed a model of cooking based mainly on the concept of *artifice* and the *mixture* of flavors. Here the preparation of individual dishes and their presentation at various points throughout the meal disclose a synthetic rather than an analytical logic: in other words, the tendency to keep things together rather than to separate them. This was also in keeping with the dictates of the dietary knowledge of the era, which considered food balanced if it contained all nutritional qualities, which were manifest in turn in the different flavors. A perfect dish was thought to be one in which *all* flavors were simultaneously present. The cook was expected to perform an intervention on "natural" products by altering their traits, sometimes in a radical way. Cooking was perceived as an art of combination that aimed at modifying and transforming the "natural" taste of foods into something different, or "artificial." This explains the mixing of flavors and by extension the systematic use of colorants (which made the art of the cook rather like that of the painter), as well as the quest for special shapes and textures through the clever use of cooking methods and technical manipulation. To gain a deeper understanding of the significance of these choices in the history of food and taste we must now step back and start from the beginning.

The Legacy of Rome

The cuisine of the Roman Empire—initially documented in several literary texts and then, belatedly but in a more organic way, in the recipe collection attributed to Apicius, composed around 400 CE—seems at first glance very distant from us. The distance shrinks, however, when we realize that many of the basic characteristics of medieval and Renaissance cooking were derived from this cuisine, and they survived until the seventeenth or eighteenth century. The combination of sweet and sour, for example, and more generally the practice of mixing different flavors had been passed down through the ages in a continuous fashion, while undergoing some important modifications, adjustments, and variations along the way. The same can be said about the use of spices and the mixing of strong, sharp flavors with sweet, salty, and bitter ones. This too was a distinctive trait of medieval and Renaissance cooking—whose origins we can easily trace to ancient Rome—and it was enriched over time with new experiences and influences. Although Germanic culture played a primary role in transforming medieval preferences in the area of food products and resources (by accentuating interest in game and in meats in general, as we have mentioned), it did not present any significant novelty on the level of taste. Here, as elsewhere, it was the Roman tradition that prevailed, conquering the conquerors.

In Roman times, "sour" generally meant vinegar, and "sweet" meant honey. Many recipes in Apicius call for the simultaneous use of both products, either as condiments or as a base for cooking. Similarly, sweet and salty flavors were mixed together, and individual preparations were flavored with doses of honey and *garum*, the famous sauce made from the inner organs of fish macerated in oil and herbs, which Apicius includes in several recipes with the specific goal of

achieving a salty flavor. Raw "rustic herbs" are dressed with oil, vinegar, and
garum,[9] and it is generally understood that "if a dish tastes too bland, add garum;
and if it is salty, add some honey."[10]

Among strong flavors, Roman cooks had a special preference for *laser*, a type
of resin harvested from silphium root that had a strong stench and tasted similar to garlic. After this plant mysteriously died out in the first century of the
Common Era, it was replaced with asafetida, which is still used today in Asian
cooking.[11] In addition, Romans used nard, sumac, costmary, and myrtle berry
(products that were rather exotic) to flavor their food.[12] The use of pepper, a genuine gastronomic novelty, also became widespread in the first century. Pliny
marvels in his *Natural History* at the acclaim pepper had begun to command.
Its success was indeed extraordinary, since almost all the recipes of Apicius,
including desserts and wines, call for its use. Other spices were also known at
the time, but they were used almost exclusively for medicinal purposes or in the
creation of perfumes.

The picture becomes even more complex in the "Excerpta," an appendix
attached to the collection of Apicius. These excerpts are supposedly culled from
the main text, though they were in fact composed a century later (at the end of
the fifth or the beginning of the sixth century) by a writer named Vinidarius,
probably an Ostrogoth living in northern Italy. Here, along with pepper, new
spices are suggested for culinary use. Notably, we find ginger and saffron. Saffron has the specific function of adding color to food, which would later become
a characteristic aspect of medieval cooking (*propter colore*).[13] Cloves are also
mentioned in the list of products added to Apicius's recipes in one of the codices
that have come down to us from medieval times.

There are significant traces of the Roman model of cooking in *De observatione ciborum*, a long letter written by the Greek physician Anthimus, who traveled to Italy to visit Theoderic, king of the Goths, at his court in Ravenna. This
was the first treatise on diet and gastronomy produced in Europe in the Middle
Ages.[14] The lingering presence of aromatic plants like nard[15] and sumac,[16] the
custom of cooking food in vinegar and honey,[17] the repeated appearance of
sauces that are typically Roman, such as oxymel (made from a base of honey and
vinegar) and eno-garum (based on wine and garum),[18] and the use of honey as
an additive to wine and water[19] are signs of a culture that, far from dead and
buried, continued to survive in a vibrant way in the customs of everyday life.
This culture would last for many hundreds of years more. In the eighth century,
garum was sold along the banks of the Po by merchants from Comacchio, and
Lombard rulers would request a payment of garum at the river port of Parma. In
the ninth century, inventories taken at the monastery in Bobbio (in the Apennines near Piacenza) record the purchase of two *congi* of garum at the market
in Genoa for the monks' dietary provisions.[20] This was probably an important
product: Comacchio and Genoa evoke the image of harbors, maritime activity,

Satisfied consumers (engravings by Giuseppe Maria Mitelli).
Source: *Le ventiquattr'hore dell'humana felicità* (Bologna, 1675).

and commerce. Establishments for the production of garum were also scattered around the Adriatic shore, in Istria (as we learn in a letter written by Cassiodorus in the sixth century), and as far away as Byzantium. It was in fact also thanks to ongoing commercial contact with Byzantium, the immediate heir of the Roman Empire and its culture, that an appreciable link with the Roman culinary tradition continued to be maintained.

The Arabs: Innovation and Continuity

The encounter with the gastronomic culture of the Arabs certainly accelerated the emergence of a new yet simultaneously ancient taste during the High Middle Ages. It was both new and ancient because it reformulated some basic traits of Roman cooking (the mixing of flavors and the taste for spices) by introducing new products and presenting older elements in a more delicate and refined manner. What the Arabs brought to this aspect of medieval civilization was completely analogous to what occurred in other areas of culture and science: the appropriation, transformation, and dissemination of basic elements from ancient Greek, Roman, and even Mesopotamian and Persian civilizations. As the most important assimilators and exporters of these cultures, the Arabs guaranteed their conservation and transmission to Europe in the Middle Ages. It was also thanks to the Arabs, rather than to an uninterrupted process of internal development, that some elements of the cuisine of antiquity survived through the centuries in revised and revitalized forms.

In the High Middle Ages the Arabs brought to the West two products that were crucial to the conservation and transformation of ancient taste. These were citrus fruit and cane sugar, which gradually took the place of vinegar and honey in cooking customs (after a period in which they were used side by side), softening the contrast between tastes and "lightening" the flavor. In areas such as Sicily and Andalusia, which experienced Arab domination directly, these changes were particularly rapid and precocious. But products tend to circulate, and in the High Middle Ages Italy already had a profusion of maritime cities and traders. In addition, for a few hundred years the Arabs, far from being disruptive to the political unity of the Mediterranean, provided a crucial point of commercial contact between Europe and the Orient through the spice markets. It was only at a later moment—beginning in the eleventh century with the launching of the Crusades—that traders, mainly from Venice and Genoa, established direct routes and ports of call in the eastern Mediterranean. Nevertheless, the importance of the Arab contribution to the use of spices that became a characteristic of European cooking traditions by the Middle Ages remains controversial. Some scholars, such as Maxine Rodinson,[21] have claimed that it was a decisive factor, while others, such as Bernard Rosenberger,[22] tend to reassess its influence. The fact remains, however, that during the Middle Ages, between the seventh and eighth century, the taste for spices began to develop a profile that was clearer and more varied than that found in the Roman tradition.

Spices

De contemptu mundi, the invective against the follies of the world issued by Pope Innocent III at the beginning of the thirteenth century, did not fail to condemn the sin of greed and the kinds of gluttony recently invented by the insane passions of humankind. The pontiff observed that it was no longer enough to harvest the good things that come from the trees, the earth, the sea, and the sky. Instead, "spices are demanded, fragrances acquired," and the strategies of the cook are engaged in the creation of every dish.

We have already noted that this was hardly a novelty in the true sense of the word. The interest in spices, already foreshadowed in late Roman cooking, had not completely disappeared during the High Middle Ages. At the beginning of the twelfth century, in praising the splendor with which Boniface of Canossa had celebrated his marriage to Beatrice of Lorraine, Donizone wrote that during the nuptial feast, which lasted three months, "spices were no longer pounded with mortar and pestle but were ground in the mill like grains of spelt."[23] Thus when the expeditions and sieges that accompanied the Crusades brought the West more directly in contact with the Orient, the spice trade exploded, responding to a demand that already strongly favored strong aromas and flavors. Italy played an important role in this turn of events, since its markets were particularly prominent in supplying spices to the West, which inevitably left a mark on local cuisine. The availability of pepper, ginger, and nutmeg ("peiver, zenzavro e moscao") was a source of great pride for an anonymous Genoese poet of the eighth century who sang the praises of his native city in a fictional dialogue with a Lombard.[24] Over time, however, Venice, not Genoa, became the dominant player in the trade of these precious ingredients.

The commercial manual complied by Francesco Balducci Pergolotti—active in Florence between 1315 and 1340—provides a list of products handled by contemporary importers. The range of spices featured here is much more extensive than in previous centuries and includes various types of pepper (black, white, and long pepper, a sweet, pungent variety highly prized in Roman times), six different kinds of ginger, cinnamon and cinnamon flowers, carnation leaves and stems, cloves, nutmeg, mace (the fibrous covering of dried nutmeg), cardamom, goat's rue, galingale (an aromatic rhizome of Chinese origin, reminiscent of ginger but without its lemony aftertaste), and saffron. Also included are aniseed, turmeric, cassia, caraway, "paradise grains" (Guinea pepper), zedoary, cubeb, cumin, aloe, and nard. Finally, sugar appears in its various shapes and guises: powdered, in loaves, candied, refined, and tinted with violets or roses.[25]

The cookbooks of the fourteenth century were the earliest documents to codify these products. To understand the success of spices,[26] we must remember that the dietary culture of the era placed a very high value on their role in the digestive process. Medieval science claimed that the "heat" radiating from spices allowed food to be absorbed faster and more efficiently by the digestive system by helping it to "cook" in the stomach. Spices were thus sprinkled liberally on cooked dishes and were also distributed as sugar-coated confections at the end of a meal, along with spiced wine. There was an additional, social value attached to this custom. Because of their prohibitive cost, spices were highly appreciated by the upper classes and became a status symbol in the gastronomy of the rich. Ultimately, they were associated with the magical aura of the Orient from whence they came. It was even said that spices grew on trees in the Garden of Eden (which many thought to be located in the Far East). Their exotic character thus acquired an even more compelling aspect, evoking visions of Edenic happiness and lost eternity. All these factors readily explain the superabundance of spices in the cuisine of the upper classes. The imaginary—then as now—played a major role in shaping food customs, and it was all the better if science could lend its support. In any case, the belief that spices were used to mask the poor quality of foods or to conceal the true nature of fish and meats that were spoiled, contaminated, or badly preserved is certainly false. Yet even though scholars have long shown this view to be inconsistent with the evidence, it continues to circulate with the irrepressible vitality typical of cliché. This historical falsehood springs from modern rationalism and from the presumption that only we moderns are able to choose the flavors that are good for us. What kind of taste would those medieval bumpkins, who did not even use forks, have been capable of developing? Yet cooking with spices, developing a cuisine characterized by strong, contrasting flavors, constituted a taste preference that had much to do with the scientific beliefs, fantasies, and fashions of the time. Necessity does not enter into the equation. It is enough to point out that the poor—who might well have had to eat decaying food—did not belong to the social environment where spices were consumed. These were reserved for the elite who could afford to pay exorbitant prices to acquire them in the market. This very limited group of consumers was certainly not burdened with the problem of spoiled or imperfectly preserved foods. Medieval custom considered only very fresh meats suitable for cooking—game on the day it was killed or meats expressly butchered at the point of purchase—at least among the social classes that could afford such items. This practice lasted for a long period of time, as we have already seen.[27] The recipe collections show moreover that spices were added to foods at the last minute: "as late as possible" is the advice of one fourteenth-century writer. There were other, more efficient, and widely practiced methods of preserving foods, particularly the custom of salting. Ultimately, it is clear that spices were used in many different ways, with the purpose of creating the *taste* desired.

Of all Italian cookbooks written in the fourteenth century, the Venetian collection provides the most precise information on the gastronomic uses of these products, which is hardly an accident, given the primacy of Venice in the spice trade. It distinguishes three basic recipes, with three different mixtures of powdered spices: a more delicate preparation for light dishes (such as fish), a heavier one for strong dishes (roasts and so forth), and a mixture of moderate flavor suitable for almost any dish. The "universal" mixture ("fine spices for everything") includes an ounce of pepper, an ounce of cinnamon, an ounce of ginger, half a quarter ounce of cloves, and a quarter ounce of saffron. The "sweet" mixture ("sweet spices for many fine, good things") is composed of a quarter ounce of cloves, one ounce of ginger, one ounce of cinnamon flowers, and a "*folio*" (which probably indicates a bay leaf).[28] The "strong" mixture ("strong black spices for intense flavor") is composed of half a quarter ounce of cloves, two ounces of black pepper, some long pepper, and two nutmegs.[29]

In other recipe collections the uses for which the spices are intended are not explicitly indicated, but they are no less evident on this account. It is also clear that some spices enjoyed special status: pepper, perhaps because of its venerable tradition as the only spice already in use for more than a thousand years, is often cited on its own, independently from other flavors. The same occurs with saffron, but for a different reason. Since dishes of a yellow hue were often deemed desirable, it was used for coloring rather than for flavoring food. "Color with saffron," is the advice given in the *Liber de coquina*, "and add other spices, if you wish."[30] The systematic distinction made in this book between saffron and other spices might lead the reader to suspect that it was a local product, and in fact we have textual evidence that saffron was cultivated in Sicily in Roman times. It was revived there in the eleventh century and spread to other regions, such as Tuscany and—as we know from Bonvesin da la Riva—Lombardy.[31] The special role played by saffron proved to be long lasting. It is indeed possible that the terms *crucum* (crocus) and *safranum* (saffron), which the *Liber de coquina* uses over fifty times, are intended to designate two different things: the "local crocus," mentioned by the physicians of the Salerno school, and saffron from the Orient.[32] In the fifteenth century Maestro Martino uses saffron in several recipes to give dishes a yellow color.[33] This chromatic variation is by far the most common. It is also the most frequently recommended, not only by Martino but by all cooks of the Middle Ages and the Renaissance. Yellow projects the image of gold, happiness, and immortality. In a certain sense, saffron constitutes the culinary alternative to the gold emblazoned on the painted tables of the era.

The use of spices continued to signify social prestige at least until the sixteenth century, as we see in Cristoforo Messisbugo's suggestion that the cost of a feast could be reduced in relation to the social status of the host: "One should know that when a gentleman of modest rank hosts a banquet, he may economize by using one-third of the quantities of sugars and spices, or one-half."[34] But tastes are changing. Although Bartolomeo Scappi continues to call for "Venetian spices" in a manner reminiscent of the culinary habits of two centuries earlier,[35] his basic mixture contains mostly cinnamon (four and a half ounces), an ingredient that was absent in the fourteenth-century text, along with two ounces of cloves, one ounce of nutmeg, and half an ounce of "paradise grains" (Guinea pepper). He adds to these five items half an ounce of saffron and one ounce of sugar[36]—ingredients often mentioned separately in other recipes. Sugar in particular sometimes appears as an *alternative* to other spices,[37] even if it is often simply *added* to a dish. What we see here is a trend toward greater delicacy or "sweetness." The preeminence of cinnamon among traditional spices seems to have similar significance; at this juncture, the combination of sugar and cinnamon tends to prevail over all others.

Sweet, Sour, and Sweet-and-Sour

We have already seen that the combination of sweet and sour was a consistent element in the history of taste for a substantial period from Roman times onward. It was reinforced on the dietary level by the logic of the "temperament of opposites" and the mixing of flavors. In mapping out this history, however, we can distinguish different phases, culturally and territorially quite distinct. In some areas, particularly Italy, we note the increasing prevalence of one flavor (sweetness) over another, while in other areas (like France), the scale always seems to tilt in the opposite direction. In addition, from the Middle Ages onward, the range of products used to create sweet and sour was articulated in a more complex manner than was customary in the cuisine of ancient Rome, where it was centered on just two flavors, honey and vinegar.

As time passed new products were added, including verjuice (obtained from unripe grapes), citrus fruits (all of which were bitter, as their Italian name "*agrumi*" suggests, for in fact the sweet orange was not introduced into Italy until the fifteenth century), and the juice of other fruits that were bittersweet by nature. For many centuries sweetness was obtained from honey, dates, and raisins, as had occurred in Roman times. The discovery of cane sugar, imported to Sicily by the Arabs and embraced by Frederick II in the thirteenth century,[38] marked an important shift and was accompanied by the diffusion of almonds and hazelnuts, used as both sweeteners and thickeners.

The view that Italian contact with Arabic culture had an influence on the revival (or simply the conservation) of the taste for sweet and sour seems substantiated by some of the recipes found in fourteenth-century cookbooks. These dishes—either known to be or thought to be of Arabic derivation—include *limonia* and *romaia*, both of which are characterized by the use of almonds, citrus fruits, and specifically the juice of oranges described as "bitter and sweet."[39] Also indicative is a recipe for "saracen broth," used to tenderize meat with "good wine and bitter juices," along with dates, seedless raisins, and almonds. This recipe is especially interesting for the fact that it is the only one, among the many broth preparations found in *Liber de coquina*, which has a sweet-and-sour flavor.[40]

In most other cases, the sweet-and-sour combination is presented as an option rather than assumed to be the most obvious choice. "If you wish to make it sweet and sour, add the juice of bitter oranges and sugar" is the final comment in a recipe for fish soup in the *Liber*.[41] The same occurs in a recipe for *scapece*, a dish of fried fish preserved in vinegar, which provides a very interesting example of the growing taste for sweetness in the course of the Middle Ages. Here, after the fish is fried in a generous amount of oil, it is allowed to cool. In the meantime, the remaining oil is used to fry some sliced onions along with sultanas, jujubes, and plums. Spices and almonds are then mixed with wine and a small quantity of vinegar, "used in moderation, so that it will not be too sour." The cook then places the fish in a dish and pours the wine mixture on top. Given the presence of both fresh and dried fruit, the recipe already seems quite sweet. Yet this is not enough. Clearly anticipating the possibility of objections, the anonymous compiler adds, "If you wish to make this a sweet-and-sour dish, add the required amount of must or sugar."[42] If we compare this recipe to that of Apicius (reduced to a single line: "In order to preserve fried fish at length, cover it with vinegar as soon as it is taken off the heat"),[43] we notice that the biggest change is the emphasis on sweetness, not mentioned in the Roman model. One could say that the preference for sour preceded the preference for sweet flavors,[44] which gradually developed alongside it. We can already see this in Roman times and again, in a more systematic way, in the Middle Ages, especially in areas where the influence of the Arabs had consolidated and relaunched the Roman tradition.

This was not, however, an omnipresent, homogenizing choice: the cooking customs of the fourteenth century carefully differentiated one dish from another, accentuating this or that flavor according to the occasion. The preferred condiment for roast crane, for example, could be a sauce made from liver, marjoram, saffron, and other "good spices, blended together in wine and vinegar along with two egg yolks and cooked must," thus creating a sweet-and-sour flavor. The sauce used for peacock could be based on the same ingredients, "with the exception of cooked must," a detail indicating that the desired flavor is sour.[45] On the other hand, a recipe might be completely sour, like the preparation for duckling in verjuice, vinegar, and the juice of oranges, lemons, or limes. Such a recipe, however, could be accompanied by a variant calling for the addition of sweet flavors: "Add the juice of bitter orange and sugar, which will be sweet and sour."[46] Bitter sauces are recommended primarily for roast meats,[47] but a full range of possible gradations unfolds before us, with the single objective of pleasing the diner's palate. In a recipe for "*peverada*" we find the following instruction: "Prepare it sweet or acidic, as you wish."[48] When dealing with spices, sugar, and vinegar, the issue was never to *conceal* a taste (as many still maintain), but rather to *invent* one.[49] "Regarding the questions discussed above, the wise cook will be informed on all matters, depending on the different customs of the realm, and will be able to vary and give color to foods in accordance with his best judgment."[50]

We must make an important point at this juncture: although the taste for sour flavors can be found in the cuisine of all social levels, sweetness was perceived as a symbol of social privilege. While citrus fruits, which were imported from southern Italy or from the Riviera, were not widely available to all, no peasant was without access to vinegar (and this must have been the "natural" destination of many weak or badly preserved wines). As for verjuice, we know that the peasants were expected to contribute quantities of unripe grapes to their landlords.[51] Sugar (though not honey, which was beginning to go out of fashion) by contrast was available only to a few and would remain so, thus becoming like many other things a sign of class difference. In the words of the writer Gentile Sermini, who lived from the end of the fourteenth to the middle of the fifteenth century, "Make sure that the peasant does not taste sweetness but only sour things. Rustic he is; rustic he will remain."[52]

It could happen, however, that a "peasant" might pretend to eat like a lord by serving up a pan "of rice with sugar." He would nonetheless be incapable of appreciating the refinement of such a dish and would treat it like a vulgar cabbage soup, topping it up with huge chunks of bread and turning it upside down "as people commonly do in the countryside." Such, at least, is the behavior of a peasant featured in a short story by Sermini,[53] and a clear ideological message emerges from this image: each person eats in the manner prescribed by his social class. At the same time, Sermini's tale begrudgingly acknowledges that some sharing, exchange, and borrowing of food customs took place between "rich" and "poor" cuisine.

The Triumph of Sugar

Between the end of the thirteenth century and the beginning of the fourteenth, the Neapolitan *Liber de coquina* still called for an abundant use of honey in cooking. Yet it is already clear that there was a tendency to replace it with sugar, which appears with increasing frequency in a wide range of uses. While honey is *added* to food, much in the same way as a sauce,[54] or is used as a dip for fritters,[55] sugar becomes part of the basic composition of the dish,[56] as well as providing a replacement for honey in its traditional uses.[57] In some cases, the choice is left to the discretion of the cook, showing that this is a moment of transition, characterized by the superimposition of one custom on another. Broad bean soup is flavored with pepper, saffron, and "honey or sugar."[58] And pancakes are sprinkled "with sugar or honey" once they are cooked.[59]

The Tuscan recipe collection from the end of the fourteenth century, directly derived from the *Liber de coquina*, confirms this transitional moment, though it emphasizes the preference for sugar,[60] attributing a more marginal role to honey by limiting it essentially to fritters and some desserts. The really important shift occurs in a group of northern recipe collections from the geographical area that reaches across Italy from Siena to Venice. Here honey appears even less often,[61] while sugar, which is increasingly characteristic, can be found in more than 28 percent of the 135 recipes, more than doubling the percentage represented in the *Liber de coquina*.[62] A recipe for *"bozolati da monege"* (small, ring-shaped cakes) establishes a sort of equivalence between the two products. "If you want [to use] honey, for every ten [that you wish to make] you need a good spoonful of honey; and if you want sugar, for every ten you need an ounce of sugar."[63] But the winner is already quite evident. Sugar is by now widely used in cooking, and it can also be added in powdered form to enhance a cooked dish: "When you are serving the food, pour some sugar into the bowl, and it will taste very good."[64]

Sugar also becomes a major feature in sauces. While the Neapolitan *Liber de coquina* and its Tuscan imitation suggested a tart sauce "with every roast," as we have already noted, the Venetian recipe collection firmly proclaims that a sweet-and-sour sauce based on spices, sugar, and vinegar is the "perfect reinforced sauce" and is "a good flavoring for every kind of roast."[65]

The triumph of sugar may be regarded as a distinguishing trait of Italian cooking, for, if we look beyond the Alps, we see that bitter flavors still prevailed in France, and Germans continued to use honey in the traditional way.[66] This was the beginning of a more delicate cuisine, explicitly acknowledged as such by those who first practiced it. The Venetian recipe collection of the fourteenth century suggests adding sugar to honey in preparing confectionery, "if you want to make it more delicate,"[67] and substituting sugar for other spices in preparing food for the sick. For example, in the recipe for *cotognata*, a quince-based confection normally made with honey and fine spices, we find the comment: "If you want to prepare this for the sick, boil it first with a little sugar instead of spices."[68] There is the general assumption that once a dish is cooked "sugar will do it no harm.[69] This foreshadows the attitude of Maestro Martino, who mentions honey on only one occasion and makes generous use of sugar in many of his recipes. Martino's friend Platina offers the following pronouncement in a recipe for *biancomangiare*: "It would not be a bad thing to add a little sugar. Indeed no dish would refuse sugar, as they say."[70]

"As they say" (*ut aiunt*): by the middle of the fifteenth century the excellence of this sweet white powder had almost become a commonplace, a universal preference that was solidly supported by medieval thinking, since the *Tacuinum sanitatis* had already proclaimed that hot, moist sugar "is good for the blood" and that it possesses the special, almost unique trait of being "suited to every temperament, age, season, and place."[71] In the sixteenth century—as we see in a comment of Costanzo Felici—the reputation of sugar had already become proverbial: "Sugar is an excellent accompaniment to everything, or one could make it such. As the saying goes, '*sugar never spoils a soup.*' [It] makes eating more refined and, very frequently, drinking also, by rendering both experiences sweet and flavorful, [for] we can truly say that this is a precious food . . . and human nature finds great pleasure and delight in its sweet flavor."[72]

Renaissance cooking became a triumph of sugar, to the great benefit of Venetian traders. Though Genoese merchants also imported sugar from Portugal, it was Venice that held primacy in its transportation, refinement, and development, a dominance that had already been in place for five hundred years. The Venetians themselves cultivated special expertise in confectionery and pastry making, while cooks in the courts and cities of Italy poured sugar into all kinds of preparations. There is hardly a recipe in Scappi's collection that does not call for its use. In fact, there is already a rather archaic ring to Messisbugo's pronouncement—regarding the preparation of a "sweet and strong green sauce"—that "if you want to sweeten it you can add honey or sugar."[73] Moreover, Messisbugo makes it quite clear that sugar, not honey, had become a symbol of social refinement, suggesting that only gentlemen of modest means, who needed to economize, should substitute honey for sugar in various preparations but not in the case of "white foods, Turkish rice dishes, white *torte*, white sauces, or other similar things that would change color with the use of honey." His final word of advice here is: "Those wishing to cut back on expenditure might use honey . . . but they should add some sugar on top."[74]

The Italian craze for sweetness has also been linked to the sweetness of local wines, which over the course of time would have accustomed the taste of the population to sweet flavors. Jean-Louis Flandrin has developed such a view, whereas he associates the contrasting preference of the French for bitter flavors to their habitual consumption of wines with a sharper taste, the inevitable result of the fact that the wines come from a different climate, where the vines were cultivated on a different soil.[75]

Certainly, Montaigne had a similar perception. During a brief stay in Florence he describes the wines served to him as possessing "a sickly sweetness, unbearable in this season." Feeling slightly dazed at the end of a meal, he attributes his state to "the sweet white wines," whose feebleness "does not quench the thirst" and thus induces one to drink too much.[76]

This was nothing new. In the thirteenth century Salimbene of Parma lists the ten qualities the French believed wine must possess in order to deserve full praise: it should be good, beautiful, white, strong, proud, fine, bold, cool, lively, and bracing. Sweetness is not among these requirements, though it is the primary characteristic of good wine according to a Maestro Morando "who taught grammar in Padua and expressed his praise for wine in these words: 'Glorious sweet wine / makes [a man] plump and fleshy / and lightens his heart.' "[77] This view is also reflected in the *Regimen sanitatis* of the Salerno school: "The best wines are white and sweet."[78] To describe wine as the "sweetest nectar," as Donizone does in his account of the wedding feast of Boniface of Canossa and Beatrice of Lorraine, is thus not merely a rhetorical flourish or classical allusion.[79]

The Humanists, Antiquity, and "Modernity"

Did the field of gastronomy experience a rediscovery of antiquity comparable to the quest pursued by writers and scholars in the humanistic and scientific fields? The answer to this question—in the negative, as we shall soon see—is an important indication of the specificity of culinary history and the need to articulate it using special criteria, independent of those suited to other histories.

Appearances would seem to suggest the contrary. Apicius is often cited by Platina and his friends in the Roman Academy, which was under the direction of Pomponio Leto. Leto's concept of living "in the ancient style" by adopting the habits and customs of antiquity, including dietary practices, inevitably invoked the manuscript of Apicius as an ideal point of reference. This document had been brought back to Italy in 1455 by Enoch of Ascoli, following the kind of painstaking research in libraries across Europe that had unearthed many other manuscripts during the same period.[80] It is hardly surprising that the pope denounced Pomponio and his colleagues not only for conspiring against him but also for immoral conduct. The pontiff accused these men of gluttony in particular, that is, of having pursued the pleasure of eating up to the point of consuming meat during Lent, thus violating liturgical obligations in order to live and cook in the style of the pagans.[81] In fact, Platina's *De honesta voluptate et valetudine* is full of suggestions of this kind. There are allusions to "Roman" meals, and "Roman" names are repeatedly assigned to dishes and diners appearing throughout the book. But is this merely an antiquarian gesture (of the type that became highly fashionable in the years that followed)[82] that was not reflected on the practical level? When the Sicilian humanist Antonio Beccadelli asks Giovanni Aurispa to show him the text of Apicius, he is told that he shall receive it but should not harbor false expectations, for his own cook is greater than Apicius.[83] Even in Platina's work, the real or assumed imitation of antiquity is mostly a formality. What prevails is pride in "modernity," a modernity that is nonetheless completely medieval, invented sometime between the fourteenth and the fifteenth century, to which conscious reference is made as an extremely innovative phase in the history of taste.

Although Platina's language sometimes mimics that of Apicius, the content is quite different, as it is derived directly from Maestro Martino's *Libro*. Broth thus becomes *jus*, soups and *torte* become *minutal* and *patina*, white flour products *leucophagium*, and compressed fish roe *ova tarycha*.[84] With surprising anachronistic virtuosity, pasta, which was unknown to the Romans, becomes *esicium*, while Apicius's term *liquamen*—which had by now disappeared from the repertoire of fish sauces—is used to designate pork fat. The dietary values attributed to foods are also completely infused with medieval beliefs. When Platina writes that "meat is the food that nourishes best, and does so in the healthiest manner, and has greatest substance,"[85] he is expressing a view that is very far from the world of ancient Rome, where a claim of this type would assign primacy to bread.[86] But his most explicit declaration of love for "modernity" is expressed in relation to *biancomangiare*, a food that Platina proposes not only as a dish in itself, in accordance with the custom reflected in fourteenth-century recipe collections, but also as an "accompaniment to meat." Platina writes: "This is a condiment I have always preferred to those suggested by Apicius. There is really no reason that the tastes of our ancestors should be esteemed above our own, because, although [our forebears] surpassed us in almost all pursuits, we are unsurpassable in matters of taste." "Our taverns" are real, authentic *gymnasia*, "where there are heated debates on the manner of flavoring dishes."[87] Platina's model here is uniquely and exclusively Martino: "O immortal gods, what cook can be compared to my Martino, from whom I have learned most of the things about which I now write?"

Even in the sixteenth century the development of the art of cooking shows substantial continuity with medieval custom. Though conscious of practicing a cuisine that was new in many respects and certainly in the vanguard when compared to the rest of Europe, Italian cooks of the Renaissance do not show any intention of challenging their predecessors (as often occurs during phases of nouvelle cuisine). On the contrary, they "prefer to adopt their precepts and assimilate their techniques, even at the cost of having to carry out corrections in order to surpass them."[88]

The Flavor of Salt

If sweetness denotes the cuisine of the elite (as it did for a long time), the food of the poor has a predominantly salty flavor. Cured and preserved foods, which are long-lasting and guarantee a minimum of nutritional insurance throughout the year, are still part of a system of exchange that supplies delicacies to the tables of the rich. Their principal use, however, is as the basis of "ordinary" eating customs, of the production and consumption of food in the home. The rich eat fresh food, and the poor do not: from the end of the Middle Ages onward this was one of the main points of contrast between the image of rich cuisine and the food of the poor. Meats, fish, cheese, and vegetables are served on peasants' tables, where they are flavored, monotonously, with salt. The great thirst provoked by salt certainly helps to explain the excessive consumption of wine (at least to our way of thinking) or of beer in other countries, which accompanied the consumption of food for many centuries.

Nutritional treatises, beginning with the work of Anthimus in the sixth century, advise those who are in a position to choose their own dietary regimens to avoid salted meats: "they should not be eaten, unless they really must be, since salt causes the fat to drain from the meats, making them dry and difficult to digest."[89] This advice also applies to fish.[90] Naturally, everyone knows that "no food is ever cooked without salt" (as we read in Platina),[91] and the physicians readily celebrate the virtues of a product that "delights the palate and gives taste to food."[92] But it is one thing to consume products preserved with salt and quite another to give flavor to fresh products by integrating salt into a symphony of flavors that come together in the cooking of dishes. Moreover, in the recipe collections intended for an aristocratic environment, salt almost never appears, except as a flavoring for salad or in the recommendation "to add salt sparingly."[93] "I will not speak of salt, because its use is arbitrary," is Scappi's abrupt comment on the matter.[94] On the other hand, instructions are given on how to desalt preserved foods. "One need not disdain the desalting of foods preserved in salt, as this is frequently practiced, especially in the kitchens of the great."[95] The flavor of salt was thus willingly left to the peasants.

Oil, Lard, and Butter

The rich cuisine of ancient Rome, which is documented in the recipe collection of Apicius, used oil more than any other type of fat; its dishes were in effect literally oozing with oil.[96] This prestigious fat, a true symbol of Roman agriculture along with bread and wine, was juxtaposed with butter and lard, which were in turn symbols of the nomadic and pastoral civilization of the "Barbarians."[97] Lard also appeared in Roman cooking, but only in that of the poorer classes, of inferior cultural status. Among the agronomists of Roman antiquity, only Cato records a few recipes—for sweets—made with clarified animal fat (unguen or adeps),[98] perhaps drawing on the traditions of the countryside.

Romans did not by any means despise pork; the Po valley, culturally rooted in an ancient Celtic occupation, was the center of pig farming, and it supplied pork even to the market in Rome.[99] Still, it was not until the third or fourth century that pork meats appeared among the ingredients that the emperors generously distributed to the masses living in the capital.[100] In the High Middle Ages the valorization of the economy of the forest as a result of the spread of Germanic culture also led to the acceptance of lard as one of the strong values of the dietary system.[101] Anthimus, the first medieval writer to concern himself with dietary science, dedicates a disproportionately long portion of his treatise to lard,[102] despite his own cultural background (born a Greek, he grew up at the court of Byzantium and traveled to Ravenna, then under the rule of the Goths). He suggests in fact that it may be used for vegetables and all other foods, particularly "if oil is not available." This specification (ubi oleum non fuerit) shows that the cultural preference for oil typical of the Romans persisted even in the sixth century. But the overall context had changed in the meantime, since the political and social advancement of the Germanic people had launched a genuine campaign to promote animal fat and animal products in general. Lard also became the preferred fat used in aristocratic cuisine. Though governed by strict rules regarding the consumption of meat, even the monastic diet conformed to the habits of the population at large by adopting pork fat for cooking green vegetables and legumes.[103] An exception was made, however, for Lent and other times of fast and abstinence, during which all animal products were completely forbidden.

The restrictions imposed by the liturgical calendar, which required all Christians, and not only members of religious orders, to abstain from animal products on several days of the year,[104] are an important element in the history of alimentary fats. On such occasions the faithful were obliged to replace lard with vegetable oil, a fact that accounts at least in part for the emergence of the unprecedented practice of alternating lard and oil in the dietary culture of the Middle Ages. This custom did not reflect different social and ideological contexts and cultures but was integrated into the very system of consumption, which was basically the same for all members of society. The encounter between Roman and Germanic culture—with the decisive mediation of Christianity—had thus produced a new system of values that somehow included both of them. When in the year 765 a priest named Rissolfo called for a free meal to be served three times a week to the poor of Lucca, he was careful to specify that the gruel (made of grains and legumes) should be flavored abundantly with either lard or oil (*de uncto aut de oleo*), alternatives most probably determined by the liturgical calendar.[105]

Transcending differences of taste and of social, cultural, and regional provenance, a system had already evolved within which each fat had its own place. Oil belonged to lean cooking, while lard belonged to fat. This system also functioned on the economic level: the same guild often oversaw the trade and sale of all kinds of fat. Oil was included among the specialties of the "lard traders,"[106] just as fish alternated with meat at butchers' shops.

The rule requiring the alternation of oil and lard is reflected in the recipes of the fourteenth century. For example, the *Liber de coquina* describes a chickpea soup flavored with "with lard or oil, as the day requires" (*sicut dies exigit*). A *pasticcio* of cabbage "is made with oil on fast days [and with fish instead of meat] and with lard on other occasions." A *pasticcio* of trout can be flavored with lard rather than oil when eaten *tempore carnis* (on days that allow meat).[107] Clearly, there were many local variations. Lard appears in 25 percent of the recipes in the *Liber de coquina*, which was written in southern Italy, in 36 percent of the recipes in its Tuscan adaptation, and in 42 percent of those in the Venetian version.[108] The alternation of fats imposed by the liturgical calendar is nonetheless the main factor determining the choice of lard or oil.

The process of integration was uneven, however, since only lard belonged to the everyday world of the common people. Olive oil was still a product of the elite and was often costly outside the regions where olives were cultivated (even though during the Middle Ages, partially as the result of an unusually mild climate, olive trees managed to grow as far north as central Emilia and the lake districts of Lombardy and the Veneto). How then could the people solve the problem of Lenten abstinence? Above all, with the help of the market, which sold olive oil of various provenance. The Venetians sold oil from the Adriatic regions (especially Apulia and the Marches), and the Genoese sold the oil from the Tyrrhenian regions (Liguria, Tuscany, Latium, and Campania). Another solution for lean days was to use oil extracted from other vegetable products, such as walnut oil, which the ancient Romans had found disgusting[109] and which nonetheless enjoyed unexpected acclaim during the Middle Ages. Finally, however, in the later centuries of the Middle Ages, the ecclesiastical authorities allowed the use of butter as an alternative to oil on lean days, sporadically at first and then in a general manner; this dispensation applied initially only to the regions of northern Europe, where butter was traditionally consumed (even if only by the lower classes and the peasants),[110] and it was later extended to the countries of the south, including Italy.

According to Flandrin, the choice of butter in the north of Europe was determined not by taste but by *dis*taste. The sharp flavor of olive oil, highly appreciated in the cuisines of the Mediterranean tradition,[111] was unacceptable to the

Man sniffing a cured sausage (engraving).

Source: Antonio Frizzi, *La salameide: Poemetto giocoso con le note* (Venice: Zerletti, 1772).

consumers of continental Europe, perhaps in part because Italian (and Spanish) merchants did not hesitate to profit as much as possible from the Lenten rules by dispatching oil of the worst quality to northern Europe (the English expression "as brown as oil" gives some inkling of what must have occurred). For this reason, the northern populations chose butter as an alternative fat, despite the "poor" image associated with it from the social perspective. In the course of these developments the status of butter changed, and it became a fashionable product. On the strength of its new image, it ultimately found its way even into the culinary practices of regions that were culturally linked to olive oil. The decisive shift seems to have occurred in the fifteenth century, and its effects were felt even in Italy. According to Flandrin, this was almost tantamount to a second invasion by northern cuisines of the culinary territories of the Mediterranean, following the initial invasion in the High Middle Ages that had brought about the triumph of lard in the dietary habits of Europe as a whole through the diffusion of Germanic customs.[112]

These two events developed, however, in very different ways and with different connotations. While the first invasion had come about—to continue the metaphor—with great deployments of troops and resources, in the form of a food culture that imposed itself through power and social dominance, the arrival of butter in the kitchens of the south by contrast happened without fanfare—indeed almost without a sound. At least at the beginning, butter was presented as a substitute for oil and thus took on the "weak" connotations of Lent and of "humble" cuisine. This is how it seems, for example, in *Il registro di cucina* (The cooking register), which was written in the 1430s by Johannes Bockenheym, the cook of Pope Martin V.[113] Here, in the section dedicated to Lent, we find a recipe for broad bean soup that includes the instruction to add olive oil or butter for flavoring. In a recipe for pan-cooked carp, Bockenheym notes that the dish should be prepared with wine, parsley, and oil or butter.[114] He also suggests butter for a *torta* of greens, a cheese *torta*, and fried eggs.[115] Meat dishes by contrast are always flavored with lard or clarified fat.

Butter also makes an appearance in the cookbook of Maestro Martino, who suggests its use for flavoring pasta, by adding it to grated cheese, which had been the most widely used condiment for pasta dishes for many centuries. This innovation was adopted and repeated in subsequent recipe collections.

Even in the fifteenth century there was the persistent belief that "butter should be used mostly by those who live in western and northern regions, where oil is unavailable," as Platina wrote, emphasizing the excellence and prestige of olive oil. But there is no longer an attitude of superiority toward the fat consumed by the "Barbarians." Citing both ancient and contemporary views on the subject, Platina concedes that butter may be used "instead of fat or oil to cook any dish."[116] By contrast, other writers—including Michele Savonarola of Padua, the author of an important treatise on nutrition that also appeared in the fifteenth century—continue to fight a losing battle against butter, deeming it unfit to appear on the tables of the nobility: "Though many use it instead of oil, butter harms the stomach and loosens the intestines, and those unaccustomed to eating it will find that it upsets their stomachs."[117]

This was not the position that prevailed in the long run, and by the sixteenth century the cuisine of the nobility regularly used butter. Bartolomeo Scappi's *Opera* too reflects a moment of adjustment or accommodation in relation to this issue, as it distinguishes three different levels in the use of fats: lard and clarified fat are used for fat days, butter for lean days (Fridays and Saturdays), and oil (olive and almond) for the vigils of holy days and during Lent. Though butter could if necessary replace all other fats, it has in fact also carved out a space of its own, which is clear and well defined.

In the course of the seventeenth century butter finally prevailed in all areas of cooking, even in the realm of meat, thus definitively shedding its Lenten associations. The cuisines of northern and southern Italy participated equally in this shift. Both Antonio Latini's Neapolitan recipe collection and Bartolomeo Stefani's, written in Mantua, frequently specify the use of butter instead of lard or clarified fat. This development also affected the preparation of sauces. Fatty sauces based on butter (or oil) now came into existence and were destined to replace the sour and spicy sauces favored by medieval and Renaissance cuisine.[118]

In this context, lard suffered a loss in prestige, as it no longer maintained the primacy it had enjoyed in the dietary culture and cooking practices of the Middle Ages. Even Vincenzo Tanara, a Bolognese agronomist who had a visceral attachment to the culture of pork (we have already mentioned his work on "the 101 ways" of cooking it), was perfectly aware of the uses of butter, though he does not treat it with the kind of attention he lavished on lard and clarified fat. Tanara writes: "Butter helps to create a certain consistency in the foods that are made with it and especially in dough, creating a faint crustiness or hardness on the surface, which is very pleasurable to bite into with one's teeth. . . . [It also] is used in the preparation of pastas, in a thousand sauces, instead of oil, or on the spit, or for *crostini*, as already mentioned, and in other ways.[119] Around the turn of nineteenth century butter attained even greater importance, and in 1840 a man named Carlotti from Verona, the owner of olive groves near Lake Garda, complained that "butter has replaced oil in many cooking preparations."[120]

At the end of the nineteenth century, reflecting on the diverse range of traditions in the various parts of the peninsula, Pellegrino Artusi delineated a geography of cooking fats without making any reference to the liturgical calendar. He wrote: "For frying, people will use the best type of fat produced in their locality. In Tuscany there is a preference for oil, in Lombardy butter, and in Emilia lard."[121] Attentive as Artusi was to placing the different regional traditions within what seemed like the national framework of Italian cuisine, he still had to maintain the utmost flexibility and openness when suggesting the use of this or that fat: "[Use] the kind of fat that you find most agreeable." "[Fry foods] according to the taste of the place where you happen to be or from where you have come." "[For fat, use oil], wherever the oil is good." "Choose between lard or butter according to local custom, which generally favors one or the other of these condiments." Artusi's well-meaning tolerance—his thoughtful invitation to his readers to respect the diversity of individual and collective tastes—may have attributed too much importance to territory (or place) in the definition of differences. In fact, other variables, of a social and cultural rather than an economic nature—liturgical obligations, the dietary imagination, the mechanisms of fashion—also contribute over time to building up complex layers of use value. Oil, which is characteristic of ancient times, lard, of the Middle Ages, and butter, of modernity, intersect with each other in cooking practices in a dynamic pattern that is not at all fixed or immutable.

During the twentieth century butter gained new ground, finally shaking off its elitist connotations and claiming a larger number of consumers. But the process was not yet complete, since at this point olive oil scored a new triumph over animal fats, thanks to the discovery (or perhaps more accurately the invention) of the "Mediterranean diet" by American doctors and journalists. The story is not yet over.

The Italian Model and the French "Revolution"

Many clichés have circulated on the splendor of Italian cuisine in the sixteenth century, of which Scappi's *Opera* represents the most complete and mature testimony. These myths are neither devoid of truth nor entirely untainted by far-fetched fantasy. Above all there is the widespread belief that Italy gave birth to the knowledge that enabled French cooks to invent a "new cuisine" beginning in the seventeenth century. This cuisine was in time to achieve cultural hegemony, parallel to the influence exerted by the court of France on every area of civil and intellectual life in Europe. There is even a line of historiographical thinking that confidently identifies the protagonists of this development as the cooks employed by Catherine de' Medici, who in 1533 married the duke of Orléans, Henri de Valois, crowned Henry II, king of France, in 1547. It was purportedly thanks to this couple that Italian cuisine made its way to the Parisian court.

There is no documentary proof for this claim. In any case, it is hardly necessary to invoke Catherine de' Medici to show that "Italian" culture was present on French soil. In the sixteenth century, as in the Middle Ages, there was a wide circulation of culinary techniques and knowledge among European countries in the guise of a cosmopolitan culture that knew no borders. The reciprocity of influences or rather "the circulation of ideas and types of knowledge"[122] between

Italy and France is clearly reflected in the recipe books of the thirteenth and fourteenth centuries. The *Liber de coquina* proposes a recipe for meats "*ad usum Francie*," for a pea soup (with Brie cheese) "*ad modum gallicorum*," and a "*brodium gallicanum*."[123] Conversely, Italian specialties are mentioned in books written on the other side of the Alps, showing a special and rather predictable interest in "Lombard" dishes, since Lombardy was relatively close to France from the territorial and cultural point of view. Jean-Louis Flandrin notes in the French cookbooks of the time a "*leche lumbard*" and a "*tourte lombarde*," a "*crustade lumbard*" and a "*rys lumbard*," as well as "*potage de Lumbars*" and a "*Bruet de Lombardye*."[124] This Italian influence increased in France in the 1400s, when Platina's *De honesta voluptate et valetudine* (and indirectly the work by Maestro Martino that provides its inspiration) became known throughout Europe, thanks to the fact that Platina wrote in Latin, an international language. Platina's treatise was subsequently translated into several Italian versions and later, beginning at the end of the fifteenth century, into French, English, and German. European culture's substantial debt to the Italian art of cooking and style of living can be ascribed to this work more than to any other source. Scappi's magisterial *Opera* by contrast was never translated into French, although it was plagiarized extensively by German and French writers.[125]

In the same period, the adjective "French" was used to describe Giovanni de' Rosselli on the frontispiece of the cookbook of which he was the presumed author but which in reality was entirely copied from Maestro Martino. This tells us that, even during the era in which Italy's elite cooking enjoyed greatest esteem, "Frenchness" was already part of the image projected by this cuisine. We must remember too that German cooks were also greatly admired, a fact that is underestimated today. In the fifteenth century Germans worked in most of the important kitchens of Italy, from the Bentivoglio household of Bologna to the court of Pope Martin V, whose chef, Johannes Bockenheym, wrote a treatise on cooking between 1431 and 1435.[126] There were also several German innkeepers in Italian territory. In the opinion of Enea Silvio Piccolomini, these were "the people who practice the art of innkeeping in almost all the cities of Italy,"[127] and in one short story we find a German cook preparing lasagne at the monastery of San Procolo in Bologna.[128] The professional pride of the "Lanzi" (as Germans were often called in the sixteenth century) is also the subject of a comic poem by Antonio Grazzini (otherwise known as "Il Lasca"), who makes his German characters speak in comically incorrect Italian.[129] Even the French admired German cuisine. When Montaigne traveled through Germany on his way to Italy, he marveled at the excellent quality of the food served in German inns and regretted that he had not brought along "a cook to instruct in their ways so that some day the cook could try them at home."[130] In short, contacts between the cuisines of Italy and France (as well as Germany and other European countries) existed from medieval times onward, before, during, and after the Medici affair.

Praising the ability of French and German cooks in preparing food, condiments, and sauces, the steward Giovan Battista Rossetti wrote in 1584 that, while much of the skill these men possessed was learned "from our Italian cooks," they had developed it to a degree of "utmost perfection" by adding "a new level of refinement."[131]

But how does this concern the French culinary "revolution"? Italian cooks might well have been masters in Europe, but what they taught (the profusion of spices and sugar, the mixing of sweet and sour) was still profoundly linked to the medieval culture of artifice, which reached its highest point of perfection on the Italian tables of the Renaissance. The technical skill of a cook of Scappi's caliber is beyond question, but the culinary reformation that occurred in France in the seventeenth century was based on radically different principles, as we discussed at the beginning of this chapter. These principles were the rejection of artifice and of the combination of sweet and sour, a drastic change in the use of spices, the invention of sauces based on fats rather than acids, and the increased value attributed to "natural" flavors. The Italian recipe collections of the fifteenth and sixteenth centuries, and the cooks who wrote and used them, cannot be considered as providing the model for a cuisine that developed from very different, even diametrically opposed, theories and practices.

Italy nonetheless made a genuine contribution to the French model, though on a different level. In reality, many scholars agree that Italian influence was more marked with regard to *food products* than with regard to *flavors*. One of the novelties of seventeenth-century French cooking was the high value placed on vegetables and garden herbs, in contrast to the emphasis on meat that had prevailed in medieval times.[132] And it was above all the Italian culinary tradition that had developed and transmitted over the centuries the preference for cooking with vegetables, as we have already seen. Fresh peas cooked in the pod, which were all the rage—the very latest in culinary fashion—at the court of the Sun King in the seventeenth century,[133] can already be found in Maestro Martino's fifteenth-century recipe collection, where they are fried along with salted meat—"Take peas as they are, in the pod, and cook them"[134]—and in Scappi's *Opera*, where peas are stewed or served with vinegar and pepper: "tender peas boiled in the pod."[135]

Besides, the seriousness with which Italian cooks approached their craft was long considered by the French as a strange eccentricity. In a well-known passage, Michel de Montaigne describes a conversation he had with a steward who had once worked for the now deceased Cardinal Carafa. Here the writer evokes the image of a man well capable of articulating his views on cooking as an art and as a science:

[I asked him about his job,] and he replied with a discourse on the science of guzzling, delivered with magisterial gravity and demeanor as if he had been expounding some great point of theology. He spelled out to me the difference in appetites: the one we have before eating, the one we have after the second and third course; the means, now of simply gratifying it, now of arousing it and stimulating it; the organization of his sauces, first in general, and then in particularizing the quality of the ingredients and their effects; the differences in salads according to the season, which one should be warmed up and which served cold, the way of adorning and embellishing them to make them also pleasant to the sight. After that he entered upon the order of serving, full of beautiful and important considerations. And all this swollen with rich and magnificent words, and the way we use to talk about the government of an empire.[136]

A man like this, says Stephen Mennell, is truly a "pioneer of gastronomy," foreshadowing the theories of "good taste" that were elaborated in modern France in opposition to medieval culture.[137] Mennell's claim could be countered, however, by pointing out that the arguments made by Montaigne's character are rooted in the dietary and culinary culture of the Middle Ages, and the reader of Platina's work and the writings of his fourteenth-century predecessors could find ready evidence of this. In fact, even Petrarch was already lamenting in his day that men spoke of nothing other than food and that they neglected literary matters, "making cooks undergo examinations but not copyists."[138]

The fact remains, however—and this was correctly emphasized by Mennell—that Montaigne's account features in an essay entitled "The Vanity of Words" as an example of useless eloquence. Paradoxically, it was along the lines of this pejorative assessment that the (negative) myth of the cooks of Catherine de' Medici came into being, a myth that Italians adopted in a positive sense. Even if a man of Marin's prominence could acknowledge, on the strength of the well-known cliché, that "Italians taught us [French] how to prepare food,"[139] the moralistic condemnation launched by the writers of the *Encyclopédie* against the artifices of cuisine—the only goal of which was supposedly "to make men eat more than necessary"—was aimed primarily at Italians. Under the entry *"cuisine,"* Louis Jaucourt accused the cooks from the far side of the Alps of spreading the mania for food and the ways to satisfy it: "Italians were the first to inherit what was left of Roman cuisine. They brought their knowledge of culinary abundance to the French, the excesses of which many of our kings attempted to repress with edicts, but in the end it triumphed over the laws made during the reign of Henri II. Then cooks from the country across the Alps came and established themselves in France, and this is one of the things we owe to that crowd of corrupt Italians who served at the court of Catherine de' Medici." As we might expect, this is followed by the excerpt we have already cited from Montaigne on the vanity of words, which includes the gastro-theological disquisition by the erstwhile steward of Cardinal Carafa.[140] This was in 1754. Soon afterward we find the same passage used to support the opposite side of the argument. The anonymous writer of *La cuciniera piemontese*, which appeared in 1771, accepts the idea that "the many cooks who followed Catherine de' Medici were the first to bring good taste to the kitchens of France during the time of Henry II."[141] A 1772 letter by Abbott Giovanbattista Roberti on "the luxury of the eighteenth century" denounces the "arrogant fastidiousness" of certain Frenchmen who, when they come to Italy and "take their first taste of one of our dishes cooked in a style different from what is customary on the other side of the Alps, declare outright that it is detestable." Poor men! Little do they realize that "in the time of Catherine de' Medici our great teachers left the hearths and pantries of Italy to instruct [that illustrious nation] in the art of sumptuous and refined food, and our cooks brought the skills of the dining table there, just as our captains brought those of the battlefield. And we read in the work of Montaigne himself of how he heard a marvelous disquisition on cooking from a cook employed by Cardinal Carafa, the like of which was unknown in all of France."[142] Francesco Leonardi went as far as to claim that "the departure of Catherine was cuisine's final farewell to Italy."[143] And so the myth was born.

"Waters, Cordials, Sorbets, and Ice Creams"

Italians were the undisputed masters in developing methods of chilling and freezing drinks. "The real way to make all kinds of waters and cordials in the Italian style" was disclosed to the French in 1692 in a chapter in Audiger's *La maison reglée*. Thirty years earlier, the same Audiger tried to obtain from the French king the exclusive right to "manufacture and sell all types of cordials in the Italian style."[144] This indicates the acknowledgment of a truly Italian invention that was already at least a hundred years old. The custom of chilling drinks—by mixing snow or ice with water, wine, or any other drink—had spread throughout Italy in the second half of the sixteenth century, though against the advice of many doctors. In larger cities this custom spread among the masses, if we are to believe a comment made by a Roman physician in 1603.[145]

The creation of sorbet resulted from experiments in chilling drinks, and it too became a matter of myth. Supposedly, sorbet was also brought to France by Catherine de' Medici (and who could doubt it?). There is no documentary evidence to support this hypothesis, however, and we cannot prove that the art of sorbet making was already practiced in Italy in the middle of the sixteenth century. Yet we certainly know that sorbets—already developed to a degree of remarkable sophistication—were sold in special shops a century later, most notably in Venice and Naples. When Antonio Latini, a native of the Marches, took up service at the court of Naples in 1659, he had the impression "that every-

one [in the city] was born with a special skill and instinct for making sorbets."
This pursuit was not limited to experts, however, but was also practiced by "persons of little learning," as Latini informs us in his brief "Treatise on Various Kinds
of Sorbets, or Water Ices." His short essay, included in the book on stewardship
and cooking that he composed at the end of his career, between 1692 and 1694,
contains the first written recipes on how to mix sugar, salt, snow, and lemon
juice, strawberries, sour cherries, and other fruit, as well as chocolate, cinnamon
water, and different flavorings. There is also a description of a "milk sorbet that is
first cooked," which we could regard as the birth certificate of ice cream.[146]

De' sorbetti, the first book entirely dedicated to the art of making frozen confections, was published in Naples in 1775. Its author, Filippo Baldini, discusses
different types of sorbets, some made with "subacidic" fruits, such as lemon,
orange, and strawberry, and others made with "aromatic" ingredients, such as
chocolate, cinnamon, coffee, pistachio, and pine nuts. A separate chapter deals
with "milky sorbets," meaning ice creams, whose medical properties are vigorously proclaimed.

Literary works echo this trend. The "sorbettiera" (sorbet maker) is celebrated
in a canzonetta written by Lorenzo Magalotti,[147] and Parini's young protagonist
(il giovin Signore) concludes each day with the sweet, cool taste of a chocolate
or coffee sorbet.[148]

Sorbets were produced side by side with the "flavored waters" that captivated
Audiger. During his visit to Italy he wrote:

> I made a vigorous effort to neglect nothing connected to confectionery
> and cordials and to perfect the art of making all kinds of waters, with flowers or fruits, chilled or not, sorbets, custards, barley waters, pistachio
> waters, and others made with pine nuts, coriander, aniseed, fennel, and
> every type of grain, and to give them a good flavor by emphasizing their
> own best qualities. I also learned how to distill all kinds of flowers, fruits,
> cereals, and other substances, distilling them in both cold and warm conditions, and to prepare chocolate, tea, and coffee.[149]

Can One Cook Without Spices?

The gradual abandonment of spices is one of the most distinctive (and culturally significant) aspects of taste and was initiated in the seventeenth century by
the "new cuisine" of France. This apparently paradoxical phenomenon is a
good example of how the fashion of the elite is determined by cost, rarity, and
the exclusiveness of the types of food consumed. Spices had indeed been the
characteristic sign of rich cooking for over a thousand years, but they now began
to lose favor at exactly the moment when their abundance made their use possible on an increasingly broader scale (as had already begun to occur). After all,

the voyages of exploration and conquest around the globe had as one of their objectives the acquisition of spices through direct access to the site of their production. But the overabundance of aromas and flavors that flooded Europe in the sixteenth century soon generated a sense of fatigue. Now that fine spices were within the reach of many, if not all, the "truly" rich looked elsewhere for signs of distinction. The royal court of France—and by extension the nobility of the realm—rediscovered indigenous flavors. Thus chives, scallions, mushrooms, capers, and anchovies began to replace spices.[150]

Sweet-and-sour sauces, to which spices were added and which inevitably accompanied meat dishes in accordance with the model of medieval and Renaissance cuisine, began to disappear along with spices. Meats were now garnished with raw salads and dressed with oil and vinegar. Salads were thus transferred from the category of appetizers, to which they had belonged for centuries in keeping with a custom repeatedly reinforced by the advice of physicians and culinary experts,[151] to the category of side dishes or accompaniments (contorni).[152] Even sugar was abandoned, or at least marginalized, by being assigned to a specific place in the meal—the final dessert—instead of maintaining a fixed presence in every course, as Italian cooks had once recommended and still continued to do, at least to some extent.

In Italy these changes occurred very slowly, above all because the art of cooking was not really regulated by cooks, as was the case beyond the Alps, but rather by stewards and "house masters." The question of taste had thus become secondary to such issues as supervising the formal aspects of hospitality, the staging of banquets, and the organization of the dinner table.[153] The complexity or rather the complicated quality of the recipes, the excess of ornamentation, and the superimposition of culinary activities that did not always follow a linear plan were traits frequently found in Italian cuisine of the seventeenth century. They are especially evident in the recipes of Antonio Latini, which also show the influence of Spanish cuisine, similarly marked by a culture of ostentation, unappreciative of simplicity and moderation. And yet Latini dared to suggest that "the way to cook and flavor foods without using spices" was to replace them with parsley, wild thyme, and other aromatic herbs. Nevertheless, his suggestion occupies just a few lines, and he quickly shifts to a more conventional position: "Since I have taught you the way to add flavor without spices, it is time to give a recipe on how to flavor complex, constructed dishes, how to create Spanish embellishments and dishes in the Neapolitan style, with the kinds of spices that are most suitable [cinnamon, coriander, nutmeg, cloves, and pepper]."[154]

Small signs of evolution are more readily discernible in Stefani's "Lombard" cooking. Stefani uses spices in moderate quantities and sugar in only a few sauces (rather than adding it to all dishes, as Latini did). He also introduces the use of anchovies in sauces (a custom that lasted in Italy at least until the nineteenth century) and makes a more consistent use of fats, especially butter.[155] Yet flavors and aromas are slow to change. Cinnamon and sugar are still used in soups, as they were in Scappi's time, along with nutmeg, cloves, pepper, and, predictably, the sweet-and-sour combination. In fact, citrus fruits, or vinegar with sugar and spices, are still the decisive elements in the majority of sauces, imparting an unmistakably ancient flavor.[156] Along with the lean sauces of the medieval and Renaissance tradition, we find a "butter sauce" made with a base of egg yolk and lemon juice and reminiscent of new creamy sauces, such as mayonnaise, in the "new" French cuisine.[157] Yet Stefani cannot resist adding nutmeg, powdered cloves, and sugar, as well as some musk and amber (the currently fashionable aromas).[158] Only in the case of "ordinary cooking," to which he dedicates an appendix in the second edition of his recipe collection, does Stefani concede that the cook might forgo the use of spices. Here beef stew is flavored simply with garlic and rosemary: "do not add spices, for when it is cooked it will be good" (and yet he also asserts that if one wants to make the dish more dignified one must add a little pepper, cinnamon, and nutmeg). The tendency toward simpler and more natural flavors thus seems ambivalent or contradictory. Still, the mental attitude that prompts Stefani to offer the following advice on the flavor of strawberries is definitely new: "Do not add anything else to this flavor, since one must be able to perceive its natural taste and smell." Similarly, in the case of wild cherries, he writes: "this taste should not be mixed with any other ingredient, because it is very flavorful on its own."[159] Nothing is added apart from sugar.

It is clear that the climate too was changing—and perhaps to a greater degree—beyond the environment of aristocratic cuisine, which was restricted by the demands of protocol and image. At the beginning of the seventeenth century the Florentine Giovanni Del Turco, a cook not by profession but "for amusement and pleasure," already expressed reservations on Bartolomeo Scappi's cooking practices—from which he nonetheless pillaged a great deal of information—because Scappi "makes much use of spices and sugar, which may not appeal to the taste of many people, as well ginger, nutmeg, and cinnamon in particular, but this may be corrected according to the judgment of each cook."[160] He suggests that "greater prudence [should be observed] regarding the influence of noble cuisine on the alimentary practices of society. . . . Assuming that a superior gastronomic model exists, its pertinence outside the framework where it is naturally expressed [the cuisine of the court and the upper classes] belongs mainly to the level of representation and the imaginary [rather than taste]."[161] In the end, power is not the measure of all things.

In the eighteenth century Italy's Enlightenment philosophers argued the necessity of banishing strong flavors from the dinner table in favor of food characterized by refinement and lightness. As Pietro Verri wrote in the journal *Il Caffé*, "no strongly-flavored food is permitted on our table." This choice is not merely gastronomic but also ideological in the broadly political sense, since it defies the old order, whose "showy abundance" had caused a sense of heaviness in the stomach and had led to the inability to think. "This is our meal, which we will conclude with an excellent cup of coffee. We are thus satisfied, well nourished, and not overwhelmed by heavy food, which wilts the spirit, spreading boredom through our society."[162]

A "bourgeois" codification of the trend toward a greater delicacy of flavors is found in the work of Pellegrino Artusi, where it is accompanied by a thoughtful observation on the shifts in taste that occur over time. Referring to a sweet made with rice flour, Artusi writes: "The composition of this dessert makes me realize that recipes too are subject to fashion, as the taste of our senses varies according to progress and civilization. Now we appreciate a cuisine that is light, delicate, and pleasant to look at, and perhaps the day will come when many of the dishes I describe as good will be replaced by other, much better ones."[163] Only the final recipe is dedicated to "fine spices" — nutmeg, cinnamon, allspice, and cloves — which must be pounded and mixed with sweet almonds in a mortar. This seems almost like a tribute to time-hallowed traditions no longer in fashion, faintly echoing the claim that "spices are stimulating, but, if used sparingly, they can help the stomach."[164]

It is mainly in the kitchens of the common people — and this is hardly surprising — that the erstwhile tastes of the aristocracy now find a welcome and where they are imitated and replicated with the belated discovery of flavors that had been beyond reach for a very long time. Take, for example, the recipes that Luigi Bicchierai (also known as Pennino), an innkeeper at Ponte a Signa from 1812 to 1873, recorded in his diary along with stories and comments on events that were happening around him.[165] To accompany a dish of "dressed squab," he recommends a sweet-and-sour sauce that we might well mistake for one of the recipes found in the collections written in the Middle Ages or the Renaissance: "Take a third part of vinegar and two parts of cooked must, and if there is not enough must, two thirds of sugar, along with spices, including cloves, and finely chopped zest of lemon, pine nuts, seedless raisins, and little salt. Boil the mixture for a quarter of an hour and pour over the squab when fried." In his recipe for a dish of fried shrimp prepared with sweet and savory flavors, Pennino notes: "Add salt, pepper and sprinkle with a touch of cinnamon. Add a hundred grams of raisins that have been macerated and then dried off, and add lemon juice also." We can detect his explicit awareness of drawing on the tradition of high cuisine: "This is an ancient recipe that was used in aristocratic cooking. It is prepared by monastic cooks and was used whenever they needed to make a good impression on an important visitor."[166]

To sprinkle sugar and spices on *tortelli* "like the falling snow" is an ancient practice that was carried out by the cooks of the nobility and can now be observed in the inns and farmhouses of the Alpine valleys. The sharp tang of

Fishmonger ("Smell How Fresh It Is!") (photograph, Naples, 1860–1880).

sweet-and-sour flavors also lives on undiminished in Cremona relish and many other preparations that have come down to us thanks to a large degree to their importance in the culinary lore of peasants.

Toward the Development of a National Taste

A strongly elitist model shaped the development of taste over the centuries, setting a trend for the consumption of rare ingredients and creating a preference

for sophisticated combinations of flavors. This model floundered when bourgeois cuisine, which was simpler and less creative, began to assume a dominant
role. In terms of the food products used, bourgeois cooking, when it first
emerged, was not unlike the refined culinary model, although it showed greater
concern with the cost of ingredients and the work that was necessary to transform them. There was in fact a significant level of osmosis operating between
these two traditions. In moving from France to Italy, bourgeois cooking took on
an air of titled nobility. We have only to remember Menon's *La cuisinière bourgeoise*, which was translated into Italian under the title *Il cuoco piemontese perfezionato a Parigi* (The Piedmontese cook trained in Paris). It was not only the
presence of prized meats and vegetables that constituted the value of a dish of
French origin but also an element of professional virtuosity, the clever management of heat sources, and the art of decoration, which represented a gastronomic surplus value and the ultimate mark of excellence. The quality of ingredients and the cost of labor were the two criteria around which bourgeois cuisine developed a model that was as different from the food served on the
cosmopolitan tables of the aristocracy as it was from the dishes served at country feasts.

The appearance of new, cheaper, and more readily available vegetables—
both fresh and preserved (in the case of potatoes and tomatoes)—on the dinner
table all year long favored this revolution. By the middle of the nineteenth century, the tomato was the basis for a sauce used universally in restaurants both
humble and grand as an accompaniment to meat and also as a sauce for pasta
dishes. Its stable, moderately acidic taste and its bright red color, undiminished
by the process of preservation, ensured its success, and it became an ingredient
that appeared equally in the dishes of the poor, the middle class, and the aristocracy. The story of the potato was somewhat similar. Although it had a poor
reputation in terms of flavor and consistency, it was nonetheless easily transported, manipulated, and combined with other foods. So the potato too became
an ingredient that was used across Italy's social spectrum, though its cultivation
was still unevenly distributed in the nineteenth century. Potatoes and tomatoes
also raised the issue of territorial provenance, since they were ubiquitous and
easily replanted and hence constituted culinary references that were not characteristic of a single place but could be considered universal.

While the food eaten by the masses was salty, as we have noted, elite food was
sweet. While the nobility dined on game, the lower classes consumed rough
grains. The cuisine of the bourgeoisie by contrast favored mild or unsalted
dishes, like pastas, potato, veal, and fish in white sauce, and they held these in
high esteem. Bourgeois cooking showed a preference for foods that have a soft
texture, a "natural" color, and flavors that were not too intense. The strongest
seasonings, such as robust red wine for a marinade and a *civet*, and sugar for an
open-faced tart, were assigned a specific, unobtrusive place and linked to a par-

ticular purpose. Preserves, and canning in particular,[167] encouraged this trend toward less intense flavors, for here the ingredient guaranteeing preservation — salt or vinegar, sugar or fat — does not constitute the dominant flavor. The use of traditional pilchards, salt cod and anchovies, dried legumes, peas and beans, and pickled foods gave a popular connotation to the same ingredients that, when placed in a metallic container with oil, like sardines, or in brine, like peas, became "elegant" foods.

While simple, strong flavors were synonymous with the cooking of the poor, complex flavors, and French sauces in particular, were treated with suspicion, as they were regarded as the outcome of deliberate falsification and as hostile to the stomach. In this case, it is not the ingredient, a spoonful of concentrated broth or some sherry, a cooking base or a base of cognac, that provokes alarm but the process of combination, the alchemy that produces an unrecognizable aroma, flavor, or color. The bourgeois culinary expert uses only one weapon, the accusation of indigestibility, to discredit both extremes in the scale of sensory values, high and low. Some exceptions to the ban on mixed flavors were allowed. For the most part, these involve dishes of regional provenance — dolce-forte salt cod, hare, and boar — thus simply proving the rule. Many of the dominant tastes of past centuries survive on the margins of the culinary heritage.

Even when beset with hunger pangs, a man can retain his prejudices or rather his ideological preferences. A well-to-do urbanized Italian who enrolled in the Giovine Italia movement before 1860 and became a nationalist later expressed distrust toward unfamiliar condiments and downright hostility toward those from abroad. Faced with exotic products his prejudice grew out of all proportion. If Bouvard, Flaubert's employee, "feared spices as though they could set his body on fire,"[168] Pellegrino Artusi gives repeated proof of a similar sense of repulsion. Seeing macaroni served on the streets of Naples, he laments the fact that the dish "is flavored with a great deal of pepper and sharp cheese."[169] His use of the adjective "sharp" (piccante) is telling. The sauces thus described in La scienza di cucina contain capers, from which the vinegar has been removed, a couple of chopped anchovies, and lemon.[170] "Sharpness" does not require pepper, paprika, or ginger, and it can be accepted only within the limits of a culinary style that is refined, soft, and oily or characterized by flavors that do not linger on the palate, quite unlike foods such as garlic, the flavor of which returns to the mouth from the cavities of the stomach.

This does not mean that the power of salt in the cooking of the masses cannot be attenuated or diminished. Although salt cod is not "suitable for delicate stomachs" (and for this reason Artusi repeatedly states that he cannot digest it), it is presented in numerous recipes as a desirable and widely available product. This preserved food is found in a large geographical area both inside and outside Italian borders (la brandade de morue, for example, appears in the book with the title "baccalà Montebianco"), and it thus merits recognition as one of the typical values of a bourgeois code of taste. Differences between one region and another can be played down with a kind of gastronomic compromise: a complicated local recipe for macaroni *alla napoletana* can be juxtaposed with a simpler version if necessary. In this case, the differences serve to bring together parts of the country with different histories into a sense of national unity that confers legitimacy on them.

Nationalism is not simply a private, bourgeois sentiment that attaches to the map of Italy images of wines and other specialties, along with their marks of distinction: pictures of salt cod on Vicenza, pickled carp on the Alpine lakes, paprika and figs on Aspromonte. The state in fact presides over the nationalistic tendency with its effort to remake Italian society from below. The armed forces were among the institutions that had the greatest influence on the leveling process, especially during the four years of World War I. Until 1916 the breakfast ration for an infantryman consisted of the following items (in addition to bread, which was measured separately): "120 grams of dried figs, or 150 grams of chestnuts, almonds, walnuts, or hazelnuts (unshelled), or 40 grams of cheese, or 30 grams of olives and sardines or herrings, or 200 grams of fresh apples." This is the hypothetical reflection of the kind of breakfast that might be eaten by peasants from different regions, as it includes traditional dried and salted preserves. Yet it was distributed to all soldiers of the same rank, including those from the cities, whose families had abandoned the countryside and dried figs centuries earlier. The items on the list are not only high in calories but also have strong flavors, with the result that breakfast tastes similar to the meals consumed later in the day. In 1917, the following year, the ration changed to include eight grams of roasted coffee and ten grams of sugar.[171] The culinary unification of all the soldiers thus countered the disparity among regional diets, in keeping with the model offered by Italy's French and English allies. The bittersweet taste of coffee, already permitted as an exception during the Crimean War in order to fight cholera and make up for the lack of wine,[172] was now (and will always be) associated with waking up in the morning and resuming physical activity. Coffee was one of the "nerve foods," along with tea and chocolate, which were officially prescribed and made available in this way during World War I with the specific objective of increasing the daily dose of stimulants.

But coffee was not the only industrial product that was provided daily to all. Dried pasta, canned meat, salt cod, cheese (Swiss, fontina, sbrinz, provolone, and ewe's cheese) also reveal a concerted effort to unify taste. What is occurring here is the creation of a dual system of values: we observe on the one hand the valorization of tradition, memory, and a sense of roots and on the other a contemporary emphasis on industry and the military front. The barracks and the trenches thus became a school of nutritional modernization and the (temporary) suspension of local traditions, since the promotion and consumption of some foods necessarily involved the elimination of others.

The development of an Italian taste resulted from this leveling process, with the bourgeois model functioning as the "high" point of reference. The "low" point is found in the consumption of rancid foods in workers' cafeterias, school refectories, and summer camps and in the kitchens of hospitals and other institutions financed by the state. It was not only the outbreak of war that imposed the same kind of food on both soldiers and civilians but also the social project of a centralized society, collectively supported by public and private forces alike. The persuasive power of this regime was all the more efficient for the fact that it made the foods consumed by the Italian lower-middle classes available to all, as we have seen in the case of coffee and sugar. It does not surprise us, then, to find clear traces of the sensory preferences that characterize Artusi's work and the recipe collections of the early twentieth century in Marshal Fornari's *Il cuciniere militare* (The military cook), written during the Fascist era. Here we note the scant presence of spices (pepper and cloves), a limited use of salt, and a tendency to moderate the use of fats. A hot, spicy sauce intended to accompany a dish of boiled meat for a hundred men calls for just one liter of vinegar and ten grams of pepper. Here too vinegar rather than pepper is equated with a hot, spicy taste. Lard or oil is suggested as a fat. Fornari recommends, however, that these be used sparingly, reminding his readers that "in the kitchens of the wealthy, the cooks completely remove the fat from gravies and sauces, first during preparation and again just before serving."[173]

The tastes of the masses developed through imitation but were consolidated in the soldiers' mess, through rationing restrictions (which were particularly severe between 1940 and 1946), and as a result of the higher living standards that enabled the widespread growth of the canning and preserving industry. It is hard to identify clear-cut patterns in an increasingly complex nutritional panorama, characterized not only by the contrast between the rural and urban populations but also by class differences in the cities, where internal migrations played an important role in altering the face of neighborhood markets. Yet if any dominant values can be distinguished, these are represented by industrial products. A can or a cube of meat extract could function as a unit of taste, both in the popular imagination and in prevailing culinary standards. The leading Italian food industries not only sought to standardize products, conditioning the tastes of consumers, but also conferred an added value on these products corresponding to the effort of cleaning and cutting, preparing and parboiling the ingredients. Cirio tomatoes and Arrigoni meat extract could be added to the panoply of time-saving, partially prepared foods and—according to the recipes advertised by these manufacturers—could be used in a great variety of preparations. The variable constituted by the specific cut of beef or by the time involved in cooking and in skimming or straining broths thus disappears thanks to a cube of meat extract with the same color and flavor in millions of servings. The same holds true of the ripening, selection, and boiling of San Marzano tomatoes. The elimination of such variables is hardly surprising, since the same ingredients were packed into cans and sent all over the world and the same finished products were destined for markets everywhere.

A dish created with the help of partially prepared foods, such as a packet of macaroni or a can of peeled tomatoes, would not explicitly compete with home-made products such as fresh pasta or with dishes from the repertoire of refined cuisine (such as a *pasticcio di maccheroni*). It too could involve variations, both at the preparatory stage—for the cook must decide how firm the pasta will be when served—and in the final flavoring. Since distinct regional traditions existed side by side in Italy throughout the twentieth century, with the single term *piccante* (hot or spicy) indicating two radically different levels of sensation in Calabria and in Emilia, what is involved here is not simply adding a condiment but adjusting the flavors. The principal ingredients were no longer those that conferred the dominant flavor (since this flavor was created in a factory and intended for everyone, it had to be of moderate intensity) but rather the secondary ones, which could be called the "discretionary" seasonings. One of the characteristics of the industrial production of preserved vegetables (typified by the Cirio Company, whose history spans the entire twentieth century) was to provide a range of similarly marketed products that the consumer could quickly transform and personalize with a few simple procedures in the final phase of preparation. With a packet of spaghetti, some peeled tomatoes purchased in a can, and some anchovies for the sauce—all available throughout most of Italy—the consumer could create a pasta dish whose real seasonings were parsley, garlic, pepper, peppercorns, and one or more cheeses, which in turn could be sliced or grated, highly salted or less highly salted, according to personal preference. It is the combination of spices, herbs, and milk products—the most ancient flavors—that constitutes the aromatic character of such a dish.

At least this was the case in what is now a bygone era of culinary history. In preparing pasta today, it is in fact quite possible to eliminate all local or seasonal variants by using garlic-flavored olive oil, a can of grated cheese or a package of the vacuum-wrapped variety, and frozen parsley for the final seasoning. Such developments have reduced both the time spent shopping and the work carried out in kitchen, attracting consumers to precooked foods that need only to be reheated. The most successful of these dishes are those that correspond to generic tastes and are increasingly recognizable at a national rather than a local level. The number of packaged Italian foods available in every supermarket in Europe continues to grow, and there is an especially strong demand for standardized items, such as *tortellini di pasta* with a hundred different fillings, giving rise to a level of uniformity in the products consumed without eliminating the existence of variants.

CHAPTER FOUR

The Sequence of Dishes

The Galenic Cook

Premodern medicine is often described as "Galenic," in homage to Galen, the second-century physician whose teachings were influential up to and beyond the seventeenth century. It was founded on a basic principle from which most of the ideas and decisions regarding the care of the body were derived, that is, that every living thing—human, animal, or vegetable—possessed a particular nature based on the combination of four qualities, hot and cold, dry and moist. These qualities were thought to reflect the four elements—fire, air, earth and water—that make up the universe. A man was considered to be in perfect health when all four elements were combined in his body in a balanced way. If one element prevailed over the others, because of temporary illness, age (young people were considered hotter and more moist, the aged colder and drier), climate, environment, the type of activities pursued, or any other circumstance, it was of the utmost importance to restore the balance with the appropriate strategies, among which the control of nutritional intake was the most important. A person afflicted with an illness that made him too moist, for example, needed above all to consume foods of a dry nature, and vice versa. A healthy person by contrast needed to eat balanced or "temperate" foods, as they were described by physicians of the time.

Cooking, which was essentially perceived as an art of combination (as we have already mentioned), thus enters the picture. Very few foods, apart from bread, were thought to possess a perfectly balanced nature. In the vast majority of cases some form of intervention—classified along a complicated scale of intensities or "degrees"—was needed to correct the nature of the food and to establish the appropriate balance. If a particular food was too hot, it had to be made colder by being combined with cold ingredients and so on, according to the two principal methods of intervention: cooking techniques and the rules of accompaniment.

This casts light on many instructions in the recipe collections for the cooking of particular foods, strategies such as adding liquid to certain meats or boiling them in water to make them moister or conversely roasting moist meats to make them drier. A strict correspondence was established between the nature of the meat (which varied according to the species, age, and sex of the animal) and the cooking method it would require. "Venison is eaten boiled," wrote Anthimus in the sixth century in his treatise on diet. "Roasting is good if the deer is young. But a roast of venison is heavy if the animal is old."[1] These customs have become enshrined in proverbs. Why indeed do people say that "an old hen makes good soup"?

This system also explains how certain culinary combinations became customary over time, some of which are still practiced even today. Why is cheese eaten with pears and ham with melon? Each of these combinations reflects premodern food practices, which viewed many types of fruit with distrust (including pears and melons) because they were thought to be too moist or cold. The function of the cheese and the ham (considered dry and hot) or of wine in other culinary traditions, such as the French, was to warm or dry out the nature of those foods. Salt was used for the same purpose, and the French still sprinkle it on melons.[2]

The extraordinary attention the Galenic cook lavished on sauces is part of the same general picture. When used in the appropriate way, sauces had the specific role of tempering meats and fish, making them both digestible and delectable. An appealing flavor was important, since another essential principle of this system of cooking and nutrition was that, in order to be properly absorbed by the body, foods should stimulate the digestive juices and provoke pleasure. According to Platina, garlic-based *agliata* sauce should be served with hard, fat meats "to make them more digestible and to stimulate the appetite."[3] It was widely believed that desire was the perceptible sign of need and that the ability to experience pleasure in satisfying this need was one of the main indications of physical health. Having cited different opinions expressed by various authors on how to temper the frigid nature of the cantaloupe, Platina opts for the solution that seems most instinctive: "As for myself, I agree with nature. After one has consumed a cantaloupe one is inclined to desire wine—good wine—which is almost like an antidote to the rawness and coldness of the cantaloupe."[4]

Maino de' Maineri, a Milanese doctor and the author of a fourteenth-century nutritional treatise, similarly declared that "what is most appealing to taste is best for the digestion."[5] In many ways Maino's *Regimen* resembles a recipe collection, given the quantity of practical suggestions offered on foods, their modes of preparation, and their possible combinations. Significantly, the chapter dedicated entirely to sauces was also circulated as an independent text with the title *De saporibus*.[6] On the other hand, it was not unusual to find examples of medical advice in recipe books: the physician and the cook are two aspects of the same culture. The fourteenth-century *Liber de coquina* gives a recipe for *agliata* (pounded almonds, garlic, and ginger moistened by a thin broth), specifying

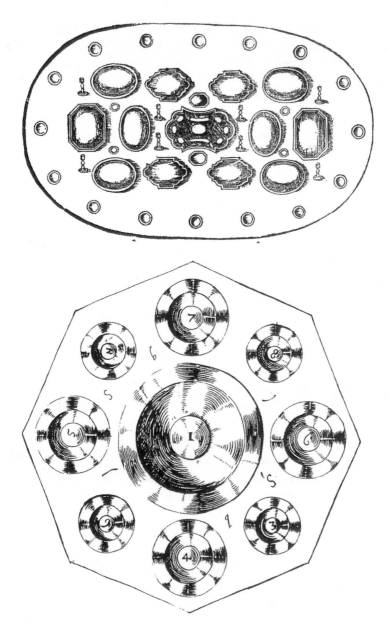

ABOVE: *Table with Sixteen Places, Service for Thirteen Diners* (engraving).

Source: *Il cuoco piemontese ridotto all'ultimo gusto e perfezione* (Milan, 1791).

BELOW: *Table Set for Eight* (engraving).

Source: Mattia Giegher, *Li tre tratti* (Padua, 1639).

that although it should be served ideally with meats ("pro carnibus"), it could also be served with types of fish that might be difficult to digest ("cum piscibus dure digestionis").[7] Such instructions are more numerous (and more explicit) in "derivative" works such as Platina's. Broad beans are cold and tend to be moist and hence are dangerous for the stomach. Yet they "seem less dangerous when sprinkled with spices."[8] Green beans are hot and moist. Their damaging potential can be tempered by "sprinkling oregano, pepper, and mustard on top" and drinking clear wine with them.[9]

Such rules were widely observed, for food science used the same language as cuisine, an idiom that was consistent with—or perhaps fully embraced—the concerns of the senses: hot and cold, dry and moist were not abstract categories but a way of theorizing perceptible experience. Hence this language permeated the entire social body and can be found in scholarly treatises and peasant customs, scientific opinions and everyday practices, reflecting different levels of self-awareness. Readers of Maino and Platina, as well as the individuals who frequented the taverns of the time, "knew" that pears, peaches, or cherries (depending on the season) were best accompanied by cheese. The meals eaten à la carte at the Albergo della Stella in Prato between 1395 and 1398 often concluded with cheese and cooked pears (or cherries in May or peaches in September, according to seasonal availability).[10] This is valuable information, since it relates to people of every social level and involves dishes served à la carte, which the diners had selected individually. There is no difference between this custom and the habitual preference of Filippo Maria Visconti, lord of Milan, who, according to his biographer, Pier Candido Decembrio, liked to end his meal with "pears or paradise apples cooked in cheese."[11] "Say, could you bring us some cheese or fruit?" Margutte asks the innkeeper in Pulci's *Il Morgante*. So the man rushes off and "puts together a pile of cheese and fruit."[12] As we observe here, even those with voracious appetites would take the rules of dietary science into account.

"The Things That Should Be Eaten First"

After the choice of appropriate cooking methods and the assessment of the proper food combinations, the third important stratagem for healthy eating was the organization of the dishes served at a meal into the sequence considered most conducive to their absorption and digestion. This was not a matter for the cook but for the steward or major domo.

Going back as early as the twelfth century, we find information on the types of dishes served at meals, though often in unexpected sources. A legal mandate issued in 1191, for example, provides explicit information on the menu that the monks of Saint Ambrose in Milan were obliged to prepare every year on the feast of Saint Satiro in honor of the local canons (a custom that someone was now attempting to contest). The list of foods served, amounting to nine items served in three courses, mentions only the meat dishes, as these are undisputedly the principal elements of the meal. Cold meats (chicken and pork) and *gambas de vino* (perhaps indicating meat marinated in wine) are served for the first course. For the second course, there are stuffed chickens, *turtuella de lavezono* (perhaps a meat *pasticcio*, baked in the oven), and beef with a *piperata* sauce. Roast chickens, sides of meat "*cum panicio*" (wrapped in bread, perhaps), and stuffed piglets are listed for the third course. No information is given on any of the other items served (the bread and wine or the appetizers, side dishes, and desserts, if any). The order in which the courses are served is clearly important. While affirming that this was the traditional menu, one of the witnesses stated that "the stuffed piglets were sometimes served with the first course and sometimes with the third; and vice versa in the case of the cold pork."[13]

A simpler and hence more complete menu recorded in an agrarian contract signed in 1266 is also more clearly intelligible from the dietary point of view. This document was drawn up by a landlord in Asti by the name of Pancia (Belly), who required some of his tenants to offer a yearly tribute of two meals for himself and a chosen companion. The document stipulates the following items: for each diner, one lemon at the beginning of the meal; next, for each diner, two pounds of fresh pork and a dish of white chickpeas, followed by one roast capon apiece, and the appropriate sauces to accompany these foods. At the end of the meal, six chestnuts and one "paradise fruit" are required per person. In addition, there is the request for as much white bread as can be eaten and as much good, pure, clear wine as can be consumed. It is also stipulated that the entire meal is to be served on a clean, white tablecloth.[14]

The lemon served at the outset of the meal may seem strange to us, but this is completely in keeping with medieval food practices, which assigned to the appetizer the task of "opening" the path to the stomach by stimulating gastric juices with acidic properties. Tart fruits in season generally served this purpose (along with salads dressed with oil and vinegar, on the subject of which a real debate developed, as we shall see). Two meat courses follow. Leaving aside the issue of quantity (two pounds of pork and an entire capon for each diner), we can assume that the first dish is cooked in a sauce stewed, and we know that the second is roasted. This was the sequence usually observed in Italy, and in France also.[15] The sauce accompanying the roast is virtually indispensable, as we have seen. Skipping the entremets—the second course—and the desserts, which compound the number of dishes and courses served at more important banquets, Pancia's simple country meal concludes, as it began, with fruit, but with fruit of a different kind, appropriate to "closing" or sealing the stomach with its starchy consistency. The "paradise apple" was also found on Visconti's table. Bonvesin de la Riva similarly attests to the practice of serving chestnuts at the end of the meal. In Lombardy, he writes, chestnuts "are cooked over the fire while still green and are eaten after the other dishes, instead of dates," which apparently are present only on wealthier tables. Alternatively, Bonvesin writes, city dwellers like to conclude their meals with walnuts.[16]

The simpler menus are the most interesting to analyze, even if fewer of them are documented, since they present a clearer picture of the meal's basic structure. One such menu appears in a short story by Giovanni Sercambi (who lived at the end of the fourteenth and the beginning of the fifteenth century). Here a peasant woman from the countryside near Lucca improvises a "well-cheesed" dish of *lasagne* and a big omelet for two hungry guests. This is preceded by a salad of greens ("*raponzori, salbastrella, primifiori*, and rocket") gathered from the field by the guests themselves and seasoned with oil and vinegar.[17] The banquet awaiting Pierbaldo and his men on their return from the hunt in Simone Prudenzani's *Saporetto* also begins with a salad—bellflower, corn salad, aniseed, wild mint, smooth sow thistle, and spelt with black pepper—followed by hare, kid, and stag with sauce. Then comes a course of veal, capon, and rolled tongue, after which "the roast is served," along with oranges, pork ribs, squab, and liver. The last of the numerous meat courses is a pie filled with the meat of small game birds, and the meal ends with candied almonds.[18] Another menu found in Prudenzani's *Saporetto* begins with *tortelli, biancomangiare*, "French soup," lasagne, and ravioli, followed by "the boiled food," comprised of chickens, boiled and stewed meats, and roast game (turtle doves, squab, and gray partridge), and concluding with cakes and pastries, cooked pears, raisins, apples, and spiced confectionery.[19]

Platina devotes an entire chapter, as well as shorter statements within paragraphs and chapters, to discussing "the things that should be eaten first." "In choosing foods one must observe a certain order, since at the beginning of the meal one may eat fearlessly and with the greatest pleasure the things that stimulate the stomach and provide light, measured nourishment." His examples are some "qualities" of apples, pears, lettuces, "and everything that is eaten either raw or cooked that can be seasoned with oil and vinegar."[20] With regard to fruit, Platina's advice is to follow the rule of starting the meal with fruits of a sweet, fragrant quality and ending it with those of a sharp, astringent flavor, such as apples, pears, pomegranates, and blackberries.[21] Melons and peaches are accompanied by a good wine "to prevent them from decaying" in the stomach.[22] In the case of citrus fruits, he recommends the sweeter types (we are reminded of the lemons stipulated in Pancia's meal; Platina assures us that these "stimulate the appetite," though he also mentions oranges and citron). If the fruit selected is found to be too tart, it may be sweetened with sugar.[23]

Another possibility is to begin a meal by serving a salad dressed with oil and vinegar. In the following century, this option is reiterated by Costanzo Felici following a long, erudite discussion where he cites Celso and Galen, the best-known physicians of late Roman antiquity. Felici also deplores the bad habit of

Table decoration with a design inspired by the Fountain
of the Rivers (engraving).

Source: *Disegni del convito fatto dall'Illustrissimo Signor senatore Ratta* (Bologna, 1693).

so many diners who are "excessively eager to begin eating" and claim that the
capacity of salad to "whet and excite the appetite" is wasted at the beginning of
a meal, when there is no lack of appetite. Such persons use salad "indifferently,
before and after the meal," to stimulate their unabated greed for more food.[24]
The debate on salad continued over the subsequent centuries in tandem with
"technical" instructions on how it should be dressed.[25] In *Il vitto quaresimale*
(Lenten food), Paolo Zacchia wrote in 1636 that salads should be eaten only
once during the meal and in moderate quantity. "Salads have no other purpose
than to stimulate the appetite of the stomach. . . . Eating [them] twice during
a meal, at the beginning and in the middle, or at the beginning and the end . . .
can only be quite harmful."[26] Obviously, these must have been customary practices, as they were still being condemned a hundred years later.

The "strong" dish in a meal was by definition the meat. This was hardly a
matter of dispute. "It is now time to discuss the dishes I call the second course,
which I maintain to be the richest. I will thus deal with meat, the food that provides the greatest, healthiest nourishment and is the most substantial."[27] Thus at
the end of a typically medieval disquisition Platina clearly expresses his own
opinion: regardless of the type of preparation (roast, boiled, stewed, or fried),
meats, or fish dishes, *are* the meal. Usually, boiled meats are served before the

roast ("post mangiamentum alessi, succedit arostus," in the regal banquet described in Folengo's *Baldus*),[28] but rules are flexible and opinions may vary. Perhaps they also change over time. In 1536, when serving a gala meal to Emperor Charles V in Trastevere, Scappi presents an initial cooked course consisting of a "thin roast," a second course "cooked in broth," and a third consisting of a "boiled dish."[29] This is clearly a Lenten meal, based on fish rather than meat, but the spirit of the menu is very different from what we might expect. "When the roast should be eaten is a matter still argued by the experts," declares the learned professor Ventronio Manduco Ciccelardofilo, a strict Aristotelian, in a satiric text written in Verona in the eighteenth century: "There are those who say it should be eaten first at lunch and last at dinner, those who say it should always be eaten last, and those who say it should always be eaten first. For this reason we must state clearly that the roast can be eaten wisely and in abundance whenever it is well cooked and browned."[30]

Platina speaks of vegetables and greens "that we usually eat with our courses," yet for a long time the inevitable accompaniment to a dish of roast meat or fish was sauce — the most suitable sauce for each type of meat and fish, determined according to the dietary-gastronomic standards we have described.

Platina calls the "third course" the one that "seals the stomach at the end of the meal." The foods served here should have an astringent capacity and preferably a hot, dry nature. If one has eaten meat, one could then eat "apples or sharp-tasting pears, depending on the season" or quince and pomegranate, "not to mention all kinds of astringent foods, such as broad beans and pistachios." One could also eat ripe cheese, since "it is thought to help seal the stomach" (while fresher cheese is used to flavor all kinds of cooked dishes). The most refined diners eat candied coriander seeds or aniseed "as a medicine for the throat and head," while "those with fewer pretensions make do with fennel." Here Platina is presumably alluding to wild fennel. The sweet variety was later prescribed by Scappi for the conclusion of *every* meal. Finally, everyone eats chestnuts, "which have a cold, dry nature" (we are again reminded of Pancia and of Bonvesin da la Riva, and we realize that some customs continued for a long time.) "Almonds, hazelnuts, or walnuts are eaten after a fish dish," however, "because their dry nature is thought to obviate the cold, moist power of the fish."[31]

In the sixteenth century a new custom developed of serving sweet dishes at the beginning of the meal as well as at the end. In the banquet described by Scappi held in honor of Charles V in 1536, the three hot courses are preceded by a course served from the pantry consisting exclusively of sweets: biscotti from Pisa and Rome, bite-sized morsels of marzipan, Neapolitan *mostaccioli*, marzipan *caliscioni* in the Venetian style, fresh *pignoccati*, sugared oranges, little cakes with almond oil, sugar, and pine-nut milk, and Roman *zeppole*, "which is to say, fritters made of red chickpeas, sugar, muscat grapes, raisins, and dates."[32]

Following a second course from the pantry consisting of fruit, sweets, cakes, ices, ricotta cheese, and sugared almonds, a second round of cooked dishes begins, preceded this time by cold savory dishes: anchovies, caviar, marinated fried fish, and salads of various types, such as borage, citron blossoms, capers, rosemary blossoms, asparagus, and lettuce.[33] This seems like a more elaborate version of the practice of serving salad "halfway through the meal" against which Felici and Zacchia had protested in vain.

The two tendencies coexisted alongside each other. The choice of savory prevailed in the simpler menus, such as those recorded by Romoli (who begins with lemons, grapes, pomegranate, and cured meats)[34] and by Frugoli (melon and cured meats).[35] Writing in 1584, Rossetti explicitly condemns the "Italian" custom of serving sweet dishes at the beginning of the meal, since he prefers the French and German models, which continued the medieval tradition of starting out with bitter or salty flavors.[36] The system proposed by Rossetti (cold dishes, meat, vegetable, cheese, fruit, desserts) is a remarkable foreshadowing of the sequence of dishes that would prevail over time in an ever more linear organization. For the moment it remained marginal, at least with respect to important banquets and their lean or Lenten versions: as Paolo Zacchia observes in *Il vitto quaresimale*, "it is customary in times of fasting to eat some foods flavored with honey or even with sugar at the beginning of the meal."[37] The savory model was perhaps still dominant at times of ordinary eating or in everyday cooking. Remembering his stay in Pontremoli, Montaigne wrote: "At table the first thing they gave me was cheese, as they do around Milan and in the country around Piacenza. Following the Genoese practice, they gave me olives without pits, prepared with oil and vinegar."[38]

The Meager Repast

In the history of gastronomy no meal is more difficult to document and interpret than the one that consists of a small portion of food consumed alone and in silence. It is difficult in the first place because until recently scant attention was paid to the diner who prepared and ate this kind of meal. The problem is also complicated by the fact that frugality can be associated with very different kinds of behavior, whether spiritual, compulsory, neurotic, or economical. Those who eat alone may be monks or nuns, prisoners, misers, or misanthropic types. There is no shortage of written testimony on the subject, even from surprising sources. Pontormo, a painter who lived in Florence in 1554, ate at home. In his diary, which begins on a day in Lent, he recorded what he ate. One evening his supper consists of "a lettuce salad and an egg-fish [an omelet]" and on another evening of "half a head of kid and soup." He drinks wine and eats about ten ounces of bread at every meal. The food he consumes with his bread is produced locally. On two occasions only he sweetens his omelet with sugar.

If he goes to eat at the inn he eats the same things, and when dining with friends he does not stint on meat, especially on religious holidays. He prepares his food himself, most often bread, eggs and salad but also dishes that require time to prepare: "a meat pie made with my own hands," "a fine head of cabbage cooked with my own hands." He is an odd character, sparing in his ways yet attentive to what he consumes and decisive in his views. He praises the pancakes his friend Bronzino made for him, while the cow that Bastiano, his servant, bought for him, "you wouldn't get the dogs to eat."[39]

Pontormo fasts rather often, a very common dietary practice required by the religious orders. His fast is modified by meals of plain water, wine for medicinal purposes, and bread. Echoing the Christian tradition of periodically abstaining from food, many books offered instruction on ways of repressing the appetite. The title of one of these, Scalco spirituale (The spiritual steward), suggests a collection of remedies for warding off the temptations of hunger and thirst. The book condemns sweetness and all other flavors that might be "pleasurable to the taste."[40] An entire chapter is devoted to bread making, the cultural resource of the pious man, as almost all other foods are considered harmful, especially if suspected of having flavor, such as walnuts, hazelnuts, almonds, garlic, and onions. What we find here are exercises in the negation of appetite through abstinence and fasting, exercises that reduce the meal to a few quickly swallowed bites of food while summoning up the image of the solitary man eating alone in the sight of God. Concerned with diet and old age, Alvise Cornaro approached these issues from a different perspective. To ensure longevity, he recommended a meal made of a single dish, accessible even to the poor though not to beggars: "bread, panatella, and egg." There is nothing simpler than panatella, a mush made from stale breadcrumbs, broth, and egg. This is the soup that Cornaro himself prepares (and that he follows with meat, poultry, or fish).[41]

Culinary texts do not consider the fact that an individual might eat alone, much less that he might deprive himself of all food except bread. Yet an entire body of writing composed of diaries, short stories, poems, and other forms of evidence attests to many different levels of intake, including the consumption of no food at all. From these texts we learn that some travelers carried food with them on their journeys so that they would not find it necessary to stop at an inn, while others would rush to an inn to devour a panful of tripe.[42] The meal was a less codified variable than one might suspect and eludes rigid typologies. In Florence at the beginning of the sixteenth century, Pontormo ate a great deal of eggs and fresh vegetables, as well as mutton, pork, or beef, stewed or roasted. He had few opportunities to enjoy sweet dishes, contrary to what recipe collections of the period would lead one to expect. Dining with others did not add much to his customary regimen, involving dishes that seem to have been passed down for generations and would be repeated for centuries to come. Some of the friends

Loggia Leading Toward the Opulence of the Great Hall (engraving).

Source: *Disegni del convito fatto dall'Illustrissimo Signor senatore Ratta* (Bologna, 1693)

who joined him for dinner at the inn also follow a pattern of consumption that is not codified yet seems habitual: "On Saturday evening we went to the tavern, Attaviano and Bronzino and I. We had fish and eggs and aged wine and paid seventeen coins a head."[43]

Unlike the banquet we will examine below, these examples of simple refreshment seem to offer little opportunity for a complex analysis of tastes, as our culinary references derive from an ancient substratum, and a continuous line reaching back from the contemporary meal allows us to identify the meal of the past. In reality, many of these dishes are described in linguistic forms that are no longer current, alluding to models of consumption and dietary values that are profoundly out of date. We should not lose sight of the environment inhabited by this Florentine artist, who obtained his food from the vegetable garden, bought oil by the barrel, bottled his own wine, and kept his market purchases to a minimum. We need to investigate his nutritional *habitus*, seeking some sense of order in his choices and reexamining his meal, which is certainly not an abundant one from the typological point of view. Such a meal provides the key to the way in which a man relates to himself and to others.

The first consideration determining the organization of dietary intake is economical. For dinner on Tuesday Pontormo had the head of a kid goat, half of which he put aside, intending to fry it the following day. All his purchases were divided into a part that was used immediately and a part that was set aside for a subsequent occasion—a portion for his apprentice and possibly another for his servant. The selection of various cuts of meat and types of fish destined for different kinds of cooking suggests the shrewd management of culinary resources. Even in situations of the most lavish abundance, of which we find examples in princely homes, we see the same principle of bringing together all resources and redistributing them in a political gesture that enabled all subjects, from courtiers to servants of lowest rank, to share some of the food. This is the most profound meaning of the meal, as an individual and collective reserve of edible objects produced by a fragile art and divided up and redistributed in order to create well-being. In order to assure a dignified progression, rarer foods followed more common foods, and different dishes appeared on the table in a sequence that took cost, appetite, and flavor into account. Some foods, like bread, were intended to nourish and satisfy the stomach, while others, such as eggs, were considered a matter of taste.

We might well ask if the simple meal, consisting of few dishes, was expected to adhere to a certain structure and to what extent this might have changed over the course of history. We note that even in Pontormo's modest meals, fruits such as cooked apples, dried figs, and grapes follow the meat and eggs. Salad, which is well seasoned and described as having "simple stimulus," precedes all other foods for the purpose of opening up the appetite.[44] These were well-known medical and dietary rules, obeyed instinctively by everyone, even in the organization of major banquets. Though the position occupied by fruit in the serving sequence remained constant from the Middle Ages to modern and contemporary times, the position of salad changed. Salad meant fresh, raw ingredients, which were sprinkled with salt and served along with the appetizers. As pickled foods, cured meats, and the sharp taste of vinegar began to lose favor with the bourgeoisie and were no longer used as appetizers, salad too suffered a decline.

It was then served as an accompaniment to roast meat, which Artusi, like the domestic cooks who came after him, prescribed for all months of the year. How could lettuce, which was considered cold, continue to exert its Galenic function when it accompanied a roast? The issue of food combinations and their longevity (which surpasses that of the therapeutic models that governed them) is one of the least investigated aspects of contemporary food practices. In fact, we have not yet completely severed our ties with ancient medicine. To be more precise, we have replaced it with another system. Beginning around 1930, the culture of vitamins led to the reintroduction of raw vegetables as appetizers (though not for their purported coldness), resurrecting an ancient custom with new motivations.

These examples lead us to consider the careful sequencing of dishes as the outcome of the quest for pleasure and good health. It would be reductive, however, to claim that these were the only principles involved. If Pontormo preferred to eat fish in the company of his friends, it was because they made the experience of dining more satisfying to him. These men shared the cost of the meal, and their enjoyment increased Pontormo's own pleasure in sitting down to eat. His diary lists a hare, a pheasant, and a couple of squabs, one at a time, as foods endowed with intrinsic prestige, capable of becoming an occasion for celebration. Eating one type of meat was tantamount to a feast. Two kinds of meat were more than a feast. Pontormo mentions a large fish served with a small plate of fried fish and, with special interest, "meat and fish," "fish and lamb," and "roast kid and fish." To combine the same ingredients prepared in different ways or to consume two different kinds of products—foods harvested from land and water, fat and lean, light and dark, moist and dry—was truly a meal. A combination based on difference or likeness, on a contrast of sensory stimuli and taste values, was the first criterion in the sequence of dishes. As in rhetoric, the creation of a dish (*inventio*), its placement on the table (*dispositio*) in alternation with other, different dishes, and the observance of the principle of variety (*variatio*) stimulated the imagination and taste. By arranging dishes on the table and regulating the sequence in which they appear, by filling the intervals with music and entertainment, the consumption of food was transformed into a sensory and aesthetic experience. The symmetry of the dishes, the harmony of volume and color, the floral decorations and sugared ornaments adorning the table were a language that stimulated eloquence, not only in terms of speech but also in terms of food. The typology of the meal, and hence the competence of the steward, served this objective.

Organizing and Presenting the Banquet

In courts and in the homes of the upper classes, the steward—or rather stewards—had the task of organizing banquets and overseeing the presentation of food at the dinner table. Most of the cooking treatises of the sixteenth century sprang from the writer's experience as a steward or as a supervisor of personnel assigned to the dining room. Each author, according to his station, had his own way of imparting his knowledge about the preparation of banquets, as he might have risen from the ranks of the cooks or might even have been born into the nobility, like the Palatine count Cristoforo Messisbugo. He thus chose the type of exposition most likely to enhance his own prestige and cast the best light on his employer, either formulating a theoretical project by proposing a system of dishes and courses that would work for any occasion or offering as instructive examples some specific cases of suppers already served, thus retracing a history of the banquets hosted at court. Scappi took the first approach, since he worked in the service of the popes and was bound by duty to modesty and reserve. Messisbugo chose the second, highlighting at every stage of the meal the generous patronage of his princely employer. Traveling in the service of Don Alfonso d'Este of Ferrara, Rossetti enriched the annals of the Este family by bearing witness, even in Paris, to the culinary culture of the court at Ferrara.[45] The patrician table is the special focus of such treatises; the tables of the principal officials and titled members of the court as well as those of the guests and strangers of minor rank are considered mere fractions of the former.

In compiling the menu, the steward must draw on two distinct forms of expertise, that of the butler and that of the cook. The butler oversees the silverware and linen; he folds the napkins in an artistic way, serves cold dishes, salads, fruit, biscotti, sweets, and confectionery. He practices a sensual art, "finding pleasure in fragrances,"[46] applying perfumed essences to the linen, embellishing the table with flowers, and arranging the decorations. He is present in the dining hall and serves the dishes destined for the beginning and end of the banquet, which are variously called "pantry courses," "cold courses," and "fruit courses." Part of the food served during the first course comes from the kitchen but has been prepared in advance, such as fish cooked in wine and roast peacock, both obviously cold. These have the purpose of stimulating the diners, allowing the cooks enough time to put the last touches on the hot dishes when the guests are already seated. He begins by bringing out salads; biscotti; fresh, sweetened cheeses; cured meats or marinated fish; caviar; and herring. At the end of the meal he sets on the table at the same moment cakes, cooked vegetables, ripe cheeses, fruit, candied almonds, and confectionery. The order in which the foods are served is partially open-ended and partially determined by taste and dietary principles. The salad and the glass of malvasia wine into which a little *biscotto* is dipped—both are appetizers—precede the cold meats, sliced sausages, or sirloin, according to the adage that requires tender foods first and hard foods later ("Mollia praemittas, hinc fercula dura sequatur").[47] The diner chooses from Pisan biscotti, marzipan *caliscioni*, and *mostaccioli*, according to preference. Each course served thus offers a selection of similar foods and a hierarchy of diverse dishes.

A team of undercooks, pastry cooks, and kitchen hands works under the supervision of the head cook, who in turn takes his orders from the steward and obtains his raw material from the supplier. The task of the head cook is to oversee the preparation of the hot courses and to ensure the cleanliness, economy, and discipline of the kitchens. The presentation of the subsequent courses is organized from the kitchen. Each course has from one to three dishes or from sixteen to twenty, depending on the occasion, but the number may obviously be reduced. The dishes are based on meat or fish and are prepared in different ways (boiled, roasted, or fried), offering an intrinsic variety of poultry and game, veal, lamb or mutton, freshwater and saltwater fish, perhaps interspersed with complementary foods and flavors, such as sweet blancmange and miniature pastries. Another type of variety is provided by serving different parts of the same species of animal. Some of these dishes disappeared only in the nineteenth century, such as the eyes of the ox or calf, for which Rossetti proposes twenty-two preparations. Pastas and noodles, flavored with cheese and sugar, along with soups and broths are served during the first or second cooked course, with the purpose of supplementing the meat or fish dishes. In the selection of dishes, there are strict rules regarding temperature, while the rules of accompaniment are extremely variable. The diners find a large array of dishes set out before them on the table, and they are able to examine and choose among them at close quarters.

The menus and styles of service modeled on the customs of other countries, which were often imposed by the ruling classes, especially in the case of aristocrats of Spanish origin, followed the same general pattern. A "German-style" banquet was served on circular tables with one or more large dishes in the center and smaller dishes arranged around it. Thus the first round of servings was within immediate view, with the second slightly further back. Breasts of veal, peacock and duck, or pork head, feet, or rinds were placed on the central dish.[48] Soup too was served at the outset of the "German" meal, unlike the "Italian" version. Domenico Romoli describes a "French banquet" as a strictly organized sequence of courses with a double set of appetizers (one from the pantry and the other from the kitchen), boiled, roasted, or fried dishes, cakes and fruit, followed by a "servitio sul tapeto" of tasty morsels and sweets for nibbling and munching. A "Spanish" banquet required that all cold dishes be displayed on the table. Following these, "a bowl of good broth with croutons, covered with a lid" was served to each diner.[49] The meal continued with servings of roast meat and appetizers. Finally, there was the "Venetian" style of presentation, where dishes were brought to the table under plate covers, which were removed in front of the guests as the food was carved and served.[50] Any one of these methods of presentation might be implemented at a banquet, depending on the type of guests to be entertained, on the historical and political circumstances, or merely out of desire for variety.

Planning the presentation of a meal involved more than determining the number of the dishes arranged on the table. It also had a ceremonial function. In a situation where the head of household might want to eat in relative quiet, with two or three guests at most, an appropriate menu would be arranged. Making allowances for proportion, this is Pontormo's supper on a courtly scale, consisting of two courses (one from the kitchen and one from the pantry) that reflect both dietary and religious concerns, the principle of variety (a fried dish, a boiled dish, a roast), and the typology of dishes (appetizer, soup, meats, and side dishes). In 1609 Cesare Evitascandalo documents such a meal in these terms:

> figs
> fried sweetbreads
> roast (or boiled) veal
> veal broth
> sliced sausage
> cabbages

and in conclusion three or four things served from the pantry:

> Parmesan cheese
> crisp pears
> almonds
> fennel
> cake (if desired)[51]

Gastronomic rules are very important in the organization of meals. This is reflected not only in the rules relating to Lenten or lean food in its various declensions (the first fast of the season on Ash Wednesday and the penultimate fast on Good Friday) but also in the variety of ways in which the foods are presented. Rossetti cites meals consisting only of pike (served in thirty-six different ways), eel (thirty-one different dishes), oysters, or sturgeon.[52] What we witness here is the display of virtuosity endorsed by the rich recipe collections, which showcased the cook's ability to select products of every age and cut, to transform them in the cooking process, and to present them in ways that distinguish them from each other. Eels "in white sauce," "in light broth," "chilled," or "with cabbage"—to mention only the first four cooked dishes offered at a meal—present clear differences in color, volume, and consistency. Offering large eels, small eels, and young moray eels—served whole, in croquettes, in pies, fresh, salted, or smoked—allowed the cook to play with the basic flavor and nutritional density of the central ingredient. The cook enjoyed and embraced the challenge presented by the thematic meal, and we can imagine the pleasure experienced by the skilled practitioner in varying the dishes and culinary formulae. Here, the artistic mastery of flavors using complex rules and producing surprising effects replaces the predictable codification of dishes. For a Lenten meal in the month of March, Bartolomeo Scappi works exclusively with sturgeon. He offers this basic ingredient in "two presentations served from the Pantry, and two from the Kitchen, consisting of five courses." There are seventeen different dishes, in all.[53]

In addition to the meal's verbal and sensory aspects, it involves a code of gestures. Both servers and diners are actors playing roles of varying importance in a spectacle that also includes fine speeches, sets, and props. The grace with which the diners use their hands, taking food from the plate and placing it in their mouths, is part of the performance. Among the actors, a special role is assigned to the carver, a prominent figure until the seventeenth century, when his functions were gradually absorbed by other servers and finally, in the nineteenth century, by the head of the household. It was the carver who cut the bread, fruit, meat, fish, and all other foods eaten by the diners, adding salt when necessary. Performing a ritual gesture perfected in the courts of Italy, he carved the roast fowl with his knife, raising the meat into the air with a fork, and then arranging the slices on a plate in a circular pattern. The diner accepted his portion and placed it in his mouth. He did this either with his hands or with a fork. The use of forks, which had been adopted some time earlier, was becoming widespread when Cervio published his treatise on the art of carving in 1581.[54] The task of the carver was mainly to divide and distribute the food. In the case of a meat stew, for example, he did this by "dividing it up, portion by portion, for each diner's plate, placing a little of the juice in each."[55] But the carver's distributive function was only one aspect of his work, for in the act of cutting he dismantled the whole to create a single part. His gesture, which echoed that of the diner, reconstructed the shape of the food at the very moment of its undoing.

The theater of gastronomy was not limited to spectacles of this sort. The decoration of the table demanded architectural constructions, emblems, figures of sugar or butter molded in human and animal shapes, gigantic landscapes and volcanoes of pasta, and a profusion of natural and artificial flowers. These items often constituted the most enduring memory of a banquet. In the description of the feast prepared by the Venetians to welcome Henry III on his return from Poland, the sugar sculptures are mentioned, while there is no information regarding the menu. At this banquet two tables were covered with entire armadas, colorful flags, horses, lions, tigers, and a host of characters paying tribute to the sovereign, as well as the candied heads "of Pontiffs, Kings, Cardinals and Doges,"[56] amounting in all to about two hundred figures. This is the final stage of the evolution of food into an object offered as a souvenir to those in attendance. The display on the table of confections made of sugar, dough, and marzipan represented not only the prince's political dominion over the products of the land but also his symbolic power over terrestrial space, over history, myth, and all living creatures.

The Choice of Wine

Water and wine have a special importance in the books written by household stewards. In these texts wines may receive a brief mention or command careful attention, especially from the dietary point of view, but they are not linked to the

Menu

Subrics de riz

Côtelettes de poulet à la Milanaise

Noix de veau rôtie

Salade

Sorbet au cacao - Pâtisserie

DESSERT

————◇◇◇◇————

Racconigi 24 Luglio 1905

Antipasto
Frittate alla marescialla
Filetti di manzo con salsa bearnese
Pollastri arrosto - insalata
Pasta millefoglie alla parigina

VINI

Corvo Casteldaccia

Barbaresco

Grande Spumante Cinzano

Racconigi 25 Ottobre 1909.

Menus used by the Royal House of Savoy, Racconigi, July 24, 1905
(in French), October 25, 1909 (in Italian).

courses presented on the menu. It was the steward, however, who decided the
order in which the drinks were presented and communicated his choices to the
wine steward and his assistants, the "cupbearers," or wine waiters. What were
the qualifications and requirements for a good wine steward? Above all "he
should be able to recognize taste, flavor, and aroma," a talent that was best
accompanied by a "merry, ruddy" face.[57] In addition to selecting the wines and
keeping them at the appropriate temperature, the wine steward was expected to
prepare the water for the meal (making sure that it was fragrant, sweet, and
cool). Assigned to a special corner in the banquet hall, along with his "drinking
vessels, carafes, and other containers of crystal and silver," he kept others from
approaching this area. He decanted the wine before passing it to the wine waiter
and took charge of the various tastings. As it was explained in the seventeenth
century, "he would never pour drink for his master without first testing the wine
and the water."[58] (This ritual was not devoid of tacit meaning and implication:
"Princes are accustomed to the practice [of tasting] . . . out of suspicion that the
wines might be poisoned").[59] The same was true for all solid and liquid foods,
without distinction. The tasting ceremony also served the function of assessing
the quality of the product, a fact that is periodically verified in the *Canevaro*,

which mentions the practice of testing "all the barrels, one by one."[60] After the wine was poured from the decanter into the drinking glass, it was not necessarily ready for immediate serving, since the wine steward might find it necessary to add water in various measures in order to temper its strength or to give it a thirst-quenching quality. Pronouncing the name of the wine, which would be repeated to the diner, the wine steward then dispatched his assistant, the wine waiter, to serve at the table.

Leaving aside the personal tastes of his employer, Romoli describes a series of accompaniments as follows: "When melons or salad are served, the first wine will be a Greco or a white Salerno; a 'wintered' malvagia, muscatel, or a vernaccia with the appetizers and the boiled or stewed dishes, and light, white wines with the roast foods, then strong, red wines with the fruit, Ippocrasso, Magnaguerra, or sweet, red Salerno."[61] Limiting himself to wines found in books, Bacci provides us with the description of each type. A Salerno wine has "a rich aroma, a very clear color; possessing a constitution that is halfway between substantial and light, it leaves no winey aftertaste on the tongue, only sweetness." Regarding Mangiaguerra, he writes: "the wine obtained from these vines is very dark . . . and one finds a broad range of gradations in its various kinds, and its richness will depend on the richness of the soil and the grapes."[62] Some of these wines had already been described in the well-known memoir of Sante Lancerio, the wine steward of Pope Paul III. Lancerio mentions a good six Greco wines, naming their relative locations, three varieties of malvasia transported from Schiavonia and Candia, and muscatel ("golden in hue . . . but pleasant") from several provinces.[63] In his writings on the role of the chief steward or housemaster, Domenico Romoli limits himself to providing a typology of wines. Based on this, the wine steward could make a more specific determination in selecting wines from the cellar.

As pointed out in a recent study by Allen Grieco, an analysis of the wines chosen to accompany the food served at table should take dietary concerns into account.[64] It must be emphasized in any case that the logic underpinning the Galenic system, which was based on contrasts, operated on principles that are diametrically opposed to contemporary custom, which tends to combine food and wine in terms of affinity rather than opposition. "The wine served with fish must be stronger than that served with meat," wrote Maino de' Maineri, the fourteenth-century physician we have already cited. For this reason Romoli's meal begins with white *amabili* (moderately sweet wines) served with melon and salad, two cold foods. For the course consisting of boiled or stewed foods there are "sweet" (malvasia) and "hot" (muscatel) wines. The meal continues with "small," cold wines intended to compensate for the nature of the roast meat and concludes with very sweet, strong wines, or even with *ippocrasso*, a mixture of wine, honey, and aromatic flavorings. Lancerio described these last wines, which accompany the fruit, as "sensuous" types. Wines are golden in color at the beginning of the meal, becoming paler, then red, and finally very dark at the end. Most of them come from the Kingdom of Naples, from Greco, Mangia-guerra, and Salerno. We must also point out that it was Paul III who gave his consent to the printing of Lancerio's *La singolar dottrina* (the special doctrine).

Citing sources such as these, we do not wish to suggest that the method of choosing wine for each course, based on its presumed appropriateness for the food served, was exclusive to the papal banquets. In offering hospitality to an unexpected visitor, a gentleman who lived with his family in a country villa between Novara and Vercelli chose to serve "a very generous white wine" with melons for the appetizer and a "very delicate claret" to accompany a meal of game, roast kid, and boar in lard broth, as well as two pairs of squabs, parboiled and roasted. While the melons and meats came from his own estate, the wines may have come from elsewhere. The man's guest, Torquato Tasso, listened with pleasure as his host expounded not only on the wines mentioned in the works of Homer but also on wines transported to Venice from the Levant, white wines from the Rhine Valley, and Greco from Naples.[65]

The issue of the correct combination of wine and food extended to the prepa-ration of dishes and drinks. Wine is found throughout the entire range of cook-ing practices, competing with must, verjuice, and vinegar, other products of the grape. Bartolomeo Scappi recommends water and wine for boiling hams, pork sausages, and ox tongue. Sauces in particular call for wine, with at least sixteen of the thirty-two cited in the second book of Scappi's *Opera* requiring its use. There are four sauces with malvasia, two with Greco. Wine is used for several purposes—for diluting, moistening, steeping, softening, flavoring, and giving body and color to food—and this means that the cook must also possess a theo-retical awareness of its properties. "Greco from Somma, Greco from Ischia, as well as Chiarello and white Romanesco are the best of all wines for making ices and also for mixing dough and for cooking on days of abstinence. Magnaguerra, Lagrima, and French wine are also good for making royal sauce."[66] The use of wine as a liquid for rendering food softer and more fragrant was not limited to cooking. At the beginning of the meal, guests were invited to dip their Pisan *bis-cotti* in glasses of malvasia and their *biscottini romaneschi* in Trebbiano.[67]

Wine was present outside meals at all times of day. It was served on awaken-ing or as refreshment during the course of a tiring journey. It was used for thirst, for hygiene, and as a remedy for ailments. If one needed a cool drink, one could economize by drinking *acquaticcio* or *acquetta*, which was made from steeped wine dregs and provided an excellent, refreshing substitute for wine. This drink, whether white or red, cooked or flavored, would typically last until the summer following the wine harvest. Given its modest price, it was available even to the serving class.[68] The wine steward also skillfully exercised the art of measuring and serving the appropriate quantities of fresh water. The true secret of his trade, however, was not really a matter of calculating, mixing, or tasting drinks but rather his keen awareness of the preferences of the prince who employed him. Only by taking into account the habits of a wine lover such as Paul III can we fully appreciate the daily commitment of Sante Lancerio, who served the pontiff malvasia wine, sometimes for dipping biscotti, sometimes "for the nourishment of his body," and sometimes for gargling.[69]

Despite these testimonies, the presence of wine in the cookbooks of the sixteenth and seventeenth centuries is merely implicit, featuring in the recipes as one of the ingredients that evaporate in cooking. There is no mention of wine in the menus prepared for banquets, and there is no support for the claim that the grape and its products were the principal elements used as the basis for flavoring. The style in which wine was handled and served at the courts of the princes and popes, however, presents a striking contrast to its consumption by ordinary citizens such as Pontormo, who bought his wine by the barrel and had it transported to his home from Radda in the Chianti region as well as from Calenzano, fifteen kilometers outside Florence. For centuries, two types of wine coexisted in the same urban context: ordinary wine, obtained from the nearest grape-growing area, and wine imported from afar, bearing the names of unfamiliar places, which the wine trade made available to the rich. This split prevailed throughout the entire span of culinary history, lasting up to and beyond the unification of Italy in the nineteenth century.

Although the practice of printing information about wines on cardboard menus in order to indicate their accompaniment to one, two, or three dishes became habitual in the second half of the nineteenth century, it was nonetheless confined to the households of the aristocracy and other ruling families. The choice of bottles varied according to taste, fashion, and the market, but there was a marked preference for national products. At the court of Savoy before Italian unification, vermouth or bitter dry wines, sherry, Madeira, or Marsala were served with oysters. Fine, sweet wines, such as Frontignan and Tokai, were served with Bordeaux steaks and fruit. Of the forty types of wine and spirits for which Vialardi (one of the few to concern himself with such matters) suggests appropriate combinations and accompaniments, only seven are of Italian origin.[70] At the royal court of Italy, a meal began with oysters and a white Capri wine, Gattinara or Barolo accompanied the meat, and Moscato was served at the end. The vineyards of the nation are thus well represented. Traces of ancient dietary custom survive in pairing warm, full-bodied wines with oysters and sweet wines with fruit. A novelty of modern wine practices is the presence of very dry champagne or sparkling wine in the place of the "small" white wines served with the roast. At the beginning of the twentieth century, some of these patterns were adopted by hotel restaurants, which assigned as much importance to wines as to food, offering a well-stocked cellar, a sommelier, and a wine list for consultation by clients after they had read the menu. Hotels and restaurants thus became the heirs of the courts of the minor nobility.

Recipe collections, however, continued to ignore wine, the dietary element that was beyond the domain of the cook. In discussing two different cuisines, French and Tuscan, Giovanni Nelli and Pellegrino Artusi, both highly regarded authors of cookbooks, show the same indifference to drinks. Even in works that include some mention of wine, its use at the dinner table is still not a central concern. In *La cucina nazionale*, Dr. Agnetti writes: "After the appetizer a dry white wine is served, and for dessert, a sweet sparkling wine. As for the rest, there is complete freedom, provided that the wine is absolutely excellent."[71] Agnetti's main interest lies in the management of the cellar and the aging of wines. He devotes more space in his book to discussing casks, the diseases that affect wine, the bottling process, and corks than to the issue of serving or even selecting the individual bottles. Among Italian culinary experts, the writers who include a discussion of wine are usually those with a special interest in issues of hospitality, such as Rajberti, who distinguishes between ordinary wine and fine wine. For this writer, an excellent wine means a Bordeaux, "the prince of serious wines," or a champagne, "the prince of comic wines."[72] In an atmosphere that was open to the rediscovery of native resources, Rajberti, who was from Monza, carefully reevaluates the wines of the major states of the Italian peninsula, mentioning wines from Lombardy, Piedmont, Tuscany, the Neapolitan hinterland, and Sicily. This is a typically bourgeois selection, in that it proposes—in order of importance—wines from the writer's own area, from the territory that was to become the Italian nation, and from the international market. Heavy, sweet wines from abroad are also included (Alicante, Madeira, Malaga, Cyprus), with a preference for sweeter varieties such as muscatels and raisin wines, which continue to be suggested as accompaniments to the final course of ice creams and pastries. The special preference for champagne remains unchanged, despite its cost. And yet if we compare the wines available on Italian shelves with those available in France, it becomes clear that the middle-class residents of a wealthy city such as Milan lacked a well-established tradition in the art of selecting wine, which would have resulted in more assured choices. Rajberti's wine remains very similar to Pontormo's, for it is still in essence a table wine. Bottled wines by contrast were opened on special occasions, generally at the end of a meal when a sense of fullness and euphoria prevailed. At this juncture, in 1850, there is still little evidence of the art of combination. What we find instead is a uniform pattern of consumption in terms of quality, with a flourishing trade in fine wines that was exclusive to the urban environment and catered to a limited clientele.

The Bourgeoisie Cuts Back

The terminology, arrangement, and sequence of courses may vary from one recipe book to the next, disclosing a meal structure where dishes were placed simultaneously on the table at several junctures, in numbers proportionate to the guests. This custom continued without interruption at the ecclesiastical and princely courts until the time of Latini (1692), who was employed at the Spanish court in Naples. Under the influence of the French, this vast service was modified with the introduction of a more complex and varied organization. A dinner offered in the month of May is subdivided by Vincenzo Corrado (1778) into two presentations: the first includes four soups, four terrines, eight hors d'oeuvres, eight round entrées, eight small entrées, and four *relevers* (the *relevé* is part of the entrée and is intended to supplement it). The second presentation involves four chilled dishes, four roasts, eight square entremets, eight entremets served in little boats, and eight round entremets. The total of sixty-eight dishes shows that the change in the style of service did not bring about a noticeable reduction in the number of dishes. Yet we see a new balance between cold and hot—since hot now precedes cold—and the introduction of a couple of elements that are destined to become the rule: soup at the outset and coffee (here in custard form) at the end of the meal. Particularly important are the small, highly flavored, creative dishes, such as the entremets or *trasmessi*, of which sixteen are made of fish and eight are sweet.[73] The balance between appetite, free choice, and obligatory selection is modified in favor of a sequence that follows an increasingly rigid pattern. In the "French" service we see the premises of the "Russian" service.

Around the middle of the nineteenth century, in the most elegant dining rooms of Italy we observe a shift to a type of meal where all dishes are offered to each diner in a preestablished order, the system that still prevails today. In this new system the diner is faced with a compulsory choice but also with the possibility, restricted by the rules of good manners, of refusing an entremets or a side dish. While the Renaissance diner could request one of the dishes placed on the table, reach directly for the one nearest him, or refuse a specially served hot dish, the nineteenth-century host now decided both for himself and for everyone else. At restaurants, where ordering precedes consumption, the opposite occurred, as each client became in a sense his own host. With the adoption of the new type of service, known as the "Russian" style, the showy, simultaneous display of several foods loses its appeal. What becomes more visible now is a sense of progression and hierarchical organization. There was a widespread impression that less food was consumed. "For a long time," wrote Alberto Cougnet, "our stomachs have been rebelling against the Gargantuan habits of our elders."[74] One might say at the very least that people began to eat differently. The organization of the service, the time taken to consume the food, and the space assigned to the diner are now measured in units that correspond to the serving of a single platter. This does not mean that different fashions were abolished. For the French, the place assigned to salads was with the roast; for Italians, it was offered before the roast. The serving of a chilled sorbet halfway through the meal, which was a requirement at the beginning of the nineteenth century, was considered inelegant by the end of the same century, as well as the serving of warm cheese in the place of "natural" cheese. There was also no shortage of dance buffets and light snacks, though here a mild degree of anarchy was still allowed to prevail. On such occasions a cup of "double consommé" was obligatory, while "assorted sandwiches, anchovy pastries, and bread stuffed with Russian salad" were optional.[75]

In recipe collections where the court banquet is not presented as the exclusive model of dining, special focus is placed on the Sunday meal. The reduction in the total number of dishes served, which was instigated by the bourgeoisie, is evident in these books, and it reflects an increasingly closer correspondence between the food served and the food actually tasted and consumed. It was not so much the decline of the aristocracy that abolished the banquet as the changing role of the dish placed on the dining table, the systematic calculation of the necessary and the superfluous, and the growing intolerance of ritual. Each social class gave special importance to its own rules, and there was an increasing reluctance to participate in official or ceremonial dining as an expression of subordination or obsequiousness. The serving class no longer mediated the relationship between the prince and the masses. Now even a meal offered by one's landlord was experienced as a heavy imposition: to have to accept an additional portion of the same food out of pure courtesy, or to limit oneself to gazing sadly at a more generous portion than was offered, and to feel hesitant to refuse a food that one does not desire to eat are only a few of the slavish behaviors that the new gourmets stigmatize.

There has perhaps been too much emphasis on the shift from "French" to "Russian" service, which is the serving of dishes one at a time. This had a special impact on the ceremonial organization of meals in the homes of the aristocrats and members of the affluent classes, the modern heirs of the princes of the past. Apart from requirements imposed by special occasions and courtly protocol, even in the most privileged households the principle of an ample, coherent meal, without waste, was now preferred. Even Ippolito Cavalcanti, a writer who did not conceal the fact that he was a duke, drew up a meal description (a "minute," or menu) in 1847 that was very different from Corrado's: "1. Shrimp soup. 2. Squid beignets (hors d'oeuvre). 3. Sturgeon, Italian style (entrée). 4. Entremets of *cannolichi*. 5. Roast of *spinole*. 6. Little pastries stuffed with *angine* fish and flavored with rum."[76] Dessert and fruit are not included. The eight courses served at Cavalcanti's Neapolitan supper on Christmas Eve may be regarded as especially noteworthy, since this meal would retain its basic composition in middle-class and aristocratic households and in restaurants up to Artusi's time and even beyond.

There are close connections between festive dining and the daily meal. The allocation of ingredients to different days of the week and the reuse of uneaten food, along with the skillful management of leftovers, which allowed diners to experience the memories of one dinner in the course of the following one, linked meals to each other just as shopping lists coordinated by a single budget also tend to do. This was hardly a new concept. We have only to remember the half head of kid consumed by Pontormo on Tuesday and the other half set aside for Wednesday. The bourgeoisie recodified this ancient custom, adapted it to the urban market, and infused it with its own national, political, and liberal values. While the recipe dictates ways to make economy an art, what emerges from the menu and the organization of the meal is a social lesson that fuses together both the nutritional and the representational function. To be sure, hospitality requires style, but this means the imposition of the style of the host. Members of the bourgeoisie thus dine serenely at home but less comfortably in the presence of others. Whether scant or lavish, the portion offered to guests in the home must always strive to find the right measure. But what measure? Physiology and hygiene consider the curve of the belly as projecting the needs of the social body, adapting taste to need and profit. The four-dish meal is not only suited to the weak stomach and the sedentary life but to the careful budget that corresponds to actual resources. The urban bourgeoisie plans every aspect of dining according to its own values, freeing it from the legacy constituted by privilege and the myths deeply embedded in the history of gastronomy: the Christian supper, the Roman banquet, the Renaissance feast, and Parisian folly.

Superstitions, with which the history of taste is replete, are certainly far from dead and are observed with a sense of resignation. In France and Italy anecdotal discourse reveals a preoccupation with the famous problem of the number of guests, which can be adjusted to any number, except thirteen. Why are twelve and fourteen allowed but not thirteen? Rajberti produces a case history, recounting the risks and the number of deaths.[77] He shows no sign of remembering the Last Supper, at which the thirteenth guest was either Judas or the sacrificial victim. Rajberti's is a secular dining table, where no blessing is pronounced when the diners sit down and no grace is recited at the end. At this meal there is much talk of excess and dying, but in jest, with the pretense of disbelief. The detachment with which the middle classes comment on traditional rituals is due to their autonomy, the same independence that makes them intolerant of the aristocratic meal and its trappings, wines, false etiquette (and especially outrageous cost), and the luxurious clothing and exotic products that remind them that values are falsified by excess and disproportion. Both the term "aristocratic" and the term "popular" ("of the ordinary people") have a negative value when attributed to the meal, the first because it evokes the slavish observance of formality, and the second because it evokes a false idea of freedom according to which "one can eat and eat," leading the diner to lose all sense of taste long before leaving the table.

The single culinary model previously adopted in the courts of popes and princes thus gave way to a multiplicity of minor models. Every member of the middle class dictated the law of his own table, adapting it to his beliefs, his work, and his family. The meal became less and less dependent on qualified servants and was managed with increasing frequency by the man of the house or by his wife. This man attributed special value to the dishes of the city or the state where he resided, and yet, as a Lombard, a Piedmontese, or a resident of the Po Valley, he recognized the common aspiration of all landowning people by serving boiled beef and everyday wine. Hygiene or health was placed above taste, and cooking became a science, that is, one could place one's entire cultural preparation at the disposal of the stomach. The bourgeoisie created a type of meal that legitimized poor cooking by gentrifying it and penalized French cooking by adapting it to provincial Italian taste.

The Death of the Appetizer and the Resurrection of Cheese

The debate on popular, bourgeois, and aristocratic cooking influenced the structure of the meal, modifying it profoundly. Many dishes were moved to a subsequent course, while others were assigned a new role. From the second half of the nineteenth century onward the order of the items noted on menus was turned upside down, leaving unresolved doubts. The place assigned to soup and to cheese, the role of the entremets, the serving of punch before the roast were also problems that the bourgeoisie inherited from the aristocratic tradition. These were resolved when they were placed in a context where, in the idiom of the restaurant, they became part of the set formula of the first, second, and third course. There was still a difference, however, between the confusion provoked by a "frozen punch, Roman style," a rarity served before the roast, and the difficulty faced in defining entremets of various types—such as gnocchi made of semolina, soufflés, savory puddings, even pork feet and *"salama da sugo"* from Ferrara—sometimes served between the boiled meat and the stew, sometimes between the stew and the roast, with a "linking" or supporting function. Raw salad, which used to appear at the start of the meal, now accompanied the roast. Cheese was a different matter. Should it be served as a separate course? Or should it appear with the fruit, after the sweet? Or should it precede both of these? These choices were not minor matters. To end with the cheese meant to uncork serious, aged wines, which certainly did not go with fruit. The reduction of dishes instigated by bourgeois cooking left the final stage of the meal in a state of uncertainty, which women, unlike their husbands, interpreted in favor of dessert and sweets. And finally there was the issue of coffee. Though it was clear that this should be served very hot, it was unclear if it should be served at the dinner table or in the living room.

Among the many issues related to form, the question of the antipasto was the most important. With its profusion of different foods, it was the only part of the

GLI AMI
CI DEL
CIRCOLO
DEGLI
ARTISTI

AL SE
NATORE
LEONAR
DO BI
STOLFI

SABATO, 24 MARZO 1923

TAGLIATELLI ALLA BOLOGNESE

SELLA VITELLO RICHELIEU

FARAONA SALMY

INSALATA PARISIENNE

CHARLOTTE RUSSE

DESSERT

GRIGNOLINO DA PASTO
CHAMPAGNE

RICORRENDO L'ONOMASTICO
DEL PROTETTORE DEI
Spend poch, mangia ben
e mai content.
Torino, 7 Novembre 1905

❊ MENU ❊

VINI

Bianco Secco

Grignolino vecchio

Champ. Americain
G. H. Moum

Antipasto variato
Riso all'Imperiale
Carré di Vitello alla Touluse
Asparagi di Rivoli al Parmigiano
Tartufi delle Breide alla Piemontese
Becaccie arrosto
Insalatina mignonette
Omelette Soufflet
Composte e Pasticceria
Dessert
Caffè à Liquori

Buffet Stazione N. 3
F. Molinari

Società "Il Drago"
PRANZO SOCIALE
Torino, 10 Giugno 1

MENU

Salade Primeur
Jambon varié
Potage Reine Margoot
Esturgeon sauce Crevettes
Tournedos à la Godard
Champignons et Tomates à la Genois
Poulet de grain à la broche
Salade Bébé
Fraises Orange et Curaçao
Gâteau Noisette
Panier de fruits
Café

Chianti
Barbaresco
Mått Trepat

LISTA DELLE VIVANDE

ANTIPASTO
RISTRETTO DI POLLO IN TAZZA
SCAMPI DEL CARNARO ALLA DUSE
RISO CAROLINA
MEDAGLIONI DI BOVE MELBA
FAGIOLINI DEL LIDO AL BURRO
SOFFIATO DIACCIO "MARIA JOSÉ"
BISCOTTI DI NOVARA
CESTINO DI FRUTTA
CAFFÈ

VINI:

CHIANTI EXTRA 1924
(MARCHESE ANTINORI, FIRENZE)
CORA - ASTI SPUMANTE

Italian menus from the early twentieth century

meal that reflected the courses offered on the tables of the aristocracy. Its evolution in the bourgeois meal continued to be tied to the stimulation of appetite and the dietary organization of the menu. The success it attained in lower-middle-class festivities, in *trattorie* and fine restaurants, and its decline at the dinner table made it all the more enigmatic, especially since its contents altered without ever changing completely. How could such a free-spirited way of combining foods fall into disrepute in a food culture that had grown increasingly less ceremonial?

From the historical viewpoint the antipasto should not really be considered in the category of hors d'oeuvre. The term *antipasto* first appears in the sixteenth century, and Domenico Romoli uses it in the modern sense to mean the initial course. The term "hors d'oeuvre" by contrast is used by Massialot in Paris in 1691 to indicate dishes, such as artichoke hearts or pork trotters, that served as a supplement to the first or second course, as a kind of entremets that could also be presented after the roast. Etymologically, as Panzini shows, if a meal is considered to be the main project (oeuvre), then preparations that are supplementary or marginal to it are considered outside (hors) its scope. *Il cuoco piemontese* (The Piedmontese cook), written in 1766, uses the term in this sense, citing two supporting soups as the hors d'oeuvre but limits its use to the first course. It was only in the following century that "antipasto" and "hors d'oeuvre" became synonymous.

Romoli reflects the appetizing function of this course by proposing fresh, unsalted cheese, capers, and little fritters, which are meant to stimulate the appetite without filling the stomach. It was initially a cold but very varied course, not devoid of an internal progression, and ending but never beginning with meat or fish. With the French reform, soup, which was considered diluting and refreshing, took the initial position at the banquet, and the hors d'oeuvres, little pastries, stuffed vegetables, fritters — all bite-size — followed this, alternating with terrines of hare and liver pâtés. This was the moment to nibble, to savor either a beignet or a sweet morsel, without worrying too much about one's appetite, which was already alert, even engaged. How long did this creative anarchy last? It is difficult to estimate, because within the tradition of aristocratic cuisine the hors d'oeuvre took on a character that was increasingly less whimsical. At the court of Savoy in the years before Italian unification we find sardines and tuna in oil, radishes and olives, mushrooms in vinegar, and, obviously, caviar, along with curls of butter, cured meats, and melons.[78] The transformation of a cold course into a great platter of preserves was thus complete. What remained was the aim of stimulating the appetite through the simple flavors contained in the products used for preserving food (vinegar, oil, and salt) and in the raw, sliced vegetables. In this sense the antipasto, whether it precedes or follows the soup, is shop-bought food, and it was used by the cleverest hosts to fill out the duller phases of the meal. To interpret it literally, by serving "the usual salami of every color and spice" and perhaps following this with other cooked sausages, would mean to destroy the appetite. To consider an antipasto that consists entirely of pork meats—much appreciated by the masses—as a vulgar custom is just a short step away from this.[79]

Rajberti is formal: salami is not part of the cuisine. Artusi, having opted for the Tuscan custom of serving the appetizers after the soup, prefers the term "*principii*" (starters) to *piatti d'antipasto*, and he proposes the serving of *crostini* (bite-sized pieces of toasted bread). The *principii* include sandwiches made of fat, cooked ham or tongue. Purportedly good to eat after the soup or to accompany a cup of tea, they have a function that is more filling than appetizing, and they do not appear on the same menus as canapés with caviar or truffles, which project a spectacular impression with their costly ingredients served in minute quantities. These judgments and subterfuges show that the problem of snaring the diner and keeping his appetite alert without tiring it, without falling into a plebeian sequence of cold, salted, acidic items, was widely shared without finding a clear solution. The popular Italian antipasto enjoyed huge success in the 1930s, although the elite, chefs, gastronomic experts, and domestic cooks deplored it. French restaurants of high quality preferred to replace it with a course composed of oysters, caviar, foie gras, or hot morsels, croquettes, beignets, tartlets, and fondu. On the other hand, housewives, who were unwilling to undertake the preparation of difficult, savory pastry, abandoned the practice completely. In a Milanese recipe book, *Il quattrova illustrato*, one of the initial chapters bears the title "Dettato contro gli antipasti in favor delle minestre" (A statement against appetizers and in favor of soups): "The idea of sitting down at the table with an appetite for the seductive and poisonous miscellany of cold dishes known as the antipasto is absolutely barbaric from every point of view." Since the antipasto is "spicy and highly flavored," it ruins the palate, making the food that follows it seem bland. Heavy and cluttered, it is indigestible.[80] Ada Boni, the epitome of Roman ladies of good breeding, notes by contrast: "The meal may begin with an antipasto, in spite of how much discussion has been devoted to whether or not this is an appropriate thing. In fact, appetizers, which are composed for the most part of spicy foods, momentarily alter the sensitivity of the palate."[81] Following the fashion of the new culture of vitamins, the attempt to reintroduce raw vegetables and salads at the beginning of the meal has had limited success and only in connection with their weight-reducing associations. In 1950 the paradox constituted by this useless, superfluous course was discussed in terms that were conditioned by years of privation. "Many culinary enthusiasts are opposed to antipasti, because, since they are so appetizing and varied, they often have a negative impact on the success of the other dishes, for, having tasted them, one ends up without an appetite for anything else."[82]

The decline of the cold antipasto marks the end of a ceremonial tradition that began with platters of different foods placed simultaneously on the table. It also marks the end of a dietary tradition that based the order of presentation on the needs of the body by reawakening or stimulating the appetite with various foods. The masses inherited the culture of cured meats and pickles, peppers and anchovies marinated in oil, eaten with quantities of bread, marking a belated and uncontested triumph. The customs of large hotels mirror this, for reasons of economy. In the historical process that brought about a simplification of the meal, the fate of the antipasto is anomalous. The culinary avant-garde abandoned it in order to reinstate other courses, including the cheese, which Il quat-trova assigns to "the interval that precedes the gentle pleasures of the desserts and follows the satisfied sense of well-being that emanates from a satisfied appetite."[83] Cheeses are fatty, salted products purchased at the store that, like salamis, require the accompaniment of bread and wine. Disassociated from fruit, they gradually carved out their place between the meat course and the dessert.

The history of cheese is a curious one. It used to be, as we have seen, a food for country folk, nibbled by doctors and cooks,[84] combined with fruit when aged, flavored with sugar when fresh. For centuries cheeses were regarded as ingredients to be used in cooking rather than as products for direct consumption, served just as they were on the dining table. Or perhaps Parmesan might be sliced and served. Or a marzolino cheese might be opened up, in the middle of the fruit display, following the compositional standards of a still-life painting. In the early sixteenth century praise for cheese is found in the work of literary authors fond of paradox or is expressed by gentlemen appreciative of the riches of herds and pastures, such as Ercole Bentivoglio of Milan and Count Giulio Landi of Piacenza.[85] When the antipasto composed of cured meats began to fall into decline, cheese was recuperated by the elite—reinforced by the gastronomic practice of the French—and it was assigned a position all its own. This shift can be noted at its inception. In the second half of the nineteenth century, when it was still a custom in noble households to start the meal by serving provola cheese "in carrozza," crackers with gorgonzola, and Reggio chizze refashioned with French names,[86] it became increasingly common to serve the cheese after the roast.

The modern way of serving cheese came into being with the awakening of interest in local, handmade products and in industrial products of longstanding reputation and with the increasing attention paid to wines. Il quattrova illustrato, one of the earliest recipe collections to launch this fashion, suggests not only Parmesan and gorgonzola cheese but also mozzarella. It was women—housewives—who liberated cheese from ostracism, refining the manner in which it was served and protecting its soft creaminess with a glass lid. In the first phase, the shape or cut of the cheese was rarely displayed on the table. The rind continued to be regarded with distaste, and the cheese was flavored (mozzarella with slices of truffle), buttered (gorgonzola), or even cooked. This presentation prefigures the emergence of the special place now reserved for cheeses, which

are now devoid of any associations of repugnance or uncleanliness. The acceptance of the natural rind constitutes a big step toward the sincere love of cheese.
With the acceptance of odors that might sometimes seem pungent or even foul,
there is also a relinquishing of the taboo against mold, air holes, gradations of
yellow, and splotches of strange colors such as blue, which were considered
unsuitable for eating. Now the custom of serving two cheeses, one sharp and the
other sweet and creamy, takes over.[87] In the last fifty years the end of the meal
has been remodeled, inserting this ancient, misrecognized product. In restaurants it now takes the place of fresh fruit and is served before dessert.

The Single Dish

The death of the antipasto and the resurrection of cheese: the articulation of the
contemporary meal seems less and less tied to the progression of dishes and
courses and freer in its choices, allowing the diner to eat only the pasta course
and a sweet or a fish dish and a cheese. The autonomy claimed by taste over the
requirements of ceremony, especially in restaurants, is matched in the home by
the choice to assemble a number of dishes in one, in particular on occasions of
relaxed conviviality or solitary dining where the choice of food and the simplification of the meal are intertwined.

At the dawn of Italian gastronomic culture as well as in our own time, the
issue of a single course, or single dish, for dinner is discussed in two different
ways. In the first sense it is either a free choice or an obligation imposed by the
environment, circumstances, or availability. In the second sense it corresponds
to a way of planning the whole meal as a single dish. In France and Italy dictionaries record this second meaning beginning in the 1980s, to indicate a substantial dish that is easy to prepare—or indeed the opposite—as a very rich and
highly appreciated dish served at a dinner among friends. By the same token the
recipe collections do not record it even in times of rationing, even though in
Germany during World War II it was imposed by patriotic principle, once a
month, in restaurants and homes, in the form of an *Eintopf*, a soup made of peas
and ham (*Erbsensuppe mit Speck*). The single dish is nonetheless documented
in earlier times, not only in Germanic countries. Philanthropic and charitable
associations have always tried to imagine nourishing foods assembled in a single bowl that could sustain the life of the individual. The hot soups of Lord
Rumford, composed of bread, barley, and vegetables,[88] belong to the same context of dietary, economic, and social planning. The polentas consumed by
northern Italian peasants show by contrast how a system of nutritional subsistence is founded on a caloric basis that can integrate every form of flavoring.
The single dish was thus initially formulated in communities, whether open or
closed, freely or rigidly structured, that are characterized by the need to find
enough food for survival at the lowest cost.

Bringing together different ingredients, each with its own cooking requirements and flavorings, the single dish merely condenses the meal into a single
portion. It is easy to imagine how, using the same products and the same quantities, one could create a greater number of individual dishes. Soup can contain
a serving of pasta or rice, a side dish of boiled vegetables, or a small portion of
meat and fats. The first Italian recipe collection to approach this subject was
Savina Roggero's *Piatto unico all'italiana* (The single-dish meal, Italian style),
published in 1977. What are the advantages of the single dish, according to this
writer? It brings together the pasta course and the main dish; it organizes the
meal in a modular way, facilitating the accommodation of additional diners at
the table simply by increasing the ingredients; and it saves the effort of serving
a course.[89] Especially noteworthy is the fact that traditional, regional formulas
prevail (salt cod with polenta, *panissa*) and that the choice of recipes is extended
to include exotic dishes from elsewhere in Europe (*quiche Lorraine*, goulash
with dumplings) and from overseas (*nasi goring* from Indonesia, *chili con
carne*). Thus the single-dish formula is compatible with an Italian tradition,
causing it to evolve toward a model of culinary encounters and exchange, borrowing elements from some countries while providing inspiration and suggestions to others. Having found a warm welcome in the world of advertising, the
single dish inspires the interest of nutritionists looking for balanced, easily combined foods. Typical examples of dishes "capable of supplying on their own the
nutritional contribution of the usual pasta course and main dish" are "pasta with
beans, stewed veal with potatoes, pasta dishes with cheese and meat sauces,
hearty soups served with grated cheese, pizza, and so on."[90] We recognize in
these not so much the product of the Mediterranean diet, as *Mangiare meglio
per vivere meglio* claims, but rather some of the cooked dishes that best represent
Italian cuisine today, with the possible exception of veal stew and potatoes.
Clearly, the recipe collections do not ignore these dishes, but they do not evaluate them in this light, while the food industry and the restaurant business have
fully understood their potential for profit.

The single-dish meal was not born yesterday, as people used to say. Among
the texts that exerted the greatest fascination on the writers of the sixteenth century there is the pseudo-Virgilian *Moretum*, a frequently translated poem that
tells of how a peasant prepares a flatcake flavored with herbs crushed in a mortar, oil, and cheese. The *Moretum* brings to the foreground a dietary tradition
based on self-sufficiency, vegetable products, and the importance of flavoring.
The fragrance of the peasant's meal comes from the crushed herbs, and its taste
and smoothness derive from the oil and cheese.[91] It would be easy, and we will
abstain from underlining it, to suggest a continuity between this flatcake and
pizza or between the herb sauce and Genoese pesto, and yet the existence of this
model of a meal of a single serving offers one of the keys for interpreting the
inventory of Italian dishes at the top of which we find those that are best known

throughout the world. Is this the revenge of the cuisine of the masses? Or is it indeed proof of the continuity of models of subsistence?

It is neither, because lunches, dinners, and breakfasts consisting of a single dish, which are always the same and yet always different, constitute a recent invention in the dining habits of the well-to-do. These are indebted to a system of production and distribution that consolidates and disseminates the image of food. Agriculture and the food industry have made dried pasta and frozen peas available throughout the year, along with flour, tomatoes, and the anchovies needed to make pizza. Without these, the seasonal and productive cycles would affect the products consumed, making their availability precarious. The first requirement of the single dish is its predictable cost and its consistent presence in the marketplace, in memory, and in verbal, written, and visual communication. For centuries bread was the complete meal par excellence, until it became the support or container for a condiment or filling, without losing the identity associated with its linguistic diminutive [*panino*, diminutive of *pane*, denotes a sandwich in Italian—Trans.]. A second requirement is that this dish should not seem linked ineluctably to the history of the individual and his environment but should transcend these concerns, addressing a broader community. It may have a precise geogastronomical origin but is reproducible everywhere. For this reason, pizza has a strong identity in places where there are no roots or memories, where it must seem merely an unpronounceable exoticism.

The third characteristic of the single dish is gastronomic versatility. Minestrone, pizza, and pasta will tolerate the most diverse ingredients. Pasta was sweetened with sugar in the sixteenth century, pizza was flavored with spike-cap mushrooms in the nineteenth century, and a minestrone made by a well-known producer of frozen foods contains up to fourteen varieties of vegetables. This is not so much a single dish as a typological one, allowing a series of chromatic and taste variations that do not affect its ability to be identified or impede its repeated consumption over time and space, and, unlike dishes such as the hamburger, it enjoys a positive nutritional reputation. All the dishes mentioned above have recently received positive dietary evaluations, not because they have been used as a cure for illnesses and found to be therapeutic but because they readily lend themselves to manipulation by culinary and scientific discourses. The slowly absorbed sugars in semola flour, the vitamins and minerals found in the vegetables, the wholesomeness of unrefined grains, the "Mediterranean" ingredients of pizza function as selling points, leaving aside the issue of individual metabolism and above all the quantities consumed.

A hearty sandwich or hamburger may correspond to a meal, but neither of them constitutes a dish. The final trace of ceremony contained in a portion of spaghetti or minestrone lies in the fact that it requires the diner to sit down at the table, using a place setting and silverware. Pizza, however, has a polyvalent status, since it may be eaten with a knife and fork or with one's bare hands. It may be consumed on the street, at work, in a bar, at home, or in a pizzeria. It is the final frontier of ritual dining: the single-dish menu and its variants, which may be typical or creative, ethnic or national. Like many "frontier foods" the pizza comes in a modest version and a luxurious one. Unlike other dishes if its kind, however, it also has a third version—"four-seasons pizza"—which is endowed with the appropriate symbolic weight of the solar and gastronomic cal- endar. A circle of dough can accommodate literally anything thousands of miles from its land of origin, changing its name slightly to "new pizza" wherever it is topped with ingredients such as Hawaiian pineapple or Canadian bacon, chili con carne, smoked pheasant, or three different types of caviar (black, red, and gold).[92] This circle, in which the order of culinary presentation is inscribed, can be renegotiated ad infinitum.

CHAPTER FIVE

Communicating Food: The Recipe Collection

The Book

The Italian word "*ricetta*" (recipe) derives from the Latin "*recepta*," which orig-inally meant a prescription prepared by a physician for patients and pharma-cists. The term is used in its modern meaning in "Ser Meoccio ghiottone" (Meoccio the glutton), a novella from the middle of the fifteenth century by Gentile Sermini. Here we find an allusion to a book "filled with cooks' recipes [*ricette*] and descriptions of all kinds of foods and delicious indulgences, the way they are cooked and flavored, and the seasons in which they are served."[1] From then on, the use of both "*ricetta*" and "*ricettario*" — to designate a recipe collec-tion — can be found in abundance. In order to understand these words correctly, however, we need to add some further clarification.

This concept of the book allows us to distinguish between an isolated recipe — a single set of instructions — and a collection of texts partially or com-pletely dedicated to the topic of food preparation. As a genre, the menu collec-tion includes a broad typology of texts under a group of identifying terms such as "*cucina*" (cooking), "*menù*" (menu), and "*casa*" (household). *Liber de coquina*, *Libro per cuoco*, and *Libro della cocina* are the titles of some of the old-est Italian recipe collections still in existence. These date from the end of the thirteenth to the beginning of the fifteenth century. The *Libro de arte coquinaria*, written by Maestro Martino in the fifteenth century, is already a fully fledged recipe book, despite the brevity of its recipes, which are often lim-ited to a list of ingredients and the description of a single phase of preparation or cooking. In 1516 it appeared in print for the first time with the new title *Epu-lario*, and authorship was attributed to Giovanni de' Rosselli. It was reprinted fif-teen times in the sixteenth century and at least eleven times in the seventeenth, continuing to appeal to readers at least until 1682, when the last edition was printed in Venice.[2]

There is no better example of the durability of a didactic genre before and after the invention of the printing press. The terms "book" (*libro*) and "work" (*opera*) serve to convey an awareness of the specific elements of cooking. Fol-lowed by a phrase referring to dishes or banquets, both terms became commonplace on the frontispieces of sixteenth-century recipe collections, of which the books written by Messisbugo and Scappi are the most famous examples. Created by men who were professional experts in specific areas of service at the courts of the nobility, these cookbooks are far from miscellaneous collections, and in the course of their publishing history they became more diversified. This can be observed both in the internal organization of the individual volumes, which are broken down into sections or chapters dedicated to different types of cooking in the strict sense—pastry making, curing and preserving, distilling—and in the creation of separate volumes with information on different aspects of professional practice.

Whether a recipe collection exists in manuscript or printed form does not in itself allow us to draw typological distinctions or to make immediate assumptions regarding the date of composition or the intended readership. The custom of recording and collecting recipes has continued down through the centuries. Clearly, we can see a correlation between the increase in female literacy in the nineteenth century and the increased production of diaries and notebooks at the time. In addition, the publication of women's magazines led to the custom of clipping, cataloging, and pasting items into scrapbooks. The practice of jotting down and assembling recipes was not an alternative to printing but if anything a custom that paralleled it, with the result that publishers producing books on topics of domestic management were obliged to leave blank pages in each volume for personal annotations and recipes. In 1950 the publishers of *Il cucchiaio d'argento* (The silver spoon) placed sheets of watermarked paper with the heading "Reserved for Personal Recipes" at the end of each chapter, bound into the body of the book.

Although the oldest cookbooks that survive today in codex form were created as early as the fourteenth century, the concept of the recipe collection in the broadest sense goes back further in time and includes the recording of pharmacological preparations, as we have already mentioned, as well as the diffusion of practical texts on household management that also offered advice on economic and hygienic matters. Nevertheless, the miscellaneous and multidisciplinary character of these works does not lead us to conclude that the genre is an ancient one. The compiler might be a physician, a household steward, or even a man of property with a general interest in nutrition, the economics of food preservation, provisions, and hygienic products such as soaps. Combining different forms of knowledge was part of the special competency required for household management. When a domestic handbook was produced in a household with a large staff, where a range of different skills was required, it was likely to offer prescriptive advice. This tradition lasted down through the years and is reflected in the publication of manuals on domestic economy, which offered sensible, up-to-date accounts of the organization of the bourgeois family with a salaried female housekeeper. Lidia Morelli's *Nuovo ricettario domestico*

Portrait of Cristoforo Messisbugo.

Source: Cristoforo Messisbugo, *Banchetti, compositioni di vivande et apparecchio generale* (Ferrara: Buglhat and Huche, 1549).

(New domestic recipe collection), written in 1935, offers 5,390 entries on topics relating to the necessities of everyday life. Here, in addition to recipes for jams, entries on subjects as diverse as dental hygiene and gaslight can be found under the appropriate headings. We even find instructions for the compilation and cataloging of recipes.

The creation of domestic notebooks and the compilation of handwritten notes also became necessary because printed books, whether illustrated or not, cost a great deal of money and were thus the province of the elite. In the 1500s treatises on stewardship, charts illustrating cuts of meat, and cooking manuals all followed various editorial criteria, which can be seen in the choice of lettering, the use of margins, and the etchings and illustrated tables accompanying the main body of the text. Books written on trades or professions and on ceremonial codes of behavior were meant to be of practical value to those who used them and thus had to be manageable, sturdy, and dignified enough to do honor to the prestige of the dedicatee. Records of hospitality had an important place in the library of the prince. These offer lavishly engraved images of festive occasions and celebrations rather than recipes or lists of provisions. A collection of such images found in Bologna bears the following inscription: "Disegni del convito fatto dall'Illustrissimo Signor Senatore Francesco Ratta all'Illustrissimo publico, Eccelsi Signori Anziani, & altra Nobiltà. Terminando il suo gonfalonierato Li 28 febraro 1693" (Drawings of a banquet given by the most Illustrious Lord Senator Francesco Ratta for his most Illustrious Audience, the most high Lord Elders and other Members of the Nobility, marking the end of his term as standard bearer on the twenty-eighth of February, 1693).[3]

Written accounts of banquets, accompanied by illustrations of sumptuously adorned tables, might also include solemn references to a royal family, principally to the Bourbon dynasty in Naples in the eighteenth century. After the description of meals and banquets organized at court and reports of financial expenditure, we find illustrations of various spectacles. Among the most noteworthy of these are images of the marvelous "machinery" of the *Cuccagna* (a spectacular display of food representing the Land of Plenty), featuring every form of bounty under the sun: fountains of wine, hams growing on trees, and flocks of chickens, all likely to be pillaged by the starving masses of Naples under the amused gaze of their noble lords.[4]

As a result of the development of printing methods that enabled the reproduction of images on a much broader scale, by the nineteenth century professional recipe collections could offer illustrations of high quality that were greatly appreciated by household stewards and pastry cooks. These images mark a distinction between "high" and "low" cuisine. The sixty-four tables in *La cucina classica* (Classical cuisine) by Urbain Dubois and Emile Bernard, published in Italian in 1877 at the expense of "an association of Milanese cooks," offer useful, up-to-date information to Italian practitioners working alongside and in competition with the French. The use of engraving techniques, and hence full-color or three-tone reproductions, though considered an expensive option in the twentieth century, yielded illustrations that facilitated more effective culinary preparation and became part of the documentary resources consulted by chefs.

Books written for housewives and housekeepers are another matter. Toward the end of the eighteenth century, recipe collections addressed to a bourgeois audience and to a literate, urbanized servant class, both male and female, began to appear in booklet form. Such booklets could be produced at low cost and distributed as almanacs or periodicals. *La cuoca cremonese* (The cook of Cremona), written in 1794, presents a calendar followed by a list of products organized according to seasonal availability, menus, individual chapters dedicated to meats, fish, vegetables, and pastry, as well as information on the value of various coins and even the postal schedule. *L'oniatologia ovvero discorso de' cibi con ricette e regole per ben cucinare all'uso moderno* (Oniatology; or, A lesson on foods, with recipes and rules for good cooking in the modern style) is the earliest known publication created from individual installments of a periodical, assembled and bound together. From 1785 to 1786 *L'oniatologia* appeared as a booklet of eighty pages three times a year. After a break, it resumed publication in 1794 and was completed the same year. Though the initial word in the title may seem mysterious, the contents of this work are far from unusual, given that it includes recipes for many familiar Tuscan dishes. *L'oniatologia* was reprinted in a single volume in Florence in 1804 and again in 1806. In the meantime, *L'almanach des gourmands* appeared in Paris in 1803. Described as an "annual calendar," this proved to be the first culinary periodical. By the middle of the nineteenth century the growing strength of advertising and the increasingly specialized nature of the publishing industry facilitated the dissemination of new books well within the financial reach of the general public.

Linking its fortunes to a type of publishing characterized by modest prices and wide distribution, the cookbook not only proved capable of influencing female domestic culture but also had an impact on the marketing and sale of merchandise. Evolving from the single-volume format—usually published under the printer's name rather than the author's—to series of books, it was ultimately assimilated with the periodical. The pamphlets published by Biblioteca Casalinga Sonzogno, whose titles all began with the number 100—*100 conserve per la famiglia*, *100 ricette di cucina vegetariana*, *100 ricette di cucina per i bambini* (One hundred preserves for family use, One hundred vegetarian recipes, One hundred recipes for children)—cost from twenty to sixty *centesimi* an issue over the course of the thirty-year period that began with World War I, anticipating the tendency of recipe collections to become kinds of memoranda, ephemeral sources of occasional advice. These cleverly titled texts, which were between thirty and a hundred pages in length, functioned like class notes. Sponsored by the national food companies (Cirio and Arrigoni) or by the office of Fascist propaganda, publications of this type were often distributed free of charge during the Fascist era, giving rise to a proliferation of brochures, fliers, and throwaway advertisements. The cookbook's miscellaneous character—as a collection of recipes that could be selected and read one at a time, as the occasion required—makes it a distinctively protean production, likely to include etchings, drawings, and photographs and suited to different kinds of binding (stapled, glued, or spiral) or even to distribution in unbound form, in files or envelopes. Whether expensive or free of charge, acquired for personal use or intended as a gift, the recipe collection thus became a distinctive genre in twentieth-century publishing.

Title, Frontispiece, and Portrait

The frontispiece guides the reader's initial approach to the book's contents. A title referring either to the subject of the volume (*Liber de coquina*) or its potential user (*Libro per cuoco*) was the earliest method of classification to gain widespread currency. *Libro de arte coquinaria*, the title used by Maestro Martino, already alluded to cooking as an art, and this term was to enjoy lasting success in the titles of Italian, French, and English publications. "Art" implicitly elevates the status of food while acknowledging the skill of the preparer.

We subsequently find frontispieces alluding either to a specific orchestration of recipes and dishes for courtly banquets, as in Messisbugo's *Banchetti, compositioni di vivande et apparecchio generale* (Banquets, composition of dishes, and general presentation), written in 1549; to the writer's qualifications and the court of his employer, as in Scappi's *Opera dell'arte del cucinare* (The work of Master Bartolomeo Scappi, private cook to Pope Pius V), written in 1570; or to the correct method of executing tasks such as the carving and serving of meat and fish, as in Cervio's *Il trinciante di M. Vincenzo Cervio* (The carver, by Master Vincenzo Cervio), written in 1581. Domenico Romoli's book examines the broad array of responsibilities assigned to household officials. As a steward expected to take care of the prince's dining requirements, Romoli had at his disposal a bursar (or "economist") in charge of provisions, a head cook (or "private cook"), and a pantry cook in charge of the preparation of fruit and salads, linens and tableware. The title of his collection *La singolar dottrina* (The special doctrine) suggests an aspiration toward the kind of elegant, erudite expression appropriate to persons of good breeding, if not of high rank. Romoli, a Florentine gentleman, was a cook before he became a steward, and hence his nickname Panunto (Oiled Bread), which appears on the frontispiece of his book, along with a lengthy inscription:

> The singular doctrine of Master Domenico Romoli, nicknamed Panunto, on the responsibility of the Steward, the seasoning of all dishes, and the seasonal suitability of all types of animals, poultry, and fish. On banquets for every occasion and the daily requirements of the dining table, all year long, at the courts of the Princes. With a determination on the quality of the meats of all animals and fish and the healthy qualities of every dish. Concluding with a brief treatise on the maintenance of good health. An extremely useful work for everyone.

This description already alludes to the duties of the steward, the cook, and the "bursar," the calendar of seasonal products, and the responsibility for organizing banquets. It also alludes to "Princes" as the principal beneficiaries of this labor. We note the inclusion of information on the quality of ingredients, menus for the entire year, and the dietary rules that must be observed. There is a striking absence of any mention of the pantry or the cellar (the domain of the wine steward). Proceeding to the table of contents, the reader observes that the entire eighth book is devoted to flavoring and the ninth to dietary science, with special reference to nutritional variety and physical movement. To take responsibility for an individual's physical health down to its most fleeting determinations—dreams—is the objective of a doctrine that is "special," both because of its complexity and variety and because its real focus was not food but rather the body of a nobleman or prelate. The dedication to Francesco Rustica of Padua offered by the printer Michele Tramezzino underlines this aspect of Romoli's work, praising the writer's status as a Florentine nobleman and his employment at the papal court in Rome.

Historical factors may affect the selection of a book's title. In naming his treatise L'Apicio overo il maestro de' conviti (Apicius; or, The master of banquets) in 1647, Giovan Francesco Vasselli pays tribute to a famous Roman epicure and to a great institution of the ancient past fondly remembered by antiquarians and men of letters. Apicius's name was also held in high esteem outside Italy. It later reemerged in the neoclassical context with Apicio moderno ossia l'arte di apprestare ogni sorta di vivande di Francesco Leonardi romano (Modern Apicius; or, The art of preparing all types of foods by Francesco Leonardi of Roma), published in 1690; Apicius Redivivus or the Cook's Oracle, printed in London in 1817; and Apician Morsels, by Dick Humerlbergius, published in London in 1829.

Other elements would similarly leave their mark on the frontispiece. The process of assigning different functions to different individuals among the higher ranks of service gradually made culinary practice more complex, to the point that the organization of the meal became a task unto itself, independent to some degree from the art of the cook. The publication of the La lucerna de corteggiani (The courtiers' oil lamp) in 1634 serves to illustrate this point. If the object mentioned at the outset—an instrument that illuminates the house or court—seems mysterious, the mystery is quickly resolved in remainder of the inscription: "The Courtiers' Oil Lamp, which presents, in Dialogue Form, a disquisition on the Courts, on the twenty-four noble offices, on a variety of foods for the entire year, for every Sunday and for other Banquets; divided into six chapters, this is the work of Giovan Battista Crisci of Naples. To his Most Serene Highness, the Grand Duke of Tuscany, Ferdinand II." Like the "special doctrine," the "oil lamp" is an instrument that casts light on the household or court. The book discusses the twenty-four most important positions in household service, including the carver and the steward, whose task is to "order food for the kitchen of his Lordship throughout the course of the year." Only the "noble offices" are included here, and both the cook and the butler are omitted. Hence, while La lucerna offers 290 pages of menus for every day of the year and descriptions of six banquet projects, it does not contain recipes. Still, it is one of the richest repertoires of its kind in existence, showing the scope and variety of ordinary meals—organized into three rounds of service (hot, cold, fruit) and comprising a maximum of eighteen dishes—in the context of the Neapolitan court.

The frontispiece is far from anonymous, since the author's presence imposes itself with great insistence. Here we find the etched portrait of Giovan Battista Crisci wearing courtly attire and displaying his coat of arms, with two oil lamps in the upper corners, and a statement of his age as forty-five. It is not unusual to find a portrait placed after the dedications and before the main body of the text, as occurs in the books by Messisbugo (1549) and Scappi (1570). These are head-and-shoulder images of mature men, which allow us to admire their flowing beards, hairstyles, and clothing. Carvers are shown in chivalric attire, complete with cape, gloves, and sword, as we see in the book by Antonio Frugoli (1638). On the frontispiece of Bartolomeo Stefani's *L'arte di ben cucinare* (The art of cooking well), published in 1662, we observe a likeness of the author, a Bolognese cook, captured in a pose that seems reserved, dignified, and devoid of ostentation. Once he had attained a position so eminent that he could mingle with courtiers who were close to the prince and, following the publication of his own book, even with literary figures, an author would frequently express his pride by displaying his coat of arms and wearing elegant attire. Vanity played a part in this custom. At the age of forty-five, Antonio Latini, who came from very modest origins,[5] had a portrait etched in which he appears younger than his years. He decided to publish this image in the 1692 edition of the *Lo scalco alla moderna* (The modern steward) but later changed his mind and replaced it with another portrait, which he inserted into the volume before the dedications and tributes addressed to him in verse. Pictured holding a copy of his book and wearing a long beard, he now looks fifty. Having obtained knighthood, however, Latini removed this version from the subsequent edition and replaced it with another portrait, where the coveted symbols of nobility are visible on his chest.

The use of the portrait is an Italian tradition that allows the reader to attribute a face to a role. It rescues the cook from the anonymity of the mechanical arts by honoring his personality. Although this custom became less frequent after the era of Antonio Latini, Antonio Nebbia chose to revive it by including in his book a portrait printed on watermarked paper that shows not only his face but also his frilled shirtfront, wig, and spectacles.[6] Here Nebbia is portrayed with his hand resting on a book placed on a table alongside an inkwell and hand-written text, thus offering us a rare image in which writing tools are featured next to kitchen burners. In the nineteenth century engravings of this kind gave way to smaller images of the chef in his kitchen wearing a floppy white headdress, which was destined to grow taller and stiffer in subsequent illustrations. This image is the prototype of the lithographic portrait or photograph of the chef still current today. Here, even when the energy level in the kitchen shifts from inertia to frenzy, the smiling cook, posing in his uniform, presides over the convivial proceedings with serene benevolence, expressing himself in gestures that grow increasingly faster and more coordinated. An alternative to this model is the image of the kitchen staff captured at the moment of greatest intensity. Reviv-

Portraits of Bartolomeo Scappi, Giovan Battista Crisci,
Antonio Frugoli, and Cesare Evitascandalo

Sources: Bartolomeo Scappi, *Opera dell'arte del cucinare* (Venice: Tramezzino, 1570);
Giovan Battista Crisci, *La lucerna de corteggiani* (Naples: Domenico Roncagliolo, 1634);
Antonio Frugoli, *Pratica e scalcaria* (Rome: Cavalli, 1638); Cesare Evitascandalo,
Libro dello scalco (Rome: Vullietti, 1609).

ing a visual trope found rarely in the older recipe collections (the exception is the *Epulario* in 1516), this picture presents cooks and maids, or head cooks and kitchen hands, hard at work. In this case it is not the individual who dominates the scenario but the work itself.

At some point around the end of the eighteenth century or the beginning of the nineteenth, a long period of iconoclasm interrupted the cult of personality found in the oldest recipe collections as well as the most recent ones. The phenomenon may be linked to the end of Italy's aristocratic era or may be interpreted as an attempt to adapt to the customs of the French, who from 1650 until the Revolution eliminated cooks' portraits from their recipe collections. The shift from visual portraiture to a simple statement of professional qualifications is also implicitly reflected in the titles of books written in the second half of the eighteenth century, which undergo a fundamental change and begin to imitate new models. Examples include *Le cuisinier françois* by La Varenne (published in Italian translation in Bologna in 1682) and *Le cuisinier royal et bourgeois* by Massialot (published in Italian translation in Venice in 1773). On the frontispiece of the translation, as in the original, we often find an allusion to the professional career of the cook, his place of origin, and his special skills. Information regarding the geographical area in which he was trained or is currently employed is also increasingly present. The cook is obviously French in 1682; he later becomes "Piedmontese, trained in Paris" and is finally "from Macerata."[7]

In addition to portraiture, there were other symbolic, enigmatic ways to celebrate the cook's personality. Heraldic emblems and coats of arms, real or imaginary, as well as pseudonyms and honorary titles may serve to enhance the portrait. These elements can be written or engraved. The Florentine nobleman Domenico Romoli appears on the frontispiece of his book along with his nickname "Panunto." Punning on his own last name, Franco Vasselli, a "household prefect," captures the attention of readers about to proceed to the recipes with an allusion to his role as a vessel on the sea of gastronomy.[8] A coat of arms located on the upper right side of the medallion that frames the portrait of Bartolomeo Scappi shows a dog running away, *escaping* from its chain, thus offering a visual pun on the writer's name by linking it to the verb "*scappare*" (to escape). To insinuate a coded message regarding an individual employed at such rank in the kitchens or dining halls of the nobility or to link his name to recondite qualities constituted a clever game of allusion that was not without an element of risk, given the "secrecy" imposed by author's position. Of all the messages that could be communicated indirectly by the frontispiece, an assertion of the book's paternity was of special importance. This was duly entrusted to the engraver. For example, paternity is communicated in the works by Latini and Nebbia (both of whom were known to be of modest birth) with the presence a book within the portrait.

These small vanities were justified insofar as the cook stood apart from the crowd of anonymous tradesmen as an exceptional character, since he was accepted into the highest ranks of those who serve. In the nineteenth century the profession broadened its scope to include employment in private homes and hotels and was reshaped into a hierarchy that became affected by the policies of labor unions toward the century's end. Operating within a precise economic sector and changing his place of work from one season to the next, the cook no longer held as his highest ambition the honor of contributing to a banquet attended by dukes and members of the royal court. Cooks now appear on the frontispieces with their places of origin: they are Bolognese, Milanese, or Neapolitan, trained in the culinary capitals of Italy, in the service of the nobility or the urban bourgeoisie. Most often their names are omitted, as if anonymity guaranteed a type of cuisine that could be both personal and communal, domestic and public. With increasing frequency female cooks appear in the titles, as in Menon's *La cuisinière bourgeoise*. Like their counterparts, these women come either from the provinces or the city—from Cremona or Genoa— and they are sometimes featured as the companions of male cooks, as was customary among domestic employees: *Il cuoco milanese e la cuciniera piemontese* (The [male] Milanese cook and the [female] Piedmontese cook). Frequently, the publishers' efforts to find imaginative adjectives to apply to these women conjure up the memory of that precious resource, the faithful female servant. Hence we find *La cuoca di famiglia* (The [female] family cook), *La cuoca risparmiatrice* (The thrifty female cook), *La cuoca sublime* (The sublime female cook). From the time of Latini onward, cooks of both sexes are decidedly *modern*, with different values. After the Congress of Vienna, they also become "Italian."[9] In the elite cuisine developed in the houses of reigning sovereigns, honorific titles appear in great profusion: "the king," "the emperor of cooks," or "the prince" or, going a step further, "the king of kings among cooks."[10] Olindo Guerrini offers the following view of such affectations and the recipes that accompany them: "As for the other King of all Cooks, the Queen of all Cooks, and other such culinary majesties, what we find here are merely translations from the French or disjointed compilations."[11]

To say that these titles are the product of fashion is a simplification. While they follow the criteria proper to the publishing tradition of culinary books, they also function as a set of social signals, aiming at a particular type of male or female readership. These titles echo each other, changing over time to resonate with the values of the emerging middle-class family. Ada Boni's *Il talismano della felicità* (The talisman of happiness) evokes the cult of fine food and successful wedded union, since a likeness of the author, created by her husband, Enrico Boni, is included in the book from the fifth edition onward, proving that the dream of female cooks to achieve eternal renown for their art had never died. On the other hand, to present a young bride with a copy of *Il cucchiaio d'argento* (The silver spoon) was to appeal to her sense of refinement, since its title alluded to an item that was traditionally one of the most expensive wedding gifts.

Dedications and Tributes

Acknowledgments feature abundantly in collections of menus and recipes. Perhaps because the cookbook emerged from smoky kitchens or was driven by the anxiety to create successful dishes or serve at important banquets, the author's dedication shows off his familiarity with persons of distinction, and the tributes he receives echo a prestigious consensus. *La lucerna de corteggiani* opens with a dedication to Ferdinand II of Tuscany and another to the Accademia degli Erranti; thirty-eight sonnets in Italian, Spanish, and Latin, along with a substantial quantity of other poetic compositions, appear at the end. These are encomiastic exercises often expressed with clever puns ("te glorioso / che quanti'altri in te cresci CRISCI cresci" [You, glorious one, that many others grow, grow, grow with you], with "cresci" [you grow] evolving into Crisci's name).[12] They are signed by noblemen and academicians, and they are explicitly addressed to Crisci: the number is perhaps exorbitant but indicative of the desire to flatter the powerful and earn admirers, to be recognized and revered. The custom of dedications was not a passing trend. The recipe collection reflects a continuous, concrete tribute to the figure of the prince. The reader should be fully aware of the fact that the skills the author shares in the volume have received their stamp of approval from a great man. Since it is a more delicate matter to offer honor to a prince of the church, in such cases authors may have recourse to typographical strategies. Thus in Scappi's *Opera* the name of Pius V appears on the frontispiece as part of his official *imprimatur*, in the dedication to the steward Don Francesco Di Reinoso, and in all the titles of the peripheral materials.

There were also other ways of announcing the benevolence of the elite. Menus declaring the name of the host and the occasion for the banquet at the top of the list of dishes served have a celebratory, propitious function. Under the heading "Lunch prepared for the second coronation of His Holiness Pius V, Friday, January 17, 1566,"[13] Scappi gives a full report of his contribution to a banquet, affirming his previously announced titles. More unusual but no less solemn is the kind of occasion in which the author himself extends an invitation to dine: "A private dinner that I prepared for His Most Illustrious Excellency, Sir Hercole, My Most Distinguished Lord, at my home on the feast of St. Anthony, January 17, 1543."[14] Only the rank of Cristoforo Messisbugo, superintendent of the duke's estate and administrator of provisions and salaries for the entire court,[15] could command such an honor. Other personal, even sentimental, reasons may be added to these professional ones. A special assignment or a memorable banquet would be regarded as the crowning glory in the life of the cook, even if his participation in this event was part of a complex organizational system. Examples of such important occasions are the conclave of 1549, in which Scappi participated, and the banquet offered in honor of Queen Christina II of Sweden by the duke of Mantua, in which Bartolomeo Stefani took part. It is true that Stefani initially hesitated to acknowledge the event, saying: "I have not worked in the kitchens of Royalty." Yet he later gave in to the pressure of those who urged him to prepare "some Royal dinner," admitting to his participation in the banquet as well as his personal admiration for the Swedish queen: "I myself served her *trionfi, refreddi*, and other dishes."[16] A "*trionfo*" (triumph) was a sculpture in sugar that on such occasions might be molded in the shape of Mount Olympus, featuring cherubs and a royal crown. The "*rifreddo*" was a dish eaten cold. If we consider the complexity of the banquet—three courses served from the kitchen and another three from the pantry, consisting of more than fifty elements, large trays of food, and bowls of cured delicacies—it is not only Stefani's presence that seems significant here but also his voice, his testimony as a living witness.

The convention of offering dedications and gratitude to patron princes and making appeals to the reader is most customary in works describing feasts, ceremonies, and banquets motivated by the good will of a patron or host. The habit of including letters written by illustrious personages to acknowledge their support or esteem is its later correlative. Vincenzo Corrado's *Il cuoco galante* (The gallant cook) carries a statement of esteem from Cardinal de Bernis, a minister and former French ambassador to Rome, who declares himself an enthusiast of "Pythagoran" (vegetarian) food. There is also a statement by a Dr. Spallanzani, who asserts his interest in the "diverse bodily sensibilities" and the "diversity of the opinions, by virtue of which, regardless of how excellent a dish might be, it will at times fail to please."[17] At the end of the eighteenth century the practice of dedication became rarer, and some of its elements were discarded. As a greater number of copies were printed, the cookbook was controlled to an increasing degree by the publisher, and beyond this relationship of specific dependency it owed its principal debt to the market. An explicit offer of services began to sound artificial. It implied on the author's part a formal request for acceptance, which the dedicatee was obliged to consider. In other words, it represented an extortion of his consent to things that had already been done. The dedication ultimately became a rarity. Or so it would seem from *La cucina teorico-pratico* (Theoretical-practical cuisine), written by the duke of Buonvicino, a rather bizarre character who rather provocatively placed the consent of the dedicatee before his own dedication. At the top of the book's opening page we find the inscription "I accept the present dedication. Trabia." A justification for this follows, along with an offer of Trabia's work. At the bottom of the page, to the left of the author's signature, the reader discovers that "Trabia" is Cavalier Giuseppe Lanza, prince of Trabia, a Sicilian minister and councillor of state.[18]

L'ARTE
DI BEN CVCINARE, ET INSTRVIRE
i men periti in quefta lodcuole profeiffione.

Doue anco s'infegna à far Pafticci, Sapori, Salfe, Gelatine, Torte, & altro
DI BARTOLOMEO STEFANI
Cuoco Bolognefe.

All' Ill.mo, (&) Ecc. mo Sig. Marchefe

OTTAVIO GONZAGA
Prencipe del Sacro Romano Imperio, de'Marchefi
di Mantoua, e Signor di Vefcouato, &c.

IN MANTOVA, Appreffo gli Ofanna, Stampatori Ducali, 1662,
Con licenza de' Superiori,

Frontispiece with portrait of Bartolomeo Stefani.

Source: Bartolomeo Stefani, *L'arte de ben cucinare, et instruire i men periti in questa lodevole professione* (Mantua: Osanna, 1662).

The increasing frequency of indirect or humorous dedications is a sign of changing times. When a book is expected to remain within the walls of the home, with no reader other than the woman of the house or the servant, there is not much scope for affectation. This also holds true of publications dedicated to professional practices. In this case the dedication is now less likely to be written by the author than by the bookseller or publisher, a figure who, from the time of the earliest culinary publications in the sixteenth century onward, had habitually taken up his pen in order to attract readers or clarify the circumstances involved in printing a particular volume. In *Il re dei cuochi* (The king of cooks) it is Legros, the publisher, who thanks Nelli (whose portrait is reproduced in the book) for his good faith, his timely revisions, and his success.[19] We find the most original dedication, however, in Pellegrino Artusi's *La scienza in cucina* (Science in the kitchen), of which the first edition is dedicated to the author's two cats, Biancani (or Biancunzein) and Sibillone. Here Artusi writes: "For both of you, because you had the habit of rubbing your stiff tails against my legs while I was trying out these dishes in the kitchen, dying to be the first to give me your opinion."[20] The publishers initially rejected *La scienza in cucina*, which the author then printed at his own expense. Hence it does not invoke protectors; as the offspring of a bachelor, the book is dedicated to his most faithful companions. Later, having achieved acclaim, Artusi reprinted his work, and the two big white cats disappeared. Nevertheless, this edition gained—if not dedicatees—a couple of godparents, in the form of two individuals of some renown, Olindo Guerrini and Maria Mantegazza (wife of Senator Paolo Mantegazza), who had immediately expressed their admiration for Artusi's work. Their letters were thus included at the end of the second edition, following the chapter dedicated to "Some Rules of Hygiene."

The growing scarcity of dedications in cookbooks coincided with a period during which it was fashionable to give dishes French names as a tribute to famous living people. This custom grew more widespread over the course of the nineteenth century and was passed on to Italians by osmosis, with titles alluding to dishes that had been created on specific occasions and were linked to the name of the host. As the custom spread, these titles became a virtual lexicon. The birth of *pêche Melba*, created by Escoffier in London in 1893 for Nellie Melba, the Wagnerian soprano, proves that hotel restaurants were capable of bestowing fame on a name by linking it to a dessert.[21] King Victor Emmanuel II and Humbert I of Savoy lent their patronage to *noix de veau Victor Emmanuel* (veal nuggets with game) and *salade à la Humbert*, respectively. Cavour's name appears in at least five dishes: a creamy rice soup (*potage à la Cavour*), stewed head of veal (*tête de veau à la Cavour*), a capon dish (*chapon à la Cavour*), a lemon ice cream (*glace de crème à la Cavour*), and a pudding (*pouding à la Cavour*).[22] This custom suggests the enthusiasm of European aristocrats and royalty for culinary creativity. It distinguishes refined cuisine from common cooking, bestows a certain dignity on a recipe, and becomes a symbolic point of ref-

erence to which those responsible for service and protocol are especially attentive. Cooks, epicures, and even restaurant proprietors were also among those
who could hope to achieve immortality by having their names bestowed on
dishes, provided that these dishes had the good fortune to remain famous. Yet
the craze for endowing foods with names did not end here. Although the hotel
where a recipe originated might claim it as its own and name the dish after its
birthplace, this practice could generate confusion. Thus we find *crêpes Excelsior*, created by Paolo Fabrizzi, a chef at the Excelsior Hotel in Naples, as well
as *petti di pollo Excelsior* (chicken breasts Excelsior), the invention of Roberto
Salin at the Venice Excelsior. Restaurant proprietors lent a sense of authenticity
to a dish by creating legends around it, as happened with the attribution of the
dish *spaghetti alla carbonara* to a "Trattoria carbonara" in Rome.[23] There is no
limit to the kinds of images inspired by these names. Tourist locations (as in
"*timballo Tivoli*"), songs (a "flaming" omelet dubbed "*O sole mio*"), and painters
("*Carpaccio*") become part of a varied and richly detailed anecdotal tradition
perpetuated by *maîtres*, managers, and restaurant owners. Issued like a copyright by cooks and gourmets, the proper name ultimately became, at least in
commercial cuisine, a sign of the inauthentic.

There is a similar trend in domestic cooking, where dishes can be named
after mothers, grandmothers, and servants, whose memory is repeatedly invoked
at table just as the diners place their food on the fork. The use of a diminutive
name in a recipe, accompanied by a short clarification, often underscores the
recognition of an individual's hardworking dedication in a personal, heartfelt
tone. Thus in his recipe for *panettone Marietta*, a title that would otherwise
remain mysterious, Artusi notes: "My Marietta [Sabatini] is a fine cook and such
a good, warmhearted woman that she deserves to have this cake named after
her, especially since it was she who taught me how to make it."[24]

The title of a dish is considered famous if it is mentioned in gastronomic texts
and repeated in culinary manuals and recipe collections. The longer it survives
its initial appearance, the more firmly its identity (or composition) is established, although its origin becomes no clearer in the process. In the 1970s the
introduction of nouvelle cuisine brought a change to this custom of French derivation by redirecting the readers' attention to ingredients and cooking techniques. The revival of the tradition of eating out in modest inns with solidly traditional, anonymous fare ultimately eliminated the practice of applying nick-
names or proper names to dishes, leaving this to the more commercially
oriented sector of the restaurant business.

The Organization of Contents and Indexes

The recipe book involves both the collection of brief didactic texts and the
arrangement of these texts in a certain order. Its organization has three variables:

the principal ingredients used in the recipe, the type of culinary preparation, and the appropriate manner of service. To facilitate consultation, the material must be arranged systematically and must be accompanied by indexes. Considering that the recipe collection provides information on banquets and menus, the indexes offer the possibility of different recipe combinations, depending on the type of celebration, the calendar, and the appropriate protocol, all of which require methodical documentation. In the light of this complexity we will now discuss the recipe collection from the perspective of its consultation by readers.

The earliest culinary manuscripts are devoid of tables of contents. Maestro Martino's *Libro de arte coquinaria*, however, organizes its content into chapters corresponding to food categories (meat, eggs, fish) or culinary preparations (soups, sauces, tortes, fritters). Yet this organization is not strictly enforced. In the first chapter different meats are featured in haphazard succession rather than grouped together according to their principal ingredient—veal, pork, or poultry. In addition, some recipes provide specific serving instructions, and this too becomes one of the methods of classification. Maestro Martino tells us, for example, that the *fritelle de fior di sambuco* (fritters of elderberry blossoms) should be served immediately and "brought to the table very, very hot." The order in which the book's contents are presented also suggests a hierarchy of dishes, giving primary importance to roasts and boiled or stewed meats. The last three recipes, which appear after a group of fish recipes, seem to have been added on to the original text, especially in the case of a rice dish and a *pastello volativo* (a pastry crust designed to contain live birds, which were set loose in the course of the banquet). When the *Libro* appeared in print for the first time in 1516 with its new title *Opera nova chiamata Epulario* (New work called Epulario) and a different author's name—the "French" Giovanni de' Rosselli—a full list of recipes in the order of their appearance was provided at the back of the book.

A book of recipes is like a systematic dictionary, since the entries are grouped according to their semantic affinity. Tables of contents, indexes, and lists of dishes allow the reader to access the information needed to prepare individual dishes or to create the desired menus. As these tools became more refined, they set the stage for the transformation of a group of recipes into a culinary encyclopedia. A century after the initial appearance of *Libro de arte coquinaria* the cookbook had begun to include a catalog of provisions and professional tasks and an inventory of cooking equipment. Though these features would vary from author to author, the cookbook generally served the function of providing a set of norms to be observed in culinary practice. Messisbugo's work, written in 1549, lists all the furnishings, provisions, and equipment needed for a banquet, in addition to the necessary spices and ingredients, household supplies, and personnel. Romoli's work by contrast separates professional skills and problems of staffing from the calendar of seasonal products and provides relevant information on quality. Finally, Scappi's book encompasses all the major points of concern: the cook, the kitchen, the quality of supplies and provisions, curing and preserving food, and a precise inventory of all permanent household equipment (the equipment used while traveling is discussed elsewhere). The inventory has both a proprietary and a professional aspect, since it serves to offer acknowledgment to the employer, to instruct culinary disciples, and to plan dining procedures.

Other lists follow. Thus we find lists of banquets and lists of recipes arranged according to ingredients and culinary preparations. To describe banquets offered by princes or prelates in precise chronological and worldly detail, encompassing the entire apparatus of production, meant to emphasize the importance of these events. On the other hand, to treat banquets apart from their social context, by focusing on them as a combination of different courses and dishes, implied a concern for the abstract model and its variants. Cristoforo Messisbugo takes the first approach in his description of the magnificent hospitality offered by the Este court in Ferrara in all its spectacular aspects. Scappi by contrast presents an alternative perspective, offering an annual calendar with a menu for each day of the year, allowing for all kinds of variables, both ordinary and exceptional. This calendar begins on April 8 and ends on Good Friday of the subsequent year, for which he proposes a lunch menu without fish.

In order to locate a recipe, the reader may consult a final, comprehensive index that lists each recipe according to page number (Messisbugo), or indexes for each volume, or even for each chapter (Scappi). As we have seen, the grouping of recipes obeys two criteria—the ingredients or the type of culinary preparation—with which other criteria may intersect. Dishes may be grouped together in a chapter if they are served in the same course or if they belong to the same season of the year or liturgical dispensation. Throughout Lent, with the exception of Good Friday, fish is mandatory, and hence the user must consult the part of the collection where fish recipes are listed under their dual classification as "fat" (with butter) or "lean" (with oil). In addition, the overlapping of medical and dietary concerns prompted Bartolomeo Scappi to dedicate an entire volume to convalescents. Here the individual sections are arranged according to therapeutic and nutritional criteria. Clear broths or consommés are provided at the outset and sauces at the end.

The order in which chapters or volumes are arranged may also vary: some authors discuss meats in the first book, others pasta. The sequence of the recipes is not arbitrary, however: if the ox is the first item introduced, all the animal's edible parts and cuts of meat are discussed in logical succession, progressing from head to foot. This systematic approach allows the reader to observe how the meat of a specific animal is transformed into its potential culinary versions. The most important treatises make a point of presenting both domestic animals (such as the calf, along with various cuts of veal) and rarer species, which might even include the bear and the hedgehog.[25] Describing purchases, various phases of work, utensils, and service, the recipe collection is organized as a list of directives and dishes, accompanied by a network of indexes that allows the reader to correlate them to each other.

This structure is modified by the distribution of dishes into the courses served at the dinner table. In the sixteenth century these were divided into cold and hot, and, following French influence, they were organized into a sequence that progressed from entrées to roasts, savory entremets, and finally desserts. The order of service in the dining room, however, does not correspond to the order of the culinary procedures unfolding in the kitchen. According to the French model, the initial information provided in the cookbook should be a description of all stocks and sauces, followed by soups and meats. This format prevailed in professional cuisine from the eighteenth century onward. Francesco Leonardi's *Apicio moderno* begins with broths, subdivided into types and degrees of concentration (*generale, suage, consome, biondo, restoran, tablette, sugo*); it then proceeds to describe sauces and discusses beef in the second chapter. For provincial cooking, we can cite the example of Antonio Nebbia's *Il cuoco maceratese* (The cook of Macerata), published in 1781, which begins with broth but immediately moves on to soups. Pellegrino Artusi also follows this model.

The alphabetical organization of the material, essentially based on the titles of dishes, offers a radically different model. An example of this approach is found in the chapter indexes and layout of the fourteenth-century collection *Libro per cuoco*. Fat and lean dishes, intended for the first or second sequence of courses, are organized in a way that suggests some kind of typological system. The twenty-two *torte* are listed together, as their titles begin with "*torta de*" and conclude with an ingredient (fish, herbs), a geographical location ("*Romania*"), an adjective indicating the inclusion of an ingredient (*sambugata*, indicating "with elderberries"), or a toponymic (French, Hungarian).[26] Some expedients can be adopted to make this method work; the synonymous use of *savore* and *salsa* (flavoring/sauce) means that we find these entries mixed with each other. Massialot's *Le cuisinier royal et bourgeois*, published in various reprints from 1691 to 1751, revived the use of alphabetic indexing in France. This was based on the presupposition that the recipe collection would be consulted for specific information and so was arranged exclusively for the cook, without taking into account the order of dishes and courses. The Italian translation of Massialot's work, *Il cuoco reale e cittadino* published in 1773 by Baseggio in Venice, while respecting the original text, adheres to this organizing principle only with regard to names and ingredients beginning with the same letter in French and Italian, as in the case of *agnello* and *agneau* (lamb), for example.[27] Because of its practicality, however, alphabetic organization became commonplace in publications destined for popular readership, as we see in *La cucina casereccia* (Home cooking).[28] The motive for this choice is clear: the simpler the meal, the rarer the recourse to a type of cooking that branches out like a tree, beginning with diluted soups or thin broths, featuring an entire series of imbricated operations and also requiring the creation of cold, preprepared or quickly prepared dishes. Alphabetical indexing nonetheless enjoyed limited success in recipe collections, insofar as it mixed lean dishes designated for days of abstinence with fat dishes considered suitable for ordinary days, soups with desserts. Hence this system was adopted exclusively by culinary dictionaries, which were intended mainly for professional use. The dictionaries, which began to appear in the second half of the nineteenth century, differ from both encyclopedic works such as the *Dizionario ragionato degli alimenti* (Methodical food dictionary) by Francesco Leonardi, printed in Rome in 1795, and domestic glossaries written in dialect, such as Puoti's *Vocabolario domestico napoletano e toscano* (Domestic dictionary: Neapolitan and Tuscan), or practical, Tuscan works such as Carena's *Prontuario di vocaboli attinenti alle cose domestiche* (Handbook of terms pertaining to domestic matters).[29] Under each entry, the culinary dictionary provided a lexical definition, a gastronomical description, and a variable number of recipes. Among the earliest was *Dizionario della cucina moderna* (Dictionary of modern cooking) by Giacomo Giardini, the president of an association of Milanese cooks and a promoter of the Italian translation of *La cuisine classique* by Urbain Dubois and Emile Bernard.[30] Published in Milan in 1885, Giardini's dictionary instructs its users in both Italian and French, discussing common foods (cauliflower) as well as rarer items (dolphin and bear), without neglecting simple dishes such as fried eggs, specially provided for neophytes. Entries relating to service are either omitted or, like menus, relegated to an appendix, while the wine cellar appears under the entry for wine.

Of the two methods of organization, the alphabetical and the systematic (by ingredients and type of culinary preparation), it was the second that prevailed in Italy. In France, by contrast, the enthusiastic reception of the *Larousse gastronomique* in its 1938, 1984, and 1996 editions sealed the success of the recipe collection structured as a dictionary.

The Recipe

The recipe is a text describing the preparation of a nutritional object. By prescribing the ingredients, instruments, and methods needed to attain this goal, it teaches the reader to make—or rather provides him with the knowledge necessary to make—a particular dish.[31] Although a recipe may be oral or written, we are concerned here only with the written variety. The recipe belongs to an ancient prescriptive genre that was developed in very diverse ways. Yet one cannot properly speak of an evolution in the genre. The recipe may in fact have emerged at the beginning of Italy's gastronomic history with some basic characteristics that were destined to remain unaltered. Take, for example, the recipe for green sauce found in a codex from the first half of the fourteenth century:

"To make green sauce, take parsley, mint, cardamom, nutmegs, pepper, cloves, and ginger, and pound them vigorously in a mortar. Add some bread crumbs, mix some garlic in as well, if available, and adjust [the mixture] with a good vinegar."[32]

The ingredients and the tools (mortar and pestle) specified here frequently reappear with various modifications. Even when the mortar is replaced by the half-moon blade or the grinder, the procedures are practically identical. The allusion to thickening (with bread crumbs) and diluting (with vinegar) is another element that was destined to last in the preparation of sauces. From the didactic point of view, the recipe's use of the imperative form of verbs indicating procedures (take, pound, add, mix) and the progression of tasks described (chopping, mixing, adjusting) can be translated into modern Italian without any alteration. What marks this recipe, in our day, as historically dated? Perhaps the lack of distinction between the two types of ingredients, spices and herbs, and above all the absence of any mention of quantity and proportion. In 1967 Anna Gosetti della Salda recorded a similar recipe, with the title *"bagnet piemontese."*[33] Here the reader is instructed to take fifty grams of parsley, a clove of garlic, and the crumbs of one bread roll. All other aspects mentioned, such as the addition of salt (absent in the ancient recipe), are to be attributed not to the original recipe but to its subsequent recodification.

The connection between taste and organization is the great variable in recipe collections. By taste, we mean the choice and combination of ingredients, the level of heat required for cooking, and in general the flavoring procedures. Garnishing and serving the dish are part of this aspect, as is the judgment of its gastronomical value. Taste involves the historical pattern of a recipe's execution. From this perspective, the distance between the earliest handwritten recipes and the recipes of the sixteenth-century collections is already significant. *"Salza verde"* (green sauce) appears in Scappi's *Opera*. He suggests, however, that it be flavored with salt and pepper, without recourse to other spices, but adds a small amount of mint. His creation takes into account the final taste above and beyond the accumulation of flavorings. In making green sauce one must achieve the right color and consistency by selecting the appropriate fresh herbs and by completing the procedure of chopping or straining.[34] Moving down through time and space, the ingredients and terminology may change, but not the recipe. In giving instructions for "green sauce *alla Reale*," Vincenzo Corrado, an eighteenth-century promoter of vegetarian cooking, brings a hint of a sweet-and-sour flavoring to Scappi's earlier recipe by adding sugar, candied citron, and lemon. A Neapolitan by adoption, he also includes basil in his selection of herbs.

From their earliest appearance recipes have had an unknown number of beneficiaries but only one privileged reader: the cook or the steward. For such individuals, the gross amounts of ingredients are not as important as their proportions. In dictating the recipe for "ravioli on meat days" Maestro Martino indicates the quantities needed for the filling (half a pound of cheese for a pound of pork belly), specifies the precise size of the *raviolo* ("as big as half a chestnut"), and suggests that the pasta be cooked "for as much time it takes to say the Lord's Prayer twice."[35] For the preparation of the dough, however, he provides neither ingredients nor amounts. In former times the cook found himself facing a dilemma: whether to assume his audience's experience and give the broad outlines of his own way of doing things or to provide conscientious instruction, oral or written. A pedagogical intent is plainly evident in *Il cocho bergamasco alla casalenga* (The home-style cook of Bergamo), an anonymous manuscript from the end of the seventeenth century intended for the instruction of domestic personnel in the home of a gentleman of relatively modest means. Here each recipe (the first of which is "to make a flavorful boiled dish") is followed by a quiz: "How long does it take to cook the piece of veal?" "Six quarter hours are sufficient, boiling it continuously as one should, but if the piece is bigger—say, for example, four pounds of rump—two hours are required." "When should the cooking commence?" "If the time of the meal is known, the cooking should be started an hour and a half in advance, so that the food can be placed on the table as soon as it is removed from the pot, eliminating the need for it to be kept near the heat, where it could lose much of its flavor."[36] What we see here, in the form of an exam administered by a domestic cook, is the didactic approach that would become very popular in women's publishing two centuries later.

There are other writers, however, who take an awareness of many concepts for granted, not only in the cook and his principal associate but also in the case of trainees. When compilers assume that customary knowledge has eliminated the need for a detailed description of ingredients and procedures, recipes become shorter and provide only the most indispensable instructions. Concise recipes are found most often in the earliest handwritten collections, from the fourteenth to the fifteenth century, but they also appear later on. Vincenzo Corrado uses the concise formula in *Il cuoco galante*. This helps him to avoid repeating himself but also enables him to indicate a dish by naming the ingredients and procedures of cutting and cooking that constitute its principal elements. His recipe for stuffed macaroni begins as follows: "Large *maccheroni*, cut into strips half a finger in width, are cooked almost thoroughly in capon broth."[37] The specification of "half a finger in width" is an important detail to allow room for the filling, while the degree of cooking ("*quasi cuocere*") is imprecise, since everyone in Naples knows how to boil macaroni.

The more culinary skill can be taken for granted, the shorter the recipe, until it almost resembles a definition. Since the beginning of the twentieth century, through French influence, the professional recipe collection has become a simple memorandum. Thus Cesare Picco's *Nuovo lessico di cucina abbreviato* (New Abbreviated Culinary Lexicon) provides no point of reference for the

LEFT: portrait of Antonio Latini; RIGHT: portrait of Antonio Nebbia.

Source: Antonio Latini, *Lo scalco alla moderna, overo l'arte di ben disporre i conviti* (Naples: Parrino e Mutii, 1692–1694); Antonio Nebbia, *Il cuoco maceratese* (Macerata: Eredi Pannelli, 1786).

shape, volume, or consistency of the gnocchi in the following: "Potato gnocchi: Mix together floury potatoes of good quality and white flour. The dumplings should be cooked in plenty of salted water. They are usually flavored with butter and cheese, meat sauce, tomato sauce, Genoese pesto, etc."[38] The same is true for other manuals. For those who are not already familiar with *gnocchi à l'italienne*, for example, it is impossible to ascertain how to make them from this simple recipe: "Gnocchi are prepared from a mixture of water, butter, and flour, to which grated Parmesan, strained potatoes, and eggs are added. Cook, and sprinkle with Parmesan and steaming butter."[39]

In sharp contrast to this, we find recipes so long-winded and digressive that they become verbose, a tendency that gained currency with the emergence of culinary publications addressed to women. The second half of the nineteenth century witnessed a significant increase in the number of books written for female servants and for women running their own households. Here economic circumstances require the careful monitoring of expenditure. In these recipes amounts are not left to guesswork, and cooking times are precise. With the development of home cooking, practiced according to the standards of the middle classes, the recipe is transformed into a timetable, a shopping list, and a description of the necessary labor. Waste and potential errors in preparation are all taken into account: if the cook uses too few potatoes or too much flour, the *gnocchi* will disappear forever into the water;[40] if the flour placed on the pastry board is insufficient, the dumplings will stick to each other.[41] The word *"gnocchi"* is synonymous with disaster: mixing hot potatoes and flour creates glue, and adding egg to the dough hardens it.

Is the recipe, then, simply a kind of memorandum, a set of working notes? Ingredients, utensils, manual procedures, and cooking methods are deployed here in the name of a very ambitious goal: the creation of tasty edible objects. The recipe's success does not depend solely on a protocol that correctly stipulates the different phases of execution. Cooks dictate or commit their recipes to writing in order to transmit their knowledge, thus elevating one of the manual arts into a noble calling. To these texts they entrust their secrets, their personal interpretation of goodness and beauty, and even the culinary judgment of their diners. An example? Ingredients do not exist in the abstract but embody specific qualities. To assess the quality of a particular fish means to be familiar with its species and habitat, to know if it originates in fresh water, whether lake, river or pond, to know its reproductive cycle as well as the best conditions for catching, transporting, preserving, and cooking it. Every type of fish has its market. Thus, according to Scappi, the eels at Comacchio are "better than in any other part of Lombardy. These are preserved in salt and brought to all parts of Italy."[42] Descriptive details concerning the nature of food products, where they are sold, and how they taste are accumulated over time, enriching the recipe collections with an encyclopedic knowledge that has become the common heritage of the entire gastronomic community. Discernment too is part of the recipe collection: "Peas are very tasty when they are tender, and when dry they are practically of no use whatever," says Corrado, who also states that "the true season for young chickens is summertime, as they are then very pleasing to the taste, tender and delicate." "Tomatoes, too, are very tasty," and it is a pleasure to observe them so red and plump, peeled and seeded, stuffed and fried.[43]

The recipe is thus subjectively prescriptive. We would be mistaken to think that modesty obliges the cook to hide his personality behind his words. Just as portraits reveal the author's pride and ambition, the texts of the recipes similarly allow his experience to shine through. Scappi writes: "At the Milan fish market I saw different kinds of very small fish, where they are known as *pescherie*."[44] His *Opera* is full of such memories, even if there is no better way to authenticate an experience than to declare it to be public knowledge. This is also Corrado's attitude. He recommends "tender and flavorful cardoons from the Salento peninsula" and broad beans of the kind "much used by poorer people, who consider them the second most important form of cereals." A native of Oria in the province of Salento, Corrado makes this comment in a tone of feigned detachment.[45]

The style of the cookbook may be personal, pedantic, or witty. Since the recipe presupposes a contract according to which the correct execution of the actions described will lead to a given result, its secret lies primarily in the art of communication. Nothing suggests that this art is unique to recent times. Certainly with the emergence of a female market for recipe collections in the course of the nineteenth century, there was a change in the language and even the identity of those who wrote such books. A sense of familiarity now begins to prevail at the expense of the professional tone of the traditional recipe collections. Eventually, as the woman of the house took over all the functions previously assigned to domestic personnel, the tone becomes direct and intimate. The writing loses its didactic edge, inviting the complicity of its female readers with nontechnical language. More and more frequently there is discussion of cost, cooking times, cleanliness, and equipment, such as stoves and sorbet makers. Artusi's great talent was in finding the right tone: polite but at the same time inclined toward personal digressions, autobiographical anecdotes, and jokes.

An important problem in culinary criticism is the issue of a recipe's authenticity. Given the anonymous aspect of cookbooks and their nature as compilations, we may wonder to what extent the recipes contained in them have been adapted from earlier texts. In addition, the status of writing with respect to printing has changed over time, and we have inherited a body of unpublished texts dedicated to household management and professional practice on which only partial research has been carried out. From the outset, Italian culinary writers habitually translated or incorporated elements from other culinary cultures. There was nothing scandalous about this, as repetition assured success and legitimacy. When we consider the possibility of compiling a chronological list of "original" recipes, however, we must establish some basic distinctions. Evidence of contact with other cultures, as in the use of American products, is easy to discern. We know that Antonio Latini transcribed a recipe for "tomato sauce, Spanish style" in Naples in 1692,[46] thus becoming the first cook in Europe to offer instruction on cooking tomatoes. It is more difficult to date the creation of other dishes. Il cuoco piemontese perfezionato a Parigi, written in 1766, translates a recipe for "soufflé" from La cuisinière bourgeoise, but with a different understanding of the term than the one subsequently adopted, since at that time soufflés were synonymous with beignets.[47] In the case of other preparations it is impossible to establish a clear date of origin. "Salsa verde" not only appears in all collections from the Liber de coquina onward, but it is possible to date it further back when we consider the "ius viride in avibus" (green sauce for fowl) in Apicius.[48]

Perhaps the earliest appearance of a recipe in writing is not the most significant occurrence (for, as occurs in lexicography, it may be exposed to continuous modification); but, its faithful reproduction in other texts. Cases involving the entire recopying of a collection written by a previous author are not unknown, as we have seen in the case of Giovanni de' Rosselli, who plagiarized Martino's Libro de arte coquinaria and published it with the new title Epulario in 1516. Here, however, the organization of the material differs from the original, which places Lenten fare at the end and concludes with fish. Each small change is important even if it does not alter the overall didactic picture. Imperfect citations are perhaps more interesting than examples of plagiarism or editorial strategies such as new titles, cuts, or the addition of recipes. These citations involve the incorporation of single recipes into a collection without mention of an author. Perfectly legitimate in household notebooks, this practice enables us to learn about domestic customs and values. When we realize that Don Felice Libera, a priest from the Trentino region, offers a recipe for "rice soup and tomato" which he copied from Nebbia's *Il cuoco maceratese*, this is mainly of interest to us because of the distance between the Trentino and Macerata, thus allowing us to hypothesize the use of tomatoes in the Alpine region in the late 1700s.[49] The translation of entire manuals with altered titles and the omission of the author's name is linked to this phenomenon. We must point out, however, that what appears on the frontispiece of a collection such as *Il cuoco piemontese perfezionato a Parigi* is not the source from which it is translated, Menon's *La cuisinière bourgeoise*, but the gastronomic model that provided its inspiration.

This is only a short step away from regarding the author of a cookbook as someone who collects recipes from different sources discovered along the way, which he has observed or heard, committed to writing, and eventually published. Artusi in fact consciously makes this assumption. Wishing to illustrate not just the cuisine of his own region but that of Italians in general—or at least a significant number of them—he exploited the initial success of *La scienza in cucina* by adding recipes sent to him by readers from all over Italy to later editions. He acknowledges his practice of borrowing from others but out of discretion does not always name his correspondent: "For this pasta [macaroni with sardines, Sicilian style] I am indebted to a very clever widow whose husband, of Sicilian origin, used to amuse himself by experimenting with certain dishes from his native region, including hake, Palermo style, and sliced, poached fish."[50] This is an especially complicated case of transmission, since the woman first learned the recipe from her husband and later, after his death, passed it on to Artusi, the culinary expert. Yet its success did not end here. Without citing Artusi, Agnetti reprinted it in *La nuova cucina delle specialità regionali* (New cuisine of regional specialties [1909]), in a chapter devoted to Sicily. Recipes also traveled by mail and through newspapers and magazines, covering huge distances, attaining a new layer of authenticity at every step. Macaroni dishes "took off from the station in Naples either in a lovely first-class carriage or in third class, or happily boarded one of the steamers in the beautiful Bay of Naples, traveling to the four corners of the earth."[51] Where will they end up? A collection printed in Hong Kong at the end of the 1930s, with facing-page text in English and Chinese, presents a recipe for "macaroni *à la Napolitaine*" in a chapter devoted to "Savories." After boiling for twenty minutes, the pasta is cut into strips and flavored with butter, tomatoes, mushrooms, and cooked ham.[52]

We might well wonder where this recipe was adopted on its way to Hong Kong. But research on the trade routes traveled by pasta has not yet begun.

The Menu

The first problem posed by the menu is a terminological one. In ancient times the list of dishes planned for a meal bore the title "lunch," "dinner," "*merenda*" (light refreshment), or "supper," followed by the date and the list of foods. The term "*minuta*," from which the contemporary Italian word "*menù*" derives, was borrowed from the French and appeared in Corrado's work at the end of the eighteenth century. It reappeared in the work of Cavalcanti, also from the Neapolitan region, and its use then spread throughout Italy. The Italian term triumphed in the 1800s but began to fall into disrepute in the early twentieth century, when purists preferred to use "*lista*" (list) or "*nota*" (note). "*Menù*" made a comeback—along with the term "*carta*," used in restaurants—after the end of World War II and was destined to stay.

There are two kinds of menus, those recorded in recipe collections and more rarely in nondidactic texts and the "free-standing" menu, which is handwritten or printed on a card and distributed individually to diners on the occasion of a special meal. Menus of the first kind are found in sixteenth-century treatises, and they have continued without interruption up to this day. Individual menus are more recent, as they have been recorded in paper format only since the start of the nineteenth century. The menu used in restaurants derives from the second type. It became established in Italy through its use in the hotel industry, which was organized along the lines of the French model.

Aristocratic households of the sixteenth century offered banquets to celebrate a wide variety of occasions, and hence the typology of the menu seems complex. In its most sumptuous version it is part of the organizational apparatus for a great festivity. On May 30, 1529, Messisbugo was commissioned to prepare a fish supper for Cardinal Ippolito d'Este, one of the fourteen banquets cited in his book. Having begun his account with the list of illustrious guests and a description of the decorations, Messisbugo inserts the meal into a sequence of festivities. More than 140 different dishes are listed, constituting several courses, each accompanied by a number of serving platters on which the food is displayed. The intervals between courses provide the occasion for musical interludes, songs, or amusing sketches. Over thirty different types of fish are presented, but there is no mention of drinks, which were the domain of the wine steward. This is an example of the menu as a project, of a type more elaborate than others, organized into seventeen "*vivande*," or rounds of service, with eight dishes apiece, ending with cheese, fresh fruit, glazed fruit, and fruit marinated in syrup.

In the absence of ceremonial occasions and the need to do honor to distinguished guests, there are menus that stewards can use as basic models, adapting them to the requirements of specific circumstances. A large part of the menus recorded by Scappi belong to this category. Each bears a date. There is a menu for every day of the year, taking into account the demands of the season and the requirements of religious observance, including the appropriate fare for fast days and meat days. Lunches and dinners are also noted, with their respective types of service, and a distinction is made between pantry courses (cold foods) and kitchen courses (hot foods). Along with the single titles there are notes of a clearly organizational type, indicating the number and duties of the personnel in charge, as well as the number of platters and the quantities required for each course. These details, which enable the reader to calculate the quantity and destination of the necessary tasks, can be ignored or left to the discretion of the steward, as Romoli suggests, reducing or increasing the number of courses and offering an "evening collation" composed of only six dishes. Other authors, such as Crisci, simplify the organization into three phases: cold, hot, and fruit dishes, each assigned to the charge of a specific employee.

As these codifications vary from one author to the next, we recognize that the menu is essentially a professional document, created by practitioners in consultation with the master of the household, an instrument for calculating what is required in the larder as well as the work carried out the kitchen. "When the Master wishes to host a banquet, the steward must learn from his Lordship, or from his superiors, the appropriate instructions and intentions regarding what has to be done for the guests, how many dishes should be served, and in what order. And the butler must be informed of all of this, along with the bursar and the cook."[53] The function of the list that "the steward must draw up for his collaborators" is to provide a memorandum showing approximate costs and the amount of work involved, while taking into account that the variety of the dishes served on a particular occasion should not be decided on the basis of a single day but in the context of the entire week to which reference is made.

Rossetti, who identifies himself as the steward of Lucretia d'Este, describes his experiences in detail: "When I began to perform the offices of the steward, I would write out on Saturdays the meals and dinners for the entire week that followed, varying things as much as possible, and then during the week I had a better memory of what I had proposed to do."[54] This was a general plan, adapted from day to day, for a variable number of guests. The precise number of diners is not stated, but it is suggested by some factors that indicate the general size of the banquet (such as the quantities of serving dishes or the number of tables to be installed). Having established the picture, the steward would check the master book in the pantry and the bursar's register showing prices and purchases. "Three dishes of six roast partridges garnished with slices of citron": the fowl would then be procured for the following day and placed in the hands of the cooks. In the kitchen, at the moment of serving the food, a banquet organizer

Portrait of Ada Boni by her husband, Enrico Boni.

Source: *La cucina romana* (Rome, 1929).

would read a list of the dishes to be brought to the table. The menu was born from this dual-purpose text, which was created as a plan to be followed and later used as a list that could be checked as the work was completed. Hence books without recipes, such as Rossetti's in Ferrara and Crisci's in Naples, were published to help stewards with their responsibilities, serving both as practical memoranda and records of accomplishment.

This approach to organizing the meals of aristocrats and prelates lasted until the nineteenth century. French influence changed these rituals very little. New

names were given to the courses served, thus restructuring them into a progression of soups, terrines, hors d'oeuvres, entrées, and relevés, as indicated on the
menus. Yet this did not alter the function of a book such as Corrado's *Il cuoco
galante*, written in the eighteenth century, which divides the banquet into two
"setups" with a total of sixty-eight dishes. The only variant is that the dishes are
now listed in numerical order, bearing witness to a progression of taste. This ritual survived up to the first half of the following century, with a gradual shift from
French service to what was called "Russian" service.[55] Giovanni Vialardi, identifying himself as the assistant head cook in the household of Carlo Alberto and
Victor Emmanuel II, prescribes a sequence of twenty dishes with corresponding
wines and seven more dessert dishes (cheese, sorbets, fruits, and so forth) with a
matching number of wines but presented in two phases of service, as was customary in France. The author indicates the number of place settings and the
progression of the dishes, noting that "each guest will have his menu written in
clear lettering, which he will consult for the order of service."[56] In this case the
menu had a dual purpose: a handwritten text was considered sufficient for those
preparing and serving the food, while the diners required the printed version.
For the first group the menu functioned rather like a musical score, while for
the second it provided some information on the program.

In the newly created Kingdom of Italy there were signs of diversification in
the menus composed for various occasions among different classes. While the
menu had once indicated the order of the dishes served at a banquet, it now
became a plan for weekday and holiday dining. The domestic recipe collection
and the household notebook record a gradual range of possibilities with regard
to size. We thus find menus for feast days, Sundays, working days, for a single
day, for dinner, for supper, for lunch, for the midday meal. Two rules seem to
prevail: on the one hand a series of dishes increasing in number according to the
circumstances and on the other a basic level that cannot be reduced. In the
everyday menus, whether printed or handwritten, the difference is scarcely
noticeable. Taking the four courses suggested by Dubini—soup, one or two
meats, or one meat and a cooked side dish, and dessert[57]—the domestic record
of a well-to-do Turinese family coincides with these numbers with regard to the
evening meal but differs at lunch, where only two courses, pasta and meat with
a side dish, are served. In such cases, fruit (which does not require work) is omitted. The domestic cook scribbles down some notes each morning that function
as a list of items to be bought at the market—items for lunch, for dinner, and for
the days that follow—indicating the number of guests that might be expected.
The detail of which dishes are served is repeated orally at table, in response to
the question "What are we having today?" and only on extraordinary occasions
is the menu written down.

The introduction of the menu printed on paper or cardboard functioned as
a call to order, as a plea for good manners within the context of an increasingly

informal style of domestic living. The written menu made its appearance between 1820 and 1835, and its presence is documented predominantly in royal households and at state banquets.[58] We can offer some hypotheses to explain its eventual success as well as its absence before the triumph of bourgeois cuisine. In the Este household where Messisbugo served, a course of ten dishes displayed simultaneously on the table was a marvel in itself. In the course of the meal this display was destined to be repeated five to ten times, in different ways on each occasion, and included the spectacle of sugar figurines and pies cut open to release live birds. Whatever information was given in advance spoiled the surprise effect. At the nineteenth-century meal, where the appetite had to be calibrated from one course to the next, or in a restaurant, where everything had to be ordered and paid for, the menu had an anticipatory character. It was thus transformed from a plan of work and service into the promise or the possibility of different dishes and courses. Once the prerogative of the cook and the steward, the menu now passes into the hands of the diner who must study it. The banquet menu becomes a lithographic text, with the names of dishes organized in a vertical column and embellished with images celebrating the household, the location or the occasion, or conjuring up the anticipated food with artistic illustrations. Now wines also appear on the menu, and, if a musical program is planned, so do the titles of the compositions to be performed.

Often the choice of language and the persons to whom the titles of the dishes allude cloak the culinary experience in an air of mystery. Rajberti complains about this, describing meals in great households where "every table setting is furnished with a list of dishes, two-thirds of them written in French and a third in English, since we are not even allowed to eat in Italian anymore."[59] But the situation is most extreme in restaurants, where only regular clients manage to understand what is going on without the need for assistance. *"Potage Nelson"* and *"consommé Sarah Bernhardt"* are listed at the beginning of a menu from the Grand Hotel in Florence in 1900, indicating, respectively, a broth made of beef fillet and ham and a broth made of chicken, asparagus tips, and champagne.[60] Such items intimidate the uninitiated and confuse the pleasure seeker, until the headwaiter resolves the mystery. Then the client consumes his cup of broth in a few spoonfuls and quickly forgets the title.

Unlike the recipe collection, which is a text that may be consulted in order to acquire competence or understanding, the menu is an official, bureaucratic, or commercial document. It is committed to writing on repeated occasions. In the domestic setting it can take the form of a memo dictated by the woman of the house and jotted down by the cook. It can be a printed card sent in an envelope to an invited guest or placed on the table beside his name card. In a hotel restaurant it can take the form of a note written by the headwaiter as he stands at a client's table, which is then conveyed to the kitchen staff, along with the name of the account to be settled at the end of the meal. What we see here is the repeated practice of recording, which confers solemnity on the appetite, anticipates its satisfaction, and sanctions well-being. Handwritten or printed, the menu is a typical nineteenth-century ritual to preserve the memory of the meal, transmitted from the aristocracy to the bourgeoisie. It is hardly an accident that on grand occasions, weddings, and anniversaries, it is obligatory. The multilingual restaurant menu divided into courses (as many as twelve in French haute cuisine)[61] is its modular, depersonalized development. Derived from this is the menu used in institutions such as the army, the navy, and maritime companies, which may take the form of a written announcement posted on general display. *Il cuciniere militare* describes the organization of food rations in the style and language of a modest restaurant, with its two set courses, both cooked, which are followed by fruit.[62] The menus used in the officers' mess by contrast show much greater evidence of gastronomic terminology.

We might well ask if menus printed on cards or paper are really necessary. The written menu has a quality that seems to run counter to many aspects of contemporary life. When used in the home it now seems a dated, obsolete way of welcoming diners to the dinner table, and its use has disappeared along with other customs, such as the place card. In restaurants by contrast the absence of a menu listing dishes and prices is unacceptable, suggesting a casual or even careless approach to business. In public everything must be written down and displayed in plain print, with illustrations provided for those who have difficulty reading or for foreigners who do not understand Italian. This is the outcome of mass literacy and an analytical consumer culture wedded to the idea of the right price. It marks the end of the tacit, personal contract. To appreciate fully the significance of the menus of the nobility or those used in the great hotels of the past we must forget for a moment their printed format and remember a phenomenon in our more recent past when, in modest country restaurants and taverns, everything was communicated by word of mouth, from the table to the kitchen, right down to the final request for payment. The proprietor had his recipes, implemented them as well as he could, and communicated them as needed. There was nothing to record in writing, except supplies and accounts, because the same dishes were offered repeatedly from one generation to the next, according to the availability of ingredients. If new dishes appeared, they too were based on ingredients that came from the vegetable garden or were purchased at the local market. The rural or bourgeois client got used to this informality. After listening briefly to what the proprietor had to say, he could ask for explanations. He could visit the kitchen, select his meal, and have it served. Nothing was written down in this setting, as the choice varied from day to day and might even be influenced by bad weather. Paolo Monelli sublimely summarizes an oral menu that was proposed, in local dialect, by the owner of a *trattoria* in Pescara: "Have a seat, and I'll take care of everything."[63]

CHAPTER SIX

The Vocabulary of Food

A Chronological Outline

Italy's culinary texts are written in at least three languages: Latin at the outset, French from the end of the seventeenth century onward, and Tuscan Italian, which is omnipresent, subject to change, and marked with inflections from regional dialects. In recipes, cookbooks, and menus, which provide most of the terminology, we can discern some indications of a linguistic chronology, reflecting for the most part the system of social and cultural exchange. Some of the didactic texts on culinary matters were written in Latin up to the middle of the fifteenth century, while the first book explicitly translated from French was La Varenne's *Il cuoco francese*, printed in Bologna in 1682. From then on the number of books that referred to a culinary experience in Paris increased significantly. So too did the importance of loan words used in the vocabulary of professional cooking, which developed into a thick web of Gallicisms. The power of the French language over culinary Italian did not begin to shift until after the end of World War II, when the influence between French and Italian cuisine became intensely reciprocal.

The writers of culinary texts adopted the Tuscan vernacular, along with regional variants, from the middle of the fifteenth century onward. This was a language common to the aristocratic courts of Italy, although it was also open to local and demotic influence, ultimately embracing terms of every provenance—including French and German—that designated ingredients, preparations, or culinary procedures. Even when servants and other personnel were unable to write, they spoke some Italian in addition to their local or native dialect. This Italian was easily conditioned by the whims and fashions of the nobility and was liable to change in response to stimuli from above or below. In the nineteenth century numerous recipe collections were titled or partially written in dialect, or they included individual recipes written in dialect. A similar pattern can be observed in a lively body of bacchic convivial texts, which undertook to revitalize the language of the hearth.

In sketching this broad outline we are not attempting to illustrate the development of a professional idiom that absorbed influences from far and near as it assimilated or adapted itself to different schools and culinary models (which were French throughout all the nineteenth and part of the twentieth centuries). Rather we wish to emphasize the open, malleable character of this language, characterized by a resistance to rules and spelling, that developed in the various sectors of hospitality, service, and dining customs, often in an irregular fashion. Precisely because of its changeable nature, despised by the literary class, the vocabulary of cooking seems indebted to the culture of servants, a tradition that is not always adequately represented in manuscripts and printed documents. The culinary idiom also reflects distinct roles, since the chef and the female domestic cook did not prepare the same dishes or describe their work in the same way. The chef used different registers of speech, similar to the language of those whose meals he provided, while the maid expressed herself in dialect, and the woman of the house functioned as her spokesperson. The language of the domestic sphere, the idiom used by women, is predominantly oral. At least until the era of compulsory schooling, this spoken language maintained a type of secret osmosis — and is therefore difficult to evaluate — with the elevated, professional language recorded in culinary texts. Ignored for a long time, the language of women has only recently been recognized in cooking manuals.

We must now add a more contemporary note to this brief outline. The attempts to impose order on the languages of cooking, particularly noteworthy after Italian unification, came to nothing. So too did the efforts of Fascist legislation to enforce a new policy of linguistic purity. Since the 1950s the Italian language has absorbed a new wave of influences from abroad, some French and some English. Yet this is hardly tantamount to foreign domination, since we can also discern a countervailing trend because of the increasing exportation of Italian skills, industrial products, ingredients, and dishes. Culinary Italian is used today in restaurants around the world, where it is colorfully emblazoned on signs and menus. The pizza—whatever its etymology—has reversed all previous biases and tendencies.

Latin

Until the seventeenth century and beyond, Latin was the educated language used by scientists writing about food. The *Liber ruralium commodorum* by Piero de' Crescenzi (1304–1309), which was translated into the vernacular between the fourteenth and the sixteenth centuries, is one example of a successful agronomical treatise composed in Latin. In the *Summa lacticiniorum* (1477), Pantaleone da Confienza, a physician, agronomist, and traveler, provides an account of his travels, written in Latin, in which he expounds on cheese-making procedures and their typologies in Italy and elsewhere in Europe. Understood by all well-educated individuals, this was the written language par excellence. Hence medical texts on nutrition were composed in Latin, at least to the end of the seventeenth century. Clearly, scientific terminology was conceived for the exclusive use of the educated classes, even if it was eventually absorbed on a broader scale and became intelligible to some degree to the unlettered population. The prescriptions written by members of the Salerno school were articulated in a rhythmic pattern using Latin words that were quite close to the Italian spoken by the people: "bona sunt ova candida, longa, nova" ("pale, large, fresh eggs are good").[1]

As was the case in other disciplines that called for a didactic literature, culinary texts were written in Latin up to the middle of the fifteenth century. This Latin was enriched by neologisms from the vernacular, which were assimilated into the system of classical grammar and syntax. It was described in Italian as *latinuccio* or *latinaccio* (coarse Latin) and in French as *latin de cuisine* or *latin rosty*. The oldest cookbook that has come down to us is the *Liber de coquina*, which was probably created for the Angevin court of Charles II in Naples around the end of the thirteenth century. In addition to international recipes — "Provençal, Teutonic, Gallic, and Hispanic" — the collection includes instructions for very modest tasks presumably delegated by the cook to the kitchen workers: "Recipe cicera et pone ad distemperandum per unam noctem in lexivio ben salsato. Mane autem, abluas bene cum aqua tepida" ("Take chickpeas, and steep them overnight in salt water. In the morning, wash them carefully with lukewarm water").[2] Latin allowed the writers to set down quick, authoritative precepts and instructions while paying attention to the simplest phases of preparation. In addition, some handwritten recipe collections composed in the vernacular, such as Maestro Martino's *Libro de arte coquinaria*, used Latin in their titles.

Latin and Italian are not used as alternatives, and neither do they seen to designate two hierarchical levels of speech and familiarity in cooking. Each is open to contamination from the other, providing stimulus for the work of translators. A recipe titled *"De la torta parmesana"* in the fourteenth-century *Libro della cucina*, by an anonymous Tuscan, begins with the following instruction: "Togli pulli smembrati e tagliati e friggili con le cipolle ben trite" ("Take dismembered, cut-up chickens, and fry them with finely chopped onions").[3] The Latin instruction in the original text, which is taken from the *Liber de coquina*, reads: "Ad tortam parmesanam recipe pullos bene depilatos et incisos vel demenbratos."[4] In the same manuscript we also find a recipe for green beans "as used in the *Marca trevigiana*": "Pone faseolos bullitos descacatos ad coquendum cum carnibus salsatis." These Latin instructions are translated into the vernacular, without much attention to grammar or the use of the article, by the anonymous Tuscan: "Metti fasoli bulliti, descaccati, a cocere con carne insalata" ("Cook trimmed, boiled beans along with salted meat"). It would be a mistake to regard Latin as a vehicular language that predated or was superior to the vernacular. Recipes written in

Latin and translated into Italian are placed side by side in the manuscript collections, but the Latin version is not presented as the refined, international version of the recipe.

The opposite phenomenon is not unusual: in *De honesta voluptate et valitudine* Platina, a humanist, translated passages from Maestro Martino's recipe collection into Latin, rendering Martino's vernacular in an elegant style that is also a model of erudite writing. The hierarchy of the two languages has an emblematic value here, without inhibiting other modes of expression. The dissemination of Maestro Martino's work did not end with the publication of *De honesta voluptate et valitudine.*[5] The *Libro de arte coquinaria* was plagiarized in Italian by Giovanni de' Rosselli in 1516. It was loosely translated into French and published in Lyons in 1505 with the title *Platine en français. Von der Eerlichen zimlichen, auch erlaubten Wolust*, a German translation, appeared in Augsburg in 1542. The transfer of recipes from one language to the other occurred not through precise translation but through a process of freely adapting or remolding a preexisting body of work. This practice is still the most common way of transmitting a recipe from one country to another, a fact that must be taken into account when evaluating the linguistic models used in recipes.

Terminology is another issue. Since similar terms were used in Italian and Latin, it was not necessary to make specific reference to one of the two languages in order to explain this or that operation: *raviolos*[6] is the Latinization of *ravioli*, closer to current usage than the variant *rafioli.*[7] Some terms, however, still seem obscure. When we find beans described as "*descaccati*" in the vernacular and "*descacatos*" in Latin, we are faced with the problem not of comparing the two terms but of determining their meaning—which is probably "shelled" or "removed from the pod."

Without going into the merits of a genre that would otherwise require analysis of a literary kind, we must acknowledge the existence of a body of writings in contemporary Latin (*latinuccio*) that could be described as mock-heroic, even before such writing became fashionable. In the work of Teofilo Folengo, alias Merlin Cocai, the vocabulary of *latinuccio* attains poetic dignity, enriched with a substratum of re-Latinized words from the Po Valley. This mock-heroic idiom does not so much enable us to measure the degree of hybridization of Latin and Italian as allow us to observe the influence exerted by dialects and the bastardization of classical culture in both these languages. Communication in Latin was not limited to early recipe collections and their ribald imitations, such as the "doctrinae cosinandi viginti," the twenty-two recipes found in Folengo's *Baldus.*[8] Latin also proved a durable vehicle for the composition of monographs and satirical pamphlets throughout Europe from the end of the sixteenth to the beginning of the seventeenth century, from *De re cibaria* by Bruyerin Campier (Lyons, 1560), a description of the panorama of French food, to *De naturali*

Frontispiece of Giovan Battista Crisci, *La lucerna de corteggiani*
(Naples: Domenico Roncagliolo, 1634).

vinorum historia by Andrea Bacci (1596), a vast encyclopedia of wines, to the *Tractatus de butyro* by the Dutchman Martin Schookius (Groningen, 1664), which is devoted to a single product, butter. In such cases we are dealing with a linguistic code that was reformulated along humanistic lines and addressed to an erudite audience. It is very different from the modest if not uncultured language used in the recipes. The custom of writing Latin poetry in the classical style with didactic and scholastic ambitions is another important thread visible in documents from the seventeenth century. The short Latin poems composed by the Abbot Gaetano Buganza on milk, coffee, and cucumbers fully belong to the historiography of food products.[9]

Finally, we must not forget an aspect of modern Latin literature that has special historical relevance. The food preferences and dining habits of ancient Rome, studied by publishers and learned men, provide early historical evidence of gastronomy, circumscribed by antiquity. This is the focus of *De triclinio romano* by Ciacconius and Fulvio Orsini.[10] It is also the topic of *De conviviis antiquorum* by Andrea Bacci, a sequel to the book on wines written by the same author, where he compares the eccentricities of the pagan world to Christian, ecclesiastical culture. Contemporary Rome was the focus of similarly vivid interest from other perspectives. *De victu romanorum* by Alessandro Petronio (1581)—translated into Italian eleven years after its initial publication in Latin as *De viver delli romani* (On the life of the Romans)—is an investigation into the environmental, dietary, and health conditions in the city.[11] With citations from classical texts and philological analyses, these scholars attempt to reconstruct all aspects of everyday life in antiquity, and, persuaded of the continuity of some basic paradigms, especially in medicine and nutrition, they proceed to compare foods and rituals. Despite their use of time-honored sources and their methodical examination of letters, laws, and memories, what we discern here is not just a historical interest but also a religious, apologetic intent (the Christian supper) and a myth: that of the unsurpassed magnificence and extravagance of a banquet that offered flamingo tongues, crests torn from live roosters, and camels' heels.[12] The level of awe and indignation implicit in the humanist reaction to antiquity is still evident in several academic texts and dissertations written years later, among which the most famous example in Italian is *Del vitto e delle cene degli antichi* (On the food and meals of the ancients) by Giuseppe Averani, published posthumously in 1761.

Rather than exerting a concrete influence on research, other writings played a purely symbolic role. This was true of Apicius's *De re coquinaria*, which, though printed in Milan in 1498 and later reprinted in Venice, was apparently unknown to Ciacconius and Bacci. Yet these writers focus on Apicius as a pretext for their reflection on the diversity of culinary models down through the ages and on the changing relationships among food, taste, wealth, and civilization. Apicius was a highly respected figure, widely recognized though rarely

read, and his name was periodically resurrected in Italian culinary writing simply to celebrate the founders of a splendid art and a didactic literary genre.

The Vernacular

In France, Germany, and England the dissemination of recipe collections in the
vernacular can be uniformly documented in the second half of the fourteenth
century. Some manuscripts in circulation were attributed to a cook (*Le viandier*,
by Taillevent),[13] while others were presented as household notebooks (*Buoch
von guoter speise*, from Wurtzburg).[14] Tuscan prevails in the recipe books produced in Italy during the same period, with some exceptions, including the
Libro per cuoco, transcribed if not composed in Venetian.[15] The *Libro de arte
coquinaria* is the first authored cookbook conceived in what was to become the
learned language of didactic texts. This is the work of Maestro Martino of
Ticino, who lived in Rome around the middle of the fifteenth century. Compared to earlier manuscripts in both Latin and the vernacular, Martino's recipes
are strikingly original, as are his use of elaborate terminology and his descriptions of products, cooking procedures, decoration, presentation, and service.
Along with well-known ingredients mentioned in the recipe titles (vegetables,
meats, and fish), there is no lack of original culinary terms: *zanzarelli*, for example, which is made from a mixture of eggs, cheese and grated bread, shaped into
"morsels," and cooked in broth.[16] Examples of the international code also
appear here, with *mirrause catalano* and the *biancomangiare* that we find in
medieval recipes written in French (*blanc manger*), German (*blamensir*), and
English (blank manger, blomanger). The writer's use of verbs (indicating culinary procedures) is especially indicative of his assured command of vocabulary,
describing various methods of cooking in their different phases as well as the
mixtures obtained by blending (*distemparando*) and incorporating (*incorpo-
rando*) various ingredients.

Maestro Martino's intellectual counterpart was Bartolomeo Sacchi, also
known as Platina, who probably wrote his *De honesta voluptate* sometime
around 1470.[17] (Platina pays close attention to Martino's creations, as when he
mentions "*zanzarelle*.") Many have suggested that this work was in fact composed by two individuals, one a cook and the other a humanist.[18] This kind of
partnership, wherein the cook would dictate his experience to an educated
scribe, often resulted in some degree of success. Alternatively, in the course of
his career a cook might acquire a level of fame, distinction, and prestige that
would allow him to sign with credibility the work sent to the printer. The roles
of those responsible for the prince's dining needs were varied, and their education was generally uneven. Stewards and carvers, who were in direct contact
with their noble masters, might even be endowed with noble titles (Messisbugo
was a Palatine count and Latini would become a "count of the Golden Spur").

There was a hierarchy among cooks, and Scappi signed himself "*cuoco segreto,*" the "secret," or private, cook of Pope Pius V. We know little of the actual transcription of their texts, since a recipe collection down to this day eludes certifiable proof of literary paternity.

The sixteenth-century cookbook incorporated two different forms of expertise: that of the cook and that of the employee in charge of the food and dining protocols of the prince or pope. It also implied the collaboration of an individual who could record the recipes on site, as well as the assistance of a learned man capable of preparing the text for printing. The organization of the material had to take into account different levels of service, market sectors, religious requirements (for fast days and meat days), dietary rules, and internal distinctions. Menus and banquet reports were coordinated with the recipes. Here the names of dishes have a special status. Since they are used in the kitchens and at the banquet table, they belong to the terminology characteristic of both service and consumption. There is a rich variety in the titles used in the sixteenth century. In Scappi's *Opera* the prescriptive model prevails for recipes ("to make dried-pea soup") and the descriptive model for menus ("pea soup with sturgeon belly"), organized according to ingredients and condiments ("cooked artichokes served with salt and pepper"), methods of preparation ("fritters"), types of cooking ("fried saltwater fish served with sliced limes"), utensils ("to cook sardines on the grill"), and so on. In summarizing the recipe the menu mentions its characteristics. It thus provides information to both preparers and consumers. A dish could be attributed to a particular culinary tradition ("French style" or "Milanese style") or might indicate the provenance of the ingredients ("Parmesan cheese," i.e., from Parma). Unlike late-nineteenth-century usage, in Scappi's work recipes are almost never dedicated to anyone, nor are the names of the cook and steward attributed to a dish. What is important is the desire to clarify the nature of the object consumed ("To roast an India hen or rooster, which in some parts of Italy are called Indian peacocks").[19]

In addition to providing a repertory of dishes and menus (which is the sole objective of works such as Rossetti's *Dello scalco*),[20] the recipe collection offers a compendium of linguistic and lexicographical knowledge. It provides definitions of food products ("Pike is a well-known fish, with a long, round shape and with a row of sharp teeth in its mouth. The large ones are mostly caught in lakes such as Perugia, Bolsena, and Vico"),[21] the appropriate terms for specific cuts ("take the loin with some of its fat") and cooking methods ("Heat the pan and, when it is quite hot, grease it with a pork rind"), and a list of instruments for cooking and serving food, sometimes accompanied by illustrations. The practice of consulting a doctor and formulating diets for convalescents and the sick ultimately makes the cook's mission a delicate one, which he embraces knowing not only that he is doing good work but that he is able to make suffering less painful. Thanks to Scappi, the recipe collection is no longer merely a memorandum used in food preparation but becomes an encyclopedia of nutritional knowledge.

We might well ask to what extent the emerging field of lexicographical research acknowledged this genre of didactic writing, which was especially prevalent in the second half of the sixteenth century. The first edition of the Crusca dictionary, published in 1612, clearly indicates how scholars kept their distance from culinary terminology. If we search the dictionary for procedures that Scappi describes in a simple way, such as the preparation of eggs, we find that it fails to acknowledge the existence of *uova barbagliate* or *uova affrittellate*. Even *frittata* is absent, either because the most commonplace words seem irrelevant outside the context of their usage or because the Crusca will see fit to include them only after they have been accepted by poets or narrative writers. The term *maccheroni* makes an appearance, since it can be traced to Boccaccio, but *gnocchi* is excluded, even though the two terms were sometimes used synonymously, if we are to judge by the title of one of Scappi's recipes: "To make a soup of *maccaroni*, otherwise known as *gnocchi*."[22] Leaving aside the Crusca, when we consult bilingual dictionaries of the period we also search in vain. Pierre Canal's *Dictionnaire françois et italien*, published in 1598, includes both gnocchi and *pappardelle*, but the first is translated as *macarons*, and the second is defined as "a type of food made with dough."[23] Though the compilers of foreign-language dictionaries acknowledged many more words from the spoken idiom, their definitions and translations were nonetheless imperfect. This terminology—for the most part orally codified and transmitted by semiliterate practitioners to men who could write and by palace authorities to scholars—thus received little attention from members of associations such as the Accademia della Crusca, who privileged fine writing and found the compilers of bilingual dictionaries lacking in expertise and hardly aware of their existence.

Lexicographical resistance to all types of professional jargon is typical of the Italian cultural tradition, reflecting the fact that the nobility linked the culture of food to the servant class. It also suggests a lack of interest on the part of the literary class in the mechanical arts and in domestic life in general. Even the body of culinary terms included in the *Grande dizionario della lingua italiana* edited by Salvatore Battaglia is limited to those provided in an anthology of texts compiled by Emilio Faccioli.[24] Certainly, Torquato Tasso's *Il padre di famiglia* is included here. We also find the complete text of Artusi's *La scienza in cucina*, though we cannot avoid the suspicion that its inclusion is linked to the author's neopurist agenda, which we will discuss below. At the same time the dictionary excludes both the terms that the stewards had borrowed from the international linguistic code and the Gallicized vocabulary used in the eighteenth century.

Recipe collections have become the subject of productive scholarly research only in the past twenty years. An examination of Cristoforo Messisbugo's vocabulary has allowed us not only to date many culinary terms back to 1549 but also to evaluate some of their basic traits: the use of Tuscan imposed by the courts and the publishing industry and uniformly adopted by all authors and the persistence of a certain number of foreign terms, among which those of French origin prevail, and a significant number of dialect words. Written in the authoritative Tuscan vernacular, though receptive to loanwords, Messisbugo's *Banchetti, compositioni di vivande et apparecchio generale* (Banquets, preparation of dishes, and general presentation) was unquestionably one of the principal works to contribute to the birth of professional culinary terminology.[25]

Recipe collections are not, however, the only linguistic source that languished in oblivion for several years before being rediscovered. Ribald literature, which incorporates abundant eating terms, was cautiously incorporated into the Crusca dictionary in 1612. Giulio Landi's *Formaggiata di sere Stentato*, which consists of satirical chapters on every kind of food capable of generating bawdy, salacious double meanings—as was the case with carrots, figs, and sausages[26]—fully belongs to literary writing, as does Ortensio Lando's *Commentario delle più notabili e mostruose cose d'Italia*, an extraordinary review of characteristic food products and local or regional dishes. The proliferation of mock-improvised poems and impertinent hymns of praise represents the other linguistically creative sector of sixteenth-century culinary literature. Here we find an aspect of food that is often ignored by the recipe collections: its consumption. These texts are omnivorous in their appropriation of the full range of gastronomical and geographical specialties, assigning a term to every product and permitting us to compare—in a discussion of preserved or cured foods—the qualities of cheeses and cured meats.[27] Taste is powerfully expressive. This is especially true when it is interpreted by those who describe the physical quality of foods, who evaluate flavor or the effect of a dish and its reception. The best interpreters, or culinary "judges," are in fact those who by virtue of their talent for writing were invited to the prince's dinner table.

Erudite men who loved to eat were not in short supply, men who assigned a grammar to flavors and praised the skill of cooks and stewards as embodied in the cuisine. The belief that the most noteworthy of these culinary practitioners—at the courts of Ferrara, Rome, and Mantua—had scant cultural preparation is belied by their writings, which, though clearly revised and corrected, required extensive knowledge of the marketplace, familiarity with the ceremonies of the court, and a keen awareness of appetites. *L'arte di ben cucinare* by Bartolomeo Stefani, a Bolognese cook in the service of the Gonzaga household in Mantua, would also prove that an elegant dedication and the display of refined wisdom in the instruction of head cooks were advantageous. Stefani possessed a fine, personal command of rhetoric, or at least he had a collaborator of high station. His presentation of his "theses on messy philosophy" to the "Most Illustrious and Excellent Lords" is worthy of a man of letters, as is his research on the best ingredients, with calendar and map in hand. His catalog of the best things in Italy rivals that of Ortensio Lando, or rather it reformulates it from a perspective that is no longer that of the curious traveler but of a person with memory, good taste, a large team of servants, and access to the purse of an affluent prince.

Did two centuries of recipes, from Maestro Martino to Stefani, leave Italian cooking with an established, long-lasting style of communication? The reply can only be uncertain. Without adequate lexicographical acknowledgment and without institutional recognition, the refined language of Scappi and Stefani, regarded merely as a reflection of courtly life, remained a fragile voice, destined at best to be copied by a few ambitious head cooks. Despite borrowings and adaptations, this language did not exert influence outside Italy, and neither was it translated even in France, where between 1570 and 1650 no new cookbooks appeared on the local scene. If we turn the terms of the problem around and impute the decadence of this genre (didactic culinary texts) to culinary models that originated in the world of banquets and feasts, the result is still the same: a body of work without parallel in Europe had no heirs after the publication of Stefani's *L'arte di ben cucinare*. Decades of silence ensued, broken only by modest translations of minor scope. Clearly, the vocabulary of the pantry, of cooking and baking, along with the description of culinary procedures and garnishing, continued to be understood and used, but changes occurred in the overall scheme of things and hence in the composition of dishes. We note the increasingly frequent inclusion of foreign terms and the acceptance of the teachings of the French canon, which, having prevailed among the diners, were now imposed on the most intelligent members of the cooking staff.

Franco-Italian

Thirteen reprintings of La Varenne's *Il cuoco francese* were published between 1682 and 1826 and eight of François Massialot's *Cuoco reale e cittadino* between 1724 and 1791. *Il cuoco piemontese perfezionato a Parigi* enjoyed even more widespread success, with twenty-three editions in Turin, Milan, Florence, and Venice between 1766 and 1855. The longest interval between any two translations was nine years. Contrary to the implications of its title, this last book is not an account of a cook's apprenticeship in Piedmont and his subsequent experience north of the Alps but a compilation "for the most part taken from Menon's *La cuisinière bourgeoise*."[28]

Italy's last great recipe collection was that of Antonio Latini. After 1694 the invasion of foreign texts began, imported in the original language and in translation. In addition, Italy's publishing centers, which used to be Mantua, Bologna, Rome, and Naples in the seventeenth century, shifted for the most part to Piedmont and would remain there throughout the subsequent centuries. The fact that there were only two German editions of Massialot's work, along with the

Parisische Kuchemeister, inspired by La Varenne and published in 1667, suggests that that the invasion of foreign texts was a specifically Italian phenomenon.[29]

What is visible here is not merely a sense of curiosity vis-à-vis Versailles, which was manifest in much of Europe from the first half of the eighteenth century onward, but a profound change in culinary Italian, evidenced in the use of translations and neologisms. A comparison between Latini's *Lo scalco alla moderna*, published in Naples between 1692 and 1694, and La Varenne's *Il cuoco francese*, printed in Bologna in 1682 and 1693, is instructive. Onion soup and rice soup become *potacchio con le cipolle* and *potacchio di riso*, respectively, signaling the success of a term derived from French (*potage*) and used by Scappi in the variant *pottaggio*. Similarly, *bisca* (from *bisque*) appears for the first time in La Varenne's text, where it is also described as *potacchio alla francese*. The titles of dishes show early evidence of this phenomenon: these names, used in the preparation and serving of food, seem, when heard by the diner, the first clear, indispensable sign of a new fashion. Incongruities arise as typical dishes, or those thought to be typical in France, are attributed to a geographical "origin": "*les caillebottes de Bretagne*" become "*rappreso di Brettagna*." Titles are doubled or extended in cases when the Italianized version fails to render a term intelligible, hence we find "*rissole specie di tortelli*" ("*rissoles*, a type of *tortelli*").[30]

Entries with foreign titles begin to make an appearance with the publication of *Il cuoco piemontese perfezionato a Parigi*. Here, of the thirty-one recipes dedicated to beef, twelve have titles containing French terms relating to types of preparation and cooking. Another title includes a term adapted from French: *carbonata o costa di bue in papigliote*. "*In papigliote*" is selected in imitation of the French *en papillotte* rather than the Italian designation *al cartoccio* to signify cooking the meat in a paper wrap. There is also one term derived from English (*beest steks a l'inglese*). The infiltration of foreign terms is even more noticeable within individual recipes, where, for example, *scaglono* (shallot) is replaced by *échalotte*. In menus and instructions for serving we find references to *entrées*, *hors d'oeuvre*, and *assiette* (a noun, erroneously transcribed in the singular, that designates the little dishes of *biscottini* and dried fruit served at the end of the meal). Repeated from one cookbook to the next, these loan words constitute a hybrid terminology that privileges bilingualism or, to put it differently, presents us with a trilingual lexicon of Italian, French, and Franco-Italian elements, transcribed freely and phonetically, with broad variations in spelling. With the publication of *L'Apicio moderno* in 1790 one could say that the Gallicization of culinary terminology was complete, even in texts written in Italian.

Born in Rome, Francesco Leonardi spent his novitiate in Paris in the kitchen of the maréchal de Richelieu before moving to Naples, where he worked for the prince of Francavilla ("all French cooking"). He then became the steward of Prince Orlov in St. Petersburg and was later appointed the chief cook of Catherine II.[31] Though he developed his career far from Rome and even from Paris, Leonardi's work clearly reflects the dominance of the French model. This provided him with a terminology that had international currency but did not prevent him—a native of Rome—from attaining fame and originality. At the beginning of the first volume he describes with the flair of an alchemist the broths that constitute the foundation of all sauces, listing "brodo generale, suage, consomè, biondo di Mongana, restoran, tablette, sugo, culì, essenza." Six of the nine terms come from French, and two are written correctly—*suage* and *tablette*—while the others are approximated. Leonardi prefers the phonetic transcription of foreign terms over the original spelling, which is impracticable for servants: "Regarding the names of dishes, soups, sauces, or other things, it is impossible to change them. Their original titles in Italian, French, or the language of another nation should be maintained. I believe that I was doing this by using French words, though in the Italian spelling. My aim is to make them understandable to those who do not know [French], for they will be amazed to find the words spelled the way they are pronounced and not as they are [usually] written" (p. xii).

Clumsy spelling, awkward accents, and phonetic Italicizations render the French spoken by the head cook a macaronic, high-flown idiom, difficult to learn and even more difficult to retain. For this reason, at the beginning of *L'Apicio moderno*, before the recipes, Leonardi offers an "explanation of some French and Italian cooking terms that the author used in the composition of this book." We will cite some of these, in the order in which they appear, to convey a clearer sense of the issue: *passare sul fuoco* (meaning in this case to fry); *gratinare* (to grate); *legare* (to bind, as in thickening a sauce); *liason* (for liaison, or binding); *mittonare* (steep or boil); *carne rosolata* (browned meat); *fior di latte* (fresh mozzarella today, but this may not have been the meaning then); *teste d'arancio* (orange slices); *coperte* (silverware); and so on (p. lxi). This type of jargon prevailed in elegant restaurants up to the end of the nineteenth century.

The first effect of this fashion, which undermines culinary conventions and terminology, was to accentuate the distance between creative cuisine and the food served in taverns or modest family homes in the provinces. The existence of two irreconcilable registers, high and low, luxurious and modest, international and vernacular, became customary, and those who practiced a style of cooking impervious to the novelties arriving from France were considered to live in the backwaters. The use of domestic notebooks, which recorded personal secrets, dishes, and preparations, was a spontaneous reaction to this state of things. A modest publishing industry dedicated to bringing out texts on domestic cooking thus established itself with some success from the early nineteenth century onward. *La cucina casereccia* (Home cooking), printed twenty-five times between 1807 and 1885 in Naples, Milan, and Palermo, is written in the version of Italian spoken in Naples, clearly distinct from both Tuscan and dialect usage. The author's most pressing concern is to ward off the condemnation of potential purists: "If, in my use of nomenclature and cooking instructions, I happened to use words that are different from those provided by our vernacular, I would have put those wishing to take advantage of my work to the trouble of using an interpreter or frequently consulting the Crusca dictionary."[32] We find some Gallicisms (*gattò* for *gâteau*, *bignè* for *beignet*, and *ragù* for *ragoût*)—though there are no terms transcribed directly in French—along with titles of dishes from Naples and Lombardy and a few from other Italian states (fritters and Roman-style *pappardelle*, as well as Genoese cockle soup). Naples was the principal city where aristocratic dining flourished, in both its French and Neapolitan versions, and where popular cooking was practiced in all its variations, in private homes and on the streets. It was also the place where the best dishes from all parts of Italy, including those from another prestigious city, Milan, were reformulated.

In *La cucina teorico-pratica* (Theoretical-practical cooking) by Ippolito Cavalcanti, duke of Buonvicino, we observe a high-flown, hybridized linguistic style that assimilates different jargons, rewriting French phonetically in Italian, rather similar to the orthographic reform promoted by Leonardi and adopted by cookbook authors (*orduvre* for *hors-d'oeuvre*, *antrè* for *entrée*). In 1846, following the advice of a priest who wanted him to add menus and recipes for Holy Week, Cavalcanti shifted to Neapolitan dialect: "e bè, mo sa che faccio, te scrivo la Semmana Santa tutta d'uoglio co la lengua bella nostra, che a te piace assaje" (And well . . . now I'm writing to you on Holy Week full of oil in our fine language that you like so much).[33] The thirty-page appendix with the title "Della cucina casereccia in dialetto napoletano" (On home cooking, in Neapolitan dialect) demonstrates that there is a linguistic problem implicit in the transmission of indigenous dishes and suggests the need to find an expressive idiom capable of connecting elite cuisine with the festive cuisine of the clergy and the middle classes.

The proposal put forward by the duke of Buonvicino seems eccentric, given the culinary culture of the Italian states where the opposite tendency prevailed: that is, using Italo-French terminology as an element of linguistic and gastronomic unification and assigning to the upper-middle culinary range, which was prevalently urban, the task of representing all traditions, local and rural. The adoption of a foreign language did not simplify communication, however, creating the problems of professional terminology mentioned above, as well as other difficulties. These include the spelling standards used in food lists or menus to be presented to guests and the issue of titling recipe books according to uniform conventions, respecting a single model. The difficulty of codification was further complicated by the fact that in the tradition of French manual writing, there was disagreement among cooks even with regard to commonly used terms. Carême wrote *magnonaise* for *mayonnaise*,[34] for example, and *béchamel* was spelled at least four different ways.[35] There was also the fact that the invention of dishes and pastries in private homes and restaurants had resulted in strange neologisms. The use of the words *"à la"* in a recipe title, followed by the name of the cook or the host, a historical figure, an actress, a city, or a state, had caused some confusion for diners consulting the menu, even in France. We find this contagious trend in Italian recipe titles also, and it becomes stranger and more confusing as one goes down the price range of culinary publications. It would take someone already familiar with French and Italian phonetics to figure out that *"dolce alla sciantile"* is the equivalent of *"crème Chantilly."*[36] The professional collections of the second half of the nineteenth century tried to restore some order to the situation. *Il re dei cuochi* (The king of cooks) gives titles in both languages, and, if a dish is Italian, Nelli translates it into French, confirming that this is the international language (*Panettone à la milanaise*).[37] Dictionaries for both professionals and amateurs began to appear, such as that of Giacomo Giardini,[38] while translations of the more authoritative manuals began to aim at linguistic elegance and propriety.[39] This pervasive aspiration was inspired by the ubiquitous presence of French cuisine toward the end of the nineteenth century: *Meisterwerke der Speise und Getranke: Französisch-Deutsch-English*, printed in Leipzig in 1893, presents one of the most complete linguistic and synoptic repertoires of elegant cooking for restaurants. Its function went beyond the basic requirements for the training of a maître d'hôtel, since it facilitated the standardization of professional terminology in restaurant dining rooms and kitchens from country to country. Its multilingual vocabulary, particularly its rendering of French terms in Italian, became a guide that enabled cooks and waiters to decipher menus where the two languages came together and overlapped and to explain terms whose origin even if recent had already been lost. With this goal in mind, Hoepli published *Il gastronomo moderno. Vademecum ad uso degli albergatori, cuochi, segretari e personale d'albergo* (The modern gastronomic expert: A manual for the use of hoteliers, cooks, secretaries, and hotel staff). This is not a prescriptive text, but it provides all that is necessary to explain and translate the name of a given dish to a waiter ignorant both of who Gambetta might be ("lawyer, statesman, and French patriot") and how *les oeufs Gambetta* are prepared ("scrambled eggs on croutons, alternating with onion purée, preserved tomatoes, parsley, and truffles"). Through the intervention of the appropriate person, the manual could resolve the Italian client's curiosity and uncertainty. Providing brief instructions on the spelling of the menu and grammatical information on the use of singular, plural, and partitive construction (*consommé au riz*), the author addresses a serious gap in the training of hotel personnel, individuals who were educated in apprenticeships rather than schools and were expected to straddle different languages at a young age. The manual, which was published in 1904, was not reprinted, showing that early pleas for a national, purist reform of the Italian language, which would put an end to the disastrous consequences of Franco-Italian usage and the jargon of the hotel trade, had begun to fall on attentive ears.

Order and Cleanliness

On December 19, 1896, Olindo Guerrini wrote a letter to Artusi, reproduced in the fourth edition of *La scienza in cucina* (1899), which provides a pastiche of a recipe by the famous court cook Giovanni Vialardi, humorously titled "*grillò abbragiato*" (braised grillò). It begins: "Once stripped of its feathers the bird is burned not boiled" ("la volaglia spennata si abbrustia non si sboglienta"). This text is tantamount to a manifesto against "translations from French and clumsy compilations" by the two culinary experts who made the greatest contribution to the reform of domestic culinary terminology.[40] Self-taught and the editor of an edition of Giusti's letters for children, Pellegrino Artusi lived in Florence, could read French, used Florentine dialect in conversation and writing, and wanted to be understood by all Italians. For this reason, he prefaces his recipe collection with "an explanation of words from the Tuscan vernacular that may not be intelligible to all."[41] He is not a scholastic purist and welcomes some French terms, occasionally followed by translations ("Are 'potatoes *alla sauté*' perhaps 'browned in butter'?") and sometimes left in the original for the sake of clarity (*quenelles*), since he does not wish to become embroiled in too many Italian neologisms.[42] A businessman little versed in foreign languages though possessing enough vocabulary to catch examples of simple correspondence, he sometimes makes a slip, such as his unfortunate use of *soufflet* for *soufflé*, probably transcribed directly from *Il cuoco piemontese perfezionato a Parigi*, which unwittingly suggests an image of defiance (since *soufflet* means a slap).[43]

Artusi took on the role that suited him: to provide a kind of paternal mediation between Italian and various dialect traditions, such as Florentine (he was a resident of Florence), Romagnolo (he was born in Forlimpopoli), and the idiom of important cities that had left their mark on culinary customs (he traveled to Naples, Rome, Bologna, Milan, Padua, and Turin). The bibliography of historical recipe books is of little interest to him, and he seems to forget the existence of an already substantial body of published work. As a guest in the homes of others, he is happy to learn new recipes, and he enjoys reading them on loose sheets of paper or receiving them by mail. He observes the work of other cooks with close attention. On the way to a fair in Rovigo, after traveling for many hours by horse, Artusi stops at Polesella, enters an inn, and asks the innkeeper what she has to offer him. The woman prepares a dish of "*risi*." Artusi listens to her, observes her closely as she works, and mentally registers every phase of the preparation, from browning to boiling, down to the final addition of a good handful of Parmesan cheese before serving.[44] "*I risi*" will end up translated as the recipe for *riso alla cacciatora* (rice, hunter style) that appears in his book. Artusi records many recipes, like this Venetian one, as he watches someone preparing the food who speaks simultaneously in dialect and whose commentary he must then translate into Italian. Two cooks help him to try out the dishes, Marietta Sabatini from Massa and Francesco Ruffilli from Bologna, both of whom knew how to write (as we see from their correspondence with Artusi) and above all how to cook.

Artusi's reform emerged in a climate of patriotic nationalism, the scholastic quest for purity, and a distinctive pedagogical sensibility. For this reason, he understands intuitively from the outset that he must not only do away with "barbaric" terms but must also adapt all cooking terms—in Tuscan and in various dialects, whether used by professionals or by servants, by women or by men—to standard Italian. "After the unification of Italy it seems logical to consider the unification of the spoken language, which few people pay attention to and which many oppose, perhaps out of vain self-regard or perhaps out of a long and inveterate habit of speaking in dialect."[45] In one area, the careful management of the dining table—ignored by educational programs and to an even greater extent by literary figures—Artusi's suggestions seem to make good sense, as they are easily absorbed and remembered. The success of his book gave him authoritative status. He accepts the dual pattern of naming fish with their Adriatic and Tyrrhenian terms and vegetables with Florentine and Italian names (*gobbi* and *cardi* for cardoons, for example); he translates a dozen Bolognese terms, choosing from the most expressive ones such as the half-size maccheroni called *"denti di cavallo"* (horse's teeth); and he reduces to the single word *"migliaccio"* the different ways of naming a dessert based on pig's blood that had been familiar to him since childhood. Offal and various cuts of meat, fats and pastas attain a municipal identity from one recipe to the next. Artusi prefers to adopt the principle of the existence of local and Italian variants rather than the idea of hegemony. His linguistic map bears a single table, triangular in shape, whose three corners are Florence, Bologna, and Forlimpopoli. The dishes that come from outside this area are already Italianized, thus gentrified. Perhaps to ennoble a sauce that his palate greatly appreciated, he graces it with the term *balsamella*, a dialect word already used by Alberto Advise, the cook of the bishop of Imola (1785–1800),[46] which, in a popular etymology and semantic analogy, suggests "balsamo" (balm) as a substitute for *"besciamella"* and *"béchamel,"* the second of which is derived from the seventeenth-century patronage of its presumed creator, the marquis Louis de Béchamel.

To provide housewives with a model of writing was probably not part of this confirmed bachelor's initial intentions, but it was the most important aspect of his success. Before Artusi's time the language of maternal cooking was an oral idiom, spoken in dialect or—as occurred in the case of Caterina Prato's *Manuale*—translated from French or German, and it stood in opposition to the language of the chefs, who were professional men. By the time women's writing was submitted to the printer it had already taken on the dry tone of scholastic Italian, the style used by the promoters of domestic economy rather than the language of ordinary women gathered around the hearth or friends conversing in a pastry shop. With *La scienza in cucina*, a familiar Italian that sounds more like a spoken than a written language and evokes the tone of a personal, informative conversation swept aside the awkward jargon thick with irritating Gallicisms that was then characteristic of culinary writing, giving voice to domestic speech. The exchange of letters and the recipes sent to Artusi from every city in Italy (from which he selected recipes for inclusion in the expanded editions of his book) provided a network through which he retransmitted his own messages. Artusi's teachings achieved their goal thanks to the broad dissemination of his book from Florence to every corner of Italy. In the course of conversations between one woman and the next, these teachings would be retransmitted in the form of recipes dictated and jotted down in pencil and would resurface later in further confidences shared. *La scienza in cucina* mixes the vocabulary of mothers and visiting ladies, dignifying the verbal style of the entire tradition of didactic writing in a minor, domestic key.

Linguistic Autarchy

The audience that welcomed Artusi's writings and the support of Olindo Guerrini, a well-known poet who was also a publisher of ancient culinary texts, helped to bring back into focus the need to reform the language and terminology of food. The acknowledgment, both direct and indirect, of *La scienza in cucina* proved a decisive factor. In a climate of cultural purism and exalted *"italianità"* (Italianness), Alfredo Panzini took a favorable position toward Artusi's ideas in his *Dizionario moderno* in 1905, paying tribute to his "native grace and purity of language that would cause many an academic writer to blush."[47] In subsequent editions of the dictionary, the tribute grows louder. This might seem a conspiracy of compatriots, since Artusi and Guerrini were born in Romagna, while Panzini was a native of Sanigallia with a house in Bellaria. In reality, however, it was the spontaneous gesture of a retired businessman, a librarian, and secondary-school teacher. The degree of nationalism that weighs on this new dictionary can be understood by focusing on one fact: there are only two dishes in *La scienza in cucina* that are described as *all'italiana* (tortellini and recooked boiled meat), while Tuscany appears in twenty-one recipe titles and Emilia in fifteen. This linguistic reform was not carried out in order to force the citizens of Italy to sit at the same table but rather to allow them to communicate their own diversity.

Artusi's name began to circulate even among the promoters of high cuisine. In 1909 Alberto Cougnet recommends him as "the inspirer of this perceptible national reform to achieve a terminology and a language that is properly Italian."[48] At the instigation of the Milanese Culinary Society, Cougnet edited *L'arte cucinaria in Italia* (Culinary art in Italy), a monumental encyclopedia of recipes for professional cooks where we naturally find dozens of birds that are *"grillettati,"* meaning cut into pieces and pan-fried. Is this a contradiction or merely the beginning of a change of heart? Perhaps the excessive use of Gallicisms was already beginning to tire Italian diners, and it was time to drop them, but the problem was how to replace them. Beginning on January 1, 1908, the menus of the royal courts were written in Italian, and the word "menu" itself underwent review. How should it be correctly renamed? *Minuta, lista, distinta,* and *gastronota* were among the profusion of proposals for replacements, but the question was redundant, as it was merely a matter of flag-waving. In reality, little had changed in the kitchens of the Savoy family, the reigning monarchs. *Consumato alla diplomatica* replaced *consommé diplomate* to describe a chicken broth thickened with tapioca. But is *consumato* not a French-based term? As Panzini observes, even Scappi used the word *consumato* to describe a broth (*"brodo ristretto o consumato"*).[49] As for the *"alla diplomatica,"* it is "a pompous term" that makes much out of very little.[50] To retranslate from French, to restore the older terms, is simply to shift the terms of the problem, creating an equally artificial vocabulary without reforming the cuisine.

This problem was again addressed during the twenty years of Fascist rule. Artusi died in 1911 at the age of ninety, but Panzini continued to expand his dictionary after World War I and included the term *balsamella*.[51] In 1929 he sat in the front row of the newly created Accademia d'Italia, which had the express mandate of stripping the Italian language of foreign elements. The project had new implications for cooking, quite different from the reforms in protocol ordained by the House of Savoy. The credit given to regional identities by the regime, the censoring of local resources and culinary traditions, the reorganization of tourist boards and the promotion of Italian products abroad gave publishers the opportunity to expand and enlarge Artusi's recipe collection, since it was now receiving the kind of acknowledgment from official sources that it had previously obtained from families. The success of the ideological training of housewives, carried out through the press and the propaganda ministry, through culinary competitions and festivals, made the dual objective of culinary self-sufficiency and linguistic self-sufficiency increasingly explicit. Women, and the servants who worked for them, were expected to give concrete form to the Fascist project even with their words. This was facilitated by the circulation of handwritten recipes, stimulated by women's magazines with the creation of a column for letters from female readers, and the emergence of the radio, which gave an element of modern prestige to oral communication. The reform of French terminology became a matter for academics, as family cooking and the food served in popular restaurants represented the capstones of Fascist gastronomy, and the unity of the spoken language began to gain ground. This was an ambitions project, given the age-old confusion that reigned among cooks, accustomed from youth to juggle with a little French and to practice their trade even on ships, and inclined to mix in a confused fashion bourgeois and refined dishes with other popular, vernacular foods, the names of which were muttered rather than pronounced and were almost always impossible to spell.

Though univocal, this national passion for the Italian language is expressed by the most diverse voices. Filippo Tommaso Marinetti, who sat in the literature class at the Accademia d'Italia with Panzini, translated what the literary pages of the newspapers and editorials repeated daily into the style of the avant-garde. After condemning pasta dishes and inserting a series of scandalous recipes, signed by "aero-poets" and "aero-painters," *La cucina futurista* (*The Futurist Cookbook*), which was published in 1932, returns to the linguistic question by providing a "little dictionary." There are Italian words to replace both Gallicisms and Anglicisms, all of which were being debated by Alfredo Panzini over the same period: *castagne candite* for *marrons glacés*, *consumato* for *consommé*, *fondenti* for *fondants*, *fumatoio* for *fumoir*, *lista* for *menu*, *miscela* for *mélange*, *sala da te* for *tea-room*. It is not so much the purist face of a noisy avant-garde movement but the spirit of linguistic reinvention that inspires these suggestions. Besides, Marinetti, a well-known and esteemed author in French also, carried on his poetic war as if autarchy provided the opportunity for resounding gunshots. In fact, the dictionary reveals some striking intuitions on his part, nonetheless misunderstood: *traidue* (between-the-two) for "sandwich" and *pranzoalsole* (lunch-in-the-sun) for "picnic," which, like *polibibita* (polydrink) for "cocktail," had an esthetic rather than colloquial success.[52] The culinary neologisms of futurism favor a process of accumulation, giving rise to *porcoeccitato* (excited pig) for a mixture of salami, hot coffee, and eau de Cologne, *dolcelastico* (elastic-sweet) for zabaglione and licorice, and *brucioinbocca* (burn-in-the-mouth) for a drink created by layering in a glass whiskey, sugar, Strega, vermouth, and alkermes. This is a way of binding terms together, like ingredients in a sauce, that is unusual in restaurant culture and has had few lasting effects, among which the most famous contemporary example is *tiramisù* (pick-me-up).

To what degree was Marinetti seriously playing this game? To make us reflect on the ritual basis of the futurist extravagances we have only to consider the strange list of dishes shown on hotel menus, thrown together and distorted in peculiar, incomprehensible ways, and the amused response to this battle of words on the part of the peaceful newspaper readers. Within the context of linguistic reform, Marinetti also has an intuitive grasp of the importance of new references and the need to adapt his neologisms to new ways of cooking and serving food. Wishing to promote art objects rather than consumer goods, his suggestions do not conform to criteria of a commercial nature. Thus the *polibibita* is not a cocktail but a mixture of spirits and other drinks according to a rule of explosive contrast—wine with quinine plus rum, plus boiling Barolo,

IL VITTO
QVARESIMALE
DI PAVLO ZACCHIA
MEDICO ROMANO.

Oue infegnafi, come fenza offender
la fanità fi poffa viuer nella
Quarefima.

*Si difcorre de' cibi in effa vfati, de gli errori, che fi
commettono nell'vfargli, dell'indifpofitioni,ch'il
lor'vfo impedifcono, de gli accidenti, che
foglion cagionare, e del modo
di rimediarui.*

IN ROMA, Per Pietro Antonio Facciotti. 1637.

Con licenza de' Superiori, & Priuilegio.

Ad iftanza di Gio.Dini Libraro in Nauona all'infegna della Gatta.

DELLO SCALCO
DEL SIG. GIO. BATTISTA
ROSSETTI,

*Scalco della Sereniffima Madama Lucretia da Efte
Ducheffa d'Vrbino,*

Nel quale fi contengono le qualità di vno Scalco perfetto,
& tutti i carichi fuoi, con diuerfi vfficiali
à lui fottopofti:

*Et gli ordini di vna cafa da Prencipe, e i modi di feruirlo,
cofi in banchetti, come in tauole ordinarie.*

Con gran numero di banchetti alla Italiana,& alla Alemana, di varie,e belliffime
inuentioni, e definari, e cene familiari per tutti i mefi dell'anno,
con apparecchi diuerfi di tauole non vfati.

*Et con molte varietà di viuande, che fi poffono cauare
di ciafcuna cofa atta à mangiarfi.*

Et con tutto ciò che è buono ciafcun mefe : & con le prouifioni da farfi
da effo Scalco in tempo di guerra.

IN FERRARA,
Appreffo Domenico Mammarello,
MDLXXXIIII.

LA CUCINA
CASERECCIA

PER ISTRUZIONE DI CHI AMA UNIRE AL
GUSTO LA ECONOMIA

CON CINQUE UTILI TRATTATI

DELLE FRUTTA, DE' VINI, DE' GELATI, DE' ROSOLJ,
E DELLA MANIFATTURA DE' DOLCI

SETTIMA EDIZIONE

ACCRESCIUTA

*Del modo di trinciare li Quadrupedi,
i Volatili, ed i Pesci*

Senza alterarne il solito prezzo di grana 25.

Di M. F.

IGIENE * ECONOMIA * BUON GUSTO

LA SCIENZA IN CUCINA
E
L'ARTE DI MANGIAR BENE

MANUALE PRATICO PER LE FAMIGLIE

COMPILATO
DA
PELLEGRINO ARTUSI

| Un pasto buono ed un meranao Mantengon l'uomo sano. | Piglia il cibo con misura Dai due regni di natura. |
| Molto cito e mal digesto Non fa il corpo sano e lesto. | Pronta digestio fa tu ore. |

IN FIRENZE
PEI TIPI DI SALVADORE LANDI
Direttore dell'Arte della Stampa

1891

Frontispieces from Paolo Zacchia, *Il vitto quaresimale* (Rome: Facciotti, 1637); from
Giovan Battista Rossetti, *Dello scalco* (Ferrara: Mammarello, 1584); from *La cucina
casereccia* (Naples: Giordano, 1828); and from
Pellegrino Artusi, *La scienza in cucina e l'arte di mangiar bene*
(Florence: Landi, 1891).

plus mandarin juice is a *decisone*—or assonance—while three ingredients featuring the vowel *a* in a prominent position are required for the *inventina*: Asti Spumante, *liquore d'Ananas* (pineapple liqueur), and *sugo d'Arancio* (orange juice). Even if none of these drinks goes beyond the confines of the avant-garde, futurist cooking had the merit of restoring linguistic initiative to Italians.

The lists of words to be substituted for corresponding words in a foreign language were issued only from 1941 onward in the "Bulletin of the Royal Academy," after stimulating a wide debate between linguists and literary experts, journalists and cooks. To create neologisms by the thousands (five thousand appear in the appendix of the eighth edition of the *Dizionario moderno* published in 1942) implied a systematic analysis of terminology as well as a major input of creativity, and this meant that the representatives of various sectors were often in difficulty or dispute with the academics. To call *marrons glacés* (glazed chestnuts) "*marroni canditi*" in Italian (candied chestnuts) meant to suppress the difference between glazed and candied products, just as to abolish the French term "omelette" meant to relinquish a term that in the idiom spoken in the kitchen meant a *frittata*, but "softer, half cooked"). Foreign words also reflected techniques of the trade, codified over time, using the vocabulary available: the difference between a parsley *frittata* and a ham *omelette* is one of cooking time and temperature, not just flavoring. Two centuries of work in French kitchens could not be swept away by an erudite list.

How many of these subtleties were apparent to the women of Italy? Many in fact, because of the existence of a system of information that traveled vertically through the kitchens giving the issue of the language question concrete meaning. The magazine industry had the task of transforming the academic tenor of the debate into a popular discussion at the national level. Product advertisements ultimately disseminated the results all over Italy. Listening was only the starting point—in a passive way, of course—of a project of reform that scholastic channels and professional training would finally render operational. The outcome of the policy on linguistic self-sufficiency (*autarchia*) was very different, as we know. In fact, as the Accademia was publishing its lists, war bulletins grew increasingly numerous, and these were followed by events that led to rationing, ration books, and finally famine. When the linguistic instrument for the unification of culinary terminology was finally made available, offering the basis for a new tradition of didactic writing on food, the country was divided, and Italians were beginning to die of hunger. American aid brought an end to the issue of foreign loan words.

Italian in the Kitchens of Babel

The fall of Fascism and the American invasion did not bring about an unfettered hybridization of culinary Italian but signaled the prudent exercise of linguistic freedom. *Arlecchini* and *polibibite* did not have the time to stick before the old word "cocktail" replaced them. Everything returned to its previous state. *L'ABC della cucina*, with which the publication of *La cucina italiana* resumed on January 1, 1952, would not have raised any objections, except to the term "*menù*," even from an academic in Fascist uniform. The monthly magazine devoted space periodically to the establishment of vocabulary, obviously without mentioning foreign expressions. Here it was not the allusion to some international sauce but the advertising, beauty products, perfumes, and Coca-Cola that foreshadowed a rupture in the language that the bourgeoisie considered one of the important aspects of its own continuity and equilibrium. There are also the reports of Arnaldo Fraccaroli: "The Javanese Meal, Lunch, Italian Style, but with Surprise Elements in Singapore."[53] Exotic travel to countries in the process of decolonization and foreign advertising were new elements, a phenomenon that sped up only a decade later, very sensitive in other, less conservative headlines of *Cucina italiana*, which brought an unexpected result.

The paradox of the last fifty years can be summed up in this way: as linguistic freedom developed in the heart of the republic and as neologisms of Anglo-Saxon origin, promoted by the food industry and fast-food chains, began to take over from French terminology, relaunched in the 1970s with nouvelle cuisine, the Italian language multiplied outside its native borders in signs and menus. This is the pizza effect. Though the term does not exist in the 1938 edition of *Larousse gastronomique*, it takes up two columns in 1984, and is the subject of two recipes. If we compare it to "spaghetti," its introduction seems all the more surprising. Under the letter *s* in the first edition of the *Larousse gastronomique* we find: salami, spaghetti, and *stracchino*. To these are added *saltimbocca*, *scamorze*, and *spalla*. The expression "al dente," referring to pasta as well as green beans, has its own entry in 1984.[54] Distortions and squabbles also grow more plentiful: "*un panini*" is given as the singular form of *panini*, and it indicates—in France in the 1990s—a sandwich toasted on the grill.[55] An American pepperoni pizza, on the other hand, features sausage not peppers (*peperoni* in Italian) among its main ingredients.

In Italy the use of culinary terms in dialect has grown rarer as the custom of local or rural dining has increased. We also see that the industry participates in this phenomenon. Adding to this contradiction is another: the persistent presence of barbarisms has not diminished with the diaspora of Italian terms abroad in a climate of total anomie, invasion, and transition. One may now teach regional cooking with the aid of the *chinois* and the court bouillon, for example, as Gualtiero Marchesi does,[56] or anglicize Piedmontese dialect expressions, as Suor Germana does with "*pollo alla baby*."[57] As a result of the invasive publishing industry and its proliferation of all kinds of encyclopedias and recipe dictionaries, a culinary vocabulary of the publishing business is what prevails today, and there is an absence of an Italian terminological handbook, with multilingual terms, definitions, and translations. This is the only instrument that could standardize the names of dishes in all parts of the world, even though the conditions necessary to bring this to pass probably do not exist.

When Artusi's work achieved the honor of being published by Einaudi in 1970, his teachings were already close to being entombed by Piero Camporesi with all the historical and local, aristocratic, and popular cooking of Italy.[58] Not that *La scienza in cucina* was lost in the rubble of the Fascist regime, but there were few women, it seems, who were fighting to revive it or imitating its style in their letters. It is no longer even mentioned. Shelves of books already satisfy every fantasy. In the past before writing down one's secret recipes one had to try them out repeatedly, and learn by making mistakes. The new dishes are simple and infallible or complicated and unachievable. The hereditary thread that allowed menus to be handed down from mother to daughter had been broken. The link between restaurants and family cooking that had kept in check the damage done by the French menu had also been broken. With the car and the highway system, the regions themselves became unified according to the model of the tourist industry, responding to a transient experience of gastronomic identity. Translated into the jargon of communication, this means that the style of the recipes dear to one's grandmother now seems obscure and antiquated, while simply reading a weekly paper or the menu at a restaurant will provide one with new culinary terms. Even without traveling, anyone can try out unknown foods, if one can manage to remember their names. When traveling one can find dishes with familiar names thousands of miles from home.

The family has maintained a level of decorum worthy of Artusi, especially in the provinces, at least at festive meals, and yet the cult of fine things seems more a question of temperament or talent than of upbringing. The myth of Paris seems rather tarnished from the culinary perspective, especially among the bourgeoisie, which in Italy distrusts everything and is not very familiar with the three-star restaurant. In addition the teaching of foreign languages is no longer a matter only for the rich, and other languages are now taught more frequently than French, the idiom in which the high cuisine of the Western world has been codified. Even the type of Italian that was spoken and written by Artusi with deliberate decorum has lost its function as a model of elegance and as a norm at the dinner table, which is now open to all forms of communication. This table, a permanent fixture in the middle of the kitchen, is increasingly casual, erratic, and attuned to the television rather than the radio, for it is situated within view of that other meal, the television commercial.

Through diaspora, the traditional image of Italian gastronomy has continued to perpetuate itself with the popular concept of the pizzeria or the Roman or Tuscan trattoria and the more refined idea of the elegant restaurant, especially since the 1980s. Internal migration has led to the dissemination of "typical" restaurants, a phenomenon that is juxtaposed with the gradual loss of older inns and eateries. External emigration on the other hand serves above all to project an echo of ethnicity under the sign of an Italian proper name. California and Florida are the areas in which the food of Italian Americans is resurrected and spreads by contagion in the most extraordinary, lavish forms. Like all hegemonic cuisines it is prepared by personnel from all parts of Italy and by others of every nationality, who learn in the course of their usually brief training the model's most rudimentary terms. In the wake of the cuisine of the fathers (the chefs), followed by that of the mothers, what we witness here is the food of the sons or rather the orphans. Gastronomic syncretism is the principal source of authenticity in a restaurant system run by those who have long left Italy behind, and it brings together at least three variables: the cuisine of the original Italian territory, that of the practitioner's birthplace, and that of the host country. Here we find a mixture of dialect, standard Italian, and another language, such as American English, for example: "Italian restaurants abroad are moving toward the creation of a pidgin menu, a lingua franca of the restaurant business."[59] This outcome is far from new. It was reflected from one end of the twentieth century to the other by the compilers of glossaries and handbooks: the language of cooks and waiters is a Volapük, a volatile Esperanto, continuously called into question and resistant to rules.[60]

When the culinary idiom seemed close to being reorganized and correctly standardized, it fell apart again as a result of the combined effect of the loss of personal, local origins, and dialects and the increasing sense of openness to all influences, so much greater for those living beyond the borders of their birthplace. Internal migration in Italy decimated the new idiom at the base, and creativity generated confusion as the new vocabulary became bloated with a profusion of invented or translated terms misunderstood by cooks and culinary experts. A similar conclusion must prompt us to reexamine the terms of the gastronomic debate and the various phases of a very uneven linguistic history. Perhaps the best proof of the illusory character of Artusi's project to provide a single, streamlined, correct language for cuisine is precisely the Babel-like image of culinary Italian both before Italian unification and after Fascism—or perhaps without interruption—amid a confusion of dialects, Gallicisms, and distortions in the first of these historical phases and the proliferation of commercial brands, Anglicisms, and contrived formulas of rural life in the second. Given this conclusion, we are faced with a paradox that might be of consolation to the cultural historian but is unproductive for those who look to the future and imagine they can hear or read its messages: only the cuisine of the nobility, in the books of Messisbugo and Scappi, spoke a language that measured up to its own ambitions.

CHAPTER SEVEN

The Cook, the Innkeeper, and the Woman of the House

Recorded Lives

Biographical information on cooks and stewards can be found in culinary writings, in the financial records of households and palaces, and in reports of festivities and banquets but rarely in autobiographical texts. Recipe collections and treatises on stewardship are important sources of information and may be read as histories of a profession, offering a cultural portrait rather than a record of individual births and deaths. These are the first texts we consult when attempting to reconstruct the lives of these men. Bartolomeo Scappi mentions repeatedly in his *Opera* that he worked principally in Rome in the service of cardinals and popes. He also claims that he once worked at the residence of a Cardinal Marin Grimano in Venice; he does not give the dates of his tenure there but notes that he had personally visited the Venetian fish market and met the fishermen from Chioggia.[1] Claims of this type are supported by information regarding ingredients and dishes specific to a particular area—the stretch of the Adriatic coast between the Venetian lagoon and Ravenna in Scappi's case—convincing us that the writer really traveled to this region and spent a significant period of time there. Although the geographical names a cook attributes to dishes and ingredients allow us to make some assumptions about his professional training and experience, they rarely constitute conclusive biographical information. Scappi's origins have been fiercely debated by critics and readers: Giancarlo Roversi thought he was from Bologna, Claudio Benporat argued that he grew up in Venice, and a stone discovered in a church near Luini seems to indicate that he was born in Lombardy.[2]

The dates of banquets and special assignments mentioned in the recipe collections provide useful points of reference. Scappi's career lasted from 1536, the year Cardinal Campegio hosted a banquet in honor of Charles V, to 1566, the year that witnessed the solemn festivities celebrating the coronation of Pope Pius V. This is a span of thirty years, the usual duration of such an appointment. The calendar of important events that punctuated Scappi's career should not be underestimated. The death of one pope, Paul III, on November 10, 1549, and the election of his successor, Julius III, on February 7, 1550, are mentioned in the appendix of the *Opera* with the objective of describing the meals served during the conclave. Information of this kind allows us to place the "secret cook" in a familiar historical context. Despite Scappi's experience in the service of cardinals and popes, his identity is merely a reflection of the instructions he provides for the preparation and presentation of excellent, attractively served food at the tables of important men. The circumstances of his upbringing and training are still unknown, along with the dates of his birth and death.

In the case of famous or high-born stewards the archives may yield more extensive information. The fact that Cristoforo Messisbugo was a rich and influential man, distinguished enough to invite Duke Ercole d'Este to dine at his home, is revealed in his *Banchetti*. Research on the management of the court of Ferrara has further confirmed that he was a personality of high profile. His travels and ambassadorships, commissioned by Alfonso I to Milan, Bologna, and Venice, his appointment as the "under-bursar of the duke," and the title of Palatine count conferred on him by Charles V constitute significant events and landmarks in a personal history that Luciano Chiappini has reconstructed with the help of archival resources.[3] Messisbugo's ascent to the position of financial manager to the duke, which was followed by damaging accusations of incorrect disbursement, adds further detail to this account, enhancing the value of his menus and recipes in the light of his role as an organizer of celebrations and banquets. The date of Messisbugo's death, November 10, 1548, completes one of the richest biographical portraits of a sixteenth-century figure.

What is missing from a life story constructed from financial documents and menus is the personal voice of the subject, an account of the various aspects of his formation as cook, courtier, and writer. What were the motives that drove him to embrace this art? How did he gain such expertise, and what role did cookbooks play in his acquisition of mastery? Even if we scrutinize them closely, financial records and recipes do not answer these questions. Rarely does a recipe tell the story of the person who created it, tried it out, and dictated it for transcription. As the outcome of a process of compilation, a recipe may be authentic and original even if not written in the cook's own hand. A cookbook, like a menu collection, is the result of a collective effort undertaken by employees of subordinate rank as well as those at the highest level of palace administration. The writing and printing of a collection also required external intervention, as these were skills not always among the cultural competencies of the steward.

These are the outlines of an area of biographical research still at its inception. The recently discovered autobiography of Antonio Latini, author of *Lo scalco alla moderna*, constitutes a surprising exception to the limits that generally circumscribe this field of inquiry. Latini's autobiography was published by Furio Liccichenti, based on a manuscript found in the public library of Fabriano that had been copied by Fra Francesco Maria Nicolini in 1690, two years

LEFT: men and women in the kitchen (engraving)

Source: Giovanni de' Rosselli, *Opera nova chiamata Epulario* (Venice: Zoppino, 1516).

RIGHT: Detail from *Supper at Emmaus*, by Raphael Sadeler
(seventeenth century).

before the publication of Latini's recipe collection. It recounts a life filled with
adventure, in which dining and cooking have only a secondary place. Latini was
born in Coll'Amato in the Marches in 1642. Orphaned at the age of five, he was
obliged to beg for food and lodging. At a very young age he became a servant by
necessity, and at sixteen he decided to try his fortune by moving to Rome. Here
he worked as cook, waiter, and wardrobe attendant in the household of Cardinal Antonio Barberini. He also learned swordsmanship and the necessary carving skills at the table of his employer, "enjoying this a great deal, and laughing
when [he] made an unsuccessful or clumsy move."[4] Before his promotion to the
highest rank of service, Latini performed every imaginable function in patrician
households, including minor administrative roles. Later, having embraced his
vocation as a steward, he served at the courts of Macerata, Mirandola, and
Faenza, and finally, as his fame grew, he moved to Naples to work in the service
of the Spanish regent, Carrillo. Earlier in life Latini had worn both the rags of
a vagrant and the clerical habit of the ecclesiastical court, and he now embarked
on the concluding phase of his career dressed in Spanish attire. After 1690, the
last year his autobiography covers, he published *Lo scalco alla moderna* and was
awarded the title of Knight of the Golden Spur. He died in 1692.

There are no menus or recipes in Latini's *Autobiography*. We learn, however, that he was sixteen when he first went to work for Cardinal Barberini's cook. His training in the various roles of service characteristic of a great household had a decisive part to play in his ascent to the position of steward, a role he first occupied in 1670 at the age of twenty-eight that became the exclusive vocation of his later years. Latini was self-taught. He learned to write from a priest-cook while working in the service of a family in Matelica, and at the age of sixteen he still expressed himself "in a countrified way," confusing singular and plural grammatical forms. He was educated over time through a process of accumulated experience, studying the ceremonies, disciplines, skills, and entertainments required in a large Roman household. The version of the *Autobiography* that has come down to us, which was revised and transcribed by a friar, raises doubts about Latini's literary abilities when compared to the quality of his recipe collection. The breadth of materials and resources reflected in this work, which comprises two volumes, inspires the highest respect.

Latini's *Autobiography* is in some ways reminiscent of another life story, written many years later by another accomplished man: Pellegrino Artusi. Artusi's book is similarly silent on culinary issues, though it provides much detail on the author's family, provincial upbringing, business dealings, political ideas, and acquaintances. Born in Forlimpopoli in 1820, Artusi died in 1911. One might well wonder w' at prompted him to record his life after he had already attained the age of eighty. He was undoubtedly inspired by motives similar to those of Latini. Both men told their life stories after they had already gained renown in a field—the art of culinary service and hospitality—that left little room for intimate confessions, literary outpourings, and expressions of frustrated pride. To tell one's personal history, beginning with the earliest years of life in the provinces, is to bring a human dimension to one's art or to hold it at a distance in order to understand it better. In both cases, the autobiography allows the writer to evaluate his own ideas and inventions, his teaching and culinary mastery, as the outcome rather than the cause of a life devoted to good taste.

In 1903 Artusi embarked on the process of recording his memories, though he later decided to keep them secret. After Artusi's time, new archival material has emerged in which we can decipher and reconstruct the lives of other men who became famous through food. For centuries, the scarcity of available documents had kept cooks and culinary experts in obscurity, but now they unexpectedly achieved a level of public fame and notoriety. The embarrassment associated with the practice of a messy, plebeian profession has long been abandoned, as have the prejudices linking this profession to the sin of gluttony. We now witness an unprecedented curiosity about these artisans—who might even be described as artists—and the ephemeral creations they produce. The publication of professional bulletins during the Fascist years not only fostered better knowledge of the workplace but granted recognition to individuals who deserved it. The articles, photographs, prizes, and obituaries published in *I cucinieri d'Italia* (The cooks of Italy) provide a useful record from that era. Along with other publications of a similar type, it offers a valuable source of biographical and bibliographical information. Magazines, guides, interviews, and recipe collections intended for a wider readership provide additional information on the training, career, and finest contributions of a particular chef, with photographic portraits of both the man and his creations. By manipulating real and hypothetical dates, journalists constructed the individual and collective histories of these culinary artists and their critics for future memory, with the obvious risk that when they wrote about a cook whose life was already legendary, they were making it impossible for future researchers to distinguish fact from fiction. Any biographical dictionary of gastronomy written in the future must take these premises into account.

The Kitchen "Brigade"

"Cook" is a collective term. Although stewards and culinary experts placed their own names and portraits in their books, the work that produced a recipe, menu, or banquet was carried out by many people. We know from the oldest surviving documents that the kitchens in patrician or ecclesiastical households were organized in a hierarchical manner. Tasks were divided among the staff, and a system of specialization enforced. There were specific spaces, dress codes, and tools appropriate to each role. While the steward was in charge of the entire production of meals, from supplies to services, the head cook was the main figure in a team that consisted of an undercook, helpers, and apprentices, all of whom had specific duties and assignments. While the undercook was responsible for the completion of a dish—a boiled meat dish or stew—the apprentice learned how to dress the meats and prepare dough. Scappi's illustrations show at least seventeen kitchen workers assigned to such tasks as "making *biancomangiare*," "working with dough," "flavoring," and "working with milk" in a cool corner of the kitchen or supervising the skewers and pans at the hearth. Knife sharpeners and dishwashers were also required. To these we must add the workers who brought in the firewood, the distributors who delivered supplies, and an indeterminate number of very young scullery hands who were responsible for cleaning.

This was and still is a difficult trade. Domenico Romoli notes that, "This is truly one of the most unpleasant occupations imaginable, as one must always be vigilant and watch out for oneself, being careful not to let any misfortunes occur." What he is alluding to is scarcely a mystery: the health of the prince and his guests, their satisfaction, the success of the banquet, the relations with other employees in service as well as those of the upper ranks, the steward, and the understeward constituted perpetual sources of anxiety. Fatigue, heat, and tension seem to be at the root of the vice most frequently attributed to the cook:

drinking. "Above all do not mingle with drunkards even if they are the most accomplished masters of cooking you can find, for, having imbibed before preparing the food, they are themselves cooked before the appetizer."[5] "It is best to stay sober because, in the midst of so much heat, excessive drink will take one's attention away from things, and from this a thousand difficulties may arise."[6] "It is best not to love wine, because those who sin through this vice will often bring down the reputation of the Steward."[7]

But drunkenness was not the only disorder witnessed in the profession, since the kitchens were prone to another endemic problem: dirt. The cleanliness and health of the entire staff, from head cook to scullery hands, were the objectives underlying the rules of correct attire, appropriate organization of space, and specific responsibilities. The *biancomangiare* had to be prepared by a designated individual, who had clean hands and wore a white hat, working in a special corner of the kitchen, separate from the others. The expectation of cleanliness encompassed everything: tables, copper and iron utensils, unused ingredients, napkins, and aprons and involved obsessive, continuous rounds of inspection and great effort on the part of all employees.

Discipline could be more strictly enforced because the kitchen is a closed space. Rossetti recommends that the head cook "must not let people gossip in the kitchen, as it is a place of too much jealousy."[8] Privacy and segregation prevent problems of theft, dirt, contamination, and poisoning, and in fact the word "secret" appears in the very title of the cook (Scappi was described as a *"cuoco segreto,"* or secret cook). Once the limits of the specific area had been established beyond dispute, one might suppose that the head cook could exercise his proper authority with ease. In the chaos of the kitchens, however, discipline was a difficult task, not only because of the confusion but also because of another factor: "everyone lives off the noble Lord and everyone steals, selling firewood, bread, trifles, and a thousand other things."[9] Scullery hands pilfered leftovers from pasta cooks, and apprentices spirited away the finest, largest types of fish, replacing them with other, smaller fish. If the items were not devoured on the spot, they were taken elsewhere. Secretively, the entire staff participated in this plunder: the servants forged strange relationships with the storeroom workers and the kitchen hands in order to gain access to the food, while the head cooks slipped away with supplies unbeknownst to the steward and the bursar. The difficulty of finding a balance between excess and bare necessity is evidenced in all the household manuals. The cook could claim the leftovers as his rightful gratuity, since he was remunerated not only in money but also in kind. Yet the excessive consumption of oil, firewood, and poultry seems to suggest that ashes and cooking fats, chicken heads, necks, hearts, and livers were being sold for profit.[10] The steward had to limit these activities through supervision and censure, forbidding theft, and giving the fullest account possible to the master of the house, without denying the tips and gifts allowed to the cooks, apprentices, and scullery workers. There have been few studies of financial archives from a perspective that would enable us to establish the existence of habitual practices or tacit agreements in the discretional management of supplies, leftovers from the banquet table, and reserves of food. In 1774 the cook Jacopo Bronzoli signed a contract with the Ginori family in Florence, a document that reveals the full complexity of kitchen management. We note that the cook, who was first obliged to serve his masters, had the right to keep leftovers but was then expected to provide food to the undercook, the maids, the male servants, the peasants, and the day laborers.[11] Food was both retribution and coin of exchange, indemnity and profit.

The cook began his day before dawn by lighting the fire, placing water on the boil, and cleaning vegetables and poultry. Later he checked the amounts and quality of the supplies and assigned various chores. The supervision of pantry service and kitchen tasks followed. All this work grew increasingly frenetic as the hour of the first meal approached, and the authority of the head cook was essential for its successful completion. He was not required to be young or old, but he needed an even temper and a great deal of experience. He had to know how to take charge, commanding the respect of the other cooks, who should be "obedient, human, lively, and, if possible, Italian rather than foreign," according to Romoli, a Tuscan.[12] The cook was trained through apprenticeship, moving up through the levels of the hierarchy, and sometimes retaining a deep devotion to his master, as witnessed in Bartolomeo Stefani's attitude towards Giulio Cesare Tirelli.[13] Apart from good professional qualifications, intelligence was an important asset in the cook's career, where organization and method were not the only qualities needed. A vast knowledge of ingredients, acquired through direct contact with markets and merchants, perfected in the course of service at different courts, and enhanced by keen sensory perception and an excellent memory, is the basis of Bartolomeo Scappi's success. Intuition allows him to put this intelligence to work to his own advantage, anticipating and satisfying the appetites of his lord, creating new dishes that are "tasty, agreeable to the palate, pleasant and delightful to the eye, with their fine color and fair proportion." For this reason Scappi is compared to an architect, with whom he shares the honor of setting up the banquet. But unlike the architect, he must also possess improvisational gifts: "if necessary, he must be able to prepare different dishes from a single thing."[14]

Above and beyond culinary fashions, the cook's profession and status had elements that were absolutely continuous. Attitude or disposition might vary from one author to the next—one seeming more modest, another more creative, and a third more attentive to the effect created by figurines built from sugar and butter than to the temperature of the food—but the professional rules that had to be respected in the collective production of the meal remained constant. Regarding the number of years required for a cook's training, Nebbia claimed

Il nuovo Cuoco Piemontese
e Credenziere Napoletano.

A cook and his helper.

Source: *Il nuovo cuoco piemontese e credenziere napoletano* (Milan, 1824).

in 1786 that an undercook should work for nine to ten years before he qualified as a household "official," that is, before he was in a position to supervise the kitchen, and this nine- or ten-year period was preceded by an indeterminate number of years as a scullery boy and apprentice. Later, at some point between the age of thirty and fifty, he would be promoted to a higher rank. These levels were not excessively rigid. Each "official" contributed to the training of others, taking on helpers who were particularly competent and effective and on whom he could depend in case of illness or other difficulty. In courts and noble households the rank of the steward, or maître d'hotel as he was known in France, was higher than that of the head cook and constituted the pinnacle of a career that had begun in the kitchen or at ceremonial functions. None of the levels of this hierarchy would alter until the end of the nineteenth century, with the possible exception of the maître, who became, at least in restaurants, the person in charge of the dining room and food service.

The pantry, which still survived in the courts of the nineteenth century, was assimilated into other departments of hotel restaurants. Hors d'oeuvres, salads, and desserts reverted entirely to the responsibility of the cook, while the butler was responsible for jellies, jams, and other preserves. The waiter or headwaiter and in rare cases the "slicer" (commis trancheur) carried out the duties of slicing, carving, and seasoning that were previously assigned to butlers and carvers of the court. The supervision of linens—tablecloths and folded napkins—and dishes fell to the responsibility of the maître. Even in regal households the arrangement of furnishings reflected a gradual reduction of services and equipment. A heavy piece of furniture was now placed against a wall and held a display rack for valuable dishes, preserving in a purely decorative way the memory of what used to be a little theater of elegance and good taste.

The new layout of the kitchen, reflecting the changes imposed by rules of service governed by French taste, was illustrated by professionals such as Francesco Leonardi (1790), who had worked in various cities of Europe, including Naples, Paris, and St. Petersburg.[15] Here we see the head cook flanked by two trusted allies, the "roaster" (rosticciere) and the pastry cook, who are not subordinate to him but responsible for separate departments. The pastry cook was a key figure during the Napoleonic era and the Restoration, and he often rose to the highest rank within the system, according to the model inspired by the French. As the new architect of the banquet, he was assigned the task of constructing emblems, trophies, buildings, gardens, and landscapes on the dining table: "A perfect cook must not only be able to draw but must also know how to fashion all kinds of shapes and decorations. Having these skills he can carry out his work with great decorum, without needing to rely on other artists, who might try to humiliate him in many ways out of envy or ignorance." Thus wrote Agnoletti, assistant confectioner and icing specialist at the court of Parma between 1821 and 1826, who was renowned for his expertise in making ice creams.[16]

In the course of the nineteenth century the culinary profession underwent a significant change. Traditionally linked to patrician households and the wealthy bourgeoisie, it shifted gradually toward the hospitality industry, of which the two central pillars were hotels and restaurants. At the height of the Restoration, just after midcentury, a new system of culinary roles and work came into prominence, inspired by the Parisian model as well as by a military image ("*brigata*," the word applied to the team working in the kitchen, was an ancient military term borrowed from the French "*brigade*"). The kitchen was now divided into separate sections, each with its own head. At the top we find the cook and the undercook, still in command. Below them we find the new figure of the sauce maker, "enlightened chemist, ingenious creator, and cornerstone of the kitchen,"[17] the most prominent of the department heads, who occupied a rank that had come into existence as a result of the primacy of sauces in French food. Each of the other departments—appetizers, soups, legumes and garnishing, fish, roasts, pastries, and iced desserts—also had its own head cook and assistant. An employee responsible for the larder and—from the early years of the twentieth century onward—for the refrigerator thus rounded out the kitchen staff. This small army was supplemented by other workers with minor roles, from the so-called family cook (who was in charge of preparing food for the staff), to the butcher, the baker, and the *casseruoliere* (a servant whose duty was to take care of cleaning all copper pots and utensils). In the case of hotels and restaurants with a restricted capacity, the number of employees diminished in proportion to need. An establishment catering to only fifty diners, for example, offered a fixed price menu, which was prepared by a head cook, his assistant, and an apprentice helper.

In this organizational scheme careers followed clear lines. The assistant head cook had been a sauce maker or had supervised the refrigerator, while the sauce maker in turn had carried out the duties of a section head. The *chef entremetier* (head vegetable cook), who occupied a rank above those responsible for the separate sectors, had been a former head of the soup department or a former assistant sauce maker. The acceptance of this arrangement in luxury hotels around the world guaranteed a broad sector of employment, bigger than that of private households, with career opportunities sometimes depending on mobility. All this was made possible by the presence of a single gastronomic model, the Parisian, to which professionals from various countries added slight variations. Work contracts in kitchens directed by French cooks, experience with prestigious chefs, and promotions in establishments of special repute are the kinds of distinctions that could counterbalance the potentially disadvantageous national identity of Italian cooks. Italian dishes, which were limited to those pasta dishes that could be classified under the heading of *légumes*, had a modest place in the repertoire of professional cooking. As a result members of the kitchen staff who were born in Italy had specific, limited competencies, requested on a sporadic basis by the clientele.

This gastronomic and organizational model prevailed until recent times or at least until the publication of the fifth edition of *Manuale dell'industria alberghiera* (Manual of the hotel industry) by the Touring Club Italiano in 1954.

Costume and Custom

To this day the professional uniforms of cooks, head waiters, and waiters observe a chromatic code strictly limited to black and white. It is clear from many sources, however, that before the nineteenth century there was great diversity in the color and style of dress worn by those who prepared and served food. Stewards were elegantly attired, displaying a degree of refinement worthy of the patrician environment in which they moved. But in the kitchens cooks and undercooks donned white aprons, rolled up their sleeves, and kept their heads covered with hats and caps. Only those assigned to the most menial tasks, the dishwashers, were bareheaded and shirtless.[18] The person in charge of food preparation and service was usually required to wear dark attire. "The steward must wear black, like a calm, serious man; he must appear clean and elegant, as befits the honor of his office."[19] He was thus obliged to wear clothes that reflected the standards of taste and style set at the court of his distinguished employer. If he worked for a cardinal he had to wear a long, flowing robe and a clerical berretta on his head. If he worked for a prince he was expected to display the sartorial elegance of a gentleman. The carver was obliged to wear a sword, and the butler, who was generally young and attractive, was expected to dress in a fashionable, up-to-date manner. In fact, the butler, who was in charge of appetizers and salads, confectionery and fruit, and really occupied a position halfway between a pastry chef and an ice-cream maker, provided the most delightful, spirited, and eagerly anticipated part of the meal. At first only the steward was allowed to grow a beard and whiskers and, from second half of the seventeenth century, to wear a wig. The lower ranks of kitchen employees were expected to be clean-shaven, but, as Scappi's engravings suggest, the youngest among them probably did not need to shave.

In courts and aristocratic households, therefore, the staff reflected the image set by their noble employers rather than a single professional code, emphasizing their masters' opulence and elegance with their style of dress. The greater the authority enjoyed by an employee, the more likely he was to wear a long wig and adopt a chivalric, princely style of dress. Wigs were worn by Antonio Latini, employed in one of the finest households in Naples at the end of the seventeenth century, and by Giovanni Nebbia, who worked in Macerata during the second half of the eighteenth century. At the outset wigs were worn long, but they became shorter in the Enlightenment era.[20] This did not mean that employees were not distinguished in ways that signaled their individual functions. The meat carver used to wear a napkin, folded lengthwise, on his left shoulder for the duration of his service at the table. This custom survived even after the disappearance of the carver, and a figure carrying a napkin under his arm or across his forearm could be seen at banquets or restaurants during the Empire period in Paris[21] and even later, right down to our own day.

The imposition of a rigid chromatic code for all employees—white for the kitchen and black and white for the dining room—was the outcome of a new approach to professional attire that came about in the nineteenth century. It was inspired by issues of hygiene and a desire for ceremonial decorum. White— used for the cook's jacket, the tablecloth, and the dishes—designated an impeccable cleanliness that was intended to make a sharp, immediate impression. Black was not entirely absent from the kitchens, but it was only permitted in foods: in gravies, squid ink, and fruit seeds. Those who served food, however, did wear black, with the specific objective of suggesting an austere, self-possessed elegance. From the sixteenth century onward black was considered elegant and authoritative and was favored by the elite, to the point that Domenico Romoli suggested in *La singolar dottrina*—as part of his attempt to tone down the eccentricities of the serving class—that the wine waiter should wear black velvet shoes rather than red ones.[22] The interdiction against garish colors occurred in parallel with the adoption of a uniform, a service livery that had already been in use at the French courts during the ancien régime and was revived during the Restoration. In deliberate contrast to the green of Napoleonic livery, Maria Luigia of Parma required her employees to wear a dark brown uniform, foreshadowing the eventual dominance of black and white.[23] During the second half of the nineteenth century the dining-room staff in every country wore a formal evening coat and white tie or, in less formal restaurants, a simple black jacket. The jacket gradually gained prominence until it replaced the tailcoat completely after the end of World War II. Only the headwaiter was allowed to wear a black tie, a distinction that associated black with a higher level of status and a greater sense of seriousness. The black waistcoat worn with the dinner jacket and the white waistcoat worn with the tailcoat in the evenings reflected a similar system of values.

Like the regulation requiring a white shirt, shirtfront, cuffs, dickey, and tie or a black jacket, pants, socks, and shoes, rigorous rules also governed the wearing of wigs. The *Manuale dell'industria alberghiera* published by the Touring Club Italiano in 1923 praised the English custom of forbidding waiters to wear whiskers and of allowing only those employed at the highest level of service to wear a trimmed beard.[24] A correlation was thus established between white and clean-shaven and between black and neatly groomed. Unseemly hair or rebellious locks implied a level of freedom conceded only to the most important employees, who, as we know, tend to treat their clients with an attitude of familiarity. In actual practice, however, many waiters wore a small moustache. We find evidence of this in group photos of the cooking teams working in hotel kitchens and on ocean liners. Here the cook may sport a dark moustache

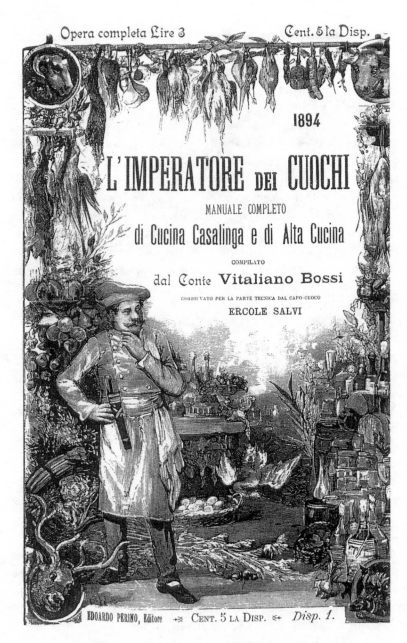

Frontispiece of *L'imperatore dei cuochi*, by Vitaliano Bossi
(Rome: Perini, 1894).

between his white hat and his clean-shaven chin. Similarly, the waiter sports a moustache between his clean-shaven chin and his neatly combed hair, which is gleaming with a generous dose of hair oil. The chromatic standards of dress, hairstyle, and grooming products were therefore in complete harmony with each other.

Only one form of headwear has survived in the food department: the chef's hat. At the beginning of the nineteenth century it was either floppy and shaped rather like a wool beret or stiff, wide, and flat. Later it grew taller, lighter, and tubular in shape, rising like a soufflé to emphasize the wearer's dedication to a superior and distinctive professional calling. If there is an adjective to describe it, this is surely "hieratic," since the hat serves as the crown of a priestly order dedicated to the health and well-being of the clientele. Its whiteness reverberates with light, delicate, high-profile values like those of poached fish, blancmange, sugar glaze, and chipped ice.

What symbolic role is embodied in the use of black attire in the serving of food? This is the color of mourning, strange, provocative, blasphemous, which Grimod de la Reynière (the first gastronomic journalist in France) used, as a young man, on his invitations to a "scandal supper." It is also the mark of masculine elegance, embodied theatrically by the waiter, who submits to a protocol but is nonetheless beyond the reach of fashion. The tailcoat, the dinner jacket, and the waistcoat only give the appearance of conforming to the dress codes of the aristocracy. In reality the waiter's dark uniform remained unaffected by sartorial trends that called for a longer or a shorter jacket, a change in the color and cut of the tie, and eventually liberated men from the funereal impression created by this type of attire.

The severe black-and-white code of the uniforms, the stiffness of the shirt-front, and the pleats of the toque also evoke something that is not unrelated to the management of restaurant life: the military code. Nineteenth-century cooks wore white double-breasted jackets, decorated with two long rows of buttons, inspired by military jackets and attached a knife pouch to their belts as a cruel mark of their trade. The waiters also seemed like soldiers, governed by a rigid discipline and strict dress code and organized into an ironclad hierarchy where everyone seemed impeccable and identical. Black and white express these imperatives, canceling out individual identities in favor of the team spirit. In the kitchen the terms chef ("chief") and chef de rang are not only a matter of metaphor.

The strangest aspect of this code is its persistence. The jacket worn by the headwaiter is unusual in today's world, as is the cook's uniform. The sommelier wears a heavy chain around his neck that seems even more antiquated. With the passing of time, and with the diminishing tendency of restaurant clients to wear formal attire, these uniforms begin to seem dated, if not downright anachronistic, and are nonetheless fully accepted. The symbolic function of the black-and-white dress code has prevailed over every other rule of taste, fashion, and convenience, emphasizing the distance between clients and staff, between audience and stage. Though shirtfronts, dickeys, and cuff links have disappeared, we still witness the vaguely nocturnal spectacle of men wearing workclothes that retain an element of anachronistic elegance, and their clients are not unappreciative of this. Thus in the field of gastronomy a conservative tone is more important than any other. Even the atmosphere of the finest restaurants is marked by time, by the restaging of a ritual. The attire worn by the staff evokes the look of a wax museum where the occupants might come to life one evening and sit down together at a banquet.

The New Innkeeper

The ship's cook and the hotel chef have been struggling for work since the beginning of the twentieth century. They have had long and difficult careers, made more demanding by seasonal moves to beach resorts and mountain villages and by extremely intense competition. They often envy their female counterpart, the household cook, who practices a steady routine and at the end of the day is better remunerated. Yet the professional cook can still look down on all others who work in the kitchen, whether alone or with the help of a servant, and who provide food and service. Innkeepers by contrast occupy a very different place in the history of cooking from that of salaried cooks. Theirs is an ancient caste, so notorious that it is invoked by Teofilo Folengo to represent hell and reappears in Collodi's *Pinocchio* in the scene set at the Inn of the Red Lobster that recounts one of the cruelest misfortunes to befall the protagonist. We have only to summon up the image of these corpulent men—squashed caps on their heads, aprons tied around their waists, and their thick hands planted on the table as they greet their clients—to understand the extent to which they have sparked the common imagination.

We have inherited an abundance of literary representations of the innkeeper, as well as travel accounts, theatrical sketches, songs, ribald poetry, and illustrations, all marked by a similarly bombastic, facetious, or denigrating tone. In public announcements of all kinds, whether issued by the police or by almsgiving associations, the innkeepers' guild has often been the target of public scrutiny. What we do not find, however, are recipe collections and handbooks associated with the innkeeper, since he works, operates, and provides his fare to the public in a casual way, deciding on whatever price suits him. He is a character that transcends time and fashion, and as such he is a dated entity, as old and as wrinkled as the countryside, with his wine and his various dishes. He can be found throughout the nineteenth and twentieth century, serving drunkards, cursing and reviling the world at large, and occasionally offering dishes that are prepared in a far from mediocre fashion. The quality of inns varied greatly.

From his demotic vantage point the innkeeper generally interpreted the social and political moods of his time and observed the growth of the city. It is particularly interesting to examine the evolution of his trade, since his way of doing business—serving food prepared in the traditional style and interpreted in different ways according to the availability of ingredients—had a profound influence on the rise of the *trattoria* in Italy. An eatery where the cook was dressed in white, like La Noce, or La Nôs, in Milan,[25] was generally called an *osteria* (inn), but the same word could also be used to describe a very humble tavern (otherwise called a *bettola*), where the owner came from the same class as the clients to whom he sold his wine.

The innkeeper's main skill was his ability to select and sell wine for his clients' consumption on the premises or elsewhere. He dedicated his commercial talents to this art, sometimes sacrificing his good name by earning a reputation as a cheat apt to dilute the wine by adding color or water to his own products. He was not always required to offer food to his clients—and in many taverns this did not occur—but the custom of cooking spread in several urban centers and smaller towns where necessity, travel, the mail coach, or the marketplace required it. Specific types of foods were typically consumed at the inn. These were above all items that were locally produced and sold at the market or, if the inn was located in the city, acquired in neighboring areas: bread, dried sausages, cheeses, as well as whatever quantity of preserved and cured foods the innkeeper might be able to obtain. The diary of Valentino Alberti of Verona (1796–1834) is illuminating in this regard. Alberti's "compote of capers" and his "compote of peppers," the preparation of which he proudly records, became so famous that he began supplying them to the kitchens of important households, even providing them for the dining table of Napoleon, who briefly visited Verona in 1807. The simplest meal Alberti customarily served was "bread, wine, salted meats, and peppers."[26] Cold preserved foods, treated with vinegar or salt, had long been considered the appropriate accompaniment of wine and were firmly linked to it. As well as selling foods, Alberti was an innkeeper in the true sense of the word, since in addition to mixing containers of wine he kept a pig and eventually cooked it for his clients. *Codeghini* (pig's feet sausages), salami, and salted meat were part of an economic system in which the tavern owner was likely to feed a pig with leftovers and fatten it up for those who frequented his establishment. When the animal was slaughtered all the clients would profit from it.

The type of innkeeper who would offer a hot meal, varying in composition and preparation according to the season and harvest, was quite another matter. Let us look, for example, at one of the individuals of this second type: Luigi Bicchierai, nicknamed Pennino, owner of the Locanda del Ponte a Signa from 1812 to 1873. His establishment was located on the bank of the Arno at a busy, navigable part of the river on the way to Livorno. In addition to the usual local clientele, visitors to the inn sometimes included important individuals passing through the area in the course of a journey. Pennino has left us a rough outline of his accounts and reflections. He worked alone in the kitchen, except for the help of a single apprentice boy. Some of his recipes reflect the local, Florentine tradition: chickpea soup, tripe with sauce, salt cod with leeks, oily omelets, beans "al fiasco," pork chops with black cabbage. Other recipes suggest economic concerns: saving the dried crusts from the croste di pan grasso (crusts of oily bread). Hunger is always lurking at the door and is alluded to in the title of his "sugo della miseria" (poverty sauce), as well as in the recipe for panzanella, described as a "dish for the poor, though very tasty and enjoyed even by noblemen, priests, and officers." Other recipes have come down to us from cooks who stopped at the inn. One of these visitors, from Asti, left Pennino a souvenir in the form of a "savoy soup," made with chicken livers, chopped vegetables, and a good ox bone. Since he had clients of all types, Pennino also had to learn to cook refined dishes, and for this reason he studied products and ingredients, experimented with them, and tasted them: "September 1, 1818. A fruit that is tasty but unsuitable for dishes served here at the inn is the pomegranate. An elderly sailor who went by ship from Livorno to the Orient tells me that in the East pomegranates are crushed for drinks, or they are boiled and strained and served with meat stew. The only thing I attempted to do with them was to serve them with fresh ricotta cheese, by mixing the seeds into the cheese, but this was not a successful idea."[27] His recipes are observations on his trade that serve as a point of reflection. Writing allows him to talk to himself and to his clients and encourages him to express himself in a conversational tone, marked with the spirit of wisdom: "1849. With all these signs of rebellion and the desire to unite Italy, when I, as an innkeeper, heard about such things and thought of Italy, which is so divided but which everyone wants to be one, I imagined [the country] as a fine big pot of stewed meats, full of trotters, tongue, various kinds of meat, and greens!! So, if Italy is the bollito, the Flag is its seasoning, a Tricolor Sauce" (p. 106). And he proceeds with the three patriotic sauces, red, white, and green.

There is nothing of the image of the sly innkeeper in Pennino. He is devout and conservative, though not without an open-minded cynicism. He gets his supplies on a daily basis, according to a schedule by which ingredients follow the same cyclical calendar as the progression of the seasons. While each product might vary in quantity from year to year, the date of its harvest stays the same. He buys ricotta cheese from the shepherds as they pass with their sheep on the way to their winter quarters. He slaughters the pig and makes blood sausage. He quotes proverbs when they are useful as a memory aid: "April 29, 1814. The farmer has put a good number of geese out for fattening. As the saying goes: 'If you want fine geese, start fattening them on Saint Catherine's Day. Then on the Feast of St. Lucy, kill them, preserve them, and set them aside for the summer, just as you would do with pork fat' " (p. 27).

With the passing of time, the construction of a railroad linking Florence, Empoli, and Livorno, the introduction of an oven for baking bread (which in 1855 marked the end of domestic baking in Signa), and the arrival of the Piedmontese, his routine varies little. The foods served at the inn come from the peasants and from local shops, rarely from afar, like the coffee beans sent from Livorno that pass through Signa on their way to Florence. However curious he might be, Pennino is a sensible sort and does not venture beyond béchamel sauce and puff pastry, served only "on important holidays." At a time when such work was usually carried out by the kitchen staff, he proved capable of doing everything himself, managing purchasing and bookkeeping, cooking the food, and serving it with simple elegance.

From the travelers' perspective, these all-purpose cooks were the very essence of tradition and local color and became the subject of increasing attention from the end of the nineteenth century onward. It was as though the presence of a type of cuisine inspired by the model of French hotel restaurants and perceived as a form of high art entailed a loss of roots, bringing about a sense of artificiality in taste. In reaction to this inns gained favor among the bourgeoisie and intellectual classes who would otherwise have been the vehicle of culinary internationalization. Modest prices, simple ingredients, and intense flavors held a powerful attraction for Italians and foreigners alike. Inns that functioned as rest stops for travelers, such as the one at Signa Bridge and others in less dignified locations, are described by Pellegrino Artusi in *La scienza in cucina* as belonging to a time when he still traveled about in a horse-drawn carriage, representing important points of reference in his memory of different tastes. When he stopped at Modigliana, Artusi was served extremely tough slices of cured pork neck for dinner, along with tagliatelle. At another inn, in Polesella near Rovigo, in a large room that served both as kitchen and dining room, the female proprietor prepared a dish of "rice, hunter's style," "which had to serve as first course, main course, and side dish."[28] Belying the assumption that the food served at inns consisted of overcooked dishes that were perpetually reheated, the poverty of these establishments meant that simple, unvaried food had to be prepared on the spot, as ordered.

But the first *osteria* mentioned in the culinary history of the twentieth century is an urban establishment. The railroad linking the principal cities of the provinces, as far south as Naples, facilitated access to the urban eateries mentioned in the earliest guidebooks. Hans Barth's *Osteria: Guida spirituale delle osterie italiane da Verona a Capri* (Osteria: Spiritual guide to the restaurant-inns of Italy, from Verona to Capri), translated from the original German with a preface written by Gabriele D'Annunzio, was first published in 1910 and reprinted in 1921. It describes the various inns and proprietors, with their wives and daughters, their wine, and some of their dishes. Since it is addressed to thirsty Italian and German tourists, it covers a broad range of establishments, among which we find trattorie, restaurants, bars, and beer houses. Other guides follow, such as Mariotti's *Quando siam dall'oste insieme* (When we go to the inn together).[29] As though embodying a manner of cooking and consuming food, the innkeepers, both male and female, emerge primarily in their physical, corporeal dimension. All are strong and stocky. It is enough to walk around Rome, step inside a doorway or under a shingle, and observe the remarkably heavy-set Sora Adele or Sora Ermelinda, "with her black hair swept up like a crow's wing, her smiling face, bewitching eyes, and the hint of downy, black fuzz on her upper lip." Similarly Sor Peppe is noted for "his imperial head and deep-set, bovine eyes."[30]

As a drinking venue the inn mainly offered wines from the Castelli Romani, which were selected, transported, and tapped by the owner, whom Hans Barth frequently pauses to praise. Sor Peppe, located directly opposite the Trevi Fountain, makes two dishes available to his clients: fettucine (*"fedelini"*) and saltimbocca, and is referred to as *"il fedelinaro"* ("the *fedelini* maker").[31] Felicetto, located on Via Mario dei Fiori, specializes in a tripe dish with sauce and a meat casserole with celery.[32] The presence of oxtail and *pagliata* alone does not guarantee "typicality," while tripe, which is found everywhere, is one of the common denominators of this type of fare in all areas. Those who dine at these inns are residents of the neighborhood. Some wineshops are located next to a fried-food shop and a pizza maker's, completing the options of their clientele. A growing interest in these establishments and their cooking explains the success of the acclaimed trattoria owners during the interwar period, men such as Alfredo, king of fettucine, located on Via della Scrofa in Rome, or Campoli, nicknamed "Il Troja," who opened a trattoria in Florence. More than mere cooks, these men were popular entertainers. Campoli had the body of a fire-eater: "Big and bulky, his enormous shadow towers over the entire table occupied by his awestruck clients. He has the shaved head of a wrestler, walks around the tables, and, with his shoulders hunched and his arms outstretched as though he were grasping for something to hold on to, he heads toward those just entering his establishment."[33] What does Campoli order for his clients? Hot croutons, penne with sauce, deviled chicken, "a rack of ribs from our own veal," a flask "of Ruffina's wine."[34] A guidebook written in 1939 offers the following review: "Campoli, known as il Troja, is the low tavern in fashion in Florence. A famous gentleman visiting from elsewhere and a little noblewoman are seated next to a common laborer. A rustic tone, clearly a place for the ordinary people, but with excellent food. All the Florentine specialties are prepared with loving care and rare ability. The Chianti and Pomino wines are excellent."[35]

There is an enormous distance between the innkeeper of Modigliana, Polesella, and Signa and his urban relative and heir, the *trattore*, or trattoria owner, who draws on a large market. The urban *trattore* can alternate his dishes over the course of the week, announcing them in advance (Monday: *pagliata*; Saturday: tripe; and so on), and can guarantee their availability all year long, over-

An Italian cook in Los Angeles (1911).
Source: Fototeca 3M.

feeding his clients if he chooses to do so. His offers huge portions, low prices, limited selections, and just one or two wines. As the modern equivalent of the innkeeper, he repeats simple recipes but has his own ideas about cooking, adjusting his procedures according to request. A fire blazing in a hearth or open grill may provide a special effect in some of these little theaters, just as dishes flamed in alcohol are served in luxury restaurants for the sake of added drama. Specialties are restricted to a very small number of dishes, such as fettucine in Rome or ribs in Florence, which are also appreciated by middle-class clients, reminding them of home cooking. These specialties derive additional appeal from the quantity of the portions, condiments, special cooking strategies, and atmosphere. Alfredo's fettucine are adorned with a double dose of butter, Troja's rack of veal ribs looks like "a kind of red valise." In comparison to Pennino's recipes, which were often inspired by the fortuitous availability of specific ingredients or the need to make ends meet on Lenten days, the cooking style that evolved in the small urban eateries was richer in content but poorer in inspiration, for it reflected the ideas held by the clients about the cuisine of ordinary people.

The difference between the country inn (the *osteria*) and the urban trattoria was significant in Artusi's time, but it began to diminish during the Fascist period. Yet the top-level establishment, the restaurant, struggled to maintain its superiority in the system if it was not part of a luxury hotel or if it lacked qualified personnel. The clientele frequenting the three types of establishment no longer selected where they went to dine merely on the basis of social class, preferring to place the importance of the type of food served above the style of service and identifying more readily with Italian regional dishes than with French cuisine. The innkeeper has been called a *trasformista* (a figure who cleverly adapts to prevailing trends). Still, the fact that he could transform himself into a *chef* (as Luigi Bicchierai did) is another of the paradoxes of Italian gastronomy. How did one of the most prestigious restaurants of Bologna come into being? Starting as a small, modest food shop with the dining room and kitchen elbow to elbow, it developed into something greater thanks to Giovanni Zurla, a career chef who returned to work in his native city. "And its special characteristics? None. Il Pappagallo is an ordinary eating house for respectable clients. It has no pretensions, and it is almost like one of those wineshops where a few regulars like to indulge methodically in drinking too much."[36] And yet the tagliatelle, tortellini, and green lasagne served here earned an extraordinary reputation, along with "Richelieu pudding," a sautéed filet of turkey with Hollandaise sauce and truffles, in no way related to the usual fare of trattoria or *osteria*.

In his later incarnation, the innkeeper or *trattore* is an independent cook, an enterprising businessman without much capital, focused on providing dishes that are generally local in character, an experimenter in his spare time, without pupils and without heirs. He perfects a small number of dishes and chooses the wines at hand. His menu? Whether it is recited orally or scribbled on a blackboard, it does not vary much but offers the advantage of pasta courses and main dishes that have certain appeal and are capable of winning a strong consensus. He is not in a position to pass this on to his heirs because unlike hotel personnel he works within a family structure and has full responsibility for the cooking. The excess and decadence of Il Pappagallo were therefore inscribed in its very origins. In modern times it is the fate of each generation of innkeepers—eternal pioneers and last of the Mohicans—to be reborn different from their predecessors and different from those to come.

From Housewife to Female Cook

One of the most heated debates in the history of Italian gastronomy is whether men or women have had primacy in cooking. This has become more intense in the twentieth century with the growing presence, and increasing importance, of popular, provincial restaurants run by women and by patterns of refined, carefully nurtured family cooking that have been identified as the mirror of good taste and authentic traditions. This debate has deep roots and involves not only the symbolic value of the female nurturer in society but the conditions in which women explicate domestic labor and the nature of their cultural and professional baggage. A chronological survey of the problem in the modern age will help us to establish the terms of the debate.

The word "*cuisinière*" (female cook) appears in the title of a recipe collection in France in 1746, though it was written and signed by a male author, Menon.[37] In Italy the work of a purported "female cook from Piedmont who teaches the easy approach to the best methods of preparing dishes both on fast days and ordinary days" was published in Vercelli in 1771.[38] In the subsequent decades rivalry between men and women for control of the kitchens and dinner tables gained momentum, with the consequence of creating two levels of competence, one highly qualified, focused on service in palaces, embassies, and patrician households, and the other, focused on the family and the middle-class environment, requiring practical experience in the vegetable garden, the marketplace, and the family kitchen. The culinary publications circulating in England and America were then almost unknown in Italy, as were the names of the legendary Hannah Glasse and Amelia Simmons, whose writings anticipated the bourgeois family model, which focused particularly on national dishes, cakes, and preserves.[39]

The Italian servant-cook, however, did not have to wait until the second half of the eighteenth century to give evidence of her talent. The good woman of the house—*la massera da be*—is the protagonist of a text written in dialect in 1554. This is a poor woman from the countryside near Brescia, who, while searching for wool to weave some clothing, knocks at people's doors offering her strong arms and substantial experience, specifying that she knows a lot about cooking. "Looking after the chopping board is something I can also do." Her areas of competence are extensive: stewed and roast meats, small and large fish, soup, *paniccia* and *vermicelli*, was well as more refined preparations such as forcemeat: "As for stuffing, don't tell me about it: *fiadoni*, *torte*, layered pies, savory custards, stuffed fritters." She knows how to bake bread and cook beans—boiled in water and in broth, dressed with oil and fennel seeds—for both servants and employers. The *massera* possesses not only the talents of the male cook but also his vices. She is greedy, drinks wine from the bottle, flirts with young men, and comes to blows with the suppliers.[40]

We do not find this character in the kitchens of the aristocracy. Messisbugo dismisses women with few words, and there is no need for other stewards to repeat his position: "I will not waste time or effort describing different soups made of green vegetables or legumes or describing how to fry a tench, or broil a fresh cod on the grill, or other similar things, which any common old woman could easily prepare."[41] These women worked in the homes of the wealthy, carrying out different tasks: attending to the fire, sweeping the floors, doing the laundry, and taking care of the hens. Since the pantry was next door to the kitchen and close to the hearth, their tasks might additionally include plucking a chicken and skinning a hare, watching over a pot of boiling meat and skimming the fat, as the frontispiece of Giovanni de' Rosselli's *Epulario* suggests.[42] The women could also be expected to prepare food for the servants and occasionally a few dishes for the gentleman on weekdays, when there were no guests in the house.

The head of the household is a paterfamilias who performs the role of host and supervises financial affairs. This family man is described in the writings of Torquato Tasso as a mature gentleman who supplies the dinner table with food from his own lands and with game caught while hunting. He gives orders for the preparation of feasts, specifying the appropriate wines and issuing commands to his servants and children. The responsibility of the male head of household lasted many years, and it was still strong in the nineteenth century. It was his prerogative to supervise the servants, his watch in hand, to order dishes, calculate costs and expenditures, select and reward the servants, though he was free to delegate some of these tasks to his wife. Senator Paolo Mantegazza, author of *L'arte di prender moglie* (The art of choosing a wife), wrote in his diary on January 5, 1895: "Every morning since January 1, I have been doing the accounts with the cook, as Marina [Fantoni, his wife] has expressed the desire that I do so."[43]

The woman of the house often supervised housekeepers and maidservants in the execution of their tasks. "It's incredible," says Adami, "how useful a housekeeper can be in a home and how quickly domestic affairs improve."[44] For centuries it was the task of the lady of the house to oversee all the servants, men and women, instructing males and females separately (as well as educating herself). She could learn a great deal from the professional cooks who were employed for special occasions. She would store up their teaching like a treasure and pass it on to her servants. As Pandolfini wrote:

Each woman should know how to cook and serve all the select dishes. She should learn from the cooks when they come to the house to prepare special meals. She should watch how these are prepared, ask questions, and learn the procedures by heart, so that when visitors arrive who need to be welcomed with appropriate hospitality, the woman will know what to do, and will order all the best condiments, and will not have to send out for cooks, which is not always possible, especially when staying at the family's country

La cucina toscana è fine e delicata.   *Il rito delle fettuccine ha inizio.*

Tuscan Cooking Is Delicate and Refined and *The Fettucine
Ritual Begins* (drawings by Novello).

Source: Paolo Monelli, *Il ghiottone errante* (Milan: Treves, 1935).

residence, where good cooks cannot be found but visitors still have to be
entertained. Not that the woman should cook, but let her direct, instruct,
and show the maids who are not as well educated how to behave in the most
advantageous fashion and how to prepare whatever dishes are required.[45]

The more modest the family the stronger the allegiance between the maid
and the lady of the house and the stricter the discipline governing the purchase
and preservation of foods, based on quality and economy. The servant-cook is
expected to provide a varied diet, with the appropriate level of decorum, comprising different elements according to the hierarchy for servants and nobles.
Homemade bread, wine, and soup are the basis of this diet, provided at little cost.

Is there a cuisine characteristic of such women? This is what Ortensio Lando
humorously suggests in his *Catalogo degli inventori delle cose che si mangiano* (Catalog of inventories of things that may be eaten). Women from the countryside had
the advantage of knowing how to prepare beans in the proper fashion, both as a "dry
dish" and as a soup, as well as chickpeas, broad beans, and famous dishes of fresh
pasta: "Libista, the Lombard peasant woman from Cernuschio, was the inventor of

ravioli wrapped in pasta as well as unwrapped morsels called '*da' Lorbardi mal fatti.*' "
"Marina da Offlaga was the inventor of *fiadoni* and *enola* ravioli." "Melibea of Mer-
bio was the inventor of *casoncelli*, *offelle*, and *salviati.*" "Meluzza from Comasco
was the inventor of lasagne and macaroni with garlic, spices, and cheese."[46] Con-
firmation of this quick catalog is provided in the poetry of Teofilo Folengo, who
lived in the Po Valley. Here Tognazzo tearfully bemoans his late wife, Bertolina, as
he remembers her culinary talents: "She was excellent at making fine, fat gnocchi
with her own hands, as well as layered pies, *tortelli*, bean soup, and womanly
polenta."[47] If Messisbugo's helpers were skilled in kneading pasta dough, simpler
versions of this art, such as the preparation of gnocchi and polenta, were left to the
women. By the same token, if a woman was left to pluck a hen or scrape the scales
off a fish, she was also allowed the opportunity to stew and roast them. Within these
limits we might say there was indeed a tradition of women's cooking in Italy, both
in the kitchens of country people and in those of patrician households.

The women were of different types, not always good. Many literary texts decry
the vices of servants, accusing them above all of dirty habits and treachery. Cleanliness is a requirement all too often invoked in modern culinary literature, as
though to ward off the suspicion that kitchens might be filthy and that foods might
be contaminated out of ignorance, neglect, or spite. In *Il fuggilozio*, a collection
of stories written by Tommaso Costo in 1596, the maid vengefully throws lasagna
strips into a pot of boiling water along with some strands of hair from the head of
her mistress. She then presents the dish, dressed with grated Piacenza cheese, to
the woman and her friends.[48] Unlike the kitchens of the courts, where each dish
was supervised by the steward, who tasted it before presenting it to his master, in
private homes the destinies of employers and their familiars were continually
intermixed or juxtaposed with each other, facilitating a type of food preparation
that mixed high and low models, enriched or impoverished by the demands of
domestic finances.

The maids' cooking style is not a minor version of the cuisine practiced by
Messisbugo and Scappi, and neither does it compete with it. It makes use of fish
and meats selected according to different standards; it draws sparingly on sugar
and spices, which are used only for sweets; and it does not aspire to formal or chromatic effects. It tempts the appetite with dishes such as sausages and beans that
are enjoyed by the servant as well the master, and when presented to the master
in a more refined version these dishes please him. If we are seeking a comparable
model we would have to move away from the environment of patrician banquets,
search in the provinces, and dust off the handwritten notebooks of well-to-do
households where the person in charge of presenting food on the table jotted
down and compiled recipes and secrets for future use. In *Il cocho bergamasco alla
casalenga* (The home-style cook of Bergamo) and in the stanzas of *La massera*,
we find recipes "of a commonplace kind" that are appreciated for the way they
are cooked, since they do not delight "the eye more than the palate."[49]

Palace cooks and scullery maids belong to worlds that remain culturally separate. The cooks undergo a period of training, they belong to a hierarchy and have their recipe books, whereas the women are illiterate, their backs bent from the effort of drawing water from the well and carrying firewood. If a certain competence developed among these women, it was not translated into a new didactic system. (By the end of the seventeenth century, "outside Tuscany" the word *massara* meant "the female servant or maid, especially in the kitchen.")[50] A misogynistic discourse rekindled prejudices, emphasizing a disparity between male and female cooks that was more moral than professional. Vincenzo Tanara, who formed his opinions from the perspective of a rural economy, criticized the laziness, dishonesty, wastefulness, incompetence, and filth of women. Female servants are all "wine-drinking, foul-mouthed, or witches" and must not even lay a hand on the hearth, leaving to "clean, faithful, and knowledgeable" men the task of preparing dishes and bringing them to the table.[51] These ideas also appear in the satirical literature produced in Italy and France around 1650, suggesting the existence of a precise hierarchy of tasks and privileges according to which the woman occupied either the highest role (employer) or the lowest (scullery maid).

Thanks to the influence of the Parisian model, as bourgeois cooking evolved the female servant was reevaluated, and she was ultimately admitted to the school of "high" (male) cooking. "My method is simple and does not require a great deal of expense," says the "female cook of Cremona." "It is also used in the great kitchens where I learned my craft from Piedmontese and French cooks and from other cooks from different places."[52] This daring statement implies that the woman knows Italian in addition to her own dialect, as well as a few words of French, that she knows how to prepare vegetable soup as well as its refined versions, with squabs and prawns, and that she keeps her serving skills up to date, adapting them as required by taste. Even though she is cited on the frontispieces of works that were really written by men, the female cook has acquired a level of responsibility that includes increasingly specific tasks, among which we no longer find baking bread for the family or preparing chickenfeed or pig fodder. Worthy cooks, such as Antonio Nebbia, specifically took on the effort to instruct this humble class of cooks: "In going to the trouble to compose this cookbook of mine, I had no other aim than to be of use to the many servants, both male and female, who aspire to or imagine being able to provide good cooking for their employers and who find that they have almost no resources to aid them in this task."[53]

Throughout the nineteenth century the idea steadily grew that female cooks could compete in the kitchen with their male counterparts, surpassing them in refinement, creating a synthesis between the cooking of ordinary people and that of the aristocrats and becoming the increasingly exclusive heir of family traditions. The particularly feminine connotation inherent in this figure is her interest in the management of provisions, preserved foods, and baked desserts. The female cook is the embodiment of two different souls: that of the scullery maid refashioned by the social system as the labor market became increasingly specialized and that of the busy, frugal housewife who is herself willing to take pots and pans in hand. Given the decrease in the number of servants employed by households, all the necessary skills had to be embodied in one person, cooking became more highly esteemed, and unexpected careers opened up. *Gianina ossia la cuciniera delle Alpi* (Gianina; or, The female cook of the Alps), a recipe collection attributed to Francesco Leonardi that was published in Rome in 1817, gives us some idea of the situation. Gianina is Austrian and the daughter of hoteliers. She marries a French cook who practices his trade in patrician households and after an international career begins his own business in Chiaja, Naples. After her husband's death Gianina takes over his work, and having liquidated his property she opens an inn on the Cenisio between Italy and France in 1789, offering a range of dishes that are partly French and partly Italian. Gianina does not seem at all like a servant. She has a small library of culinary texts, and she herself is the author of a book. The tourist industry and the postal routes are factors that facilitate her vocation as a businesswoman and a chef. How many women like Gianina can be found in Italy? Few, though the numbers are increasing, judging from the emergence of recipe collections like this one, which were written by men who preferred to hide behind a pseudonym of the opposite sex. This trend became more frequent in the second half of the nineteenth century, whatever the contents of the books might be: *La cucina economica moderna* (Modern economical cooking), first published in 1843, was retitled *Il cuoco bolognese* (The male cook of Bologna) in the 1857 edition, and retitled again in the 1874 edition, as *La cuciniera bolognese* (The female cook of Bologna).[54] The recipes are identical in all editions.

The feminine connotations attributed to a type of everyday, economical cooking gained ground amid many difficulties, not least of which was the transmission of information so familiar that it seemed to merit scant verbal elaboration. *La cuoca cremonese* and *La cuciniera bolognese* do not describe the preparation of pasta dough even once, as they venture into a field filled with terms of French origin. It is all too evident that these works constitute the simplified version of a male-dominated way of writing. Paradoxically all didactic texts on gastronomy continue to use this kind of language, giving greater importance to refined dining, the special holiday meal, and elaborate recipes than to the daily practice of making pasta and broths. Yet the recipe collections began to include in increasing numbers recipes for dishes that women really prepared at home. To mention only one in this line of publications, there is *La cuciniera maestra* (Mistress of cooking), printed in Reggio Emilia in 1884, where we find tagliatelle along with complete instructions for preparing the dough, beginning with the flour. Following the initial section, which describes the refined version of

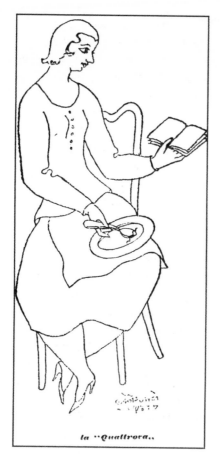

La quattrova and *La cuoca letterata* (drawings by Giò Ponti).

Source: *La cucina elegante ovvero il quattrova illustrato* (Milan: Domus, 1931).

the cuisine of Reggio, there is a section describing economical ways of cooking, and we then find local specialties like *scarpazzone*, a pie filled with herbs, as well as interprovincial and regional dishes such as "pork feet with lentils."[55]

The presence of the dual register represented by modest and refined cooking can be explained when we realize that up to the time of Artusi three people generally worked together in the kitchen: a male cook, a female cook, and a gastronomic expert. The male cook was the direct or indirect guarantor of the elevated style and was capable of providing dignified meals for possible guests. In Artusi's version this "holy trinity" consists of Francesco Ruffilli of Bologna, Marietta Sabatini of Massa, and Artusi himself, a culinary expert influenced by his background in Tuscany and Romagna. Artusi chooses to honor his collaborator Marietta Sabatini in a special way, by naming a panettone after her—and this is no small acknowledgment. "My Marietta is a fine cook and such a good, warmhearted, woman that she deserves to have this cake named after her, especially since she taught me how to make it."[56] "Marietta's panettone," "Bartola's cutlets," "signora Adele's cheese mold," and "Luisetta's soufflé" are all dishes named after women. In the use of these first names the hierarchical order begins to dissolve, mixing bourgeois housewives with their maids.

The decline of the large servant class, assigned to a thousand separate functions, reinforced the collaboration between the maid and her female employer, a pair that might have to be reestablished from scratch from one year to the next. Because of her own peasant origins, the maid had few dishes in her repertoire but had a great need to work, and the housewife too had to start from nothing on the day of her marriage. The loss of staff, far from dissolving the ties of dependency, reinforced them. To recruit the likes of Marietta Sabatini as his collaborator was a difficult task for Artusi, and he achieved it after progressing through an earlier selection of rebellious, querulous, capricious, hostile, and thieving women. The problems experienced in searching for the appropriate servant were part of the management of domestic labor that continued without interruption for more than a hundred years: from the middle of the nineteenth to the middle of the twentieth century. How was one to select a female cook? This might seem obvious: by trying her out. In reality every cook is molded by the household of her employers, and for this reason other factors had to be considered, such as her origins, accent, character, and appearance. The maid was required to disclose only two facts when first taken on by a household: where she was born and where she had last worked. The first answer allowed the employer to evaluate the level of her culinary awareness, and the second suggested a guarantee of competency. She had to learn to prepare for her employer's family food that was served according to a model that was not native to her. Coming from another province or another region she would learn all the dishes customarily selected by her employer. She would not be asked to compete with the elegance of the woman of the house but rather to guarantee a sound, agreeable standard of cooking. With a hint of irony, Emma Vanzetti, writing in 1936, suggests checking the woman's hands: "The hands of a good cook are short, wide, pink, clear, and plump, with square fingertips (revealing the woman's hardworking dedication and energy)."[57]

As patterns shift from the great household or country residence to the bourgeois family home with only one or two servants, we notice that the misogynistic denigration of female servants begins to lose its currency and bite. The female cook begins to prevail over the male cook, who is seen as costly, foppish, and the enemy of good health. Women are said to be attentive to regional culinary values and not only to those of their birthplace. Giulia Ferraris Tamburini of Milan is a practical woman: "Tortellini, said to be of Bologna, are eaten in broth and can be found preprepared and available for purchase, so I will tell you only how to cook them."[58] The market makes up for deficiencies in skill while offering the diner the pleasure of appetizing dishes that come from elsewhere. With this kind of support the regionalization of dishes that occurred in the twentieth century came to involve all female cooks and flourished throughout Italy.

Three cultural models come into play in the formation of the cook-housewife: the culinary tradition, contemporary gastronomic adjustments, and domestic economy. Traditional dishes are those that require manual skill but no imagination: broths and boiled foods, fresh pastas, and uncomplicated sauces. The use of leftovers for meatloaves and gravies, not to speak of the multiple techniques for recycling stale bread, can also be said to belong to this category. What is expressed here is domestic and local custom, the safeguarding of a simple, uncomplicated identity in the intermingling of different generations. This is the aspect of domestic culture that was most seriously challenged in the second half of the twentieth century with the rise of urbanization and the increasing exodus of women from the home to the workplace, and it survives today only in the archaic layers of the social body.

The printed recipe collection brought something new to this conservative substratum in the form of a dish that is attuned to bourgeois cuisine, more Italian than local and more urban than rural. Stuffed meat rolls, timbales, soufflés, pies, puddings, and savory canapés are the signs of a process of renewal undertaken by the domestic cook, expressing the desire for modernization. Even the dishes that come from one region, are adopted by another, and are disseminated in an uneven pattern across the country are part of this kind of consumption. The shift from a local, monotonous culture devoted to a particular pasta dish to the diversified use of pastas and sauces (which is stimulated by the availability of recipe books and women's magazines) reveals an ongoing tendency on the part of the housewife-cook to indulge in imaginary travels with her pots and pans. This trend has continued right up to the present.

Domestic economy is the most ideologically charged of the three models. The daughter of hygiene and Taylorism, it neither encourages the conservation of local tradition nor stimulates gastronomic change. Rather it expresses the primacy of good management over taste, of health over pleasure. Domestic economy was a subject taught in Italy's trade schools. International conventions, like the meeting held in Berlin in 1934, and the advent of the policy of autarchy confirmed its importance.[59] In the course of the twenty years of Fascist rule, in the principal cities of Italy, Milan, Florence, and Turin and in provincial capitals of the north, such as Udine and Bergamo, there were rural schools and daytime and evening training centers, as well as boarding schools, orphanages, and convents, where girls studied a type of cooking based on the bourgeois model. What did a woman who aspired to be a cook learn there? "To serve with love," is the response given in the title of a Catholic manual.[60] This means to shop for provisions, to learn the appropriate quantities, prices, and necessary cooking times, and to communicate creatively with inexpensive, healthy dishes, using preserved foods and economically prepared desserts. Through this curriculum, vitamins, minerals, and calories entered the cook's nutritional baggage.[61]

Tradition, innovation, and domestic economy are not the external features of a system that was consolidated once and for all, but they reflect the search for balance witnessed in Italian society up to the 1960s. This balance was rendered more precarious by the very nature of domestic work, variously perceived as duty, social service, temporary servility, and professional employment. It was the housewife-cook, with her local dishes, recipe collections, and managerial abilities, who created Italian family cooking. Over the past thirty years she has gradually handed it over to the food industry, which guarantees its ongoing survival, if only in an artificial way. With the disappearance of the permanent housemaid, the teaching of domestic economy also died out, and the housewife found herself again without a cook. Now both have to cook for themselves. The decline in manual skills, the reduction in time available for cooking, and easy recourse to meals prepared outside the home constitute the basic canvas onto which the woman and her spouse or partner project their knowledge of cooking in an increasingly spontaneous and amateurish way. The number of inexperienced, hesitant, monotonous cooks has grown along with the number of Italians employed in the workforce. So too has the throng of eager sandwich eaters, frenzied amateurs, and occasional gastronomic experts. An era of androgynous culinary art has thus begun, but not without a sense of perplexity.

CHAPTER EIGHT

Science and Technology in the Kitchen

Tradition and Progress

In the past there were basically two scientific models for the study of food and its preparation: the medical/dietetic approach, practiced continuously from antiquity down to the present, and the more recent physical/chemical approach. From the end of the seventeenth century onward the physical/chemical model gave rise to many important experiments with raw materials and preservation processes, heat sources and cooking utensils. In the field of gastronomy, however, the concept of progress is often misleading. The correlation of ingredients, labor, and implements does not affect the food in any direct, uncomplicated way. The most archaic procedures may turn out to be superior to modern techniques. Today meat grilled over a wood fire is considered preferable to meat cooked with electricity. Similarly, polenta has more flavor when prepared in a deep pan over an open fire than when it is reconstituted by adding water to a packet of yellow powder. Taste is never simply a reflection of innovation.

There is an issue of continuity here: from one end of Italian culinary history to the other, from Bartolomeo Scappi to Pellegrino Artusi, the tin-lined copper pan was considered the most appropriate vessel for cooking directly over the open fire (a heat source that had to be continuously replenished), and it was filled with water that came first from the well, then from the aqueduct, and finally from the kitchen tap. In order to evaluate the level of progress attained in the management of heat sources and in the metal alloys used in cooking vessels and utensils, we must take into account some variable factors as well as some constants, including those of a social or demographic nature. Without the work of the scullery boy or maidservant, who habitually took care of the fire and kept an eye on the embers, carried in the logs and briars, and trimmed the branches, it would be impossible to explain the longevity of the ancient kitchen. Ippolito Nievo described this age-old space, which survived up to the beginning of the nineteenth century: "[It was] dark, almost black with ancient soot, in contrast with the bottoms of the pots, the dripping pans, and carafes that were hanging there on a nail, glinting like the eyes of the devil."[1] The modernization of the household kitchen, which took place over a long period of time, fought a difficult and sometimes losing battle with traditional practices and forms of resistance. The kitchen hearth in the castle at Fratta, where dripping pans are placed strategically under the skewer, evokes a sense of nostalgia—nostalgia for a tradition that, when confronted by novelty, underwent a transformation but died out in the process, along with so many recipes and flavors. Yet the dirt of this dark, unhealthy kitchen, which was freezing in some areas and very hot in others, evokes a very different sensation, inevitably alienating our modern taste and sensibility. The contradictions between hygiene and cooking, hearty flavors and good health are in fact worthy of a separate study.

The uneven pattern of progress witnessed in different aspects of culinary practice is another important historical factor in a country where, as we will see, energy sources, both public and private, privileged some forms of consumption and restricted others. In the nineteenth century there were ongoing efforts to perfect the production of domestic heat sources, but refrigeration did not become accessible in private homes until the subsequent century. This imbalance also affected cooking customs. When municipalities began to distribute gas to urban residents, cooking systems became increasingly homogeneous. At the same time, however, the seasonal fragility and perishability of food products, especially meats, could not be remedied even by storing them on ice. For decades the use of controlled refrigeration remained a luxury, while heat was available in the kitchens of all urban households. The industrial production of foods suited to this infrastructure (i.e., the availability of the gas stove and the inaccessibility of the refrigerator) is reflected in dishes such as pasta with tomato sauce, which involves two types of preserved foods, one dried and the other semiliquid. It was only in the 1950s that a balance was found between the two poles of energy supply, hot and cold. The refrigerator was thus installed in domestic kitchens alongside the stove, which had already been in place for a period of fifty years. The consequences were not merely a matter of individual convenience but involved the entire field of food consumption. We see this in the relationship between the production of frozen goods and the spread of preprepared dishes and meals. Frozen prebaked lasagna now replaced pastasciutta.

Although the history of food is closely linked to the infrastructures of domestic life, we will examine only the aspects of those infrastructures that have special relevance for us here. To evaluate individual discoveries and innovations, we must return to the space historically assigned to the cook, observe it in its intimate details, reexamine its structures and utensils, and imagine the men who worked there, comparing them to other men who repeated the same tasks in subsequent years—or were no longer obliged to repeat them thanks to the invention of a machine. Before bringing the scientist into the kitchen, we will first take a look at the kitchen par excellence, that of Bartolomeo Scappi. This will make it easier to appreciate mechanical innovations—the introduction of

In the kitchen (engraving).

Source: Bartolomeo Scappi, *Opera dell'arte del cucinare* (Venice: Tramezzino, 1570).

simple machines and new materials—and especially to observe the role of heat, which was first produced by human labor, then by combustible fuel, and finally by increasingly sophisticated equipment. The kitchen is in fact a laboratory for physical experiments. It provides a fire source and requires a significant supply of water. It produces hot edible objects that undergo transformation as the temperature changes from hot to lukewarm or from cold to freezing. Heat conduction, the control of steam, and above all the ability to calculate temperatures became part of the cook's store of knowledge before science provided him with objective measuring tools. Yet it would be an error to contrast the cook's empirical knowledge with the method of the scientist. Both practitioners repeatedly carry out experiments on the same raw materials, but their goal is different. For the scientist the primary concern is not the value or taste of an object but the process through which the ingredients are transformed into this object. This process can be observed by studying heat sources and conductors with thermometers and densimeters or by using chemical substances or creating mechanical devices. There are further analogies and discrepancies between practitioners of the mechanical arts and scientists. The distiller who produced spirits and the butler who created sugar concoctions were clearly alchemists, just as the carver who displayed his dexterity in slicing up a roasted carcass of meat was a worldly anatomist.

The Pope's Saucepans

When we enter the kitchen illustrated in Scappi's work, we find ourselves in a place that looks as though it belongs in Sleeping Beauty's castle. Although there must be great deal of commotion and smoke here, the characters seem to have been stuck in the same place for four hundred years, waiting to be brought back to life. Work spaces are located in the middle of the kitchen, and fireplaces, stoves, and sinks are placed against the walls at an appropriate distance from where dishes are prepared or completed. The engravings in Scappi's book suggest the array of utensils used here, and information on the materials these are made of is provided in the inventory of equipment found at the beginning of the volume. Knives, spoons, skewers, stands, trivets, and frying pans are made of iron. All the pots are of tin-lined copper. The other materials are of little importance. Paddles and pins for rolling and stretching out the dough are made of wood. Mortars are made of bronze and marble. The tubular syringes used in making butter and the containers for vinegar are made of tin. In the battery of kitchen utensils iron and copper are the most common materials, and they would continue to dominate for a very long time. These metals conduct heat well. The saucepan lids not only protect the contents of the pans but also reflect back the heat, browning the top of the food. For this reason the lids were not equipped with handles (which isolate heat) but with soldered rings that could be grasped with the help of a rag or a hook.

In the ancient kitchen we find pans that can be placed directly over the fire. We also find some machines. There are three versions of the spit: the first was rotated manually by a man who stood on the other side of a low, protective wall in order to shield himself from the flames. A more advanced type of skewer involved a fan that, when set in motion by the hot air rising above the flames, caused a cylindrical cogwheel to rotate; this in turn moved the serrated wheel attached to the rod. The third, more complex variation is a "machine with three skewers" that allowed for the roasting of foods on three different levels. This instrument, which reflects the advantage of a large kitchen, also appears in the frontispiece of some seventeenth-century editions of Vincenzo Cervio's *Il trinciante* (The carver): here, with the help of the heat alone, the food is allowed to cook slowly, with prized meats, the most appetizing of ingredients, rotating around each other on the spit. In the papal kitchens these implements also included a grindstone, a pulley for the sink, a lever to raise pots from the fire, and a peasant instrument, the *zagola*, but all of these were dependent on muscle power. The spit alone reveals that there was a potential energy source in those kitchens—heat—and hence a future laboratory of innovation.[2]

The objects made in the kitchen are above all manufactured products. Kneading, mixing, chopping, whipping, pulverizing, and pounding are all actions entrusted to human hands. Only in the nineteenth century was such effort supplemented with machines. Sixteen people, assigned to different tasks, worked in contact with food. Given this number and the amount of dishes that were prepared in the kitchen, the availability of labor was not the principal worry of the master cook. His greater concern was managing the heat source and adapting it to the work under way. It was no accident that Scappi compared himself to an architect.[3] Heat and cold occupy opposite poles not only in dietary science but also in the layout of the kitchens, where they are organized according to a system of gradual progression: first there is the open fire, then the stove, then the little brick wall that holds the burning fuel, the tongs, and so on, and finally the plate warmers. In an antechamber we find the cold dishes or those of delicate color: fresh milk, whipped *fior di latte*, and honeyed milk. The circulation of air, which is regulated by various means—high ceilings, windows, stove hoods, and chimneys—allows these polar opposites to complement each other, diffusing or eliminating smoke, odors, dust, ashes, and flour particles. In the nineteenth century this was the aspect of the culinary process that fell under the iron rule of hygiene, interpreted as the need for fresh air and meticulous cleanliness. The designation of different spaces for cooking, kneading, working with chilled or cold foods, steeping fish in brine, plucking poultry, and skinning animals (the coal shed, the woodpile, and the employees' lavatory are elsewhere) is part of a type of organization that supervised both food and refuse. Each employee had a specific task in an assigned space. One would turn the spit. Another, working at the opposite side of the kitchen, would take care of the *biancomangiare*, and another would work with milk products in a cold room. The assignment of separate tasks did not necessarily mean individual professional freedom for each employee. The apprentices lived and worked together, as their sleeping quarters were in an adjacent room.

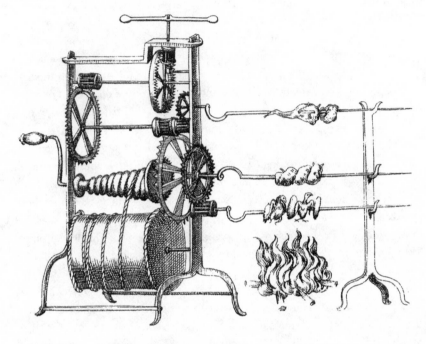

Molinello con tre spedi che si uolta dasse per forza de ruotte con il tempo a foggia di orologio come nella presente figura si dimostra

Spit for cooking meat (engraving).

Source: Bartolomeo Scappi, *Opera dell'arte del cucinare* (Venice: Tramezzino, 1570).

The kitchen is a microcosm. None of its copper utensils would appear on the dining table, and none of the iron knives would be used to slice the meat in front of the prelate. The pans gave their shape to food that was eventually transferred to other containers. Even the most delicate creations could emerge from hell to be served in heaven, without revealing a trace of the sweat and heat endured in their preparation. There was, however, an intermediate space—the small dining room, the *tinello*, where the dining-room officers ate meals with their guests—but this was a private, restricted space, and it was not always located next to the kitchen. If anything, its existence reinforced the idea of a hierarchy among those whose supreme goal was to serve the needs of their noble masters. Scappi attributed an intrinsic dignity and a specific form of attire to individual roles: dish-washers worked bareheaded, their arms uncovered. Those who handled food were expected to wear a cap and an apron. Almost all of them rolled up their sleeves in order to work as cleanly as possible.

How are these details, especially the concerns of culinary physics, reflected in the recipes? Let us take the example of a recipe for flour gnocchi and grated bread,[4] starting with the utensils. Although Scappi's recipe provides a detailed plan of work, there is also an implicit need for manual labor (for kneading the dough), for a large pot (to boil the water), and for a slotted spoon or strainer (to extract the dumplings from the water), not to mention a sieve to sift the flour, a table for kneading, and a grater for shaping the surface of the gnocchi. The bowl into which the cooked gnocchi were placed had to be made of pottery or wood, materials that prevented the dumplings from sticking to each other. The temperatures appropriate to the preparation of this dish are also clear: the dough had to be made with boiling water and would be cooked in boiling water. The recipe thus indicates the heat of the ingredients and the utensils on which the quality, appearance, and consistency of the dish depend. As a microcosm of a microcosm, dumplings and noodles reflect the physical order of the kitchen.

A Virtual Discovery: The Pressure Cooker

The history of inventions that had lasting effects on culinary labor has paradox-ical aspects. We will discuss two that are particularly relevant to physics: artifi-cially produced heat and its convection in food preparation. As we have seen, the importance of these issues was fully recognized long before new forms of production were studied and made available. Denis Papin's invention of a type of saucepan that controlled the use of steam was undoubtedly the first instru-ment responsive to the dual necessity of reducing cooking time and consuming a lesser amount of combustible fuel. Instructions for its use are found in *La manière d'amolir les os et de faire cuire toutes sortes de vivandes en fort peu de temps & à fort peu de frais* (How to soften bones and cook all kinds of dishes in a short time and at minor cost).[5] This is a log of experiments carried out with a "machine" that consisted of a double cylinder made of iron—the lower part for boiling water, the upper part for steaming food—sealed hermetically with screws and rods. There is a chapter dedicated to instructing cooks on the use of this apparatus, which was especially suited to cooking meats, indicating the quantities of fuel needed, cooking times, and results. Among the ingredients that could be cooked this way, we find bones, which had been regarded as waste. Cooking bones allowed for the creation of broths and gelatins for charitable, philanthropic purposes. Denis Papin, a member of London's Royal Society and a well-known personality in Europe, was living in Venice as a guest of Ambro-gio Sarotti in 1681, the year in which the news of his invention became widespread. A scientist of fame, he introduced his discovery, which he called a "digester," to the scientific academies.

The first "pressure cooker" was, however, only a prototype and was adopted for both experimental and commercial objectives. From 1750 Ambrogio Sangiorgio, a Milanese spice merchant, used it to extract concentrates and medicinal broths.[6] Wilke perfected its design in Stockholm in 1773, using the internal pressure of the steam to create a seal and inventing a kind of tap that functioned as a valve.[7]

Looking for a simpler way of sealing the pot, which was secure but not hermetic, Abbot Ottolini revisited the problem of regulating the steam. Timing the process with his watch, he was the first to claim that he had cooked beef "in less than an hour," "an aged capon in a quarter of an hour," and "rice in three minutes" in "Papin's digester."[8] In spite of improvements the saucepan was dangerous and difficult to close without a valve. It was not widely adopted in Italy, meeting with resistance even in the charitable organizations for which it was intended. A full century later it reappeared, bearing the name of its inventor, in Caterina Prato's *Manuale di cucina* (Cooking manual), which was translated from German into Italian. In addition to economical advantages, other motives were added in promoting its use: "It improves the texture and aroma of the foods, and the liquid does not overflow."[9]

The history of the pressure cooker is a perfect illustration of the gap between invention and commercialization, and by examining it in detail we can understand why it was so difficult to introduce this type of utensil into domestic kitchens. In fact, it was not used on a broad scale until the twentieth century, when energy supply became more stable and reliable and when long cooking periods and the need for protracted supervision of the stove became problematical. It would be an error, however, to consider the pressure cooker independently of the larger picture of energy planning and heat supply. As the open hearth—which remained a primary source of heat only in peasant society—was gradually abandoned and gas lines were installed for widespread domestic use, heat became the subject of several studies with the objective of producing clean, economical, and readily available energy. More than a century after Papin, Count Rumford relaunched research on cooking systems in a series of projects on kitchen equipment, steam convection, the improvement of chimney flues, and the preparation of economical soups. In a climate of secular philanthropy and organized charity, what had originally been conceived as a project for constructing a machine that would produce broth or bone gelatin economically was now reformulated and relaunched in a more complex way. With financial support from the public sector, Rumford, an American physicist, organized an entire chain of production—from combustible fuel to heat source, from soup to consumer—in several European cities, including Munich, Paris, and Verona, where "the kitchen of the Pietà Hospital is the best I have ever created."[10] No detail escaped his attention: when he discovered that barley tended to stick or burn in the cooking process, he designed a double-bottomed saucepan with an insulating function.[11] Once he had planned the practical details, he dedicated himself to the study of foods, particularly the preparation of meals for the poor, exploring various ingredients and recipes for what would become known internationally as "Rumford soup."

Though his initial interest was in managing and transmitting heat in the preparation of balanced, nutritional food, Rumford was soon confronted with the problem of flavor. Ingredients such as potatoes, which were ideal from the economic perspective, met with resistance from his impoverished consumers. He devised a way to overcome this by adding appetizing elements such as dry bread, which offered a pleasant contrast to the thick but still liquid meal, and encouraged chewing. Though working on a basis of individual commissions, Rumford considered nutritional formulas to be exportable since, like steam, they could pass unhindered through borders. Hence he undertook the study of less costly national dishes, for which he planned an international system of distribution. Inspired by the popular consumption of pasta in Naples, he created recipes for macaroni, and the popularity of this dish throughout Europe at the beginning of the nineteenth century demonstrates a successful alliance of philanthropic and gastronomic values.[12]

Artificial Refrigeration

The study and production of artificial refrigeration have different implications. Sixteenth-century treatises on beverage temperatures trace the ancient origins of chilled drinks and praise their civilizing values. The use of snow, stored in ice pits and mountain trenches and transported to the city by night during the summer season, was a pleasure enjoyed by the ancient Romans and a small luxury that never went out of fashion. At the conclusion of the *Trattato della natura de' cibi et del bere* (Treatise on the nature of foods and drink), by Baldassarre Pisanelli, a physician of the sixteenth century, we find a chapter on the "effects of cold drinks" that discusses the flavor, digestive properties, and ability of chilled beverages to lower feverish body temperatures.[13] Considering the consumption of cold drinks to be an environmental necessity, Pisanelli suggests the use of water, wine, and chilled fruits, secure in the conviction that he is voicing a common social aspiration: "Today every poor tradesman wants Bread, Wine, and Snow." More than the well and possibly the wine cellar, snow beds furnished the raw material for cold drinks. Pisanelli declared that the use of saltpeter was "of little use" and fit "for sailors only,"[14] thus dismissing the value of chemical processes — saltpeter is hypothermic — which were regarded as an inferior device.

It was, however, the chemical study of salt that led to the boom in chilled beverages and ice-cream products in the eighteenth century with the production of artificially generated refrigeration. Filippo Baldini, the author of the first Italian tract on sorbets (De' sorbetti) wrote: "Having examined the value of salts, Monsieur Réaumur, his thermometer in hand, found that almost all of them caused a slight level of freezing, except for sea salt. See the Memorandum of the Academy of Sciences, 1732. Wishing to economize, one could use sodium, which is ash of alica, as this chills almost all liquids in a much more efficient way than sea salt."[15]

Baldini prescribes the exact amount of salt, ice, and sugar used in making sorbets, offers a disquisition on citric acids (from citron, lemon, and orange), and introduces a new type of fruit recently arrived from America: the pineapple. With this treatise he succeeded in popularizing a chemical procedure that had culinary applications by weighing its value from the perspective of flavor and nutrition. This scientific information was tacitly circulated among ice-cream manufacturers (Naples, the city where the treatise was printed, was the home of the best ice-cream makers in Europe) and consumers. The consumers in turn consulted Baldini, a medical professor, for further information, asking his opinion on a number of things, including chocolate sorbet, the most sought after concoction of all, "made of cocoa powder, cinnamon, sugar, and sometimes vanilla, especially when it has to be frozen."[16] The sorbet maker was part of the equipment used in making preserves and was suited to the processing of fruits and flowers, coffee and zabaglione. It was made of iron or tin and was submerged in a tub of refrigerating solution.[17]

The history of refrigeration is unique. The availability of natural snow and ice in summer, even in areas with a hot climate, delayed the application of scientific research to new production processes, which began to boom in the field of food preservation with the creation of a huge international meat market in the second part of the nineteenth century. The chemical procedure that prolonged freezing temperatures took hold because of its simplicity and low cost without affecting broader, collective interests, particularly the preservation of products. Unlike the pressure cooker, it would enjoy success and longevity.

Appert in Italy: The Flavor of Preserved Foods

Up to the eve of the French Revolution, the diffusion of these scientific concepts was entrusted for the most part to physicians; they were addressed exclusively to the elite and were accepted as a phenomenon whose social role could be recognized at a distance. In 1765 Voltaire had pointed to the existence of red currant sorbet and ice creams as tangible signs of progress,[18] but on the question of natural, chemical, or artificial ice few were capable of expressing an opinion. Steam and saltpeter still had the status of trade secrets. Toward the end of the eighteenth century, however, a new climate developed among scientists, public authorities, and citizens, and a series of innovations is reflected in gastronomic literature. Count Rumford, an expert on fireplaces, ovens, and kitchens, was one of the individuals who contributed to the reconceptualization of cooking in terms of energy and heat conservation. His soups, recommended by Parmentier,[19] became popular in Italy. But Rumford was not the only one concerned with cooking equipment. Parmentier had in fact already perfected the "American saucepan," which was a simple pan for steaming food. Water was placed in the bottom of this receptacle, and the food was then arranged on a disk of perforated tin and placed over the water. Parmentier studied the effects of heat on ingredients that do not dissolve in liquid but remain firm while retaining their color. Starting with the intention of boiling a potato that would not fall apart, he redefined the taste standard of cooked vegetables and fruits, completing experiments that brought him far afield. Among other things he recommended rice prepared in the Chinese manner. Parmentier's work also showed the advantages of a type of cooking that could be carried out with salt water when traveling at sea. His report was published in Milan in 1787.[20]

Italians had a great interest in the way the French treated potatoes. Parmentier's comments on the potato, along with those of Cadet-de-Vaux and Rumford, were frequently translated into Italian.[21] These texts would help to promote the consumption of potatoes and enhance their culinary appreciation. Nevertheless, the scientific process that genuinely revolutionized household management—the practice of applying heat to foods sealed in glass jars in order to preserve them—virtually ignored the potato.

A grocer named Nicolas Appert sold his highly appreciated products— legumes preserved in fresh condition, without added salt, vinegar, or sugar—to Parisians long before he decided to divulge the secret of their preparation. Peas, artichokes, asparagus, and fruit of all kinds were thus available out of season. A vegetable farm and processing plant in Massy and a store in Paris constituted the basis of Appert's system of production and distribution, and he promoted his products in a catalog and in newspaper advertisements. His discovery became widely known in 1810, when he won a substantial prize from the Ministry of the Interior. The same year, the Italian translation of *L'art de conserver pendant plusieurs années toutes les substances animales et végétales* (The art of preserving for several years all animal and vegetable products) was published in Siena, and a German translation of the same work appeared in Koblenz. The English version appeared two years later.[22]

Before Appert's discovery, the usual procedures for preserving food were either physical or chemical. They involved primarily the use of cold or heat. Meats and fish were smoked, dried, or kept on ice. These methods had many inconveniences. If foods had been dried, they needed to be rehydrated before use. To keep them cold, it was necessary to secure a freezing environment or the appropriate quantity of ice (which was expensive in temperate climates). There was also the possibility of using additives: brine and salt were used for pickling cucumbers and herrings and curing pork meat. Other options were oil or vinegar or, for fruit, liquor and even honey and sugar. Obviously the cost varied according to the method employed, and the use of additives could be expensive but had the advantage of being very appetizing. Sometimes the food product itself provided material for its own preservation: goose or duck fat, having congealed in the cooking process, could be placed in jars along with pieces of the cooked meat. The substance to be preserved could undergo one or two procedures at varying cost, but these treatments had one element in common: the alteration of the natural properties of the fresh product. The color and texture of fish would change, for example, as each additive brought about different modifications. Fruits gradually lost their color when submerged in alcohol; smoke pierced the surface of hardened meat. Preserved foods also had a specific taste that seemed desirable in its peculiarity—the sharpness typical of salt, the pungency of vinegar, the inebriating nuances of liquor, or the rich properties of animal fats (goose, for example) and vegetable oils. Each edible substance, when desalted or rehydrated, drained or wiped off, retained the unmistakable flavor of a condiment along with the vague aftertaste of its original properties. The original aroma, however, was inevitably absent, replaced by a distinct odor of the sort that prevailed in food stores. It was possible to adjust excessively strong flavors not only through cooking but also through judicious combinations. Wine could dissolve and eliminate salty residues in the mouth, just as it was used to wash down mouthfuls of food in which the concentration of juices was too intense. The art of drinking was fundamental for the full enjoyment of preserved foods, dissolving their harshness at a very visceral level.

Clearly, dried and rehydrated peas could never pass for fresh products. Appert's procedure, however, provoked a different result, and it was surprisingly simple and repeatable: parboiled root vegetables and fruits were placed in bottles, carefully sealed, and boiled in a *bain-marie* for a period of time that varied according to the ingredients. At the end of this process the contents were sterile, and the jars could be stored on shelves for months or years before being sold. When opened, the peas seemed naturally green and still a little crisp, with a familiar fragrance, appearance, and taste. The claim made by the Societé d'encouragement pour l'industrie nationale was quite clear: the new method "does not add any foreign body to the substance intended for preservation." Appert understood none of the scientific reasons for this outcome, a fact that presented no difficulty to him from a commercial perspective. His method of production, which he carried out on a small scale, was adapted for industrial development and was also suitable for domestic use. This led to its immediate success all over Europe.

In Italy Appert's discovery became known through the publication of manuals translated from the French. *L'arte di conservare gli alimenti*, which appeared

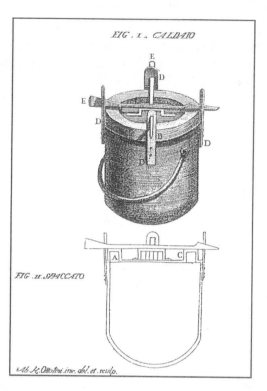

ABOVE The pan (engraving).

Source: Girolam Ottolini, *Il digestore di Papino* (Milan, 1770).

BELOW: Newspaper advertisement for a "new American sorbet maker"
from the late nineteenth century.

in Italy in 1824, presented his method of sterilizing and sealing food in jars—along with more traditional procedures—and publicized the recent development of containers with tin lids in England.[23] To appreciate the diffusion of Appert's procedure in cookbooks that described its applications around the middle of the nineteenth century, we have only to consult the writings of Agnoletti, a cook and food preserver who worked in Rome, in Tuscany, and at the court of Maria Luigia of Parma. In 1814, when his *Nuovissima cucina economica* first appeared, he was unaware of the new methods. Here, for bottling tomatoes, he suggests sealing the jars carefully and placing them in a cool place or drying the tomatoes out in the sun or on the stove. In the *Manuale del cuoco e del pasticciere* (Manual for the cook and the pastry cook), which was published in 1832, by contrast Agnoletti reveals that he has caught up with the trend: "For better preservation, boil the sealed bottles in a *bain-marie* for sixteen minutes, and allow them to cool in the same liquid." He may have learned of Appert's method sometime between 1821 and 1826 when he lived in Parma, where French cooks plied their trade, or at a later date.[24] Either way, thanks to the testimony of the book he published in 1832, we know that the new method of preserving tomatoes was integrated into elite cuisine by that juncture. Developments within the domestic environment would have occurred at a later stage.

We must underline a dual aspect of Appert's system: pulses were preserved without additives—salt, vinegar, or oil—that would have altered their flavor. When cooking a product preserved in this way, it could be treated as though it were fresh, and it might even pass as fresh. It was thus in cooking—with peas, asparagus, beans, and artichokes—that the advantages of this procedure were most evident, though in the case of potatoes the results were disappointing and costly. Fruit, or other foods served cold on the sideboard, did not yield similar results: red currants were resistant to this mode of preservation, and strawberries lost consistency and fragrance, requiring the addition of sugar. To limit these drawbacks, ripening, harvesting, and processing had to follow each other in quick succession. A different kind of advantage is achieved in the preparation of various sauces. In the case of the tomato, which was used above all as a condiment, the new method guaranteed constant availability at a steady cost, summer and winter, without waste. In Italy this would be the preserved food par excellence, spreading to all parts of the country and becoming an aspect of national identity. Italy's canning industry was created after national unification, consistent with the level of progress achieved elsewhere in Europe, and the labels attached to the cans were adorned with the image of this fine red fruit.

The widespread use of preserved foods had profound consequences for taste. The market value of products dropped, reducing the difference between early and later seasonal varieties. Costs became more moderate, and flavors were standardized. There was a big difference between the appearance, and especially the color, of these preserves and the results obtained with traditional methods of dehydration. The new method could be applied to game, which now became available at times of the year when it would otherwise be impossible to find, thus allowing consumers to have constant access to woodcock and pheasant, roasted or jugged, after they had been heated in saucepans and stored in jars. Common pulse vegetables and prized meats were subject to the same techniques. Always available, preserved vegetables enjoyed growing favor in restaurants, where they were used, openly or surreptitiously, as substitutes for dishes or side plates prepared from fresh foods. Eternally fresh spring vegetables traveled everywhere in cans and were widely welcomed. We have only to read the menus to find that "Argenteuil asparagus" was served at the Grand Hôtel d'Italie in Florence for Christmas dinner in 1900 and at the Hotel Continental in Moscow during the month of January 1901.[25] These vegetables kept their name, their prestige, and even their place of origin. The fact that they were accepted even by diners who dictated culinary taste led to the posthumous transfiguration of the grocer Nicolas Appert into a master cook and pastry expert.

The diffusion of preservation and its application to the market sectors of highest demand (soups, fish, pulse vegetables, fruit with syrup, jams, and so on) led to the democratization of elite values. Based on the premise that each basic foodstuff was theoretically suitable for Appert's method of processing, advertisers began to claim that the freshest and most natural vegetables were those in a can. The place of origin now became part of the brand name: the San Marzano tomato functions as the symbol of a national industry, the Cirio Company, based in Naples. After World War I the canning industry monopolized the publication of educational texts on cooking as well as communication with homemakers. Cirio was Italy's best-known culinary publisher up to the 1960s, producing recipe books by acknowledged authors that were organized according to specific themes (particularly the tomato), household notebooks, coloring books for children, and albums with competitions. Among the individuals who wrote prefaces for these books was Lidia Morelli, known for her contribution to the field of domestic science.[26] An element common to all these books was the insertion of at least one canned or preserved product and one fresh product among the ingredients listed in each recipe while underscoring the recipe's cost advantage, speed of execution, and uniformity of taste. The main promotional theme was not convenience, however, but rather the natural, sensory aspect of food. Color is regarded as a compelling feature: the greenness of peas and string beans and the redness of tomatoes are the marks of an evolutionary continuity, from garden to can to dish. The preserved product thus becomes a universal value in a can. Its ingredients and recipes and even its container do not vary. By combining peeled tomatoes and dried pasta, one obtains a pasta dish that, thanks to a distinctive mode of preservation, is identical from one end of the country to the other. This canning policy, which was identical to Fascist policy, had obvious implications. By proliferating maps of Italy showing the location of processing plants and depots, reflecting regional and local traditions in recipe titles, and combining typical ingredients from different areas with the famous peeled tomatoes, a culturally diverse country became unified through its gastronomic values.

The Oven, the Sorbet Maker, and Simple Machines

Cookbooks reflect innovations in the field of preservation primarily from the perspective of application. In their concern for the infrastructures of cooking, the authors place greater importance on the invention of new dishes than on the introduction of new utensils. Yet knowledge and experience allowed the home cook to master the use of ancient stoves and enabled the professional cook to supervise his staff in controlling heat and cold. The cookbook does not concern itself with physical location except on a purely theoretical level, highlighting only two related concerns: the choice of ingredients and the equipment needed for cooking. The use of open fireplaces and brick containers of live coals to provide heat gave way in time to cookers that regulated heat in a more uniform way. From the second half of the eighteenth century to the twentieth, the greatest problem implicit in heat sources—the regulation of low and high temperatures—underwent several stages of development.

Among the items that reflected this evolution was the oven, which in the early nineteenth century was heated by controlling the quantity of firewood and evaluating the temperature with empirical methods. Only the pastry cook's complete familiarity with the heat source guaranteed good results, and all advice offered to the public was of necessity approximate. Vialardi suggested placing "a damp rag at the tip of a long stick" in the oven and withdrawing it five minutes later to see if it had burned (in which case the oven was too hot) or simply browned (in which case the temperature was right for pastry dough and meat dishes with grated cheese topping). When *Trattato di cucina pasticceria moderna* (Treatise on modern pastry making) was published in 1854, German and French ovens, which provided constant heat, were already available and were recommended by Vialardi "for private kitchens."[27] The fate of domestic pastry making, including its most delicate applications such as soufflés, depended on the progressive refinement of this resource, both in homes and restaurants, which had developed over time from a simple bell-shaped structure, to the country range, to this new model. The introduction of the cast-iron, charcoal-fueled kitchen range meant that as many as eight burners could be accommodated on the same surface, and underneath this there was room for two ovens, two stoves, a tank for hot water, and two broilers with a spit.[28] By opening and closing the doors of the range, the cook could access the desired compartment without coming in contact with hot ashes, excessive smoke, or live flames. The advent of municipal gas would refine the process of heat regulation without overheating the environment surrounding the stove, fulfilling one of the main objectives of a functional appliance: a clean, cool kitchen. One must not exaggerate the changes, however. Taking into account the simplicity of contemporary domestic arrangements, Pellegrino Artusi suggests cooking a chocolate soufflé in a Dutch oven or on a simple burner between two heat sources.

Natural ice was still used in the preparation of sorbets and ice creams. The techniques suggested by Baldini were still in fashion in Vialardi's time, though the freezing mixtures were now more effective, as they consisted of water and ammonia nitrate, which could make the temperature rise above or fall below −10°C to −15°C, depending on the proportions applied. When the tin sorbet maker was submerged in this mixture, the cook could still stir the ice cream in the container. The problem presented by the production of cold temperatures evolved in a specific way. In the nineteenth century the commitment to freezing mixtures, and hence to the transportation of natural ice, still prevailed. This custom began to decline in the southern part of the USA after 1890 with advances in the refrigeration industry.[29] Refrigerators and refrigerated warehouses did not make their appearance in Italy until the twentieth century, with the advent of World War I. Examination of the monthly magazine L'industria italiana del freddo (The Italian refrigeration industry) shows that by 1928 there was already a broad national network of private and state-run factories for the processing of chilled food, preserving it with artificial ice.[30] Since there was no cooling network available to private homes, which were still without refrigerators, those who made ice cream at home continued to practice the older techniques, though some mechanical improvements were added: Artusi recommends the "American sorbet maker" with its triple-action mechanism, as it allowed the user to freeze the mixture in a faster and more uniform manner than other devices.[31] Moreover, the artisans who specialized in making ice cream lacked the capital to invest in costly appliances. Between the publication of Grifoni's Trattato di gelateria in 1911 and Hoepli's manual in 1922 there is no evidence of any evolution. Both recommend the use of a tub for the ice and salt, with a cylinder in the middle and a handle to turn the rods inside. Giuseppe Ciocca, the author of the Hoepli manual who was one of the best-known experts on ice cream in the 1930s, and Amedeo Pettini, the famous cook who wrote the preface, both noted the empirical aspect of the sorbet-making process, while consoling themselves in their status as heirs to a time-honored tradition: "We can easily foresee that one day the mechanical preparation of frozen mixtures will be carried out with different methods than those used today. But whatever the technical procedure might be in the future, the historical fact is that we were the first to introduce ice cream to civilization, and Italians were for centuries the foremost ice-cream makers in the world."[32]

More noticeable advances were made in the simple appliances used in establishments without a fireplace, but these correspond in many ways to a more

ancient concept. Comparing Scappi's battery of utensils in 1570 to that of Giovanni Nelli in *Il re dei cuochi* in 1868, we find gridirons and fish kettles, stewpots
and mortars in both. The saucepan used for steaming green vegetables is of
more recent origin, as we have seen, and so is the tool for fashioning vegetables
known as the *presse julienne*. By pressing a lever, this utensil can mold and slice
long, thin strips of vegetables (such as carrots) into the shape desired. Among
the appliances introduced into the home, many had a hand-operated screw
mechanism, such as the meat grinder, which Artusi soon replaced with the
lunette. In Caterina Prato's *Manuale* we also find a mill for grating stale bread.
The potato masher is fairly widespread, but the tool for removing the stones in
plums much rarer. During the Fascist era, some modest progress could be
observed in the kitchen with the introduction of a machine for cutting green
beans, the juicer,[33] the vegetable strainer, and the handle-operated eggbeater
(electric beaters were seen only in dairy shops). The list can be extended,
though not by much, if we include hotel kitchens, where there were juice
extractors (for fruit as well as for the carcasses of game birds), slicers, and puree-
making machines, reflecting the needs of a more complex system of service.[34]

These minor inventions were not intended to function with electrical power,
but this did not prevent women from dreaming of the possibility of powering
them with automatic batteries. The modesty of the utensils was supplemented
by their users' genuine pleasure in being part of an up-to-date domestic economy. Sponsored by the major industrialists from Borletti to Ginori, ENIOS, the
National Office for the Scientific Organization of Labor, was established in Italy
in 1926. One of its tasks was to promote the efficiency of domestic labor.[35] This
meant adopting the American model in the hope of encouraging private investments. Its initial project—the remodeling of the domestic space—was assigned
to the architect, and the housewife was called on to imagine the furnishings, the
tables (for dining, working, and ironing), and the dresser on which each dish
would be assigned its proper place. As the kitchen walls filled up with various
items, it became clear that even the smallest details had a symbolic value. A
scale and a clock were present in every kitchen, since recipes specified cooking
times and the quantities of ingredients in numeric terms, as though their transmission anticipated a collective memory loss, with a simultaneous loss of confidence in experience and analogical intuition. With its white tiles and white
wood furniture, the kitchen now looked like a laboratory, and the careful organization of plates, dishes, pots, and pans also bore tribute to the cult of personalized practicality.

Among the many virtually useless machines found in this laboratory-theater,
only one gives us reason to pause—the "mechanical mixer" designed for preparing sheets of pasta dough that Lidia Morelli had mentioned in 1935.[36] This con-
traption, made of metal cylinders operated by a handle, raises complicated questions: is it additional proof of the alienation of a new generation of women from

domestic work, or does it rather bear witness to the diffusion of pasta making outside its geographical and anthropological area? In the eyes of the culinary experts, the machine's success was synonymous with the increasing rarity of the art of the rolling pin and symptomatic of a diminishing respect for the quality of the kind of dough that could only be produced by hand. In reality the pasta maker flourished just as shops selling fresh pasta were becoming widespread in the major cities, and more than a call to revive traditions it suggests support for their conservation. The abandonment of certain fundamental elements and the replacement of handmade pasta with dried pasta were already under way in 1935, along with the commercialization of regional pasta specialties.

Metal Alloys and Ice Cubes

A complex evaluation of small domestic appliances supports the claim that the manual labor of the woman of the house was still important. The convenience offered by the new gadgets was of minimal importance when considered in relation to the overall length of time needed to prepare a meal. The preparation of foods continued to be carried out by hand, from basic ingredients to the final presentation of the dish. What began to increase on a modest scale was the market for partially prepared foods (such as stock cubes or preserved items) and food that was ready for cooking (such as fresh pasta). And yet there were some major innovations. Ovens, stoves, and sinks were renovated in the space of twenty years, bringing about a significant labor-saving advance. From 1880 onward the homes of Italy's major cities were connected to the municipal gas supply, and by 1930 electric stoves had already begun to appear.[37] The imbalance between country and city before the spread of the gas cylinder grew more marked, and no one questioned what was seen as an innovation of enormous importance. "The miracle starts early in the morning: we no longer begin the day by setting the fire but by placing something on the fire!"[38] In the modern kitchen the air is clean, the temperature is cooler, and the age-old polarization of hot and cold disappears. Water and fire, at opposite ends of the kitchen in Scappi's engravings, now appear side by side. Electricity, or heat without flames, followed the availability of gas. Once running water became available, so too did hot and cold water, which could be mixed at will. The electrical boiler made its appearance during the Fascist period, taking over yet another of the basic functions of the hearth. Water was no longer placed in a pot on the burner but was heated in a container and became available with the turn of a faucet. The handling of new elements, inflammable gases, and electric wires was certainly not more difficult to master than the earlier arrangements, but it implied a different awareness of movements and gestures, and often, as a result of the reduced need for domestic staff, there was a sense of loneliness that had not been experienced in the kitchen in previous times. The economy of combustible fuel depended on the turning of handles or knobs and the calculation of abstract parameters, and it was the woman of the house who gave direct instruction to the maid on its consumption.

The energy potential meant there was an increase in the number of hot points in a self-regulated house. The electric stove had three or four burners and an oven that could be used without long delays since it involved minimal supervision and presented few demands for intervention. Tasks such as adding liquid to a pot, turning the food, rotating it, removing it from the heat, uncovering it, and covering it up again were automatically eliminated by regulating the oven. One could even avoid the possibility of liquid bubbling over or food sticking to the bottom of the pan. In addition to the stove-top burners, one could also use an electric hot plate for the coffee maker. Where? Near the electrical outlet, on top of any table. All this could be achieved by connecting a plug, turning switches, and pressing buttons, without firewood or coal. The old pots and pans are replaced in accordance with the new energy sources, which are clean, safe, and temperature-controlled. Copper pans suddenly seem antiquated. They are difficult to polish on the outside and to coat on the inside. Iron survives only in frying pans. The ancient kitchen of the past now faces its demise. For slow-cooked dishes, stews, and thick soups, cast iron prevails, which is excellent to use and easy to clean. The thick aluminum pan with an insulated handle dominates the battery of pots and pans because of its lightness and affordability. In 1899 Dr. Formenti, following a visit to Switzerland and Germany, announced the success of this pan and anticipated the use of aluminum in the manufacture of stockpots, saucepans, stewpots, skimmers, small shovels, ladles, and so on.[39] Within a few decades a revolution had taken place, as aluminum became the material that was universally adopted by refectories and mess halls, hotels and patrician residences. This new pale metal lent itself to all kinds of uses and prompted the housewife to develop a real interest in materials. Nickel, though costly, offered all the advantages of copper but did not need to be lined with tin and polished. The enamel pan also appeared, though it seemed delicate. But the marvel that captured everyone's imagination was the *pirofila*, a Pyrex casserole dish produced by Ginori. Bright, transparent, and lightweight, the *pirofila* brought a distinctive design to ovenware. It was nonetheless a fragile object and would have to be replaced in the long run, unlike copper pans, which last forever. After World War I these were the kinds of cookware that broke a sacred taboo, since they did not make a sharp distinction between kitchen pots and serving dishes or between the realm of the servants and that of their employers. The Pyrex dish allowed the food cooked in the oven or on top of the stove to be placed directly on the dining table. As attractive as a soup tureen, it could be handled and cleaned with greater ease. None of these artifacts, which were high on the list of wedding gifts, precluded competition in the middle-class household. If aluminum was light, solid, and conducted heat well, enamel and Pyrex were fragile, washable, and attractive to look at. All seemed equally necessary, including even the ancient earthen stewpot used for cooking beans.[40]

La cucina elegante, a recipe collection for the most refined sector of Milanese society, immediately adopted this new style. A porcelain container capable of withstanding the heat of the stove was judged to be indispensable for "Beef *au gratin*," "Mushroom-stuffed tomatoes," and "Fish soufflé." Modernization makes some recipe titles sound outdated or inappropriate, such as "partridges in a stewpot," which are now cooked in a Pyrex dish, transferred from the oven to the stove top for deglazing, and then placed directly on the dining table.[41] In bourgeois homes the arrival of the new kitchenware signaled the triumph of the woman of the house, who was responsible for structural investments and for obtaining the kinds of equipment that would involve the expenditure of small amounts of capital. Such purchases foreground the value of domestic work and can be exhibited to guests with pride, as a sign of hospitality. Since objects of this kind are designed for the family meal, they are clearly distinguishable from the tableware used in restaurants, designed for serving individual portions. There was also the advantage of time saving, since time could be used in a more concentrated, efficient way. Three or four burners could be used simultaneously for the same meal. Cooking procedures that seemed to last forever became mere memory when everything could be achieved in a quicker fashion. Canned and preserved foods were successfully integrated into these transformative processes: a can of peas or peeled tomatoes needed only brief contact with the heat, since they were already preboiled or blanched. Legumes requiring lengthy cooking procedures, such as beans and lentils, could now be removed from the jar and placed in a saucepan for just a short interval before the heat was turned off. Food could be acquired precooked (in the case of beans) or preroasted (in the case of peppers), and the goal was to finish off a process that was begun elsewhere and to beautify the final presentation. In addition, a cube of meat concentrate could supplement a stew or fortify a broth, and boiled meat, which was mainly used as the basis for soups, sauces, and fillings, took on an increasingly prestigious role, becoming tantamount to a fine course in itself. Energy, electrical appliances, preserves, and canned foods thus altered the tempo of meal preparation, with ever-increasing recourse to external sources of food and energy.

The housewife of the Fascist period had a space to fill in her kitchen, the space still occupied by the icebox, a large, enamel-plated container. For Rina Morelli, writing in 1935, the secret aspiration of replacing it still seemed too farfetched: "Electrical refrigerators are now available, most of them imported from America. Not only is it unnecessary to place ice inside them, but they themselves produce ice cubes. Unfortunately, the cost prohibits their widespread accessibility."[42]

The icebox was filled with blocks of ice that were delivered to the home on summer mornings. Its natural extension was the *moscarola*, an aerated safe that was often placed on the balcony and used to keep foods cool. In homes without a cellar—the coolest indoor space available—food was exposed to variations in temperature and soon lost its chill. Milk spoiled, butter melted, and fish had to be cooked no more than six hours after purchase. But the middle-class housewife armed herself against the climate and was ready for disaster. The importance given by lexicons of home cooking to ice-cream making, with reference to such techniques as loading the ice-cream maker, softening the mixture, surrounding the molds with ice, and blending the mixture over ice, seems surprising today. This domestic art—or rather this special fascination with coldness— would soon be rendered obsolete with the introduction of a freezing compartment for popsicles, sorbets, and ice creams. But in the 1930s it had a signal importance. Since few could own a refrigerator, the Electrolux seemed like a magical ice factory, the dream of an automatically functioning icebox.

This "compression" machine is responsive to the capacity of some gases, particularly anhydrate sulfur, to produce cold by evaporation after they have been compressed and liquefied. The use of the refrigerator in large establishments, on ships, in meat storage, and in storehouses of perishable goods goes back to the late nineteenth century. It spread rapidly in the United States and England and slowly and laboriously in Latin countries. Shown at all the universal exhibitions held at the end of the nineteenth century, the refrigerator was installed in maritime warehouses and railway depots by the end of World War I. In geographical terms it spread first in north-central Italy, which is cooler than all other parts of the nation. Created to meet the needs of the community at large, it was installed in large hotels in the form of chambers and in more modest lodging houses in the shape and size of a simple cupboard. Gas, electricity, and artificial refrigeration were first tested and installed in the largest hotels, then in smaller ones, and down the scale in terms of size until they reached private homes. The *Manuale dell'industria alberghiera* (Manual of the hotel industry) published by the Touring Club Italiano in 1923 takes this situation for granted. Here we observe ten pages of advertisements for refrigerators, almost all of them placed by German-owned outlets.[43] This is an indication of the progress already achieved in the technology of refrigeration and its belated availability for domestic use.

Many understood that the refrigerator was used to preserve food, but few had experienced its capacity directly. It was nonetheless evident to all that this magic box produced water in a solid state. The symbol of the refrigerator is the ice cube, obtained by placing little metal trays filled with drinking water in the freezer. The refrigerator was one of the marvels of the hotel bar, where all utensils for making drinks were in evidence, including the shaker and the ice shaver. But was ice ever served at home? Almost never, given the backwardness of the infrastructures and the types of beverages consumed. Even water was artificially

ABOVE: The kitchen of Baron Lerchenfeld of Munich.

Source: Benjamin Rumford, *Essais politiques, économiques et philosophiques* (Paris, 1802).

BELOW: Ideal kitchen.

Source: Lidia Morelli, *La casa che vorrei avere* (Milan: Hoepli, 1931).

gaseated with the addition of powder before it was placed on the table. The practice of mixing drinks met with open hostility from the gourmets: "It is really disgusting to see some individuals drinking a cocktail before meals."[44] And yet the "little block of pure ice" was featured in all promotion campaigns, in the advisories issued to users, and in magazines or newspaper sections devoted to the ideal home. It even made an appearance in a recipe book, without it being clear to the reader whether this object was to be purchased or produced in the home. *Il talismano della felicità*, the *Quattrova illustrato*, and books instructing readers on how to receive guests all reserve a chapter for ice cubes and appetizers. In fantasies of the home that one might wish to have, there was even a furnished corner consisting of a domestic "American bar" or, lacking that, a piece of furniture on wheels on which glasses and bottles were placed.[45] The cocktail, like the ice cube, evokes America, its contradictions (Prohibition was repealed in 1933), and its extravagance. The Accademia d'Italia, alarmed by its success, suggested replacing the word "cocktail" with "*arlecchino*" (Harlequin), while Filippo Tommaso Marinetti suggested "*polibibita*" (polydrink) instead.

In photographs from the 1930s we see that all kitchens are equipped with a clock. This is the household god presiding over culinary work, allowing one to calculate the labor of the housewife against the cost of the machine. The revolution in cooking materials and food preserves, in utensils and heat sources is increasingly legitimized by a gain in time. This would be underlined with even greater emphasis in the project of universal electrification that took place in the 1950s. And yet in praising the value of time lies the ambiguity of modernity. The relationship among edible objects, manual labor, and machines, far from being simplified, becomes increasingly complex. This is due primarily to the increasing rarity first of home cooks and later of maids, and hence the end of a dream: since machines were not capable of producing food on their own or, in other words, since they could not provide a service equal to the input of a cook or a maid, almost any cooking project meant for the woman of the house a burden that was not much lighter than the previous one. The refrigerator and the electric stove were dreams of an assisted domestic life. Without assistance they are containers to be filled and emptied mechanically. Semiprepared foods and preserved foods that were ready to eat became increasingly available as the refrigerator grew larger and as heat sources became progressively more powerful, instituting an ever greater connection between the microcosm of the domestic space and the macrocosm of the hypermarket.

How were recipes and dishes transmitted in this setting, which was cleaner and more efficient than the traditional space? This is difficult to assess, insofar as the updating of domestic infrastructures coincided with the growing availability of semiprepared products ready for consumption. As family cooking was carried out with a growing battery of equipment, the importance traditionally attributed to experience began to diminish. Was it industry that created the crisis in manual work, or was it manual work that abandoned industry? Over the past thirty years, in the midst of contemporary urban life, the work carried out in the kitchen has taken on an increasingly varied aspect, representing both an accumulation of "overtime" hours snatched from one's leisure time and a refined art to be practiced during one's spare moments. The everyday transmission of a gastronomic legacy is no longer guaranteed, though the demand for traditional dishes—especially those that that require time and patience—has remained steady. The utopian ideas that presided over the modernization of the kitchen have turned against their beneficiaries. Hygiene, functionality, safety, speed, economy, and the very notion of progress today seem generic ideals, not necessarily compatible with gastronomical values.

The Magic Formula

A slow and profound transformation of foods accompanied the alteration of the kitchen space brought about by clean energy and electrical equipment. The shift from an artisanal product, an object made by hand, to something produced with steam, boilers, and motorized power represents the first phase of industrialization. The most important consequences of applied scientific research are noted, however, at the moment when new nutritional principles are patented and foods are reconstituted. Gastronomy drives this process through the consumption of new products, but at the same time it submits to the effects of chemicals that guarantee convenience, hygiene, and moderate cost. One of the consequences of this is the presence in apparently traditional foods of ingredients that are not perceptible to the human senses or conceivable to the gastronomic sensibility. This hidden, indirect effect of research is manifest in cooking at a time when the transformation of the culinary environment is still in process. Yet unlike electricity or pots and pans these novelties are less evident to sense perception, and advertising minimizes the structural evolution of the nutritional object. Behind this procedure lies the suspicion of falsification in a society that is anchored by education to the humanistic myths of the good and industrious countryside. The originality of the new industrial culture is its use of technology for the creation of foods, both old and now, as we will briefly outline below.

First published in 1891, Artusi's *La scienza in cucina* promoted a rational gastronomy with specific attention to physiology and hygiene. The term "science," accompanied by the qualifier "applied," was synonymous with industry, but Artusi himself proved to be a modest user of industrial conveniences and products. His book mentions the pickled foods that he purchased in Reggio. Here he also bought cheeses, such as Parmesan, and dried pasta—spaghetti and macaroni—but he chose to process his preserves at home, sterilizing them in sealed jars. He consumed beet sugar and drank coffee and beer. He did not avoid using Liebig meat extract as an alternative to broth.[46] This product, which he describes as "one of the few food preparations recommended by scientists," was produced in Uruguay from 1863 onward. Prepared from beef gristle, salt, and water, it was shipped to Munich and sold from there to the world at large. It had a shelf life of up to fifteen years.[47]

Italy's two best-known industrial products, which were exported all over the world, were pasta and tomato preserves. Three machines were essential for the production of pasta: the mixer, which amalgamates flour and hot water; the kneader, either hand-operated or motorized, which completes the mixing process by incorporating all the tiny grains of semola into the dough; and finally the *trafila*, or press, which compresses the dough and gives it a particular shape before it is submitted to the process of artificial dehydration. At the beginning of the twentieth century all these phases were mechanized. Contents are shown on the packaging in different languages, along with the seal of inspection (for glutinated pastinas) and cooking instructions. Taking into account the possibility of export, the recipes for macaroni are written in French or in English. The instructions stipulate the quantities of water and pasta but not the boiling times, which are shorter in the south and longer as one travels north. The accompanying sauces are described in English, French, and Italian with a series of recipes that range from the fastest and simplest to the most complex, emphasizing the value of pasta as a complete meal (and not only as a side dish). According to the information on one label:

When boiled, [macaroni] can be served in different ways:
1. With grated cheese sprinkled on top and a few dashes of pepper;
2. With fresh butter, grated cheese, and additional butter according to taste;
3. With tomato sauce, meat sauce, or ragout, specially prepared each time, and grated cheese on top.[48]

Renato Rovetta, son of an industrialist from Brescia, compiled *L'industria del pastificio* (The pasta industry), the Hoepli manual dedicated to the production of pasta. He also produced *Il pomodoro* (The tomato), another manual by the same company. Tomato processing required a strainer and a crusher, a boiler for cooking, and equipment for concentrating the tomato pulp in a vacuum. Metal cans were then filled either by hand or by machine. Prepared for export, tomato sauce and tomato concentrate also included a recipe on the packaging label.

The Hoepli manuals describe all phases of the modernization of the Italian food industry from 1890 to 1940, providing information on planning, equipment, canning, and even tasting instructions. The commercialization of food production facilitated the development of an Italian gastronomic model that was compatible with the resources and taste preferences of foreign countries (for example, butter was the only fat used in cans of tomato sauce bound for France).

The recipes attached to the manual on rice (*Tecnologia del riso*) are as detailed and as thorough in their instructions as any of the pamphlets produced for domestic use. The recipes take into account not only the ways in which rice can be served (including soups and sweet fritters) but also the various regions where it is consumed (from the area around Milan to the Veneto, from Naples to Sicily).[49] The function of the recipe is threefold: to confirm the continuity between manual and mechanical forms of production, to demonstrate the suitability of the industrial product for traditional culinary use, and to offer simple and widely applicable models of preparation.

Naturally some products, such as Liebig extract used to make broth, did not simply replace other foods but functioned as integrators without the consumer being aware of their specificity. For example, powdered milk was used in 1929 in the manufacture of *biscotti* and chocolates, in luxury cakes and pastries, and in many products for children.[50] The use of instant chocolate had anticipated this trend. With this type of ingredient there is no longer any continuity between handmade and industrial products. What we see instead is an exclusively industrial reformulation, with results that are difficult to assess from the standpoint of taste as well as gastronomy. Milk was a special focus of experimentation in Italy and in other, advanced countries. Its use in fermented drinks, yogurt, and low-fat cheeses such as *quartirolo* and, to an even greater degree, in caseine, which was destined for the manufacture of plastic, demonstrates how scientific applications were expanded within and beyond the food sector.

Industrial preparations enjoyed a remarkable degree of success in the pastry-making sector during the 1930s. Beginning with a small packet of yeast and another of vanilla-flavored sugar (the basis of all sweet baked goods), the idea developed of creating packaged desserts of both Italian and foreign origin that could be assembled by the consumer with minimal domestic outlay (eggs, butter, and milk). The immediate availability of a stove or an icebox thus made possible the creation of a *ciambella* (ring-cake) or a sweet pudding. Bertolini, Elah, Royal, and Maizena, all respected brand names, soon published their own recipe collections for desserts, as Cirio had done for canned products. Artusi's chocolate pudding was suddenly outdated, but it did not die out. This revival of recipes, now dedicated to milk and sugar, has a traditional aspect. Here the cook is implicitly a mother, the consumer a child, and her preparations are inevitably served at home. These values could be enhanced with the addition of special nutritional properties, as in the creation of baby foods and soups—along the lines of the project sponsored by the Dahò company—fortified with oats, tapioca, refined flour, and carefully trimmed legumes. There was a strong demand for healthy industrial products among the middle classes from the beginning of the twentieth century onward, and this would become more widespread with the rise in living standards.

Thanks to these "magic" packets, the food industry asserted its power in terms of speed and ease of execution. It promised success yet allowed the able consumer to claim the credit. The range of packaged items soon multiplied, as products became available for leavening, sweetening, and flavoring or as a substitute for eggs (Ovocrema). Containers of bicarbonate of soda could be used for cooking dried legumes, preparing desserts, preserving broth, making sparkling drinks, and even for footbaths. This chemical magic was easily accepted since it was integrated into the culinary craft of the home. The housewife's relationship with industrial processes, however, remained ambivalent. On the one hand she was optimistic, since she had faith in yeast and in the pasteurized milk produced by central dairies. On the other she felt confused. Although milk inspires confidence, it is difficult to assess the quality of butter. Manuals appeared to protect the consumer from some of the products in daily use: "Butter is one of the most falsified food products. Theoretically one could say today that truly genuine butter can no longer be found commercially."[51] The presence of greater quantities of water than allowed or the use of unlawful colorants or inferior fats such as margarine and coconut oil is not often perceptible to taste and smell. What was the consumer to do in these circumstances? Trust the brand name was the advice given by the director of the municipal chemical laboratory of Milan.[52] This is how self-certification became common practice.

· The war years in Italy (from 1917 to 1918 and again from 1940 to 1944) also brought a sense of ambivalence to the relationship between public authorities and the food industry. Obligatory food rationing followed the outbreak of war, and this resulted in the recourse to substitutes (such as saccharine, chicory, barley coffee, and synthetic oil), "poor" cooking (vegetable broth and chestnut meal), the practice of making-do (with recycled fats, for example), and the deliberate falsification of rationed products. In response to the pressures of need and availability, culinary creativity flourished in this climate, with a special emphasis on ritual and on the possibilities offered by leftovers. These extraordinary times eliminated all free markets other than the black market and turned the consumer back in the direction of the countryside, where it was still possible to buy food, even if prices were high. The food industry suffered during this period almost as much as the consumers. Yet it reemerged unblemished in the postwar years with growing supply and demand. The publication of promotional recipe collections was then resumed by Carli olive oil and the Cirio canning company, barometers of middle-class dining.

But changes were even more evident beyond the domestic sector. A look at the dessert industry at this juncture is illuminating. In 1950 "Algida and Motta placed *ice cream* on the market; in 1951 Motta invented *sticks* [ice lollipops or popsicles], and in 1955 Pavesi and Motta brought out *crackers*."[53] At a time when the refrigerator was becoming widely available and the food industry was attempting to invent new ways to fill it, homemade ice cream disappeared, and the production of crackers and breadsticks began to compete with bread making. Sachets of yeast now seemed dated, and the expression "homemade" was less and less applicable to common foods. Ice creams and crackers in fact became snacks consumed independently of mealtimes. Eaten purely for pleasure, they are symbols of a new industrial trend that emerged in response to the decrease in domestic baking and the simultaneous increase in consumption outside the home.

The capitalism of food and agriculture instigated the synthesis of domestic modernization (from the refrigerator to the microwave oven), the increasing tendency to delegate culinary operations elsewhere, the trend toward occasional consumption, and the need to salvage a culinary identity. It produced long-lasting items (such as frozen lasagna) as well as products suited for quick cooking (spaghetti). Successive layers of industrial history peacefully coexist. By concentrating on the wide-ranging craft of pasta making, the Barilla Company triumphed, without tomato canning companies being swallowed up. The dairy sector grew, following the pattern of product differentiation already embarked upon and capturing consumers from all age groups. The most successful food and agriculture groups, however, are those that combine different product sectors and guarantee their international distribution. To what extent were gastronomic culture and practices affected by this phenomenon?

The food industry quietly insinuates itself into recipes through the requirement of specific ingredients and domestic equipment, but it does not dictate the law for the basic food model. It offers a finished product (frozen pizza) or ensures convenient assembly (a box of pizza ingredients) without bringing an end to the domestic production of the kind of pizza dough that is first leavened and then covered with the necessary flavorings. It encourages exotic experiments. In the area of public and private distribution it also teaches ways of consuming food that are foreign to Artusi's gastronomy: eating without knives and forks (fried potatoes), spreading substances on bread (mayonnaise or Nutella, a chocolate-hazelnut spread), licking (an ice-cream cone), and throwing away beverage containers.

In the course of the past fifty years domestic values have reasserted themselves while industrial values have undergone equally important variations. A product such as a soup, when prepared by hand from the selection of ingredients to the moment of serving, is an expensive item in terms of time and money if compared with the frozen version, despite the difference in taste. In the handmade soup, the formula is personalized, whereas in the frozen version the ingredients are more numerous and the result can be modified (by adding water and various flavorings, for example). Between the two extremes other products, such as canned minestrone or ravioli, which seem rather outdated, are still on the market. Like cooking, industry is a stratified culture, offering a progressive range of products, and over time it takes stock of its own history. Factories celebrate their birthdays and express pride in the past: "1887–1932: Like a solid old house, it helps you to protect the health of your loved ones"—this is the title of a pamphlet released by Buitoni to publicize pastina made with gluten flour.[54] Front-rank producers boast of long experience and hence their continuous presence in the marketplace.

The food industry also stresses continuity in the matter of taste. While Appert's goal was to preserve foods without additives that would alter them, thus salvaging the illusion of a fresh product, freshness is still one of the principal concerns of the industry today. In response to consumers who value rapid cooking times and consume raw food with increasing frequency, lower temperatures are now used. Other values and concerns also influence research, some ancient and others more recent, such as nutritional lightness, based on the findings of dietary science, the crunchiness that has made crackers such a big success, the palatability of cheeses, and the addition of natural or synthetic aromas. Combining the criteria of taste and good health, calculating needs and opportunities for consumption, new food products are created while older food products are revived. Invention has an important part to play, especially in relation to the market sector most recently captured.

Whatever its function and its implications for consumers, industrial food is a fully planned object. Constructed through the use of additions and processes of transformation, this product derives its value from its sensory, economic, and nutritional characteristics, as well as its appearance. Volume, color, and consistency stimulate the appetite and invite consumption and are additionally emphasized by the packaging. In fact, the packaging not only protects and preserves the product; it represents it, renders it appealing, and informs the public on its possible uses with the help of pictures and written instructions. These same aspects of production and marketing were present at the beginning of industrial history, but only recently have they come together in a single process, ranging from raw materials to motivating consumer choice and beyond, offering gadgets and free gifts that confer additional prestige on the act of purchase. Removed from traditional sensory stimuli—smell and especially touch—manufactured food exists outside the cycle of the seasons; it does not vary in time and space. It is the objective synthesis of the process of production. And its life cycle is established commercially, lasting from its packaging date to the time of its death, the expiration date printed on the label.

CHAPTER NINE

Toward a History of the Appetite

The Hearty Eater

Until very recently the appetites of the body were central to the discourse of gastronomy. A lusty appetite, when accompanied by the means and capacity to satisfy it fully, was the foremost indicator (and instrument) of good health and a sign of social privilege.[1] A well-nourished belly, perhaps even a protruding one, communicated an image of well-being, wealth, and security. To describe a dinner table as "fat" was to declare its excellence. In praising Milan the writer Matteo Bandello declared it to be "Italy's most opulent and bountiful city, where one is most likely to find a fat dinner table, abundantly laid with food." Similarly there was no mockery intended in Bologna's traditional designation as "Bologna the Fat." The same was true of individuals or social groups who were described as fat. A fat man was in fact a source of envy. Far from being viewed as obese he was regarded as a vigorous and imposing person, well capable of satisfying his appetites. During the Middle Ages prosperous Florentine merchants referred to their own class as *"il popolo grasso"* (the stout people), communicating a state of collective well-being on the social and political level that was immediately translated into a body image. The use of the term "fat" to connote "nourishing" also had a positive meaning in writings on gastronomy and dietetics. Platina advises Scaurio and Celio, two of his friends in the Academy, to eat a "meat pie," for "they would do well to trade their thin looks for a bit of fat." Meat pie, he adds, "is very nutritious, fattening, and good for the liver."[2]

Voluntary abstinence from food is difficult to understand unless it is contextualized within this way of thinking. If the rule of monastic life claimed that resistance to the pangs of hunger was the best way to guarantee reward in the next life,[3] it was because the monastery itself was part of a broader collective culture that placed food at the center of human desires. Renouncing food was thus the greatest form of sacrifice.

The exaltation of fat (as nourishing food or as the highly nourished body) was the other side of a sad history, the history of starvation that threatened both mind and body. This took the form of perceived deprivation or the fear of being without food as well as real starvation that had to be combated day after day with labor and ingenuity. Only a very small number of privileged individuals could truly consider themselves safe from its grasp, and for these an "expansive table"[4] was the primary indication of social difference, of their elevated social status, which had to be communicated and proven to others. "Before the dishes were presented on the table, they were carried around the square with great pride, passing in front of the palace and within the sight of the common people who could thus witness their magnificence." Thus writes the chronicler Cherubino Ghirardacci, describing the sumptuous banquet organized by Giovanni II Bentivoglio to celebrate the marriage of his son, Annibale, to Lucrezia d'Este in Bologna in 1487.[5] The display of such "magnificence" was not only for the benefit of the common people but also for that of the numerous distinguished guests, many of whom would have limited themselves to *watching* the phantasmagoric parade of dishes carried to the table in a series of servings that lasted from eight o'clock in the evening to three in the morning. No one was expected to eat everything, for this would have been physically impossible. As always occurred in such cases, a great part of the banquet was purely theatrical. In earlier centuries a powerful man was expected to be above all else strong and brave in battle, and thus his capacity for ingesting mountains of food seemed a "natural" attribute and in a sense a necessary virtue. By the end of the medieval period, however, the image of the great eater that had characterized earlier models of aristocratic life gave way to a more mediated image, where abundant food continued to be considered an essential attribute of the powerful but in a form that evoked rights rather than duty. The gentleman of the late Middle Ages and the early modern period was a courtier, politician, and diplomat but not a warrior. He did not present himself primarily as a hearty eater but rather as an organizer of banquets, which enabled him to show off his status (acquired by birth), his wealth (with teams of cooks and highly prized foods), and his culture (with refined, highly imaginative preparations served from the kitchen and pantry).[6] Yet even within this altered scheme of things abundant food was still a value that was highly appreciated and widely upheld from a social point of view, and the appetite when present was not regarded as unseemly.

There also existed a type of abundance "for the poor."[7] Such abundance was always desired and occasionally became a real experience. In literature and popular fantasy from the Middle Ages to the present, we find the significant recurrence of the myth of La Cuccagna (Cocaigne), a land of plenty bursting with untold quantities of food within the reach of everyone, where giant pans of gnocchi are poured onto mountains of grated cheese, vines are held in place with sausage links and wheat fields are fenced off with joints of roast meat, and plump geese perpetually rotate on the spit. Only the imagination (or interest) of the small population of the elite would have been capable of generating images of happy poverty and a type of contented, self-satisfied frugality. The genuinely hungry have always wanted to fill their stomachs to bursting, and in reaction to hunger they envision a utopia of abundance.

This utopia was not only a matter of fantasy. The land of plenty took on concrete form from time to time, becoming a real place where abundance genuinely prevailed. On important religious holidays (such as Christmas or the feast of a patron saint) and important occasions in family life (such as weddings and christenings), lavish quantities of food were displayed, almost to the point of excess, in a ritual laden with rich foods and symbolism, as compensation for everyday deprivation and as an expression of the desire for a dignified level of survival. On such occasions everyone was required to witness and acknowledge the spectacle of abundance. In eighteenth-century Naples a team of town criers came through the streets shouting out lists of the animals slaughtered and the quantity of foods devoured during the Christmas celebrations. As Goethe reports in his travel journal:

> The Christmas holidays are known as banquet days. The whole city of Naples becomes a land of plenty, and it seems that five hundred thousand men have come to a common agreement. Via Toledo and several piazzas in the vicinity are decorated in the most appetizing manner: one sees garlands of foodstuffs hanging in the streets, great hoops of golden sausages tied with red ribbons, and turkeys sporting a red weathervane on their bottoms. . . . A huge number of donkeys laden with vegetables, capons, and kid goats pass through the city and the marketplace, and the eggs assembled in huge heaps here and there constitute an unimaginable quantity. It is not enough for all this to be simply devoured; instead every year a police official patrols the city on horseback, accompanied by a trumpeter, stopping in every piazza and clearing to announce the thousands of oxen, calves, kid goats, lambs, and pigs that the Neapolitans have consumed. People listen carefully and are enormously pleased with the huge numbers. Everyone remembers with satisfaction the part he played in such enjoyment.[8]

This way of reveling ostentatiously in food, abundance, and the satisfaction of the appetite shows a deep similarity between popular and aristocratic culture. What the Neapolitan masses experienced at Christmas was not very different from the daily customs of the court. It was the ethics of the middle classes that succeeded, much later, in imposing the contrasting values of leanness, frugality, and restraint, which were not unlike those upheld by monastic teaching. But this did not prevent the "expansive table" from exerting an ongoing fascination, especially among social classes long excluded from the banquet. In 1850 Giovanni Rajberti wrote:

> The main fault with the feasts beloved by the lower classes is that they do not respect the great axiom "*ne quid nimis,*" so advisable even in the best

of circumstances. What dominates is a certain fear of not being able to do justice to oneself, giving rise to a general frenzy, where people abandon that wise and well-calculated sense of moderation that constitutes the principal element of beauty in all art. Thus we find huge quantities of overseasoned and highly flavored dishes and a predominance of foodstuffs with an excessively hot and stimulating character.

For Rajberti, all too often in the course of such occasions "the meals to which the guests are invited are so oppressively long and offer such an overabundance of food that they seem to have been prepared with the appetites of elephants and whales in mind."

To Stimulate the Appetite

Is it still possible to eat in a moderate, balanced way in a culture where abundance is both a subjective and collective value? To answer this question we must consider some of the issues linked to the physiological consumption of a meal. An individual is capable of swallowing much more than he is capable of digesting, or he may find by contrast that he is able to eat much less than he might desire. What stems from this is the need to balance the quantity and assimilation of food by identifying a standard, by consulting an indicator that regulates timing, quantities, the types of foods eaten, and their effects. This indicator is the appetite. A doctor can evaluate the meal eaten by his patient and his fellow diners, evaluating symptoms of pleasure and satiety and paying special attention to the end of the digestive phase, which alone allows for the commencement of a new meal. Guided by theoretical principles and his own empirical observations, he is the "physic" who supervises his patient's sleep, his movements, the timing of his meals, the composition of the dishes he consumes, and even the choice of his wines.

The task is not an easy one. One can eat without being hungry or before one has properly finished the digestive process. One can be fooled by a false sense of appetite, lured by flavors and sauces that stimulate desire even when the stomach has already had enough. Sometimes a lazy stimulus and sometimes a spontaneous, violent one, the appetite is externally manifest in the continuous cycle of ingestion and expulsion. It is present when the stomach is empty and also, inappropriately, when it is quite full. The mechanism that regulates the appetite is not merely endogenous. Physical activity, the time of day, and the sight of food on the table can rekindle it. The "sumptuous sheen" of tablecloth and napkins or the sight of a whetted knife "can make a person with no appetite begin to develop one."[9] The doctor is not always capable of controlling these stimuli and their effects. Moreover, the princely banquet, which is the aristocratic version of the popular Cuccagna, calls for a gastronomic approach. This must be carried out with due dignity, and the pleasures of dining must be administered with appropriate expertise. And at this point the cook and the literary man can come to the doctor's aid.

The cook and the man of letters do not necessarily occupy identical positions, and we cannot generalize on the basis of Platina's collaboration with Maestro Martino. What is striking in the encounter that we have already described between Michel de Montaigne and the steward who had worked in the service of the deceased cardinal Carlo Carafa is not only the difference between the two men in terms of disposition, culture, and especially taste but also their different approach to the basic problem of the appetite and its role in the ritual of dining.[10] Let us reread Montaigne's words:

> He spelled out to me the difference in appetites: the one we have before eating, the one we have after the second or third course; the means, now of simply gratifying it, now of arousing it and stimulating it; the organization of his sauces, first in general, and then in particularizing the qualities of the ingredients and their effects; the differences in salads according to the season, which one should be warmed up and which served cold, the way of adorning and embellishing them to make them also pleasant to the sight. After that we entered upon the order of serving food.[11]

Montaigne's confusion in the face of his impertinent and loquacious interlocutor shows the staunch independence of a learned gentleman who views the meal in terms of a personal, subjective harmony between and among the body, diet, and hunger, without needing to take into account a doctor's prescriptions or a steward's devilish calculations. But the literary man also plays a part in the debate on the appetite, especially at the banquets of princes or cardinals, where he has an active and absolutely original role to play with his conversation, his poetry, and his emblems, which are transformed into candied ornaments. Platina already claimed that the role of the learned man was not to "weigh the amount of foods that each of us must eat from day to day" or to "furnish new instruments of lust" but rather to "provide [the banquet table] with the presence of a cultured man who desires good health and food of a decorous sort" in accordance with the wisdom of his humanistic learning and the capacity of his pen to transmit it.[12] The cook, the doctor, and the learned man thus find themselves implicated in a diatribe focused on the human body, which is to say, the body of the prince. Each of them adopts a different position in this debate on one issue in particular: the value assigned to the desire for food. The learned man places intellectual and aesthetic values first and considers the meal in the context of a cultural system of the past and present, contemplating the effect of the appetite constituted by personal, subjective taste in all circumstances, even in the private dining experiences of princes and cardinals. He is the only one who describes his personal position in writing and records his own experience with elegance and acumen.

The Tree of Plenty (Italian woodcut of the sixteenth century).

Management of the appetites does not rely solely on considerations of a physiological and intellectual sort. If the cook has to take into account his master's temperament and modify his art accordingly by calculating the needs of a hot or cold
complexion, his area of concern goes well beyond the natural requirements of
physical sustenance. To stimulate the appetite of a healthy man or an invalid
involves a quest for balance within the norms constituted by the impulse toward

adequate and abundant nourishment. Frictions and disagreements are inevitable between doctors and stewards, and yet no writer of culinary treatises fails to search for some form of compromise, even if he ultimately subordinates the considerations of others to his own. Domenico Romoli adopts this approach, presenting the advice of a physician after he has already articulated his own views, by relegating the translation of Robert Grospré's *Trattato del reggimento della sanità ridotto della sostanza della medicina* (Treatise on the maintenance of health based on elements of medicine) to an appendix at the end of his own book *La singolar dottrina*.[13] The management of the appetite, of the lust for food, and of the well-disposed stomach is the task of the steward, who must be careful to seek counsel from the doctor. Indeed without such guidance the diner may do himself harm, choosing foods that are not good for him and rendering the art of cooking futile. The learned man can assist both the doctor and the steward with a suitable style of expression, reestablishing the harmony of the court around the prince.

The existence of this debate can be observed even in cookbooks, enabling us to consider in a different and more complex way the problems posed by the "expansive table." A sumptuous course served at a meal does not imply a monstrous appetite but rather a solemn and polite attempt to stimulate it. The approach to the table must be adorned with many delights that offer pleasure to the eyes rather than the palate. In this regime of temperate freedom it is also necessary to provide a delicate diet for those who are obliged to abstain from heavy food. In the sixth and final book of Scappi's *Opera* we find recipes for convalescents organized into a meal of several courses featuring "boiled waters," broths, soups, roasts, eggs, cakes, and finally sauces (which are considered very dangerous), all of which are listed in order of delicacy and delectability. Scappi's employment in the service of cardinals and popes, who were often of advanced years and not always of sound constitution, obliged him to make special use of this skill, perfectly summarized in the first eighteen recipes for broths and gelatins. It is not the most serious part of his book, but it is perhaps the most ingenious. The function of the good cook is neither to tempt nor to castigate but to prove his discernment. The listless, the weak, those without appetite, and even the sick merit his full attention. A well-skimmed capon broth has a "little strip of ham" added to it for just one hour during the cooking process to provide some taste. Afterward the meat is carefully removed, and the cooking continues as the liquid is reduced through boiling.[14] It is hardly an accident that this section of the book more than the other chapters seems to have been born and conceived in Rome. Lenten rules, the practice of fasting, and ecclesiastical prudence come together in Scappi's cuisine, which is respectful of prohibitions but nonetheless serene. The aim of the recipes is always to restore good health and to revive the body's original appetites.

The sixth book of the *Opera* seems to have been written in order to help the "Most Reverend Cardinal of Carpi during his Illnesses." But each recipe bears the

memory of a dedicatee, either implicitly or explicitly. In his instructions for making "a chicken broth of hearty substance reduced in ice," Scappi declares that "it
is served to convalescents when they are very thirsty, and I prepared this for the
most Illustrious Reverend Cardinal Andrea Cornaro in 1551." Prompted by the
same concerns, Sante Lancerio, the wine steward of Pope Paul III, who lived to
the age of eighty-one, served his master malvagia wine that Cardinal Cornaro had
ordered for the pontiff from Venice.[15] The name Cornaro reappears in the dining
annals of the Curia, where it refers to a very different character, Alvise Cornaro,
the author of the work *Trattato della vita sobria* (Treatise on temperate living).
This document proposes low food intake as the secret of achieving a venerable
age, remaining intellectually vigilant and physically sound, with abundant offspring. "How appropriate it is for an old man to eat little!" Cornaro exclaimed.
What he means is not a mystery: "These are my foods: first bread, then *panatela*,
or light broth with an egg, or other equally good little soups. For meat I eat veal,
kid, or lamb. I eat chickens of all kinds, partridge, and small birds, such as the
thrush. In addition I eat fish. For example, among saltwater fish I eat golden
bream and similar types and among fresh-water fish I eat pike and similar types."[16]

One way of looking at the art of cooking is to consider it as the qualitative
multiplication of loaves and fishes. Another way is to place value on the selection of ingredients and their special qualities without overwhelming them with
excessive flavors and condiments. Cornaro's diet has something in common
with convalescent cuisine in the special value attributed to bread (which provides simple nourishment) and soup (which cleans and purifies the intestines).
"Quantity and quality" is Cornaro's defense against the kind of appetite that
reduces the human lifespan by years. He proposes a combination of modest
servings (twelve ounces of solid food and fourteen ounces of wine each day)
with appropriate nutrients as the secret of a light and flavorful cuisine.

The management of desire is a goal the steward shares with writers, philosophers of the dinner table, physicians, and many others who love life. The difficulty of establishing the proper balance between hunger and appetite, between
the experience of emptiness and that of fullness, is shown, however, by those
who exclude others from the banquet table or are themselves excluded. Paradoxically both the monk who inflicts penance upon himself and the hungry
peasant are present here too, watching the nobles, each chewing on his own
thoughts. In the room next to the dining hall where the guests are seated at the
table, the monk preaches hunger, and the peasant embodies it, acting as its
bogeyman. Since the banquet is a kind of theater, with intermezzos and stage
sets, it is not difficult to see how all roles can be played out in this environment.

The cuisine of the cardinals and the secretly organized catering arrangements for the conclave held from November 29, 1549, to February 7, 1550,
which is described by Scappi, are part of a ritual that mixes prayer and culinary
indulgence. They are in fact its most spectacular manifestation, prompting a

reflection on the kind of nourishment that is subject to constant moderation. Not only does medicine teach the church that there are sensual solids and liquids; it provides it with fearful weapons against itself, and the church expresses a strange attitude of veneration and condemnation toward dining. The worst enemy of the collaboration of medicine, cuisine, and Mother Nature is not the glutton but the man who preaches renunciation, one who hates food in large quantities and even the nature of food itself. This enemy has a name, Father Enrico da San Bartolomeo del Gaudio, and a title, *Lo scalco spirituale* (The spiritual steward). Claiming the impossibility of both complete self-denial and a compromise of the sort advocated by Cornaro, he distinguishes greediness from hunger. The first is generated by "excessive nourishment," and the second is easy to appease. The lust for food is a temptation, and its opposite, the feeling of revulsion toward food, is not a form of renunciation but the result of excessive indulgence, fullness, or the kind of phenomena well known to naturalists, such as the experience that follows the ingestion of a large amount of capers. Only a diet of bread and water can remedy this vicious cycle. The spiritual importance of hunger and thirst is championed by members of religious orders, who are not the only ones who steer away from the banquet table, distrusting its insidious lures.

The art of cooking has, in addition to its spiritual enemies, real adversaries of an even greater number. "Marza sic fame crepabo?" (Must I die like this, executed by hunger?), cries the peasant Zambello, railing against the compelling desire to eat that consumes him as he stands alone in the middle of his fields at daybreak.[17] He feeds on garlic and onions and would gladly sink his teeth into a crust of moldy bread or a rind of cheese. He would devour anything he could grasp within his clutches. Hunger has deprived him of the light of reason, as greed deprives the sensual man, but unlike the latter he has nothing to fight with other than the hard-working hands with which he cultivates his clumps of earth and his beanstalks. There is no real place for peasants at the banquet table. In this setting they are merely imagined. They make an appearance in the satiric poetry of Folengo, or they are evoked by costumed actors and musicians carrying scythes and pipes,[18] or they are featured in Arcadian sugar sculptures and in other mythological or idyllic elements adorning the table. Here the rural world evokes the earthly origins of food and sanctions the luxury of the dining table, which represents all of creation, even its most humble elements, with its edible figurines in animal and human shapes.

The body and its appetites are part of the banquet. They are the telluric forces shackled to the table, to be tamed and gentrified. Hunger and fasting are the ghosts that interrupt this feast of the flesh with their curses and prayers. In this respect the dining table is a site of mediation between heaven and earth, where the prince and the cardinal prevail with their authority and with their retinue of cooks, literary men, and scientists.

"Indigestion Does No Harm to Peasants"

After heralding the introduction of the potato as a solution to the hunger of peasants in *La pratica agraria* (Agrarian practice), a treatise on practical agrarian science written in 1778, Giovanni Battarra of Rimini pauses to explain the possibility of making bread from the pulp of this strange tuber. He suggests that it is
sufficient to mix the pulp with a little wheat flour to obtain a very delicate and
flavorful bread that is "fit for a lord." Mignone, son of the fictional peasant who
is the mouthpiece of Battarra's teachings, asks if one could make bread simply
with potato flour, without adding wheat. Certainly, his father answers, adding
nonetheless that "they say that bread made this way is rather hard to digest."
Surprisingly, this detail does not bother Mignone in the slightest. Indeed it fills
him with joy, because, he explains, "indigestion does no harm to peasants. In
fact it gives them the sensation of being fuller."[19] The moral of the story is that
what the peasant truly desires is a hearty indigestion in order to distance himself
as much as possible from the frustrating desire to eat.

Naturally this is the landlord's point of view. No peasant from the eighteenth
century (much less from earlier times) has managed to communicate his food
preferences in his own words, and since taste and custom are not exactly the
same thing, it is difficult to abandon the impression that the culinary model
attributed by intellectuals to the peasant population corresponds more to the
force of circumstances than to choices freely made. The peasant's praise for
indigestion is a cliché that goes far back in time. Agostino Gallo from Brescia,
the author of an important treatise on farming, invokes it in his discussion of
polenta. In the process of giving a recipe for this dish, his character, the unlettered peasant Scaltrito, explains to two noblemen from Brescia that millet is the
best flour to use here and that it is unwise to use wheat, "in order not to make a
polenta that is too fine and also because it is too easily digested."[20]

Thus the peasant's body desires heavy foods that stagnate at length in the
stomach, weighty foods that do not stimulate the appetite but on the contrary
suppress it. In Giulio Cesare Croce's *Bertoldo*, when court physicians try to cure
the illness of a "countryman," coaxing him with rare and delicate foods, he
swears that "if they could bring him a pot of beans with onions in it and turnips
cooked in the ashes, he would certainly get well by eating those foods." But his
request is refused, and Bertoldo dies, according to his epitaph, "with harsh
pains, as the result of not being able to eat turnips and beans."[21] We could simply find this amusing if Croce's text, published at the beginning of the seventeenth century, were not a parody of successful scientific theories that were
authoritatively articulated in treatises on medicine, botany, and agronomy produced in the preceding centuries.[22] At the beginning of the fourteenth century
Piero de' Crescenzi, a famous agronomist of Bologna, observed that wheat was
by far the best grain for making bread. He advised those who worked hard, how-

ever, using the most energy, to eat bread made with less refined grains, such as sorghum, most suitable for feeding peasants, as well as pigs, cows, and horses. Giacomo Albini, a physician at the court of Savoy, warned of the pains and illnesses experienced by those who ate foods inappropriate to their rank. He claimed that the rich should abstain from heavy soups, such as those based on legumes or organ meats, which might require a complicated digestive process. The poor should avoid refined food, as their coarse stomachs would have difficulty assimilating it. This theoretical justification of dietary privilege in the name of science was echoed by many intellectuals of the era, who were willingly complicit in the interests of the powerful, as has often happened throughout history. Michele Savonarola, a native of Padua who wrote a successful treatise on diet in the middle of the fifteenth century, was similarly attentive to the distinction between meals "for courtiers" and meals "for country people." He wrote, for example, that kid "is a meat for delicate stomachs and not a food for peasants." He describes parsnips as "a food for the poor man and the peasant." The correspondence between the "quality of food" and the "quality of the consumer" is not perceived as a simple empirical fact, associated with circumstances of wealth or need, but postulated as an absolute truth of an ontological sort. To eat well or badly, lightly or abundantly, is an attribute intrinsic to man, just as his social status is considered an intrinsic (and, it is hoped, immutable) aspect of his being. Every transgression of this state of things constitutes not only a risk to one's personal good health but also an attack on class privilege. When at the end of the seventeenth century Girolamo Cirelli writes in a pamphlet that peasants, "except on feast days," eat "like pigs," there is no sense of wonder in his tone or any hint of regret. The title of his pamphlet (*Il villano smascherato* — The countryman unmasked) clearly demonstrates the perspective from which reflections of this kind arise: the way in which individuals eat reveals or unmasks their social status. It is thought natural and appropriate that a countryman should eat and behave "like a pig." As long as this is the case, the social order is secure.

The ruling classes of the eighteenth century, imbued with a philanthropic spirit and an attitude of enlightened paternalism toward the poor, are different from those of two or three centuries earlier, who were entrenched in the defense of their privileges and intent on shaping an ideology of social difference that was tied to particular styles of living and dietary practice. It is at this juncture more difficult to discern any overt intention to exclude the poor from the enjoyment of food of high quality. The cruel cynicism of the powerful and many intellectuals has softened by now at least to some degree. But there is still something quite sinister, or at least grotesque, in the *Avvisi ai contadini sulla loro salute* (Advice to peasants on their health) proposed by Marco Lastri, who wrote a number of instructional pamphlets on agricultural topics at the turn of the eighteenth century. Lastri's "advice" forms an appendix to *Regole per i padroni dei poderi* (Rules for the owners of farmlands). Reading it, one infers that peasants eat badly (which is hardly a surprise) and that they really do not know how to eat at all, because in order to economize ("*rea* economia," the author specifies) they are apt to consume even spoiled products and prefer heavy, indigestible foods (a timeworn cliché) to save on quantity and thus keep hunger at bay. Lastri writes, "One can scarcely praise the custom of certain peasant men, fathers of families, who for economic reasons have large quantities of bread made at the same time, so that when it grows stale and hard less bread will be consumed."[23]

In other words if peasants eat badly it is because they want to eat badly. The ideological picture has by now abandoned the concept that prevailed in the fifteenth and sixteenth century, according to which bad food and indigestible cooking were an essential and inevitable fact of peasant life. Yet the consequences of the newly proclaimed freedom of choice are to say the least paradoxical from the cultural point of view. According to a French dictionary of the time, "Peasants are usually rather stupid, because they nourish themselves on coarse foods."[24]

The Diet of the Literary Man

Alvise Cornaro offers the following judgment in favor of moderation: "Writing after eating never does me harm, nor is my intellect ever better than it is then, nor do I feel sleepy after eating, because a small quantity of food cannot send fumes to my head."[25] His voice would echo for centuries, valorizing the choice of a personal, secular, and philosophical way of life. This had the advantage of restoring the act of dining to the measure of the healthy man, by considering nutrition as a temperate activity. Many studies, especially in the eighteenth century, lent their support to this line of thinking, which was espoused mainly by urban professionals and the well-to-do. The thesis defended by the twenty-year-old Dr. Scopoli in 1743, *De diaeta littérateur*, which describes the diet of the literary man, discusses among other topics the nature of foods. Scopoli recommends delicate foods, of moderate taste, allowing acidic or pungent flavors only in very small quantities. The literary man is taken as his point of reference, a man who pursues sedentary, intellectual work of great importance but with little expenditure of physical energies.

This typology was well known to dietary science, which was to occupy a central place in social consumption, proposing inexpensive products of good quality, with excellent properties from the organic point of view without being rare. The day begins with a light broth, a cup of chocolate, or perhaps a cup of herbal tea. This is a liquid diet, observed in the privacy of the home,[26] and it continues, from the morning on through the day, in pauses and light snacks, taking advantage of the properties of tea, which opens the paths to the brain and relaxes the nerves. Even the wine accompanying the meal is of good quality. It is clear,

Banquet (woodcut).

Source: Cristoforo Messisbugo, *Banchetti, compositioni di vivande et apparecchio generale* (Ferrara: Buglhat and Hucher, 1549).

pleasant, amiable, fragrant, and penetrating but neither old nor new, just as beer (mentioned because Scopoli had studied in the Tyrol) should be slightly sweet and slightly bitter.

Thirst rather than appetite preoccupies the eighteenth-century doctor, who makes use of botanical antidotes, both homegrown and exotic. This new attention to liquids, not necessarily of nutritional value but having an effect on the nerves, is part of a general reassessment of the meal that gives a central role to foods that used to be marginal and distributes juices, herbal teas and brews at intervals throughout the day. It is based on an understanding of blood circulation that favors hot drinks capable of stimulating the blood (the abuse of coffee, tea, and brews will prompt a reconsideration of this principle, given their effects on the nervous system). Vegetable products in every form have a privileged place here and are thus revived. The practice of having chocolate for breakfast, coffee after lunch, and tea between meals became widespread from the end of the seventeenth century onward, to the point that Scopoli considers them "very common in modern times" (*moderno vero tempore ita usuales*). A new dose of hot and cold liquids, of bitter and sweet flavors, reshapes the habits of taste. But this involves a slow process of adaptation, and it stimulates a sense of curiosity about a broad range of products, from the tomato (acidic) to the potato (insipid and floury). The learned men who promoted these vegetable-based innovations ultimately supported the nutritional experts whose diets seemed most agreeable to them. The translation of *La santé des gens de letters* by Dr. Tissot was published in seven editions between 1768 and 1791. In contrast to Scopoli, this doctor from Geneva, who cites Cornaro, severely curtails substances affecting the nervous system and prescribes three meals a day: a quick breakfast and a light lunch and dinner.

In the sixteenth century the appetite was first awakened by a fresh salad served with a large amount of salt and was then drawn to sugary fruit, followed by anchovies in oil and vinegar and mullet roe, also salted. Two centuries later the same stimulants no longer arouse the appetite. The issue is now reversed, according to Tissot,[27] since the pursuit of study absorbs the literary man to such a point that he loses all desire for food. Lack of appetite, listlessness, and distraction are typical symptoms of the type of organism for which work occupies the most important place, subordinating all other activities. The solution is a gastronomic one, matching the inclinations of the literary man, protecting him from those dishes that would have soporific or violent effects. Creamy dishes and oily fritters are discouraged, as well as all vinegar-based flavorings, so loved by gluttons. Smoked meats and dried legumes were also forbidden, and they are reserved for those who undertake demanding physical activity. What should the literary man eat instead? Fresh ingredients with a moderate flavor, served in season. Vegetables and fruits bring about a more gradual awakening of the senses and have a more delicate effect on the taste buds. In 1743 the "Mugellan" doctor Antonio Cocchi described this diet in an essay that provoked a great stir in the scientific community:[28] "But vegetable foods are not really distasteful to the senses. Rather, experience shows us that someone who abstains from wine and highly flavored foods for a long time acquires a finer and more delicate sense of taste, since the taste buds of the tongue and palate are not overwhelmed, nor is their action overstimulated by the excessive quantity of the small, flavor-bearing corpuscles that are abundantly contained in meats, aromatic herbs, and hard, oily foodstuffs."[29] The Tuscan dinner composed of vegetables and the nutritional habits of the Florentine masses, "who ate little meat because of poverty," are cited as examples of healthy nutrition.

The transmission of these models from medical practitioners in contact with the lower and middle classes to the culinary culture of the wealthy and aristocratic classes occurred thanks to Vincenzo Corrado, who in 1781 wrote a book on "Pythagorean food, or greens, principally for use by such noblemen and literary persons," in which he states: "Both because of the modesty of the expense involved and the simplicity of the food, composed only of greens, this could very well confer a longer life on literary men, who, in their dedication to a life of study and to the sciences, digest little and need more delicate foods."[30]

To explain such a recipe collection we must remember that members of the international medical community make reference to the same authors (a Genevan, such as Tissot, would cite Cornaro in order to praise him, just as Cocchi would cite him to argue against his views), and, more important, it applies the undisputed theories of Galen in such a way that they could be accepted everywhere. The social rank of those implied in this system, the nobleman and the scholar, is complicated in the Neapolitan context by environmental factors particularly favorable to a diet of vegetable products, thus facilitating a version of the diet that could even be used in formal dining. "Inexpensive" and "easily digested" are terms used to indicate a diet that stimulates the appetite of the senses with flavors that are sometimes delicate and sometimes intense. It is not difficult to find cultural motives to enhance a diet that is already beneficial from the economic and medical point of view. These motivations emphasize the myth of lightness and simplicity, the stimulating, aromatic, and nerve-enhancing properties of greens, and the image of nature spontaneously offering its entire productive cycle to the dinner table in the form of leaves, flowers, and fruits. "Pythagorean food" modifies the dietetic chart and the tenor of culinary judgments. The use of herbs and flowers opens the door of upper-class cuisine to the condiments favored by the masses. The chapters on the tomato as a "universal sauce" and on the eggplant "of which the Jews make much use" are the first indication of a particular discourse on vegetables that would continue to the time of Artusi and beyond.

The new diet, developed to cope with problems of weak appetite and dietary imbalance, presents an original nutritional program that, when properly integrated with fish and meat products, was also suitable for the wealthy classes. It was created for an audience that, by virtue of its intelligence, sensibility, and social prestige, could authoritatively criticize lavish culinary habits. This audience is the interpreter of a new culture of food that restores the balance between intelligence and sensuality in a subjective fashion, tempers consumption, and allows for the preparation of a sumptuous meal without the help of a stable of cooks. The French gastronomic experts of the early nineteenth century, men of letters for the most part, recognized themselves in Tissot's theories, which restored to them their role as leaders. In the light of a lucid, critical and selective enjoyment of food, they transcend and reformulate the bourgeois culinary code, eventually expanding its boundaries, along with their own waistlines.

The Bourgeois Belly

The distinction between appetite and hunger, between appetite and greediness, and the analysis of their diverse implications constitute the premise on which the birth of modern gastronomy is based. This is facilitated by the principle of freedom to which ritual must conform and by a subjective understanding of the meal. How much should be eaten is not only a question of good manners but also a problem of taste, which is in a certain sense personal and modifiable. In bourgeois cuisine, from the beginning of the nineteenth century onward, the gastronomic expert sits at the head of the table and dictates all rules. This character emerged in France under the Empire in the fateful year of 1801, when Joseph Berchoux published a poem with the title *La gastronomie*, a new word created from the ancient Greek words for "rule" and "stomach."[31] The number of gastronomic experts grew in every European capital as the urban way of life became widespread. The gourmet has a house of his own and a maid, though he often eats out when invited by others, and he frequents the best restaurants. Without ever having dined at court, he is the dinner guest who is most often invited and most attentively acknowledged by the good host. He does not belong to an unknown human species, for he is one of the well-to-do, but he displays a liberal culture. He lives to procure pleasure, though not haphazardly. In some instances a bachelor and in others a married man, a lover of women and cats—the divinities that preside over domestic life—he considers his situation emblematic; he holds forth after listening to his appetite, which should be ample but not out of line, and caresses his stomach with pride, since it is capacious and must be adequately filled. This elite cadre of pleasure seekers, whose prototypes were Grimod de la Reynière and Brillat-Savarin in France and the Milanese physician Giovanni Rajberti in Italy,[32] is encapsulated in the figure of a man who understands products and spices, who knows how to prepare and serve foods, and is able to assess the value of wines. He is often a bachelor by choice, like Pellegrino Artusi. He is in fact a selfish man (he thinks of his own intestinal pleasure) and a moralist (he preaches both physiological and economic restraint). He avoids the kinds of orgies that would ruin his health and dinners that would consume his inheritance. From the beginning of the nineteenth century onward, the myth of the feasts of imperial Rome begins to fade and lose its concreteness. What replaced it was the cult of intimate dining and a body displaying a pot belly and a waistcoat. A sense of laziness, the slight sensation of fatigue that signals the first stirring of the appetite, the immediate awakening of taste memory at the sight of the first dish served, and the torpor that radiates from the inner organs are feelings that are attributed to the man of excellent taste, the *buongustaio* (the nineteenth-century Italian equivalent of the very French *gastronome*).

In his *Arte di convitare spiegata al popolo* (The art of conviviality explained to ordinary people), published in 1850–1851, Giovanni Rajberti of Milan, on the basis of having read the French essayists and of his own experiences in life as a forty-five-year-old, offers a lecture on convivial well-being.[33] He is a doctor and an essayist and, as we shall see, a good household man. Proceeding in proper order, he consults the clock, listens to his appetite, and interprets what he learns from the perspective of the people, which in this case means the middle class. Receiving guests at home, being entertained in the homes of others, inviting guests out to dine, and being invited in return require judgment and tact and constitute an art. He provides the following example: At five o'clock it is time to sit down to eat. A little savory food, perhaps some raw salami, to pique the appetite? Nothing would be more counterproductive. This is rustic stuff, worthy of families who eat in the kitchen. "Lunch must always, always, begin with a soup," and then, as a good physician, he explains, "in order to prepare the stomach and lubricate the inner passages." He distinguishes two kinds of soup, one "noble, or the cook's," and the other "plebeian, or the maid's." The first is extremely light, and the second substantial. As well as mirroring the diner's desires, lunch is a model to which all social classes aspire, and for this reason he welcomes all worthy suggestions, from the lowest to the highest: "a plebeian soup placed at the beginning of an aristocratic meal would constitute a felicitous mixing of elements, the best fusion of opposite principles that modern incivility can ever obtain." This is the exact opposite of a vulgar celebration where, weary of eating "*riso in cagnone*,"[34] the diners throw themselves upon a plate of big, cooked sausages and stuff themselves to bursting point. It is true that the traditions of the lower classes are also appetizing to the rich. For Mantegazza, a polenta, which was a source of pellagra and meant death for the underclass, is an ineffable food, "steaming and golden, if scooped up and served with pale Milanese cream."[35] But Giovanni Rajberti, like Professor Mantegazza, pursues a comfortable style, and after the soup we find the obligatory trio of "fried, boiled, and roast meats," followed by dessert or ice cream. The bourgeois dinner table is destined to blend together all other styles of eating, ultimately refining or simplifying them, and to create a universal aspiration toward goodness.

Beyond the pleasure and social value assigned to food, there is a strong preoccupation with health, understood as a form of personal capital and as the aspiration toward lavish meals. The way in which the gastronomic expert views food is quite particular, whether he happens to be a doctor or not. Among the cookbooks published in Milan in Rajberti's time, the most sought after was Angelo Dubini's *La cucina degli stomachi deboli* (Cooking for delicate stomachs), which was reprinted at least twenty times between 1857 and 1899. The formula or rather the term "weak stomach" enjoyed great success, to the point of inducing Pellegrino Artusi, on the occasion of the fourteenth edition of his *Scienza in cucina*, to add an appendix with this title. What is a weak stomach? To interpret any menu in a literal way (*riso in cagnone*, smoked ham, potatoes with cream, *mascarpone*, English style)[36] would be a contradiction in terms, an ironic figure of speech suggesting the stomach of an ostrich. In reality a weak stomach is one that very much needs to eat but is afflicted by a "slow and continuous irritation" of the intestines, which have been submitted to incessant traffic, worn out by slow gastritis and similar afflictions, by weaknesses and idiosyncrasies. Among the urban middle class, already familiar with overeating and with poorly functioning intestines and which cultivates the refinement of tradition and attempts an Italian version of French dining practices, the narcissism of the gourmet (the *buongustaio*) has two faces, one smiling and the other preoccupied. His constant dialogue between head and stomach enables him to remember dietary rules that go back to the Salerno school ("Si tibi deficient medici, medici tibi fiant haec tria: mens laeta, requies, moderata diaeta")[37] and French proverbs ("Apaise la faim, ne jamais l'irriter"),[38] along with prognoses taken from the best and most up-to-date medical science. His humanistic culture makes him his own doctor. Thus, just as the dinner table knows no borders between one part of Italy and another or between Italy and France, health is an absolute value, immune to seasonal changes and differences in social circumstances, a value that legitimates eating well. The person who has a weak stomach, the convalescent, and even the hearty eater all care about their health, fork in hand, without falling into a vicious cycle that swings from the desire to eat to a distaste for food.

Attention to the body and to energy-giving food tends to limit the *buongustaio* to the walls of his own home. In his home progress means modest quarters, corresponding to the architecture of the urban building, floor, or apartment. For the middle class only country residences still mirrored the aristocratic concept of life. In the city, restrictions were imposed by costs and convenience. In these homes the kitchen was even bigger than the bathrooms, constituting the center of all heat sources, provisions, and serving staff. The owner's nose was guided by its fumes and odors. The restaurant or the trattoria were for emergencies, for days of travel or solitude. The café and the club were places suited to occasional masculine conviviality, while the kitchen and the dining room offered a safe refuge on ordinary days and holidays alike. Even in the absence of a wife or housekeeper the presence of a cook, male or female, was considered indispensable. The attributes of the cook went well beyond simple nutrition. According to Mantegazza, the cook "is more useful than the doctor." He (or she) must understand the health qualities of foods, must be honest and clean, apart from being able to prepare delicious meals. "If you have found a treasure of this sort, hold on to him (or her) dearly."[39] This warning is already part of the art of good family management and would be well heeded.

What were the effects of this domestic culture on gastronomy? To cite only a few: the ever more intimate link between masculine taste and the type of food prepared by women; the central role of bourgeois family cooking, adopted even at court and imitated by institutions out of necessity; the abandonment of elaborate, ostentatious preparations, in favor of courses whose abundance is their principal appeal. Since he has a comfortable home and can invite his own hosts in turn to dine with him, the *buongustaio* chooses his living quarters as the setting for his greatest indulgences. Because of a lack of resources he manages without a French chef, who would cost him ten francs a day, making do with a house-maid who earns ten francs a month. Since he has a small staff, he has to tolerate delays during the meal and must reduce the number of courses. He ignores complicated recipes, often of French origin, but, since the dinner table is only a few feet away from the kitchen, the dishes he offers, whether Neapolitan or Milanese, are served piping hot and cooked to exactly the right point. From time to time he allows himself to be lured into attending a "formal meal with printed invitations," wearing a stiff collar and starched tie for the occasion, but he then gladly returns to his own table, where he sits down to eat in his shirtsleeves (with the ladies' permission).[40] The fathers of Italian cooking in the newly united Italy emerged from this bourgeois family revolution. It should be evident that these were not the forefathers of the single-course meal or pioneers of do-it-yourself cooking, since they had demanding palates and prosperous bellies.

In the Kingdom of Italy, aristocratic cuisine did not abandon ceremonial dining, though it became Italianized after 1910. But all indicators (menus, society pages, cooks' manuals) show that the shift from the system of multifaceted courses to the system of serving single dishes one at a time, which was initiated in France in the second half of the nineteenth century and rapidly adopted at all royal tables and hotel restaurants, put an end to monumental gelatin compositions and decorative pastries. Elegance of style was now represented more by the custom of serving a champagne punch halfway through the meal and by a careful combination of wines than by the ostentation of presenting several dishes simultaneously. In Italy during this period the wine cellar remained a more aristocratic than bourgeois value. Yet the dishes served during a private lunch given by the Italian royal family for Kaiser Wilhelm II in 1908 are no more than six in number:

Risotto with sauce
Milanese asparagus
Loin of veal, *primavera* style
Capon with gelatin: Venetian salad
German pastry with *zabaglione*
Breadsticks with cheese
Wines: Castel Calattubo—Castel Perina—Grand Spumante Cinzano[41]

A court menu with the same number of dishes as a bourgeois holiday meal gives a measure of the relationship that was being established between appetite and ceremonial practice, the latter no longer constituting a purely theatrical function but corresponding to actual consumption.

LEFT: *The Glutton* (engraving by Giuseppe Maria Mitelli).

Source: *Le ventiquattr'hore dell'humana felicità* (Bologna, 1675).

BELOW: *They Expect a Lot, Those Middle-class People;
They Want to Eat Too!* (drawing by Bartoli).

Source: *Numero*, 1915.

With regard to quantity, culinary literature usually provides the major points of reference, omitting fasts and broths, half portions, and the serving of dishes left over from the day before. If a meal is skipped or if some snacking occurs, this does not seem worthy of going on record. Hero of the modern dinner table, the glutton does not escape epic celebration: Artusi cites men from his native Romagna who boast of having eaten a hundred *cappelletti* at one time.[42] But such a hero is condemned not only to a heart attack and social shame but also by new standards of taste. Quality is not measured by body weight. A line of thought implying an increasing value placed on tallness and slimness links Rajberti and Artusi, the fathers of elegant cooking that can be practiced in urban settings, to Guerrini, a cyclist and gourmet, Monelli, a traveler and journalist, and even to contemporary arbiters of taste. In modern times indigestion becomes a more and more dated symptom, outstripped by variety and choice, by the quest for balance among the good, the rare, and the economical. Within these parameters of judgment the gourmet cannot hope to make do with the fruits of his own land, not even with foods found at the local market. He must study the stores, the schedule of deliveries, and the seasons; he must use the postal system with care, select the most promising holiday destinations, and put the railroad at the service of his palate.

The quest for products and places of high quality begins at the moment in which the cuisine of the immediate locality gives way to a national-regional cuisine. It is stimulated by various phenomena: the variability of products, including the best and the worst; the fragility of local traditions eroded by emigration; the awareness, or the fear, of a decline in taste; and the lowering of standards caused by the mixing of styles and ingredients or by the uncontrollable flow of tourism. In order to satisfy the appetite appropriately it is necessary not to have to live on a fixed income, and so the gourmet goes into action again. He gives up sitting at home, and in order to fulfill his needs he goes looking for exciting curiosities. He must now chase after food and have an agile body. Since he believes in progress he travels by train and by automobile, searching for those serene locations, those ancient dinner tables, that the train and the car were about to destroy forever. This vicious cycle is the outcome of progress. It was anticipated by Mantegazza with a far-seeing metaphor in his criticism of the growing craze for the stimulants contained in coffee, tea, and alcohol: "Food is the steam that propels the locomotive; the nerve stimulant is the regulating device that controls its movement."[43]

Down with Pasta!

A generation gap separates the huge men of Romagna—those who began their lunch with portions of a hundred *cappelletti*—from Pellegrino Artusi. Or perhaps it is a gap of a different sort, a psychological and cultural shift. In the years that followed Artusi's death the rift grew deeper. The belly was regarded less and

less as the organ of taste, sending out signals of satisfaction and voluptuous gur-
gling and showing signs of material well-being through a bulging waistcoat. Its
rule came to an end because of the Great War and its courageous supporters,
because of changing times, because of the futurists, or perhaps for none of these
reasons. The demise of the belly may simply have been due to the consolidation
of bourgeois well-being in a society where fat is superfluous. As the stomach
shrinks, excessively organic symptoms of satisfaction provoke increasing embarrassment. When Artusi writes about a dreadful minestrone consumed in
Livorno in 1855 that caused him "a terrifying bodily turmoil," he betrays a way
of thinking that already belongs to the past, his own past, when excess of input
as well as output could become the subject of amusement at the dinner table,
even if the diners were consuming a bowl of more carefully prepared minestrone. This past, characterized by mountains of *cappelletti* and diabolical
attacks of diarrhea, became increasingly undesirable and was deemed to be a
vulgar fantasy.

Recounting a culinary journey undertaken in the first decade of the Fascist
era, the journalist Paolo Monelli describes the popular and regional cuisine of
Italy from one trattoria to the next. Well-known characters show up in succession: a fat man in Carpi (who ate a thousand tortellini); Troja, the Florentine
innkeeper, silent, irritable, and immense; and the Roman matrons with "bottoms wide enough to block the alleyways." A portly Italy, which contends with
a poor, short, skinny, sober, and southern one. All these actors play ancient roles.
Their bodies are different from those of the Milanese writers. Vaguely redolent
of a fairytale, they recall the wildest dreams of plenty entertained by a population smitten by famine. The gourmets keep themselves light, they travel and
taste different foods, they move from one region to another. When they escape
the danger of having to eat a *panarda* of thirty courses in the Abruzzo region,
they smile with relief.[44]

During the Fascist regime, as a result either of military propaganda or of
political and aesthetic idealism that identified the pot-bellied bourgeois as a par-
asite, dietary values changed. Marinetti's campaign against pasta, launched in
La cucina futurista (Futurist cooking), which he published in 1932, is inspired
by a prophetic intuition and implemented in the name of speed and poetry.
"Macaroni, ugh!"[45] This was the formula that summed up his rejection of heavy
dishes and stuffed bellies and his characterization of the Italian as a "solid,
leaden block of blind and opaque density." He condemns pasta but absolves
rice—the National Organization for Rice is in the front line of the autarchic
revolution—and formulates a very nimble diet. The names of his dishes recall
other symbols of speed: the bomb, the airplane, the automobile, and skis. Their
forms range from the banal shape of the female breast ("strawberry breast," "Italian breasts in the sun") to the Roman fasces, symbol of the Fascist regime
(sheaves of celery arranged on a hemisphere of rice) and also include fuselages

("fuselage of veal"). It was the ingredients and their combinations—raw salami, boiling-hot coffee, and eau de cologne for *"porcoeccitato"* (excited pig), for example—rather than the quantities that unleashed cries of disgust and blistering broadsides. Without these reactions *La cucina futurista* would have made no sense, as the attacks launched by Marinetti's band were aimed at the entire panorama of indolent, provincial, self-satisfied gastronomy. The contradictions in the food policy decreed by Fascism, the battle of wheat and autarchy, dietary planning and the promotion of country inns, are reflected in the culinary field and in the different positions espoused by intellectuals, some of them modernists and futurists, others, like Monelli, softened and seduced intellectually by the plump dreams of hungry, provincial Italians.

The fact that many things were changing can be seen in the increasingly sharp criticisms launched against the sacrosanct sequence of the Italian meal: antipasto, pasta, and main course. Rajberti already noticed this. The start of the meal is taken seriously, because it serves to stimulate the palate and prepare for a lengthy assault. To pique the appetite with a soup is to honor the stomach. In the Fascist years there was much criticism of the antipasto, bread eaten with pickles, and marinated foods. Criticisms come from futurists, who had their own ideas, from gourmets, and even from housewives. The same fate befell stimulating beverages: rich wines to enliven the appetite, chilled punch served halfway through the meal to stimulate the flagging stomach. The sequence of three meat dishes ("fried, boiled, and roasted") now gives way to the simple selection of one or another. Still, piping hot coffee retains its place and is said to contain properties favorable to the stomach. The entire system of alternating hot and cold, liquids and solids, tonics and stimulants, which regulated the syntax of the banquet according to the model of the bodily regime, now seems obsolete. To nourish oneself quickly, with avant-garde foods—as the futurists desired—means to attend to the brain rather than the intestines and hence to demote the rituals of digestion. And the appetite? It remains a curiosity, to be satisfied with a *passo di corsa* (racing speed), a dish made of rice, rum, and red pepper.[46]

The main consequence of the repression of the body and the appetite and of their perceptible manifestations in the course of a sumptuous meal is a certain relaxation of the rules. The rhythm of the courses served is abbreviated, and the interval between breakfast and lunch loses the unaltered character that it maintained in the nineteenth-century diet. The cookbooks clearly do not preach anarchy, but they are silent about its consequences. Snacks, picnics, improvisations, quickly prepared dishes, cocktails, slices of buttered bread, and sandwiches have already become part of the domestic rhythm of a patrician household during the years of Fascism. By the middle to late 1950s they were passed on to the entire urban middle class. At dinner no one mentioned health and medicine. Clearly the weak stomach did not disappear after World War II but

rather, because of the effects of protracted malnutrition and the new impact of
the prosperous free market, food and the body embarked on a different kind of
relationship with each other. Was it perhaps a consequence of rationing that
desire continued to be separated from the capacity of the stomach? Or was it the
new sense of well-being that made the memory of deprivation unacceptable?
For five to seven years Italians had been obliged to fill their stomachs furtively,
quickly, and whenever possible. When this emergency began to abate it was difficult to reconcile physiological balance and ritual order. The Italian middle-
class citizen of the 1950s is disoriented. The big plate of pasta denigrated by
Marinetti now seems tempting to him, although he would prefer something
more refined than ordinary *pastasciutta*, something like tortellini, perhaps. He
is no longer willing, however, to go back to the sequence of meats served "fried,
boiled, and roasted," and he no longer thinks it necessary to consume huge portions. Avoiding both extremes—gastric frailty and the exaggerated display of
hunger—he relegates the large meal and the kinds of behavior typical of excess
(such as second helpings) to major holidays. He also revises the proportions he
consumes every day through a process of subtraction, balancing the relationship
between lunch and dinner and between workdays and holidays. And yet on special occasions his nostalgia for the abundant meal of old resurfaces.

Perhaps women experienced a greater change than husbands, sons, or bach-
elors, since female nourishment was rarely the subject of systematic observation
in recipe books until the twentieth century. Only pregnant women, new mothers, and those who were breastfeeding merited attention and received advice.[47]
From the 1950s onward the housewife also suffered from a type of nervousness
that was different from that experienced by her father and grandfathers, for her
dilemma was not whether to eat more or less, to eat quickly or slowly, or to put
off the tastiest dishes for special occasions. Rather she is now obsessed with gaining greater freedom inside and outside the home, and above all she thinks of her
own appearance in terms of communication and social relationships. The "thin,
streamlined, figure" suggested by the magazine *Quattrova illustrato* in 1931
becomes a model that is gradually adopted by all classes, and it is the woman of
the house who now refuses the dish of pastasciutta (as Marinetti had done earlier).[48] She begins to think of herself when she cooks for the family, when she
receives guests, and when she finds herself in her own company. The menu and
the preparation and presentation of the meal, previously shared with servants, are
simplified when only one servant is available, and they lose their solemnity as
they are transformed from acts of duty into occasions for demonstrating affection.

The woman discovers herself as a consumer with an absolutely original profile. In *Il cucchiaio d'argento* (The silver spoon), the first important cookbook
of the postwar years, this is translated into more than a thousand recipes and a
final chapter titled "Dietetica della bellezza" (Eating for beauty).[49] After skimming through four hundred pages of recipes for different constitutions, for

patients suffering from diabetes, hepatitis, and arthritis, one turns the page and finds the kind of food suitable for what is really important: the aesthetic result. Nutritional principles are provided for various parts of the body (skin, complexion, hair, teeth, eyes, and figure). Reddish eyelids can be remedied with lettuce, oily skin is treated with vegetable juices and salads made of carrots and oranges. On the subject of the "ideal figure," we notice a gap: the word "appetite" appears only once. The reason is clearly indicated: "one must eat first what is necessary and then what is appealing."[50] By removing the role of the eyes and mouth, nostrils and tongue, and, along the way, all stages of the intestinal process, the body is deprived of the very sources of nutritional conflict, that is, the dilemma between what is good and what is indigestible. Only one form of discipline is found efficient: the repression of instinct. The result: to obtain the ideal figure one must realize that "the midday meal should consist exclusively of salad."

An ethics of self-deprivation, based on sacrifice, can only be rationalized by invoking ideals that are acceptable as models of health and success. These ideals, with which we are thoroughly familiar since they have been replicated ad nauseam in the dietary and culinary teachings of our own day, were promoted in 1950 with the inauguration of a "Beauty Day," dedicated to the body. Sleep, relaxation, and walking are freely allowed, but solid foods are completely eliminated:

Noon: Vegetable broth.

2:00 P.M.: A cup of light herbal tea (mint or verbena) with a few drops of lemon or honey.

6:00 P.M.: Broth, as desired.

8:00 P.M. (or at any hour of the evening, if hungry): Another vegetable or fruit juice, herbal tea, and vegetable broth.

The authors of *Il cucchiaio d'argento* attribute to this ascetic, liquid regimen the power to transform both body and soul. "This is how film stars manage to look fresh." During the most dynamic years of Cinecittà, described by many as the years of the *maggiorate* (shapely actresses), the tabloids were filled with beauties who seemed simultaneously fat and thin, with protruding breasts and tiny wasp waists, disproportionate because they were created in accordance with both hypertrophic and dystrophic standards—the very same standards as those intrinsic to the diet.

Far from gaining ground, the autonomy of medical and aesthetic recipe collections faded, thanks to the pangs of appetite. The disappearance of the belly's dominance yielded to the limiting of foods, evoking above and beyond food a false identity, constructed with suggestive scientific allusions: "The renowned beautician to top film actresses, Dr. Benjamin Gaylord Hauser, taught the stars to eliminate salt in cooking."[51] The name of the doctor has a magical ring, as though he too were a star, and it confers value on his dietary teachings. Salt produces thirst, an effect synonymous with hunger, and is therefore damaging. All the premises of subliminal communication are present here. Thanks to this and other similar messages accumulated in cookbooks, the rift between past and present is complete, and the hegemony of the slimming diet begins, initiating a predictable vicious cycle.

The Repression of the Body and the Virtual Dish

After the fall of Fascism and its dietary regime planned along political and economic lines, the end of World War II, and the gradual repression of hunger, poverty, and lean times, an age-old balance was broken for the middle classes that had once celebrated the abundance of the appetite. The body, pleasure, taste, and gradually the various forms of conviviality no longer availed themselves of a discourse in which they found coherence and harmony. Though these concepts are the theoretical basis of any cookbook, no recipe book addresses them directly. Their place has been usurped by a sense of opulence evoked by photographs, by the measurements of the ideal figure, film stars and their doctors. What is most astounding in the shift from autarchy during the years of Fascism to the rationing system in the postwar period and from this to 1950, the year in which the first signs of an economic upturn become perceptible, is the speed of transformation: in just twelve years the management of the body shifted from sanctions to rationing cards, from recourse to the black market to the art of making do, from a period of recovery among the ruins of bourgeois decorum and the arrival of the American diet to the consumer boom. The pattern of hunger, appetite, and satiety characterizing this period meets a cultural evolution that by virtue of its speed marks a rupture with the past. Added to this is the collapse of an Italian regime supplemented by vegetable gardens and orchards on the outskirts of the cities, by American aid, by food products deprived of coherence. After years of hunger, what returned was not only the appetite but the need to forget and the desire to gather various people around the dinner table and nourish them in a new way. The system on which the dietary rules of the future were constructed could be summarized in these terms.

The pot belly and the double chin, badge of honor of the early gourmets, now seemed not only implausible but ridiculous. Greasy lips, dilated nostrils, and the brandishing of a bone or chicken leg became as inappropriate as Artusi's comments on his intestinal problems. Worse yet, the lively new body turned its back on its own history, opposing the dietary and gastronomic models that had once weighed it down. Diets for losing and gaining weight listed in *Il carnacina*, edited by Luigi Veronelli in 1961, are followed by a "dissociated diet."[52] Its nutritional principles are subdivided into three groups: (a) carbohydrates (pasta); (b) proteins (fish, meat, eggs); and (c) vegetables and fats. "The dissociated diet condemns beyond question the typical Italian meal (pasta plus meat) but allows an infinite range of combinations. In practice, one may combine A with B and B with C, while one should drastically reduce A and B."[53]

Along with the dissociated diet, several surprising prescriptions begin to appear. Some reflect American dietary norms, others revise and update the treatises on hygiene from the nineteenth century: "Invert the order of foods, beginning the meal with fruit"; "Chew thoroughly. To assimilate food means to gain weight." It goes without saying that the originality of this prescription lies in the fact that one idea contradicts the other: "Avoid fasting once a week!" is the imperative of *Il carnacina*, in opposition to the advice that *Il cucchiaio d'argento* offers to young brides. It is especially difficult to reconcile such premises with the fact that Luigi Carnacina, a master cook from the school of Escoffier, represents the continuity between French and Italian gastronomy and reintroduces an elegantly balanced cuisine for the restaurant business that can be replicated in the home. This dissociation ultimately reflects the clash between the culinary and the medical models. It is as though the cook gestures emptily toward the advice of the dietician, without understanding exactly how to integrate it into his own art. If the role of the literary man in the sixteenth-century court consisted in ennobling and giving persuasive power to the quest for health and sensual pleasure, the role of the publishing industry ultimately created confusion in its readers. The diet industry, together with direct and indirect advertising of products purported to be "slimming" and the generic or inappropriate use of culinary models, diminished the ability of consumers to manage the appetite and the body.

These consumers do not know where to turn: they dutifully count calories, proteins, and vitamins, eat apples one week, give up butter the next. Then they get bored with this diet and miss the splendid balance of the good old days, when eating a great deal also meant enjoying good health. Recipe books are of little help. The same is true of gastronomic literature and press campaigns. These merely generate new myths, such as the Mediterranean diet, simultaneously revealing new contradictions that were unknown in earlier diets, given the preponderance of carbohydrates and particularly of pasta. Faced with the impossibility of making the right choice, one must adopt an attitude of tolerance, according to which all nutritional behaviors have some reasonable legitimacy. In cookbooks this becomes possible only by resorting to a subterfuge: that is, by accepting different systems of consumption and sacrificing the appetite, which is the unifying principle of health, pleasure, and taste. No recipe collection mentions the appetite now.

In a jungle of medical advice, harmful or merely functional food products, clinics and gyms, pills and shakes, one may continue to eat only with one's eyes.

ABOVE: Peasants from the Agro Romano seated at table, 1900
(photograph by Francesco Chigo).

BELOW: Lunch on the terrace, Rimini, ca. 1925.

Source: Photo Archive of the Biblioteca Gambalunghiana.

This is apparently the only form of consumption that is without negative side effects. We cannot tell what Pellegrino Artusi's dishes looked like unless we prepare them ourselves. Yet all the books published in the postwar period focus on the opposite, on the image of the virtual dish, ultimately destined for domestic preparation. It seems a cliché to repeat that refined cooking and nouvelle cuisine, free recipes and promotional recipes, have been endorsing the visual consumption of food since the 1960s and that this is often incompatible with any other kind of consumption. We nonetheless believe that this trend probably does not spring from simple marketing logic or from the new language of gastronomic communication but has its origin, as we have shown, in the repression of the body and its desires, in the denial of a unique principle, the appetite, which is capable of reconciling balance and pleasure, nutritional science and cuisine.

NOTES

[*Unless otherwise noted, all translations are mine—Trans.*]

INTRODUCTION: IDENTITY AS EXCHANGE

1. Romano, *Paese Italia. Venti secoli di identità.*
2. For some useful observations on the subject, see Schiavone, *Italiani senza Italia.*
3. *Cronica romana*, cited in Montanari, *Convivio*, p. 396.
4. Montanari, *La fame e l'abbondanza*, p. 85.
5. Rebora, "La cucina medievale," p. 1518.
6. Queyrat, *Los buenos quesos argentinos*, p. 31.
7. Prezzolini, *Maccheroni & C.*, p. 15.

1. ITALY: A PHYSICAL AND MENTAL SPACE

1. See André's analysis in *L'alimentation et la cuisine à Rome.*
2. Lopez, *La nascita dell'Europa*, p. 12.
3. Schiavone, *Italiani senza Italia*, pp. 61–62.
4. Montanari, *La fame e l'abbondanza*, p. 12 ff.
5. As Pirenne nonetheless maintained; see *Mahomet et Charlemagne*. See also Montanari, "Maometto, Carlo Magno e lo storico dell'alimentazione."
6. Montanari, *Convivi e banchetti*, p. 333.
7. Paolo Diacono, *Storia dei Longobardi*, 2:5.
8. Le Goff, *L'Italia fuori d'Italia*, p. 1939.
9. See Messedaglia, "Leggendo la cronica di frate Salimbene da Parma," p. 406.
10. *Liber de coquina*, chap. 1, sects. 5, 19–20, 35; chap. 2, sect. 62; chap. 3, sect. 3; chap. 5, sects. 4, 8.
11. Ibid., chap. 5, sect. 9 (see p. 183 for a likely meaning of the term). See Zambrini, *Il libro della cucina del sec. XIV*, p. 25: "According to the Lombards, carobs may be added."
12. Zambrini, *Il libro della cucina del sec. XIV*, p. 56.
13. Frati, *Libro di cucina del secolo XIV*, pp. 66–67.
14. Rebora, "La cucina medievale," pp. 1493–96.
15. Flandrin, "Internationalisme," pp. 80–81.
16. Mulon, *Deux traités inédits.*
17. Laurioux expresses some doubts on the issue. See *Le règne de Taillevent*, p. 210.
18. *Liber de coquina*, p. 21 ff.
19. Reprinted in Zambrini, *Il libro della cucina del sec. XIV.*
20. Laurioux, *Le règne de Taillevent*, pp. 210–12.
21. Reprinted in Morpurgo, *LVII ricette.*
22. For example: "Prepare the soup, add spices, *and serve to the noble lord with peacock or other fowl*" (Zambrini, *Il libro della cucina del sec XIV*, p. 56; emphasis added).
23. Rebora, "La cucina medievale," pp. 1470–71; Redon, "La diffusione in Italia di una tradizione culinaria senese."
24. Montanari, *La fame e l'abbondanza*, pp. 82–83.

304

1. ITALY: A PHYSICAL AND MENTAL SPACE

25. Laurioux, *Le règne de Taillevent*, pp. 211–12.
26. Frati, *Libro di cucina del secolo XIV* (Venetian cookbook); Guerrini, *Frammento* (Bolognese cookbook); Rebora, "La cucina medievale," pp. 1528–60 (Ligurian-Provençal cookbook); anonymous southern writer, *Due libri di cucina*.
27. Laurioux, *Le règne de Taillevent*, p. 189 ff.
28. Benporat, *La cucina italiana*, pp. 42–43.
29. Laurioux, *Le règne de Taillevent*, pp. 213–15.
30. See Faccioli, *L'arte della cucina*; and Benporat, *La cucina italiana*.
31. Benporat takes the first position (*La cucina italiana*, p. 72); Laurioux the second (*Le règne de Taillevent*, p. 215).
32. Benporat, *La cucina italiana*, p. 34.
33. Platina writes: "What other cook could compare to my Martino, from whom I learned most of the things I have written about?" (*Il piacere onesto e la buona salute*, p. 141). See "The Humanists, Antiquity and 'Modernity' " in chapter 3 of this volume.
34. Platina, *Il piacere onesto e la buona salute*, p. 154.
35. See M. Alberini, "Bartolomeo Scappi: Maestro di tutti i cuochi," *L'Accademia italiana della cucina* 83 (1998): 9.
36. Scappi, *Opera*, chap. 350.
37. Apart from those mentioned above, many notations alluding to origin are applied to fish. Sea fish include turbot from the bay of Ravenna (widely praised since antiquity), plaice from Chioggia, red mullet from the beaches near Rome, crabs from the shores of Ancona and Senigallia, mussels from Rome and Genoa, scallops from the beaches and harbors of Genoa, razor clams from Civitavecchia and Chioggia, sweet clams from Genoa, and sea snails from Ancona. River fish include sturgeon from the Po ("many are caught in the Stellata near Ferrara, where the river Po divides into two separate streams") and the Tiber, rudd and lamprey from the Po, the Tiber ("best of all"), the Arno, and the Oglio; and little eels from the Tiber. Fish from the valleys include gray or common mullet from Comacchio and from Tuscany, as well as from the ponds of Ostia and Civitavecchia (where scorpion fish were also found). With regard to lake fish, there is a mention of silversides from Bolsena, perch from the lakes of Lombardy (particularly Lake Maggiore), and tench and eels from Marta (Bolsena). No mention is made of the frogs from the area around Bologna.
38. Meats from livestock include Milanese beef (or "Lombard ox"), veal from Trento ("from calves that weigh no more than eighty pounds") and "*Romanesca*" veal (from animals that are "considerably heavier"). As for poultry, there are "Roman hens" and squab from Terni. Game birds include "little birds" (i.e., fig eaters and ortolans) from Romagna and the Marches, francolins from Sicily, swans from the Po, and wild storks, "many of which I have seen between the Comacchio valley and the Po" (with regard to domestic storks, those raised "in Milan and other locations in Lombardy" are considered preferable).
39. Ferrarese "*mortatelle*," "*salsiccioni bolognesi*," "*salsiccia lucchese e modenese*" (sausage from Lucca and Modena), and Milanese "*seccaticcia*"and "*cervellate*."
40. In addition to Parmesan (grated or finely sliced), Riviera cheese, and the varieties of Raviggioli and Marzolini from Tuscany already mentioned, Romagnolo (produced in "limoncelli" shapes) and Romanesco cheese are also recommended. Among fresh cheeses, mozzarellas from the Roman area appear, along with Neapolitan *cacciocavallo* cheeses and "*provature*" from the south.
41. Among the the vegetables that were commercially transported from great distances, most references are to cabbages from Bologna or Milan, marinated German cabbage sold in the markets of Treviso and Venice, dried pumpkins from Savona and Genoa, and salted mushrooms from Genoa.
42. Roman cherries and Florentine pears are the fruits most often cited, along with olives, for which many areas of origin are recorded: Genoa, Tortona, Bologna, "Tuscany," Tivoli, Monterotondo, Naples, and Sicily.
43. Roman and Pisan biscotti (always served with sweet Malvasia wine), little marzipan cakes and pine-nut sweets from the Roman area, "*berlingozzi*" from Siena, Neapolitan "*palmette*," and Milanese, Roman, and—"best of all"—Neapolitan "*mostaccioli*."
44. Rice should come from Salerno or Milan, the semola flour "from the Kingdom" (of Naples).
45. Rossetti, *Dello scalco*, pp. 508, 509.

46. Montanari, *Nuovo convivio*, pp. 14–18.

47. Stefani, *L'arte di ben cucinare*, pp. 142–43.

48. *Il cuoco piemontese perfezionato a Parigi*, pp. 77, 210, 221.

49. *La cuciniera piemontese*, pp. 90, 108, 67, 61.

50. *Eminenza, il pranzo è servito*, pp. 125 (cappelletti), 145 (balsamella), 183 (cotechino).

51. *Libro contenente la maniera di cucinare*, pp. 52 (cappelletti, spongata), 58 (mestocchine), 60 (coteghini).

52. Corrado, *Il cuoco galante*, p. 87.

53. Leonardi, *L'Apicio moderno*, 2:226–34.

54. Odescalchi, *Il cuoco senza pretese*, pp. 93 (maccheroni), 125 (vitello tonné).

55. *Il cuciniere italiano moderno*; Brizzi, *La cuciniera moderna*; *Il cuciniere italiano*; Santi Puppo, *Il cuciniere moderno*.

56. Artusi, *Autobiografia*.

57. Collodi, *Il viaggio per l'Italia di Giannettino*, p. 25.

58. Agnetti, *La cucina nazionale*; idem, *La nuova cucina delle specialità regionali*.

59. Roggiero, Ricchieri, and Ghisleri, *Testo-Atlante*, p. 66.

60. "L'Italia gastronomica."

61. A.B.C. *Cirio* (a coloring book for children).

62. Notari, *Il giro d'Italia*.

63. Monelli, *Il ghiottone errante*.

64. Piovene, *Viaggio in Italia*, p. 338.

65. Giorgio Bini, introduction to Keys and Keys, *Mangiar bene e stare bene*, vi.

2. THE ITALIAN WAY OF EATING

1. Montanari, *Alimentazione e cultura nel Medioevo*, pp. 47 ff; idem, *La fame e l'abbondanza*, pp. 19–23.

2. Zambrini, *Il libro della cucina del sec. XIV*, p. 10.

3. Montanari, *L'alimentazione contadina nell'alto Medioevo*, p. 467.

4. Montanari, *Convivio*, pp. 494–96.

5. Messedaglia, *Vita e costume*, 1:224.

6. Frati, *Libro di cucina del secolo XIV*, p. 2.

7. *Liber de coquina*, chap. 1, sect. 6, p. 110.

8. Zambrini, *Il libro della cucina del sec. XIV*, p. 13.

9. Ibid., p. 90.

10. Frati, *Libro di cucina del secolo XIV*, p. 55 (recipe 105).

11. Zambrini, *Il libro della cucina del sec. XIV*, p. 67.

12. Laurioux, *Le règne de Taillevent*, p. 261.

13. Rebora, *La cucina medievale*, pp. 1. 504–506.

14. Zambrini, *Il libro della cucina del sec. XIV*, p. 4.

15. Platina, *Il piacere onesto e la buona salute*, pp. 87–88.

16. Felici, *Scritti naturalistici*, p. 24.

17. Basile, *Lo cunto de li cunti*, first day , seventh entertainment, p. 144.

18. Castelvetro, *Brieve racconto*, p. 37. See Montanari, *La fame e l'abbondanza*, pp. 140–41.

19. Castelvetro, *Brieve racconto*, pp. 19–21. The reader is instructed to plunge the greens into a basin of water and to rinse them well.

Do not drain the basin (as the sand will have settled at the bottom), but remove the herbs from the water by hand. Repeat at least three or four times. Shake the water off the greens and dry them, then place them "in a dish with a little salt. Sprinkle more salt on top, and add a generous amount of oil. Then toss the greens thoroughly with very clean fingers or with a knife or fork, which is the more decorous method. They must be mixed in this way so that every leaf can absorb some oil, and it is unlike the procedure followed by Germans and other foreigners. As soon as they have washed the leaves, these people pile them into a bowl and throw a small quantity of salt and oil on top, but they also add a great deal of vinegar, without mixing [the ingredients] together [as their main concern is to produce an attractive-looking dish], while we Italic people are more concerned with pleasing Madame Mouth.

And one should avoid pouring vinegar on the leaves before the oil is added, as many "foreigners" do, because "greens that are already soaked with vinegar cannot absorb oil," and if the leaves are not mixed together, "most of them end up as as nothing more than unadorned greens, suitable for duck feed."

20. Montanari, *Nuovo convivio*, p. 21.
21. Messedaglia, *Vita e costume*, 1:236.
22. Bonvesin da la Riva, *De magnalibus Mediolani*, p. 84.
23. Gibault, *Histoire des légumes*, pp. 16–20 (see Messedaglia, *Vita e costume*, 1:233).
24. Mattioli, *I discorsi*, 3:14.
25. Felici, *Scritti naturalistici*, p. 90.
26. Benporat, *Storia della gastronomia*, p. 65.
27. Ibid., p. 136 (added by Fusoritto to the second edition of *Il trinciante*, by Vincenzo Cervio [1593]).
28. Montaigne, *Travel Journal*, pp. 968–969.
29. Zacchia, *Il vitto quaresimale*, chap. 5, cited in Montanari, *Nuovo convivio*, pp. 206–7.
30. Messedaglia, "Per la storia delle nostre piante alimentari: La melanzana."
31. Mattioli, *I discorsi*, chap. 78.
32. Felici, *Scritti naturalistici*, p. 89.
33. Frugoli, *Practica e scalcaria*, p. 245.
34. Tanara, *L'economia del cittadino in villa* (1644), p. 244.
35. Artusi, *La scienza in cucina* (1891), p. 178.
36. Tanara, *L'economia del cittadino in villa* (1644), pp. 238–39. See Messedaglia, *Vita e costume*, 1:256–57.
37. See Benporat, *Storia della gastronomia*, p. 126.
38. Montanari, *L'alimentazione contadina nell'alto Medioevo*, p. 159.
39. Mattioli, *Commentarii in libros sex pedacii Dioscoridis*, p. 479; de Acosta, *Historia naturale e morale delle Indie*, p. 219.
40. Felici, *Scritti naturalistici*, pp. 89–90.
41. Latini, *Lo scalco alla moderna*, 1:444; 2:55, 162.
42. Benporat, *Storia della gastronomia*, p. 169.
43. See "The New Innkeeper" in chapter 7 of this volume.
44. Camporesi, *Alimentazione folclore società*, p. 76.
45. Benporat, *Storia della gastronomia*, p. 170.
46. Montanari, *La fame e l'abbondanza*, p. 173.
47. Montanari, *Nuovo convivio*, p. 344.
48. See "Polenta, Soup, and Dumplings" in this chapter.
49. Benporat, *Storia della gastronomia*, p. 295.
50. For all this, see Montanari, *L'alimentazione contadina nell'alto Medioevo*, pp.109 ff.
51. Ibid., p. 158.
52. p. 299.
53. Messedaglia, *Vita e costume*, 1:132, 157.
54. Ibid., p. 131
55. Gallo, *Le vinti giornate dell'agricoltura*, pp. 241–42:

To prepare this for three people, take three to four pounds of millet flour . . . and put it in a pot containing four or five pounds of water boiling over the fire, making two cuts in the shape of a cross on top of it with a stick, to allow the flour to rise to the top. Leave it to cook until it swells up and separates from the bottom. And once it is removed from the fire, it should be well stirred with a round stick and in a careful fashion, until it is well broken and refined. Then take it out of the cauldron, cut it into nice thin slices with a wire, and eat it hot with cheese, or with ricotta only.

56. Messedaglia, *Vita e costume*, 1:138.
57. *Liber de coquina* , chap. 1, sect. 33.
58. Zambrini, *Il libro della cucina del sec. XIV*, p. 79.
59. Redon, Sabban, and Serventi, *A tavola nel Medioevo*, p. 258.
60. Scappi, *Opera*, chap. 71v ff.
61. Ibid., chap. 156.

62. Messedaglia, *Vita e costume*, 1:175 ff.

63. Ibid., 2:427–28. According to Folengo, the dumpling is a "coarse, vulgar, and rustic *pulmentum*, made from flour, cheese and butter."

64. See, for example, Guerrini, *Frammento di un libro di cucina del sec. XIV*, p. 33.

65. Montanari, *La fame e l'abbondanza*, p. 119.

66. Ibid., p. 123. See Montanari, *Nuovo convivio*, p. 163.

67. Messisbugo, *Libro novo*, chap. 52: "To make ten macaroni dishes."

68. See Scappi, *Opera*, chap. 70v.

69. Manzoni, *I promessi sposi*, p. 102.

70. Messedaglia, *Il mais e la vita rurale italiana*.

71. Castor Durante, *Herbario nuovo*, p. 217.

72. Carletti, *Ragionamenti del mio viaggio intorno al mondo*, pp. 58–59.

73. Montanari, *La fame e l'abbondanza*, pp. 169–70.

74. Tanara, *L'economia del cittadino in villa*, cited in Benporat, *Storia della gastronomia*, p. 169.

75. Montanari, *Nuovo convivio*, pp. 341–45.

76. Scappi, *Opera*, chaps. 70v, 359.

77. Benporat, *Storia della gastronomia*, p. 169.

78. Cited in Montanari, *Nuovo convivio*, pp. 288–90.

79. Anthimus, *De observatione ciborum*, 70, p. 74.

80. *Liber de coquina*, chap. 2, sect. 16.

81. See the recipe collection of the late fourteenth century by the anonymous Tuscan (Zambrini, *Il libro della cucina del sec. XIV*, p. 87): "Rice for the sick: Cook the rice in water in which the feet of kid goat have been boiled, and add almond milk and sugar."

82. Maestro Martino, *Il libro de arte coquinaria*, p. 159.

83. Montanari, *Nuovo convivio*, p. 184.

84. Redon and Laurioux, "La constitution d'une nouvelle catégorie culinaire?"; idem, "L'apparition et la diffusion des pâtes sèches en Italie."

85. Apicius, *De re coquinaria*, book 4, p. 14.

86. Rodinson, "Recherches sur des documents arabes relatifs à la cuisine."

87. Montanari, *La fame e l'abbondanza*, p. 176; Sada, *Spaghetti e compagni*, p. 19.

88. *Liber de coquina*, sect. 2, chap. 62, p. 144: "De tria ianuensi."

89. Perhaps these are the "*millefanti*" (literally, "thousand foot soldiers") that Paolo Zacchia remembers. See below.

90. Montanari, *Convivio*, p. 273.

91. *Liber de coquina*, chap. 3, sect. 64.

92. Montanari, "Le posate."

93. *Liber de coquina*, pp. 45–46; Rebora, "La cucina medievale," p. 1499. See Flandrin, "Les pâtes dans la cuisine provençale," p. 68.

94. *Liber de coquina*, pp. 45–46, 176.

95. Maestro Martino, *Il libro de arte coquinaria*, p. 158.

96. Maestro Martino, *Il libro de arte coquinaria*, p. 154.

97. Sorrentino, "Maccaroni romaneschi."

98. Maestro Martino, *Il libro de arte coquinaria*, p. 154.

99. Messisbugo, *Libro novo*, chap. 52; Scappi, *Opera*, chap. 70.

100. Maestro Martino, *Il libro de arte coquinaria*, p. 158. See Platina, *Il piacere onesto e la buona salute*, p. 163.

101. Sabban and Serventi, *A tavola nel Rinascimento*, p. 77.

102. *Liber de coquina*, chap. 2, sect. 62.

103. Scappi, *Opera*, chaps. 228, 254, 291, 241v.

104. Messedaglia, "Leggendo la cronica di frate Salimbene da Parma," p. 385.

105. Sacchetti, *Il Trecentonovelle*, story 124, pp. 387–90.

106. *Liber de coquina*, chap. 3, sect. 9: "Sciendum est quod tam in laxanis quam in crosetis *debet poni magna quantitas casei gratati*" (emphasis added).

107. Ibid., chap. 2, sect. 62: "Superpone species et collora, asapora sicut vis; cum istis potes ponere casseum gratatum vel incisum."

108. See "Milk Products," in this chapter.

109. See "Flavors and Fragrances from the Vegetable Garden" in this chapter.
110. *Liber de coquina*, chap. 3, sect. 3: lard and spices to flavor the "Apulian semola."
111. Messedaglia, *Vita e costume*, 1:182–83.
112. Cirelli, "Il villano smascherato," chap. 6, cited in Montanari, *Nuovo convivio*, p. 251.
113. See "Eating 'Lean' Food: The Liturgical Calendar and the Cooking of Fish" in this chapter.
114. Zacchia, *Il vitto quaresimale*, chap. 5, cited in Montanari, *Nuovo convivio*, pp. 204–5.
115. Montanari, *La fame e l'abbondanza*, p. 178 (also for what follows).
116. For a full account, see Sereni, "Note di storia dell'alimentazione nel Mezzogiorno: I Napoletani da 'mangiafolia' a 'mangiamaccheroni.' "
117. Cited in Montanari, *Nuovo convivio*, p. 358.
118. Mantovano, *L'avventura del cibo*, p. 83.
119. La Cecla, *La pasta e la pizza*, pp. 27–28.
120. Alberini, *Storia della cucina italiana*, p. 176.
121. See *Liber de coquina*, chap. 2, sect. 26: "*pastillum* sive *coppum*"; Zambrini, *Il libro della cucina del sec. XIV*, p. 66: "coppo, or pastello."
122. The "*patinae*" envisioned in book 4 of Apicius are for the most part prepared in a pan (hence their name), *frittate* or "*sformati*" without the support of any dough. This appears in just two instances (book 4, p. 14: "*patina apiciana*"; book 4, p. 15: "*patina cotidiana*") but indicates that the practice was not unknown. Still, these are exceptions, not characteristic foods, and it is thus impossible to accept the idea put forward by Alberini (*Storia della cucina italiana*, p. 74) that the "Renaissance-era" *pasticcio* (which was in fact from medieval times) is a rediscovery of an ancient method.
123. See the text (translated by Giacomo Leopardi) in Montanari, *Convivio*, pp. 65–69.
124. Laurioux, *Le règne de Taillevent*, p. 38.
125. Montanari, *Convivio*, pp. 273–74.
126. Martellotti, "The Parmesan Pie." On Mesopotamian cooking, see Bottéro, *Mesopotamian Culinary Texts.*
127. *Liber de coquina*, chap. 5, sect. 3.
128. Rebora, *La cucina medievale*, p. 1513 ff.
129. See the introduction.
130. Messedaglia, "Leggendo la cronica di frate Salimbene da Parma," p. 387.
131. Platina, *Il piacere onesto e la buona salute*, p. 181.
132. Montanari, *Alimentazione e cultura nel Medioevo*, p. 86.
133. *Liber de coquina*, chap. 2, sect. 22 (*De coppo avium*).
134. Ibid., chap. 5, sect. 4 (*De torta aliter facta*).
135. Montanari, *Nuovo convivio*, p. 144.
136. Scappi, *Opera*, chap. 349r–v.
137. Already formalized at the beginning of the fifteenth century, if, as it seems, this is what Lorenzo Sassoli, physician of Francesco Datini, refers to, advising his patient against eating "all kinds of meat pies" and suggesting instead a "well-made tart of good meats" (letter written in 1404, cited in Montanari, *Convivio*, p. 459).
138. The Milanese recipe adds ricotta cheese made from cow's or ewe's milk to the grated Parmesan, and the Bolognese recipe adds "struccioli," or "cheese freshly made the same day." In the Milanese recipe, unlike the Bolognese version, a pinch of clove or nutmeg is added, along with pepper and cinnamon.
139. Redon, Sabban, and Serventi, *A tavola nel Medioevo*, p. 79.
140. *Liber de coquina*, chap. 5, sect. 4.
141. Zambrini, *Il libro della cucina del sec. XIV*, p.78.
142. This is perhaps what the Tuscan author of the *Libro di cucina* had in mind when he defined "crispelli di carne" (meat crepes) as "tortelli" and "ravioli" (Zambrini, *Il libro della cucina del sec. XIV*, p. 38).
143. *Liber de coquina*, chap. 2, sect. 50.
144. Ibid., chap. 2, sect. 56.
145. Zambrini, *Il libro della cucina del sec. XIV*, p. 60.
146. Redon, Sabban, and Serventi, *A tavola nel Medioevo*, p. 78.
147. Messedaglia, "Leggendo la cronica di frate Salimbene da Parma," p. 385.

148. Scappi, *Opera*, chap. 354v.

149. Del Turco, *Epulario e segreti vari*, p. 27.

150. Scappi, *Opera*, chap. 210 r: "Young stuffed capons Lombard style, boiled and covered with *ravioli* without dough wrapping."

151. Artusi, *La scienza in cucina* (1899), p. 94.

152. Alberini, *Storia della cucina italiana*, p. 80.

153. Lando, *Commentario*, p. 126.

154. Messedaglia, *Vita e costume*, 1:110.

155. Sabban and Serventi, *A tavola nel Rinascimento*, p. 24.

156. Montaigne, *Journal de voyage*.

157. Montanari, *La fame and l'abbondanza*, pp. 19–20; idem, *L'alimentazione contadina nell'alto Medioevo*, p. 232.

158. Galloni, *Il cervo e il lupo*.

159. Montanari, *Convivio*, pp. 235–36 (from *La cronaca della Novalesa*).

160. Romagnoli, " 'Guarda no sii vilan.' "

161. Montanari, *Alimentazione e cultura nel Medioevo*, p. 63 ff.

162. Montanari, *La fame e l'abbondanza*, pp. 96–97.

163. Cited in Mazzei, *Lettere a Francesco Datini*, p. 370 ff (also cited in Montanari, *Convivio*, pp. 458–60).

164. Decembrio, *Vita di Filippo Maria Visconti*, 52, pp. 100–101.

165. Grieco, *Classes sociales*.

166. Montaigne, *Travel Journal*, p. 995.

167. Platina, *Il piacere onesto e la buona salute*, p. 104.

168. Ibid., p. 97.

169. Messisbugo, *Libro novo*, chap. 4.

170. The approximation of peacock with turkey is not only symbolic and functional but is also a question of terminology. See Scappi, *Opera*, chap. 61r–v: "To roast an India hen or rooster, which in some parts of Italy are called Indian peacocks." The comparison recurs. "The India hen or rooster has a much larger body than our own peahen or peacock. . . . The already mentioned rooster and hen follow the same seasonal cycle as our native peacock."

171. Scappi, *Opera*, chap. 17.

172. Ibid., chaps. 17–34.

173. Stefani, *L'arte di ben cucinare*, pp. 11–24.

174. Messedaglia, *Vita e costume*, 1:172.

175. Cirelli, "Il villano smascherato," chap. 6, cited in Montanari, *Nuovo convivio*, p. 250.

176. Tanara, *L'economia del cittadino in villa* (1665), pp. 186–87.

177. Scappi, *Opera*, chap. 11v.

178. Ibid., chap. 35: "If the animal is older, first parboil the top of the breast."

179. Cf. ibid.,. chap. 53v: "If you wish to roast an old capon, it should be rather gamey."

180. Pesce, *Macelli moderni*, p. 264.

181. Ulivi, *L'industria friggorifera*, p.165.

182. E. Vacandard, in *Dictionnaire de théologie catholique*, s.v. "Carême (Jeûne du)" (ca. 1742).

183. See Montanari, *La fame e l'abbondanza*, p. 98 ff.

184. On the function of alternating fat and lean as a vehicle of gastronomic homogenization on a European scale, see Flandrin, *Il gusto e la necessità*, p. 53.

185. André, *L'alimentation et la cuisine à Rome*, p. 219.

186. Montanari, *La fame e l'abbondanza*, p. 100.

187. Scappi, *Opera*, chap. 102v.

188. Ibid., chaps. 1v–2.

189. See "Oil, Lard, and Butter" in chapter 3 of this volume.

190. *Liber de coquina* , pp. 22, 29.

191. See comments on Ravenna's *schola piscatorum* in Montanari, *L'alimentazione contadina nell'alto Medioevo*, p. 289.

192. Scappi, *Opera*, chaps. 102v ff, 313v ff.

193. Montanari, *La fame e l'abbondanza*, p. 101.

194. Bonvesin da la Riva, *De magnalibus Mediolani*, 3, 30, p. 68.

195. Maestro Martino, *Il libro de arte coquinaria*, pp. 196–210.
196. Platina, *Il piacere onesto e la buona salute*, p. 215.
197. See " 'Lists of Things . . . Generally Used in Italy' " in chapter 1 of this volume.
198. Platina, *Il piacere onesto e la buona salute*, p. 215.
199. Scappi, *Opera*, chap. 117.
200. Latini, *Lo scalco alla moderna*, 2:1–3.
201. Platina, *Il piacere onesto e la buona salute*, p. 50.
202. Camporesi, *Il formaggio maledetto*, p. 52 ff.
203. Naso, *Formaggi del Medioevo*, p. 72.
204. Nigro, *Gli uomini dell'Irco*, p. 167 ff.
205. Moulin, *La vita quotidiana dei monaci nel Medioevo*, p. 70.
206. Zambrini, *Il libro della cucina del sec. XIV*, pp. 66–67.
207. Naso, *Formaggi del Medioevo*, p. 77.
208. Bentivoglio, *Le satire et altre rime piacevoli*, chap. 16r.
209. Messisbugo, *Libro novo*, chap. 5.
210. See " 'Lists of Things . . . Generally Used in Italy' " in chapter 1 of this volume.
211. Platina, *Il piacere onesto e la buona salute*, p. 51.
212. See "The Invention of Pasta" in this chapter.
213. da Confienza, *Summa lacticiniorum*, 2, 1–3, cited in Naso, *Formaggi del Medioevo*, pp. 114–16.
214. Romoli, *La singolar dottrina*, 7, 47, cited in Faccioli, *L'arte della cucina*, p. 397.
215. Zambrini, *Il libro della cucina del sec. XIV*, p. 73.
216. Scappi, *Opera*, chap. 47.
217. From a Tuscan recipe collection from the fourteenth century (Zambrini, *Il libro della cucina del sec. XIV*, pp. 73–74):

   Dei tomacelli, ovvero mortadelle: Take the pork liver and boil it, then mince it vigorously and thoroughly or grate it with a grater as though it were cheese. Then take marjoram and other fragrant herbs, well pounded with pepper. Add the liver, and moisten in the mortar with enough egg to thicken. Then take some pork net and shape it into little round balls, cover, and fry in the pan with lard. When cooked, place them in a new pot. Take some spices along with saffron and pepper, mix them with good wine, and add them to the pot. Boil properly, and eat.

   An analogous recipe is found in Scappi, *Opera*, chap. 48.

218. Scappi, *Opera*, chap. 50r–v.
219. Stefani, *L'arte di ben cucinare*, pp. 142–44.
220. See chapter 1 in this volume.
221. Frizzi, *La salameide*, pp.62–70.
222. Apicius, *De re coquinaria*, book 1, p. 9.
223. Montanari "I luoghi della cultura alimentare," p.368.
224. Zambrini, *Il libro della cucina del sec. XIV*, p. 75.
225. Maestro Martino, *Il libro de arte coquinaria*, p. 210.
226. Scappi, *Opera*, chap. 129v. See " 'Lists of Things . . . Generally Used in Italy' " in chapter 1 of this volume.
227. Montaigne, *Travel Journal*, p. 968.
228. Tozzi, *Pennino l'oste*, p. 91.
229. Marchi, *Il maiale*, pp.481–91; Marchi and Pucci, *Il maiale*, pp. 408–19.
230. Carpegna, "Altre rilevazioni di salumi tipici," p. 340 ff.
231. Queyrat, *Los buenos quesos argentinos*, p. 50: "Since both Gorgonzola and Roquefort are made from cow's milk in Argentina, it is very difficult to distinguish them from each other there."

3. THE FORMATION OF TASTE

1. Harris, *Good to Eat*.
2. Flandrin, *Il gusto e la necessità*.
3. Montanari, *La fame e l'abbondanza*, pp. 104–15.

4. Ibid., p. 148.
5. See " 'The Things That Should Be Eaten First' " in chapter 4 of this volume.
6. Felici, *Scritti naturalistici*, p. 27.
7. Cited in Montanari, *L'alimentazione contadina nell'alto Medioevo*, p. 159.
8. Sabban and Serventi, *La gastronomie au Grand Siècle*, p. 67.
9. Apicius, *De re coquinaria*, book 3, p. 16.
10. Ibid., book 4, pp. 2, 25: "si fatuum fuerit, liquamen adicies; si salsum, mellis modicum."
11. Salza Prina Ricotti, *L'arte del convito nella Roma antica*, pp. 221–22.
12. On the use of spices in Roman cooking, see André, *L'alimentation et la cuisine à Rome*, p. 205 ff.
13. See Laurioux, "De l'usage des épices dans l'alimentation médiévale."
14. This work is dedicated to Theodoric, king of the Franks. It can hardly be considered "the first book of French cuisine" on this account, as Grant has claimed in his introduction to Anthimus, *De observatione ciborum* (p. 28). Rose offers the hypothesis that the language used here is an Ostrogoth dialect of northern Italy (ibid., p. 16). In any case, France and Italy are completely anachronistic concepts in the historical context under discussion. The cultural environment that was taking shape at the time was that of medieval Europe, where Roman and Germanic traditions intersected with each other. See "From the Mediterranean to Europe" in chapter 1 of this volume.
15. Both stem and leaves are used: "spicam nardi vel folium" (Anthimus, *De observatione ciborum*, 13, p. 54). For information on its use in Roman times, see Dosi and Schnell, *A tavola con i romani antichi*, p. 203.
16. This is how Grant understands the *"ros Syriacum"* in the text (67, pp. 72–73).
17. Anthimus, *De observatione ciborum*, 3, p. 50.
18. Ibid., 34, p. 62.
19. Ibid., 15, p. 56.
20. Montanari, *Alimentazione e cultura nel Medioevo*, pp. 152–55.
21. Rodinson, "Recherches sur des documents arabes relatifs à la cuisine."
22. Rosenberger, "La cucina araba e il suo apporto alla cucina europea."
23. Cited in Montanari, *Nuovo convivio*, p. 269.
24. Anonymous Genovese writer, "De condicione civitate Ianuae," p. 244–45.
25. Scully, *L'arte della cucina nel Medioevo*, p. 26.
26. For what follows, see Montanari, *La fame e l'abbondanza*, p. 76 ff.
27. See "The Pleasure of Meat" in chapter 2 of this volume.
28. This interpretation is from Redon, Sabban, and Serventi, *A tavola nel Medioevo*, p. 286.
29. Frati, *Libro di cucina del secolo XIV*, nn. 73, 74, 75.
30. *Liber de coquina*, chap. 2, sect. 4.
31. Bonvesin de la Riva, *De magnalibus Mediolani*, 4.
32. *Liber de coquina*, pp. 74–75.
33. Montanari, in *Maestro Martino da Como e la cultura gastronomica del Rinascimento*, pp. 39–43.
34. Messisbugo, *Libro novo*, chap. 39. See Sabban and Serventi, *A tavola nel Rinascimento*, pp. 22–23.
35. For example, Scappi, *Opera*, chap. 110: "an ounce of Venetian spices."
36. Ibid., chap. 8.
37. For example, Scappi writes that "pies such as these [cabbage *torte*] need more spices than others and no sugar" (ibid., chap. 362v).
38. *Liber de coquina*, p. 79.
39. *Liber de coquina*, chap. 2, sects. 11–13.
40. This is not true in the case of the *provincialico*, flavored with herbs, spices, and dried fruit (pistachios) and sweetened with honey, but without a tart base; nor is it true in the case of the *"martino,"* flavored with herbs and spices, such as "Teutonic" and "Hispanic" broths, while "Gallic" broth has only garlic and spices. Dishes that are designated as "saracen," however, evoke the *difference* constituted by the combination of sweet and sour.
41. *Liber de coquina*, chap. 4, sect. 14.
42. Ibid., chap. 4, sect. 2. Similarly, in the Tuscan book: "If you prefer it sweet, add either

cooked wine or sugar, in the appropriate measure" (Zambrini, *Il libro della cucina del sec. XIV*, p. 29).

43. Apicius, *De re coquinaria*, book 1, p. 9.
44. Redon, Sabban, and Serventi, *A tavola nel Medioevo*, pp. 38–39.
45. *Liber de coquina*, chap. 2, sects. 32–33. Cf. Zambrini, *Il libro della cucina del sec. XIV*, p. 80.
46. *Liber de coquina*, pp. 30–31.
47. Ibid., p. 79: "Pound basil in the mortar, and add pepper, and distemper it with verjuice. This flavor is good with all roast meats . . . and lacking this add bitter oranges, citrons, or lemons" (cf. *Liber de coquina*, chap. 2, sect. 61). This is true for kid goat, lamb, veal (*Liber de coquina*, chap. 2, sect. 37) and above all large game—boar, stag, roebuck, bear—that require sauces that are more or less strongly spiced but with a distinctively bitter flavor (*Liber de coquina*, chap. 2, sect. 41).
48. Zambrini, *Il libro della cucina del sec. XIV*, p. 42. See also the recipe for *suppa* (slices of bread fried in the pan): "sprinkle sugar on top, or tart-tasting juices, and eat" (ibid., p. 55).
49. Redon, Sabban, and Serventi, *A tavola nel Medioevo*, pp. 39–40.
50. Zambrini, *Il libro della cucina del sec. XIV*, p. 81.
51. Messedaglia, *Vita e costume*, 2:298 (Pact of Verona, 1458, according to which the peasants were committed to "producing two pails of verjuice every year").
52. Sermini, *Le novelle*, 2:600.
53. Ibid., 2:521.
54. *Liber de coquina*, chap. 1, sect. 33: "Add honey (and oil fried with onions) to the broken broad beans"; chap. 2, sect. 3: "Honey and spices in Provençal broth."
55. Ibid., chap. 2, sect. 56: "Fried ravioli dipped in honey"; chap. 3, sect. 5: "Having added honey, eat the sweet fritters."
56. Ibid., chap. 2, sect. 12: "Sugar in *gratonea*"; chap. 2, sect. 14: *festigia* is cooked in water and sugar; chap. 2, sect. 16: "white sugar" is used in the preparation of *biancomangiare*; chap. 2, sect. 48: sugar and spices are scattered on pork intestines; chap. 2, sect. 59: sugar and powdered spices are added to the meat *mortarolo*; chap. 4, sect. 10: and to anchovy and sardine broth.
57. Ibid., chap. 3, sects. 1 and 7: "sugar added to sweet fritters" ("gratoneia lactis, crespellas").
58. Ibid., chap. 1, sect. 33.
59. Ibid., chap. 3, sect. 5. Cf. Zambrini, *Il libro della cucina del sec. XIV*, p. 36: "Put sugar or apples on top, and eat."
60. Flandrin, "Internationalisme," p. 86 (illus.). Sugar is added to a mince of vegetables and tench (Zambrini, *Il libro della cucina del sec. XIV*, p. 4), to boiled pears (p. 10), broken beans (p. 22, with honey), mustard (p. 26), "fish broth" (p. 29), roast duck (p. 31), "gratonia" (pp. 35, 45), Ubaldo's fritters (p. 36, as an alternative to honey), "crepes stuffed with meat" (p. 39), *biancomangiare* (p. 49), *festiggia* (p. 49) and so forth.
61. Frati, *Libro di cucina del secolo XIV*, p. 11, vinegar and honey in "*civiro de lepore*"; p. 13: "a little honey" in fish "cisame"; p. 70: cooked honey in "ranciata"; p. 68: a confection of dried fruit, cooked in honey; p. 72: quince pudding (*cotognata*).
62. Flandrin, "Internationalisme," p. 86.
63. Frati, *Libro di cucina del secolo XIV*, pp. 68–69.
64. bid., p. 5 (poultry soup).
65. Ibid., p. 37.
66. Laurioux, *Le règne de Taillevent*, p. 243. On the "conservative" quality of German cooking, see Martellotti and Durante, *Libro di buone vivande*, p. 56.
67. Frati, *Libro di cucina nel secolo XIV*, pp. 68–70.
68. bid., p. 73.
69. Ibid., p. 74.
70. Platina, *Il piacere onesto e la buona salute*, p. 141.
71. Scully, *L'arte della cucina nel Medioevo*, p. 61.
72. Felici, *Scritti naturalistici*, pp. 135–36.
73. Messisbugo, *Libro novo*, chap. 87v.
74. Ibid., chap. 39v.
75. Flandrin, "Vins d'Italie, bouches françaises."
76. Montaigne, *Travel Journal*, pp. 929, 1006.

77. Cited in Montanari, *Convivio*, p. 332.

78. "Sunt nutritiva plus dulcia candida vina" (*Regimen sanitatis*, 11, cited in Firpo, *Medicina medievale*, p. 82).

79. Cited in Montanari, *Convivio*, p. 269.

80. Laurioux, "Cuisiner à l'antique"; idem, *Le règne de Taillevent*, p. 247.

81. Laurioux, *Cuisiner à l'antique*, p. 35.

82. Milham, "Toward a Stemma."

83. Laurioux, *Cuisiner à l'antique*, p. 30.

84. Ibid., pp. 36–37.

85. Platina, *Il piacere onesto e la buona salute*, p. 96.

86. See "From the Mediterranean to Europe" in chapter 1 of this volume.

87. Platina, *Il piacere onesto e buona salute*, p. 141.

88. Sabban and Serventi, *A tavola nel Rinascimento*, pp. 28–29.

89. Anthimus, 12 (with reference to beef).

90. Ibid., 43 (with reference to pike).

91. Platina, *Il piacere onesto e la buona salute*, p. 180.

92. Bergier, *Una storia del sale*, p. 124 (with reference to the physicians of the Salerno school). See Montanari, *Alimentazione e cultura del Medioevo*, p. 183 ff.

93. Martellotti and Durante, *Libro di buone vivande*, p. 83.

94. Scappi, *Opera*, chap. 393v.

95. Zacchia, *Il vitto quaresimale*, chap. 5.

96. André, *L'alimentation et la cuisine à Rome*, p. 183.

97. Montanari, *La fame e l'abbondanza*, pp. 12–13.

98. Cato, *De agricultura*, 79, 80, 121. See André, *L'alimentation et la cuisine à Rome*, pp. 184–85.

99. Polibio, *Storie*, II, 15; Strabone, *Geografia*, V, 12, 218.

100. Mazzarino, *Aspetti sociali del quarto secolo*, p. 217 ff. See also Corbier, "Le statut ambigu de la viande à Rome," p. 121.

101. See "The Pleasure of Meat" in chapter 2 of this volume.

102. Anthimus, *De observatione ciborum*, 39–47. See Montanari, *Alimentazione e cultura nel Medioevo*, pp. 206–8.

103. Anthimus, *De observatione ciborum*, pp. 79–80.

104. See "Eating 'Lean' Food: The Liturgical Calendar and the Cooking of Fish" in chapter 2 of this volume.

105. Montanari, *L'alimentazione contadina*, p. 158. See "Polenta, Soup, and Dumplings" in chapter 2 of this volume.

106. With respect to Verona, see *Olio ed olivi del Garda veronese*, pp. 30, 38. The oil vendors were organized within the guild of lard makers, which oversaw the entire market of alimentary fats.

107. *Liber de coquina*, chap. 1, sect. 24; chap. 1, sect. 10; chap. 4, sect. 6.

108. Flandrin, "Internationalisme," p. 85 (table).

109. Pliny considered it "iners et gravi sapore" (*Naturalis historia*, XXIII, 88).

110. Flandrin, *Il gusto e la necessità*, p. 59 (and note 108, p. 79).

111. Ibid., p. 57.

112. Ibid., p. 52.

113. Laurioux, "Le 'Registre de cuisine' de Giovanni Bockenheym."

114. Ibid., p. 740 n. 61 pp. 740–41 n. 63.

115. Ibid., pp. 736–37 n.42; p. 736 n. 41; p. 736 n. 38.

116. Platina, *Il piacere onesto e la buona salute*, p. 52.

117. Savonarola, *Libreto de tutte le cosse che se magnano*, p. 148.

118. See "Can One Cook Without Spices?" in this chapter.

119. Tanara, *L'economia del cittadino in villa* (1665), p. 174.

120. *Olio ed olivi del Garda veronese*, p. 43.

121. Artusi, *La scienza in cucina* (1891), p. 100.

122. Sabban and Serventi, *A tavola nel Rinascimento*, p. 34.

123. *Liber de coquina*, chap 1, sect. 9; chap. 1, sect. 29; chap. 2, sect. 6.

124. Flandrin, "Internationalisme," pp. 89–90.

125. Sabban and Serventi, *A tavola nel Rinascimento*, p. 32.

126. Laurioux, "Le 'Registre de cuisine' de Giovanni Bockenheym."
127. Cited in Mantovano, *L'avventura del cibo*, pp. 73–74.
128. Cited in Montanari, *Convivio*, p. 500 (a novella by the fifteenth-century writer Sabadino degli Arienti).
129. Cited in Montanari, *Nuovo convivio*, pp. 135–36.
130. Montaigne, *Travel Journal*, p. 882.
131. Sabban and Serventi, *A tavola nel Rinascimento*, p. 32.
132. Flandrin, "Scelte alimentari e arte culinaria," pp. 512–13.
133. Sabban and Serventi, *La gastronomie au Grand Siècle*, pp. 13, 23.
134. Maestro Martino, *Il libro de arte coquinaria*, p. 152.
135. Scappi, *Opera*, chaps. 73, 204.
136. Montaigne, *Essays*, pp. 221–223.
137. Mennell, *All Manners of Food*, p. 71.
138. *De remediis utriusque fortunae*, book 1, p. 43, cited in Laurioux, *Le règne de Taillevent*, p. 231.
139. *Les dons de Comus*, p. xvii. See Benporat, *Storia della gastronomia*, p. 145.
140. See Montanari, *Nuovo convivio*, pp. 308–9.
141. *La cuciniera piemontese*, p. 3.
142. Cited in Montanari, *Nuovo convivio*, p. 335.
143. Leonardi, *L'Apicio moderno*, 1:xxii.
144. Sabban and Serventi, *La gastronomie au Grand Siècle*, p. 23.
145. Ibid., p. 27.
146. Latini, *Lo scalco alla moderna*, 2:169–72.
147. Camporesi, *Il brodo indiano*, p. 74.
148. Montanari, *Nuovo convivio*, pp. 321–22.
149. Cited in ibid., pp. 29–30.
150. Flandrin, "I tempi moderni," pp. 437–38.
151. See "From the Mediterranean to Europe" in chapter 1 of this volume.
152. Sabban and Serventi, *La gastronomie au Grand Siècle*, pp. 64–65.
153. Ibid., pp. 35, 53.
154. Latini, *Lo scalco alla moderna*, 2:153–54.
155. Ibid., pp. 54–55.
156. Stefani, *L'arte di ben cucinare*, p. 53: "Take a small pan and place in it an ounce of cinnamon stick, a half ounce of cloves, three ounces of sugar, and a glass and a half of vinegar." These are the ingredients for "royal sauce," which are simmered on a slow fire until the mixture is reduced by half. The sauce is served "with all kinds of roasts."
157. Ibid., p. 54.
158. Sabban and Serventi, *La gastronomie au Grand Siècle*, p. 55.
159. Stefani, *L'arte di ben cucinare*, p. 63.
160. Del Turco, *Epulario e segreti vari*, pp. 5–6.
161. Ibid., p. 37.
162. Cited in Montanari, *Nuovo convivio*, pp. 284–85. See Camporesi on the "enlightened reform of the dinner table," *Il brodo indiano*, p. 49 ff.
163. Artusi, *La scienza in cucina* (1891), p. 290.
164. Ibid., p. 357.
165. Tozzi, *Pennino l'oste*, p. 53.
166. Ibid., p. 76. *Dolceforte* is also recommended for game (hare or boar): "Put fifty grams of currants in a glass, along with bitter chocolate, pine nuts, pieces of candied fruit, all amounting to thirty grams, add fifty grams of sugar, and as much vinegar as is needed" (p. 120).
167. See "Appert in Italy: The Flavor of Preserved Foods" in chapter 8 of this volume.
168. G. Flaubert, *Bouvard et Pécuchet* (Paris: Garnier, 1954), p. 5.
169. Artusi, *Autobiografia*, p. 63.
170. Idem, *La scienza in cucina* (1891), p. 66.
171. Zingali, "Il rifornimento dei viveri dell'esercito italiano," pp. 537–38.
172. Baroffio and Quagliotti, *Alimentazione del soldato*, 2:1110.
173. Fornari, *Il cuciniere militare*, p. 27.

4. THE SEQUENCE OF DISHES

1. Anthimus, *De observatione ciborum*, 6, p. 52.
2. Flandrin, "Condimenti, cucina e dietetica tra XIV e XVI secolo," pp. 389–90.
3. Platina, *Il piacere onesto e la buona salute*, pp. 56–60.
4. Ibid., p. 26.
5. Flandrin, "Condimenti, cucina e dietetica tra XIV e XVI secolo," p. 387.
6. Scully, "The 'Opusculum de Saporibus' of Magninus Mediolanensis."
7. *Liber de coquina*, chap. 2, sect. 63, p. 144.
8. Platina, *Il piacere onesto e la buona salute*, p. 148.
9. Ibid., p. 149.
10. Nigro, *Gli uomini dell'Irco*, p. 167 ff.
11. Decembrio, *Vita di Filippo Maria Visconti*, 52, pp. 100–101.
12. Montanari, *Convivio*, pp. 492–93.
13. Ambrosioni, "Contributo alla storia della festa di San Satiro a Milano," pp. 83–84. The text appears on p. 95: "In primis pullos frigidos et gambas de vino et carnem porcinam frigidam; in secundo pullos plenos et carnem vaccinam cum piperata et tutellam de lavezolo; in tercio loco pullos rostidos et lumbolos cum panicio atque porcellos plenos. Porcellos vero pelnos quandoque in prima appositione et carnem porcinam frigidam in tercia apositione habebant, et e converso."
14. Montanari, *Convivio*, p. 319.
15. Redon, Sabban, and Serventi, *A tavola nel Medioevo*, pp. 17–19.
16. Montanari, *Convivio*, pp. 368–70.
17. Sercambi, *Novelle*, story 123, pp. 545–48.
18. *Il "sollazzo" e il "saporetto" con altre rime di Simone Prudenzani d'Orvieto*, p. 116.
19. Ibid., p. 123.
20. Platina, *Il piacere onesto e la buona salute*, p. 24.
21. Ibid., pp. 31, 32, 38–39, 25.
22. Ibid., pp. 26, 45.
23. Ibid., pp. 28, 41–42.
24. Felici, *Scritti naturalistici*, p. 27.
25. See "Flavors and Fragrances from the Vegetable Garden" in chapter 2 of this volume.
26. Zacchia, *Il vitto quaresimale*, chap. 5.
27. Platina, *Il piacere onesto e la buona salute*, pp. 95–96.
28. Messedaglia, *Vita e costume*, 1:341–42.
29. Scappi, *Opera*, chaps. 320–21.
30. Cited in Montanari, *Nuovo convivio*, p. 268.
31. Platina, *Il piacere onesto e la buona salute*, pp. 246–47.
32. Scappi, *Opera*, chap. 320v.
33. Ibid., chap. 322.
34. Benporat, *Storia della gastronomia*, pp. 120–21.
35. Alberini, *Storia della cucina italiana*, p. 121.
36. Benporat, *Storia della gastronomia*, pp. 125–148.
37. Cited in Montanari, *Convivio*, p. 202.
38. Montaigne, *Travel Journal*, p. 1032.
39. Pontormo, *Diario*, pp. 36 and 53.
40. Henrico da S. Bartolomeo del Gaudio, *Scalco spirituale*, p. 395.
41. "Compendio breve della vita sobria del Mag. M. Alvise Cornaro," in Cornaro, *Scritti sulla vita sobria*, p. 113.
42. "Capitolo in lode dell'hosteria," in Berni, *Il secondo libro della opere burlesche*, pp. 37, 41.
43. Pontormo, *Diario*, p. 82.
44. Massonio, *Archidipno*, p. 8.
45. Rossetti, *Dello scalco*, p. 180.
46. Ibid., p. 28.
47. "Eat soft foods first, then proceed to more solid foods" (*Regimen sanitatis*, p. 79).
48. Rossetti, *Dello scalco*, pp. 104 and 109.

49. Latini, *Lo scalco alla moderna*, 1:31.
50. Ibid.
51. Evitascandalo, *Libro dello scalco*, pp. 16–17.
52. Rossetti, *Dello scalco*, pp. 199–204.
53. Scappi, *Opera*, chap. 313v.
54. Marchese, *L'invenzione della forchetta*.
55. Cervio, *Il trinciante*, p. 113.
56. De Nolhac and Solerti, *Il viaggio in Italia di Enrico III re di Francia*, pp. 316–17.
57. Rossetti, *Dello scalco*, p. 29.
58. Liberati, *Il perfetto maestro di casa*, p. 72.
59. Cervio, *Il trinciante*, p. 49.
60. Liberati, *Il perfetto maestro di casa*, p. 79.
61. Romoli, *La singolar dottrina*, p. 7.
62. Bacci, *De naturali vinorum historia*, V, pp. 31 and 24.
63. *I vini d'Italia giudicati da Papa Paolo III*, pp. 38–41 and 36.
64. Grieco, "I sapori del vino," p. 182.
65. Tasso, *Dialoghi*, p. 34.
66. Scappi, *Opera*, chap. 8v.
67. Ibid., chaps. 229 and 175v.
68. Tarugi, *Prerogative dell'acquaticcio*, pp. 47–55.
69. *I vini d'Italia giudicati da Papa Paolo III*, p. 36.
70. Vialardi, *Trattato di cucina*, pp. 5–6.
71. Agnetti, *La cucina nazionale*, p. 201.
72. Rajberti, *L'arte di convitare*, p. 569.
73. Corrado, *Il cuoco galante*, pp. 206–207.
74. Cougnet, *L'arte cucinaria in Italia*, 2:803.
75. Ibid., 2:806.
76. Cavalcanti, *La cucina teorico-pratica*, pp. 180 and 464.
77. Rajberti, *L'arte di convitare*, p. 486.
78. Vialardi, *Trattato di cucina*, pp. 9–14.
79. Rajberti, *L'arte di convitare*, p. 517.
80. *La cucina elegante ovvero il quattrova illustrato*, p. 23.
81. Boni, *Il talismano della felicità*, p. 836.
82. *Il cucchiaio d'argento*, p. 51.
83. *La cucina elegante ovvero il quattrova illustrato*, p. 88.
84. See "Milk Products" in chapter 2 of this volume.
85. Landi, *Formaggiata di sere Stentato*; Bentivoglio, "Del formaggio." See also Rossi, *Elogio del formaggio di grana piacentino*.
86. Cougnet, *L'arte cucinaria Italia*, 1:294.
87. *Il cucchiaio d'argento*, p. 40.
88. Parmentier, *Estratto delle opere del conte di Rumphort sulla maniera di comporre minestre sostanziose ed economiche*.
89. Roggero, *Piatto unico all'italiana*, p. 7
90. *Mangiare meglio per vivere meglio*, p. 26
91. *Moretum.* Alberto Lollio brought out the first Italian translation in 1547 (*Il moretum di Virgilio tradotto in versi volgari sciolti*). A second translation by Vincenzo Rai was published in 1571. For Giacomo Leopardi's translation, see Montanari, *Convivio*, pp. 65–69.
92. McNair, *Pizza*.

5. COMMUNICATING FOOD: THE RECIPE COLLECTION

1. Cited in Montanari, *Convivio*, p. 451.
2. The principal bibliographical source used here and in other passages is Maria Paleari-Henssler's *Bibliografia latino-italiano di gastronomia*.
3. *All'angelo custode* (Bologna, 1693).
4. See, e.g., *Narrazione delle solenni reali festi fatte celebrare in Napoli da Sua Maestà il re delle*

due Sicilie Carlo Infante di Spagna Duca di Parma, Piacenza . . . per la nascita del suo primogenito Filippo Real Principe delle due Sicilie (Naples, 1749).

5. Latini, *Autobiografia*, p. 16.

6. Nebbia, *Il cuoco maceratese* (1786).

7. La Varenne, *Il cuoco francese; Il cuoco piemontese perfezionato a Parigi* (1766); Nebbia, *Il cuoco maceratese* (1781).

8. "Del signor N.N. alludendo al cognome dell'autore," in Vasselli, *L'Apicio overo il maestro de' convito,* n.p.

9. Leonardi, *Il cuciniere perfetto italiano;* idem, *Il cuoco italiano economico;* idem, *Il cuciniere italiano moderno.*

10. The most famous is Giovanni Nelli's *Il re dei cuochi* (The king of cooks), whose title is echoed in *Il re dei cuochi, ossia l'arte di mangiare al gusto degli Italiani.* In addition, in 1895 the Betti publishing house in Turin brought out a book by Jean-Marie Parmentier with the title *Il re dei re dei cuochi* (The king of kings of cooks). Vitalino Bossi wrote *L'imperatore dei cuochi* (The emperor of Cooks), which was reprinted in 1895 with a new title, *Il principe dei cuochi* (The prince of cooks).

11. Cited in Artusi, *La scienza in cucina* (1899), p. 17.

12. Crisci, *La lucerna de corteggiani,* n.p. (358).

13. Scappi, *Opera,* chap. 286.

14. Messisbugo, *Libro novo,* chap. 28.

15. Chiappini, *La corte estense alla metà del Cinquecento,* p. 50.

16. Stefani, *L'arte di ben cucinare,* p. 135.

17. Corrado, *Il cuoco galante,* pp. 7–10.

18. Cavalcanti, *La cucina teorico-practica,* pp. 5–6.

19. Nelli, *Il re dei cuochi* (1889), pp. 5–6.

20. Artusi, *La scienza in cucina* (1891), p. v.

21. Escoffier, *Souvenirs inédits,* p. 125.

22. Borgarello, *Il gastronomo moderno,* pp. 52, 98, 199.

23. Wymann, *Des maîtres de l'art culinaire du monde entier vous parlent,* pp. 323 (crêpes), 344 (chicken breasts), 335 (*carbonara*).

24. Artusi, *La scienza in cucina* (1899), p. 389.

25. Scappi, *Opera,* chap. 42.

26. Frati, *Libro di cucina del secolo XIV.*

27. Massialot, *Il cuoco reale e cittadino.*

28. *La cucina casereccia* was published nineteen times between 1807 and 1974 in Naples alone.

29. See also Fornari, *Il nuovo Carena;* Sergent and Gorini, *Nuovo vocabolario italiano domestico.*

30. Dubois and Bernard, *La cucina classica.*

31. Greimas, "La soupe au pistou."

32. Anonymous southern writer, *Due libri di cucina,* p. 14.

33. Gosetti della Salda, *Le ricette regionali italiane,* p. 6.

34. Scappi, *Opera,* chap. 94v.

35. Maestro Martino, *Il libro de arte coquinaria,* p. 137.

36. *Il cocho bergamasco alla casalenga,* p. 11.

37. Corrado, *Il cuoco galante,* p. 164.

38. Picco, *Nuovo lessico di cucina abbreviato,* p. 94.

39. Hering and Andreuzzi, *Lessico di cucina,* p. 395.

40. Artusi, *La scienza in cucina* (1891), p. 52.

41. Gosetti della Salda, *Le ricette regionali italiane,* p. 23.

42. Scappi, *Opera,* chap. 136r.

43. Corrado, *Il cuoco galante,* pp. 144, 51, 139.

44. Scappi, *Opera,* chap.137v.

45. Corrado, *Il cuoco galante,* pp. 17, 36, x.

46. Latini, *Lo scalco alla moderna,* 1:444.

47. *Il cuoco piemontese perfezionato a Parigi* (1995), pp. 233 and 334.

48. Apicius, *De re coquinaria,* p. 65.

49. Libera, *L'arte della cucina*, pp. 87, 281 (table comparing Libera's culinary repertoire and that of A. Nebbia).
50. Artusi, *La scienza in cucina* (1899), p. 89.
51. Agnetti, *La nuova cucina delle specialità regionali*, pp. 165 (macaroni with sardines), 47.
52. *Culinary Art*, p. 11.
53. Latini, *Lo scalco alla moderna*, 1:14.
54. Rossetti, *Dello scalco*, p. 8.
55. See "The Bourgeoisie Cuts Back" in chapter 4 of this volume.
56. Vialardi, *Trattato di cucina*, p. 3.
57. With eighteen editions in the course of the nineteenth century, Dubini's work is a significant source of reference, even if the menus recorded in the volume are far from systematic. Dessert is sometimes eliminated in order to accommodate a second meat or fish dish (*La cucina degli stomachi deboli* [1862], pp. 151–160). For handwritten records we have consulted the collection compiled in the household of Baron Crova in Turin between 1888–1926, which will be the subject of a future study.
58. Alberini, *Mangiare con gli occhi*, p. 33. For the attribution of the dates 1820–1835, see Meldini, *Pranzi di carta*, p. 7. For a typology, see the collection by Cerini di Castegnate, *I menu famosi*.
59. Rajberti, *L'arte di convitare*, p. 522.
60. Borgarello, *Il gastronomo moderno*, pp. 306–7.
61. Escoffier, *Le livre des menus*, pp. 23 ff.
62. Fornari, *Il cuciniere militare*, p. 34.
63. Monelli, *Il ghiottone errante*, p. 161.

6. THE VOCABULARY OF FOOD

1. *Regimen sanitatis*, p. 118.
2. *Liber de coquina*, p. 114.
3. Zambrini, *Il libro della cucina del sec. XIV*, p. 59.
4. *Liber de coquina*, p. 164.
5. Printed in Rome by Uldaricus Gallus, no date provided but probably from 1473–1475.
6. Anonymous southern writer, *Due libri di cucina*, p. 5.
7. Frati. *Libro di cucina del secolo XIV*, pp. 34–35.
8. Faccioli, *L'arte della cucina in Italia*, p. 252.
9. Buganza, *Poesie latine*.
10. Ciacconius, *De triclinio romano*.
11. Petronius. *De victu romanorum*; Petronio, *Del viver delli romani e del conservar la sanità*.
12. F. Orsini, in Ciacconius, *De triclinio romano*, p. 97; Bacci, *De conviviis antiquorum*, p. 37.
13. Laurioux, *Le règne de Taillevent*, p. 115.
14. Martellotti and Durante, *Libro di buone vivande*.
15. Frati, *Libro di cucina del secolo XIV*.
16. Maestro Martino, *Il libro de arte coquinaria*, p. 150. The term *"zanzarelli"* reappears in Platina's *Il piacere onesto e la buona salute*, p. 143.
17. Ibid., p. vii.
18. Recently, Laurioux, *Le règne de Taillevent*, p. 213.
19. Scappi, *Opera*, chap. 61.
20. The systematic list of dishes and utensils provided in the appendix of Giovan Battista Rossetti's *Scalco*, pp. 451–547, is especially important.
21. Scappi, *Opera*, chap. 134.
22. Ibid., chap. 70v.
23. Among the entries dedicated to names of pastas we find "lasagne," "gnocchi," "maccheroni," and "pappardelle."
24. References to the work of Messisbugo and Scappi are based on the 1966 edition of *L'arte della cucina*, edited by Emilio Faccioli.
25. Catricalà, *La lingua dei banchetti di Cristoforo Messisbugo*.
26. Berni, *Il secondo libro delle opere burlesche*, pp. 17 ("Capitolo del Molza de' fichi"), 64 ("Capitolo sopra la salsiccia"), 110 ("Le terze rime di Mattio Franzesi sopra le carote").

27. Landi, *Formaggiata di sere Stentato*, p. 45.
28. *Il cuoco piemontese perfezionato a Parigi*, p. 7.
29. Weiss, *Gastronomia*, pp. 340, 570.
30. La Varenne, *Il cuoco francese* (1693), pp. 4, 9 ("pottacchio di riso, con la cipolla"), 5 ("pottacchio alla Francese detto Bisca"), 165 ("rappreso di Brettagna"), p. 331 ("rissole").
31. Leonardi, *L'Apicio moderno*, 1:xxii–xxiii.
32. *La cucina casereccia*, p. 5.
33. Cavalcanti, *La cucina teorico-pratica*, p. 437.
34. Carême, *L'art de la cuisine française au XIXe siecle*, 3:131.
35. Höfler, *L'art culinaire français*, s.v. "béchamel."
36. Santi Puppo, *Il cuciniere moderno*, p. 67.
37. Nelli, *Il re dei cuochi* (1889), p. 888.
38. Giardini, *Dizionario della cucina moderna*.
39. See, especially, *La cucina classica* by Urbain Dubois and Emile Bernard, published in 1877 at the expense of the Association of Milanese Cooks.
40. Artusi, *La scienza in cucina* (1899), p. 17.
41. Artusi, *La scienza in cucina* (1891), pp. ix–xi.
42. Artusi, *La scienza in cucina* (1899), p. 17. There are thirty-four terms, such as *"baba," "beignet," "brioches," "latte brûlé," "canapé,"* and *"ciarlotta"* (for *"charlotte"*), in French or in Italian translation.
43. Artusi, *La scienza in cucina* (1899), p. 424. "Soufflé" is spelled incorrectly as "soufflet" in *Il cuoco piemontese perfezionato a Parigi*, p. 233.
44. Artusi, *La scienza in cucina* (1899), p. 58.
45. Ibid., p. 203.
46. *Eminenza, il piatto è servito*, p. 137.
47. Panzini, *Dizionario moderno* (1905), s.v. "glassare."
48. Cougnet, *L'arte culinaria in Italia*, 1:ix.
49. Panzini, *Dizionario moderno* (1905), s.v. "consumé." Cf. Scappi, *Opera*, chap. 397: "Per fare brodo consumato di carne di Vitella" (To make a "consumé" of veal).
50. Artusi, *La scienza in cucina* (1891), p. 64.
51. "Artusi, who is an expert on gastronomy, translates it as 'balsamella,' claiming that a good béchamel with a sauce of finely chopped meat is the secret of fine cooking" (Panzini, *Dizionario moderno* (1923), s.v. "béchamel").
52. Marinetti and Fillìa, *La cucina futurista*, pp. 247–52.
53. *La cucina italiana*, July and November 1952.
54. Montagné, *Larousse gastronomique*; Courtine, *Larousse gastronomique*.
55. Robuchon, *Larousse gastronomique*.
56. Marchesi, *La cucina regionale italiana*, p. 425.
57. Suor Germana, *Quando cucinano gli angeli*, p. 98.
58. Artusi, *La scienza in cucina* (1970).
59. La Cecla, *La pasta e la pizza*, p. 75. See also Corti's comments on culinary syncretism in the United States, "Emigrazione e consuetudini alimentari," pp. 718–19.
60. Borgarello, *Il gastronomo moderno*, p. 3.

7. THE COOK, THE INNKEEPER, AND THE WOMAN OF THE HOUSE

1. Scappi, *Opera*, chaps. 64, 120.
2. G. Roversi, introduction to Scappi, *Opera* (Bologna: Forni, 1981); Benporat, *Storia della gastronomia*, p. 94. On the recent discovery of the stone marker at Luini, see "Lists of Things . . . Generally Used in Italy" in chapter 1 of this volume.
3. Chiappini, *La corte estense alla metà del Cinquecento*, pp. 42–50.
4. Latini, *Autobiografia*, p. 26.
5. Romoli, *La singolar dottrina*, chap. 5.
6. Rossetti, *Dello scalco*, p. 32.
7. Latini, *Lo scalco alla moderna*, 1:9.
8. Rossetti, *Dello scalco*, p. 31.

9. Ibid., p. 32.

10. Liberati, *Il perfetto maestro di casa*, pp. 87–88.

11. Montanari, *Nuovo convivio*, p. 338.

12. Romoli, *La singolar dottrina*, chap. 5v.

13. Stefani, *L'arte di ben cucinare*, p. 6.

14. Scappi, *Opera*, chap. 2.

15. Leonardi, *L'Apicio moderno*, 1:xxxv.

16. Agnoletti, *Manuale del cuoco e del pasticciere*, 1:xii. See Zannoni, *A tavola con Maria Luigia*, pp. 69–70.

17. Touring Club Italiano, *Manuale dell'industria alberghiera* (1923), p. 529 (the quotation is attributed to the marquis de Cussy, a famous Parisian gourmand of the first half of the nineteenth century).

18. Scappi, *Opera*, tables.

19. Reale Fusoritto da Narni, *Aggiunta fatta al Trinciante del Cervio*, p. 204.

20. See the respective portraits in Latini, *Lo scalco alla moderna*, and Nebbia, *Il cuoco maceratese*.

21. Nisbet and Masséna, *L'Empire à table*, pp. 92 (*Dîner à l'Hôtel de Ville*, lithograph by C. Motte), 99 (*Le Restaurant de Justa*, gravure by Opitz).

22. Romoli, *La singular dottrina*, p. 14.

23. Zannoni, *A tavola con Maria Luigia*, p. 90.

24. Touring Club Italiano, *Manuale dell'industria alberghiera* (1923), p. 416. These comments are not included in the fifth edition of the manual (1954).

25. Barigazzi, *Le osterie di Milano*, p. 94.

26. *Il diario dell'oste*, p. 145.

27. Tozzi, *Pennino l'oste*, p. 58.

28. Artusi, *La scienza in cucina* (1891), pp. 24, 39.

29. The volume is dedicated to the memory of Hans Barth.

30. Barth, *Osteria*, pp. 137, 138, 123.

31. Mariotti, *Quando siam dall'oste insieme*, p. 245.

32. *Osterie romane*, p. 37,

33. Monelli, *Il ghiottone errante*, p. 112.

34. Mariotti, *Gastronomia alla ventura*, p. 136.

35. *Trattorie d'Italia* 1939.

36. Mariotti, *Quando siam dall'oste insieme*, p. 160.

37. Menon, *La cuisinière bourgeoise*.

38. *La cuciniera piemontese*.

39. The first edition of *The Art of Cookery*, featuring Hannah Glasse's name, was published in London in 1747. The recipe collection by Amelia Simmons, *American Cookery*, was printed in Hartford in 1796.

40. dagli Orzi, *La massera da be*.

41. Messisbugo, *Libro novo*, chap. 39v.

42. Rosselli, *Opera nova chiamata Epulario*.

43. Mantegazza, *Giornale della mia vita*.

44. Adami, *Il noviziato del maestro di casa*, p. 214.

45. Pandolfini, *Del governo della famiglia* (1446), VIII, p. 117.

46. Lando, *Commentario delle più notabili e mostruose cose d'Italia*, pp. 126–27.

47. Folengo, *Baldus*, p. 208.

48. Costo, *Il fuggilozio*, p. 292.

49. *Il cocho bergamasco alla casalenga*, p. 9.

50. Ottonelli, *Annotazioni sopra il vocabolario degli Accademici della Crusca*.

51. Tanara, *L'economia del cittadino in villa* (1665), pp. 175–177.

52. *La cuoca cremonese*, p. 3.

53. Nebbia, *Il cuoco maceratese* (1781), p. 3.

54. P. Moroni Salvadori, foreword to *La cuciniera bolognese*, pp. 5–7.

55. *La cuciniera maestra*, pp. 33 (tagliatelli), 53 (trotters with lentils), 87 (scarpazzone).

56. Artusi, *La scienza in cucina* (1899), p. 389.

57. Vanzetti, *Il doppio quattrova ovvero la cucina elegante*, p. xiv.
58. Ferraris Tamburini, *Come posso mangiar bene?* p. 400.
59. Valvassori, *Enciclopedia domestica*, p. 11.
60. Gallia, *Servire con amore*.
61. Morelli, *Massaie di domani*, p. 222 ff.

8. SCIENCE AND TECHNOLOGY IN THE KITCHEN

1. Nievo, *Le confessioni di un italiano*, p. 8.
2. For a commentary on the illustrations in Scappi's work, see Firpo, *Gastronomia del Rinascimento*, pp. 59–68.
3. Scappi, *Opera*, chap. iv.
4. Ibid., chap. 156 ("To prepare and cook macaroni in many in different ways for Lenten days").
5. Papin's book was published in London in 1681 with the title *A New Digester or Engine for Softening Bones*. A French translation was published in Paris in 1682.
6. Sangiorgio, *La macchina di Papinio riformata all'uso economico e farmaceutico*. The author claims to have used Papin's machine for twenty-five years (p. 318).
7. *Estratto d'una memoria sulla macchina papiniana*, pp. 243–46.
8. Ottolini, *Il digestore di Papino*, pp. 201–3.
9. Prato, *Manuale di cucina*, p. 7 (with an illustration). For a brief history of the pressure cooker, see Samarelli, *Omegna paese di pentole e caffettiere*, pp. 16–27.
10. Rumford, *Saggi politici, economici e filosofici del conte di Rumford*, p. 122.
11. Rumford, *Saggio sopra l'alimento de' poveri*, p. 205.
12. Rumford, *Essais politiques, économiques et philosophiques*, p. 288.
13. Pisanelli, *Trattato della natura de' cibi et del bere*, p. 176.
14. Ibid., p. 179.
15. Baldini, *De' sorbetti*, p. 19. For a history of the consumption of snow, see Planhol, *L'eau de neige*, p. 17 (on chemical methods).
16. Ibid., p. 76.
17. *Il confetturiere piemontese*.
18. Voltaire, *Les anciens et les modernes*, p. 751.
19. Parmentier, *Rapport au ministre de l'intérieur*; idem, *Estratto delle opere del conte di Rumphort*.
20. Parmentier, *Della pentola americana del Sig. Parmentier*, p. 321.
21. Parmentier, *Dei pomi di terra ossia Patate*; Cadet-de-Vaux, *Istruzioni sul miglior impiego del pomo di terra*; Rumford, "Maniera di far bollire i pomi di terra," in *Saggi politici, economici e filosofici*.
22. The Italian translation was entitled *L'arte di conservare tutte le sostanze animali e vegetabili*, the German *Die Kunst, alle thierische und vegetabilischen Nahrungsmittel meherere Jahre volkommenen Geniessenbar zu erbalten*, and the English *The Art of Preserving All Kinds of Animal and Vegetable Substances for Several Years*.
23. This is the translation of an anonymous work that appeared in Paris the same year. For a discussion of Appert's invention and the "English Can" (*la scatoletta inglese*), see pp. 10 and 14 ff.
24. Zannoni, *A tavola con Maria Luigia*, p. 303.
25. Borgarello, *Il gastronomo moderno*, pp. 307 and 326.
26. Cirio, *Pomodoro fresco a ogni stagione*; A.B.C. Cirio; Cirio, *Nuovi orizzonti per la vostra mensa*.
27. Vialardi, *Trattato di cucina*, p. 409.
28. Nelli, *Il re dei cuochi* (1889), pp. 46–47.
29. 128.
30. *L'industria italiana del freddo*, May 31, 1928, p. 124.
31. Artusi, *La scienza in cucina* (1891), p. 347. All subsequent editions up to 1911 recommended the use of the American ice-cream maker.
32. A. Pettini, preface to Ciocca, *Gelati, dolci freddi e rinfreschi*, p. xxv.
33. Guglmayr, *Encyclopedia casalinga ultramoderna*, pp. 47 and 50.
34. Touring Club Italiano, *Manuale dell'industria alberghiera* (1923), p. 543.

35. Giacobone, Guidi, and Pansera, *Dalla casa elettrica alla casa elettronica*, p. 14.
36. Morelli, *Nuovo ricettario domestico*, p. 207.
37. Giacobone, Guidi, and Pansera, *Dalla casa elettrica alla casa elettronica*, p. 17; Roanelli, Laudani, and Vercelloni, *Gli spazi del cucinare*, p. 24.
38. Guglmayr, *Enciclopedia casalinga ultramoderna*, p. 97.
39. Formenti, *L'alluminio*, p. 205.
40. Morelli, *Nuovo ricettario domestico*, p. 204; idem, *Massaie di domani*, p. 184.
41. *La cucina elegante ovvero il quattrova illustrate*, pp. 58, 71, 160, 166.
42. Morelli, *Nuovo ricettario domestico*, p. 207.
43. Touring Club Italiano, *Manuale dell'industria alberghiera* (1923), p. 252.
44. "I cocktails," *La cucina italiana*, January 15, 1930, p. 4.
45. Morelli, *La casa che vorrei avere*, pp. 430–31. The drawing of the bar is by Gio Ponti, illustrator of *Il quattrova*.
46. Artusi, *La scienza in cucina* (1891), p. 194 (Lasagni Delicatessen Products in Reggio Emilia), p. 123 (Liebig meat extract).
47. Franceschi and Venturoli, *Conservazione delle sostanze alimentari*, pp. 71–74.
48. Rovetta, *L'industria del pastificio*, p. 183.
49. Dal Buono, *Tecnologia del riso*, pp. 160–76.
50. Fascetti, *Caseificio*, p. 316.
51. Bajla, Gagliardi, and Formenti, *Vade-mecum del consumatore*, p. 75.
52. Ibid., p. 76.
53. Gallo, Covino, and Monicchia, "Crescita, crisi, riorganizzazione," p. 276.
54. Publicity brochure published by Buitoni in 1932. It contains a section dedicated to the "marriage" of industry and science.

9. TOWARD A HISTORY OF THE APPETITE

1. Montanari, *La fame e l'abbondanza*, p. 206.
2. Platina, *Il piacere onesto e la buona salute*, p. 187.
3. Montanari, *Alimentazione e cultura nel Medioevo*, p. 63 ff.
4. Camporesi, *Il brodo indiano*, p. 137.
5. Cited in Montanari, *La fame e l'abbondanza*, p. 117.
6. Ibid., pp. 30 ff., 115 ff.
7. Ibid., p. 118 ff.
8. Goethe, *Viaggio in Italia*, pp. 140–41 (1787).
9. Platina, *Il piacere onesto e la buona salute*, p. 20.
10. See "The Italian Model and the French 'Revolution' " in chapter 3 of this volume.
11. Montaigne, *Essays*, pp. 222–223.
12. Platina, *Il piacere onesto e la buona salute*, p. 6.
13. *Il regimen sanitatis Roberti Grospretii* was published in Ghent in 1538 and was reprinted in Paris two years later. It falls on pp. 359v–376 of Romoli's *Singolar dottrina*.
14. Scappi, *Opera*, chap. 393v ("To make consumé broth from tasty capons").
15. *I vini d'Italia giudicati da Papa Paolo III*, p. 36.
16. Cornaro, *Scritti sulla vita sobria*, p. 113.
17. Folengo, *Baldus*, p. 126.
18. "And as this dish was presented the Pipers played a *moresque*, and some peasants pretended to cut the grass in the garden with their scythes" (Messisbugo, *Libro novo*, chap. 13v).
19. Battarra, *La pratica agraria*, pp. 133–34.
20. Gallo, *Le vinti giornate dell'agricoltura et de piaceri della villa* (1575), pp. 241–42. See Messedaglia, *Vita e costume*, 1:129.
21. Croce, *Le sottilissime astuzie di Bertoldo*, pp. 74–75.
22. See Montanari, *La fame e l'abbondanza*, pp. 109–110, for what follows.
23. Lastri, *Regole per i padroni dei poderi verso i contadini*, pp. 31–39.
24. Cited in Montanari, *La fame e l'abbondanza*, p. 186.
25. Cornaro, *Scritti sulla vita sobria*, p. 112.
26. Camporesi, *Il brodo indiano*, p. 120.

27. Tissot, *Della salute de' letterati*, p. 24.

28. Meldini, "La tavola pitagorica."

29. Cocchi, *Del vitto pitagorico per uso della medicina*, p. 74.

30. Corrado, *Del cibo pitagorico ovvero erbaceo per uso de' nobili e dei letterati*, p. xi.

31. *La gastronomie* was translated by Eridanio Cenomano and published, in facing-page text, as *La gastronomia ovvero arte di belpranzare*, by Omobono Manini in Milan in 1825. In 1838 it was retranslated by Jacopo Landoni and printed in Ravenna by the Roveri printing company (*La gastronomia cioè l'ammaestramento ai bravi mangiatori*). The term was introduced into Italy in 1825.

32. Italians read Grimod de la Reynière's *Manuel des amphitryons* (1808) and especially Brillat-Savarin's *La physiologie du goût* (1826) in the original French editions. The first Italian translation of the latter was published by Salani in 1914.

33. Rajberti, *L'arte di convitare* (1964), p. 463.

34. Boiled rice is sautéed in oil or butter with anchovies and onions and flavored with cheese (*La cucina casereccia*, p. 48). This Milanese recipe is well known in different variations in other Italian states.

35. Mantegazza, *Almanacco igienico-popolare: Piccolo dizionario della cucina*, p. 89.

36. Dubini, *La cucina degli stomachi deboli* (1862), p. 151.

37. "If doctors are unavailable, three things will work as well as a doctor: a happy mind, rest, and a moderate diet."

38. "Subdue hunger, never stimulate it."

39. Mantegazza, *Almanacco igienico-popolare: Igiene del lavoro*, p. 51.

40. Rajberti, *L'arte di convitare*, p. 526.

41. Cougnet, *L'arte cucinaria in Italia*, 2:802–3.

42. Artusi, *La scienza in cucina* (1891), p. 8.

43. Mantegazza, *Almanacco igienico-popolare: Igiene d'Epicuro*, p. 9.

44. Monelli, *Il ghiottone errante*, p. 162.

45. Marinetti and Fillìa, *La cucina futurista*, p. 55.

46. Ibid., p. 172.

47. Leyrer, *La regina delle cuoche*, pp. 210, 226.

48. *La cucina elegante ovvero il quattrova illustrato*, p. 4.

49. *Il cucchiaio d'argento*, p. 407.

50. Ibid., p. 418.

51. Ibid., p. 419.

52. Veronelli, *Il carnacina*, p. 54.

53. Ibid., p. 55.

BIBLIOGRAPHY

A.B.C. Cirio. San Giovanni a Teduccio: Società generale delle conserve alimentari, 1925.

Accademia della Crusca. *Vocabolario degli accademici della Crusca*. Florence, 1612.

Acosta, G. de. *Historia naturale e morale delle Indie*. Venice: Basa, 1596. Reprint, Verona: Cassa di Risparmio di Verona, 1992.

Adami, A. *Il noviziato del maestro di casa*. Rome: Facciotti, 1636.

Agnetti, V. *La cucina nazionale*. Milan: Società editoriale milanese, 1910.

——. *La nuova cucina delle specialità regionali*. Milan: Società editoriale milanese, 1909. Reprint of *La cucina dell'età giolittiana*. Rimini: Guaraldi, 1977.

Agnoletti, V. *La nuovissima cucina economica*. Rome: Poggioli, 1814.

——. *Manuale del cuoco e del pasticciere*. Pesaro: Nobili, 1832.

Alberini, M. "Bartolomeo Scappi: Maestro di tutti i cuochi." *L'Accademia italiana della cucina* 83 (1998).

——. *Mangiare con gli occhi: Storia del menù*. Modena: Panini, 1987.

——. *Storia della cucina italiana*. Casale Monferrato: Piemme, 1992.

All'angelo custode. Bologna, 1693.

Ambrosioni, A. "Contributo alla storia della festa di San Satiro a Milano." *Archivio Ambrosiano* 23 (1972).

André, J. *L'alimentation et la cuisine à Rome*. Paris: Belles Lettres, 1981.

Anonymous Genoese writer. "De condicione civitate Ianuae." In *Poeti del Duecento. Poesia didattica del Nord*, ed. G. Contini. Turin: Einaudi, 1978.

Anonymous southern writer. *Due libri di cucina*. Ed. I. Boström. Stockholm: Almqvist & Wiksell, 1985.

Anthimus. *De observatione ciborum—On the observance of foods*. Ed. M. Grant. Blackatown, Devon, U.K.: Prospect, 1996.

Apicius. *De re coquinaria—L'art culinaire*. Ed. J. André (with French translation). Paris: Les Belles Lettres, 1974.

Appert, N. *L'art de conserver pendant plusieurs années toutes les substances animales et végétales*. Paris: Patris, 1810.

——. *The Art of Preserving All Kinds of Animal and Vegetable Substances for Several Years*. London: Black, Perry, and Kingsbury, 1812.

——. *L'arte di conservare tutte le sostanze animali e vegetabili*. Siena: Onorato Porri, 1810.

——. *Die Kunst, alle thierische und vegetabilischen Nahrungsmittel meherere Jahre volkommenen Geniessenbar zu erbalten*. Koblenz: Pauli, 1810.

L'arte di conservare gli alimenti tanto vegetabili che animale impiegati particolarmente dell'economica domestica pel nutrimento dell'uomo. Milan: Tipografia del Commercio, 1824.

Artusi, P. *Autobiografia*. Ed. A. Capatti and A. Pollarini. Milan: Il Saggiatore, 1993.

——. *La scienza in cucina e l'arte di mangiar bene*. Intro. and ann. Piero Camporesi. Turin: Einaudi, 1970.

——. *La scienza in cucina e l'arte di mangiar bene: Manuale pratico per le famiglie*. 1st ed. Florence: self-published, 1891.

——. *La scienza in cucina e l'arte di mangiar bene: Manuale pratico per le famiglie*. 4th ed. Florence: Landi, 1899.

Averani, G. *Del vitto e delle cene degli antichi* Genoa: Ecig, 1992. (First published in *Lezioni toscane* [Florence, 1761].)

Bacci, A. *De conviviis antiquorum deque solemni in eis vinorum usu atque ritu coenrum Sumptuosissimo* (1597). In Gronovius, *Thesaurus graecarum antiquitatum*. Lyons, 1701.

———. *De naturali vinorum historia.* Rome: Mutii, 1596.

———.*De naturali vinorum historia.* Trans. Mariano Corino, Turin: Toso, for the Ordine dei cavalieri del tartufo, 1990.

Bajla, E., G. Gagliardi, and O. C. Formenti. *Vade-mecum del consumatore.* Milan: Popolo d'Italia, 1931.

Baldini, F. *De' sorbetti.* Naples: Stamperia Raimondiana, 1775.

Bandello, M. *Novelle.* 9 vols. Milan: Silvestri, 1813–1814.

Barigazzi, G. *Le osterie di Milano.* Milan: Mursia, 1968.

Baroffio, F. and A. Quagliotti. *Alimentazione del soldato.* 2 vols. Turin: Zoppis, 1860.

Barth, H. *Osteria: Guida spirituale delle osterie italiane da Verona a Capri.* Rome: Voghera, 1910. Reprint, Florence: Le Monnier, 1921.

Basile, G. *Lo cunto de li cunti.* Ed. M. Rak. Milan: Garzanti, 1986.

Battaglia, S., ed. *Grande dizionario della lingua italiana: Indice degli autori citati.* Turin: UTET, 1968.

Battarra, G. *La pratica agraria distribuiti in vari dialoghi.* Rev. ed. Cesena: Biasini, 1782.

Benporat, C. *La cucina italiana del Quattrocento.* Florence: Olschki, 1996.

———. *Il cuoco mestiere d'arte.* Milan: Il Saggiatore, 1999.

——— *Storia della gastronomia italiana.* Milan: Mursia, 1990.

Bentivoglio, E. "Del formaggio" and "In lode del vino." In *Le satire et altre rime piacevoli.* Ferrara: Sate, 1977.

———. *Le satire et altre rime piacevoli.* Venice: Giolito de' Ferrari, 1557.

Berchoux, J. *La gastronomia cioè l'ammaestramento ai bravi mangiatori.* Trans. Jacopo Landoni. Ravenna: Roveri, 1838.

———. *La gastronomia ovvero arte di belpranzare.* Trans. Eridanio Cenomano. Milan: Manini, 1825.

———. *La gastronomie; ou, L'homme des champs à table, poème didactique en quatre chants.* Paris: Giguet, 1801.

Bergier, J.-F. *Una storia del sale.* Venice: Marsilio, 1984.

Berni, F. *Il secondo libro delle opere burlesche.* London, 1723.

Boni, A. *Il talismano della felicità.* 7th ed. Rome: Preziosa, 1941.

Bonvesin da la Riva. *De magnalibus Mediolani: Le meraviglie di Milano.* Ed. M. Corti. Trans. G. Pontiggia. Milan: Bompiani, 1974.

Borgarello, E. *Il gastronomo moderno: Vademecum ad uso degli albergatori, cuochi, segretari e personale d'albergo.* Milan: Hoepli, 1904.

Bossi, V. *L'imperatore dei cuochi.* Rome: Perini, 1894. Reprint of *Il principe dei cuochi.* Naples: Bideri, 1895.

Bottéro, J. *Mesopotamian Culinary Texts.* Winona Lake, Ind.: Eisenbrauns, 1995.

Brillat-Savarin, A. *Fisiologia del gusto.* Florence: Salani, 1914.

———. *Physiologie du goût.* Paris: Sautelet, 1826.

Brizzi, G. *La cuciniera moderna.* Siena: Mucci, 1845.

Buganza, G. *Poesie latine.* Florence: Pagani, 1786.

Cadet-de-Vaux, A. *Istruzioni sul miglior impiego del pomo di terra nella sua co-panificazione con le farine di cereali.* Naples: Trani, 1817.

Campier, B. *De re cibaria.* Lyons, 1560.

Camporesi, P. *Alimentazione folclore società.* Parma: Pratiche, 1980.

———. *Il brodo indiano: Edonismo ed esotismo nel Settecento.* Milan: Garzanti, 1990.

———. *Il formaggio maledetto.* In *Le officine dei sensi*, pp. 47–77. Milan: Garzanti, 1985.

Canal, P. *Dictionnaire françois et italien.* Paris: Chouet, 1598.

Carême, A. *L'art de la cuisine français au XIXe siècle.* Paris: Au comptoir des éditeurs réunis, 1847.

Carena, F. *Prontuario di vocaboli attinenti alle cose domestiche.* Florence: Galileiana, 1840.

Carletti, F. *Ragionamenti del mio viaggio intorno al mondo.* Ed. P. Collo. Turin: Einaudi, 1989.

Carpegna, C. di. "Altre rilevazioni di salumi tipici." In Istituto nazionale di sociologia rurale, *Atlante dei prodotti tipici: I salumi.* Milan: Franco Angeli, 1990.

Castelvetro, G. *Brieve racconto di tutte le radici, di tutte l'erbe e di tutti i frutti che crudi o cotti in Italia si mangiano.* Ed. E. Faccioli. Mantua: Arcari, 1988.

Catricalà, M. "La lingua dei banchetti di Cristoforo Messisbugo." *Studi di Lessicografia Italiana* 4. 1982.

Cavalcanti, I. *La cucina teorico-pratica.* Naples: Gemelli, 1837.

Cavazza, G. *Itinerario gastronomico ed enologico d'Italia.* Milan: Banco Ambrosiano, 1949.

Cerini di Castegnate, L. *I menu famosi.* Milan: BE-MA, 1988.

Cervio, V. *Il trinciante con l'aggiunta di Reale Fusoritto.* Florence: Il Portolano, 1979.

Chiappini, L. *La corte estense alla metà del Cinquecento: I compendi di Cristoforo di Messisbugo.* Ferrara: Belriguardo, 1984.

Ciacconius, P. *De triclinio romano: Fulvi Ursini Appendix.* Rome: Georgium Ferrarium, 1588.

Ciocca, G. *Gelati, dolci freddi e rinfreschi.* Milan: Hoepli, 1922.

Cirelli, G. "Il villano smascherato." Ed. G. L. Masetti Zannini. *Rivista di storia dell'agricoltura* 7, no. 1 (1967).

Cirio. *Nuovi orizzonti per la vostra mensa: 300 ricette scelte fra le 1224 premiate su 18.000 inviate al concorso pomodori pelati Cirio.* Portici: Società generale delle conserve alimentari, 1936.

———. *Pomodoro fresco a ogni stagione.* Naples: Società generale delle conserve alimentari, 1939.

Cocchi, A. *Del vitto pitagorico peruso della medicina.* Florence: Moucke, 1743.

Il cocho bergamasco alla casalenga. Bergamo: Italia nostra, 1979.

Collodi, C. *Il viaggio per l'Italia di Giannettino.* Part 3, *L'Italia meridionale.* Florence: Paggi, 1886.

Il confetturiere piemontese. Turin: Re, 1790.

da Confienza, Pantaleone. *Summa lacticiniorum.* In I. Naso, *Formaggi del Medioevo,* pp. 85–141. Turin: Il Segnalibro, 1990.

———. *Trattato dei latticini.* Trans. E. Faccioli. Milan: Consorzio Grana Padano, 1990.

Corbier, M. "Le statut ambigu de la viande à Rome." *Dialogues d'histoire ancienne* 15, no. 2 (1989): 107–58.

Cornaro, A. *Scritti sulla vita sobria: Elogio e lettere.* Venice: Corbo e Fiore, 1983.

Corrado, V. *Del cibo pitagorico ovvero erbaceo per uso de' nobili e de' letterati, opera meccanica.* Naples: Raimondi, 1781.

———. *Il cuoco galante.* 3d ed. Naples: Raimondi, 1786.

Corti, P. "Emigrazione e consuetudini alimentari." In *Storia d'Italia, Annali 13: L'alimentazione.* Turin: Einaudi, 1998.

Costo, T. *Il fuggilozio.* Rome: Salerno, 1989.

Cougnet, A. *L'arte cucinaria in Italia.* Vol. 1. Milan: Wilmant, 1910

———. *L'arte cucinaria in Italia.* Vol. 2. Milan: Wilmant, 1911.

Courtine, R. *Larousse gastronomique.* Paris: Larousse, 1984.

Crisci, G. B. *La lucerna de corteggiani.* Naples: Domenico Roncagliolo, 1634.

Croce, G. C. *Le sottilissime astuzie di Bertoldo.* Ed. P. Camporesi. Turin: Einaudi, 1978.

Il cucchiaio d'argento. Milan: Domus, 1950.

La cucina casereccia. Naples: Giordano, 1828.

La cucina elegante ovvero il quattrova illustrato. Milan: Domus, 1931.

La cucina italiana. 1st ser. (1929–1943).

———. 2d ser. (1950–).

La cuciniera bolognese. Bologna: Forni, 1990.

La cuciniera maestra. Reggio Emilia: Bassi, 1884.

La cuciniera piemontese. Vercelli, 1771. Reprint, Turin: Soffietti, 1798.

Il cuciniere italiano. Florence: Canale, 1848.

Il cuciniere italiano moderno. Leghorn: Vignozzi, 1832.

I cucinieri d'Italia: Rassegna dell'associazione italiana cucinieri (I). Milan: Associazione italiana cucinieri, 1924–1936 (volumes available for 1924–1926, 1934–1936).

Culinary Art Including Choice of Oriental Dishes. Hong Kong: Ministering League, n.d.

La cuoca cremonese che insegna a cucinare con facilità qualunque sorta di vivande: Almanacco utile e dilettevole per l'anno 1794. Cremona: Manini.

La cuoca di famiglia. Venice: Coen, 1976.

La cuoca risparmiatrice. Venice: Andreola, 1813.

La cuoca sublime. Venice: Coen, 1873.

Il cuoco italiano economico. Leghorn: Vignozzi, 1827.

Il cuoco milanese e la cuciniera piemontese. Milan: Lombardi, 1853.

Il cuoco piemontese perfezionato a Parigi. Turin: Ricca, 1766. Reprint. Ed. S. Serventi. Bra: Slow Food, 1995.

Dal Buono, U. *Tecnologia del riso*. Milan: Hoepli, 1921.

Decembrio, P. C. *Vita di Filippo Maria Visconti*. Ed. E. Bartolini. Milan: Adelphi, 1983.

Del Turco, G. *Epulario e segreti vari: Trattati di cucina toscana nella Fienze seicentesca*. Ed. A. Evangelisti. Bologna: Forni, 1992.

De Nolhac, P. and A. Solerti. *Il viaggio in Italia di Enrico III re de Francia*. Turin: De Roux, 1890.

Il diario dell'oste: La raccolta storica cronologica di Valentino Alberti (1796–1834). Ed. M. Zangarini. Vicenza: Associazione veneta per la storia locale, 1997.

Les dons de Comus. Paris: Prault, 1739.

Dosi, A. and F. Schnell. *A tavola con i romani antichi*. Rome, Quasar, 1984.

Dubini, A. *La cucina degli stomachi deboli, ossia pochi piatti non comuni semplici, economici e di facile digestione*. 1857. Reprint, Milan: Bernardoni, 1862.

Dubois, U. and E. Bernard. *La cucina classica*. Milan: Association of Milanese Cooks, 1877.

Durante, C. *Herbario nuovo*. Rome: Sessa, 1602.

Eminenza, il pranzo è servito: Le ricette di Alberto Alvisi cuoco del card. Chiaromonti Vescovo di Imola (1785–1800). Ed. A. Bassani and G. Roversi. Bologna: Aniballi, 1984.

Encyclopédie; ou, Dictionnaire raisonné des sciences, des arts et des métiers. Vol. 4. Paris, 1754.

Eridanio, Cenomano. *La gastronomia; ovvero, L'arte di ben pranzare*. Milan: Manini, 1825.

Escoffier, A. *Le livre des menus*. Paris: Flammarion, 1932.

———. *Souvenirs inédits*. Marseilles: Laffitte, 1985.

Estratto d'una memoria sulla macchina papiniana semplificata per l'uso esonomico del Sig. Wilcke prof. di fisica a Stoccolma. Opuscoli scelti sulle scienze e sulle arti. Milan: Marelli, 1779.

Estratto delle opere del conte di Rumphort sulla maniera di comporre minestre sostanziose ed economiche colle esperienze fatte dalla Società agraria, ad istruzione e vantaggio del popolo piemontese. Turin: Pane e Barberis, 1800.

Evitascandalo, C. *Libro dello scalco*. Rome: Vullietti, 1609.

Faccioli, E., ed. *L'arte della cucina in Italia*. Milan: Il Polifilo, 1966. Reprint, Turin: Einaudi, 1987.

Fascetti, G. *Caseificio*. Vol. 1, *Latte*. Milan: Hoepli, 1929.

Felici, C. *Scritti naturalistici*. Vol. 1, *Del'insalata e piante che in qualunque modo, Vengono per cibo del'homo*. Ed. G. Arbizzoni. Urbino: Quattro Venti, 1986.

Ferraris Tamburini, G. *Come posso mangiar bene?* Milan: Hoepli, 1900.

Firpo, L., ed. *Gastronomia del Rinascimento*. Turin: UTET, 1974.

———. *Medicina medievale*. Turin: UTET, 1971.

Flandrin, J.-L. *Chronique de Platine: Pour une gastronomie historique*. Paris: Odile Jacob, 1992.

———. "Condimenti, cucina e dietetica tra XIV e XVI secolo." In *Storia dell'alimentazione*, ed. J.-L. Flandrin and M. Montanari, pp. 381–95. Rome: Laterza, 1997.

———. "Le goût et la nécessité: Sur l'usage des graisses dans les cuisines d'Europe occidentale, I." *Annales ESC* 38 (1983): 369–401.

———. *Il gusto e la necessità*. Trans. L. Saetti. Milan: Il Saggiatore, 1994.

———. "Internationalisme, nationalisme et régionalisme dans la cuisine des XIVe et Xve siècles: Le témoignage des livres de cuisine." In *Manger et boire au Moyen Age* (proceedings of the Colloque de Nice 1982), 2:75–91. Nice: Belles Lettres, 1984.

———. "Le pâtes dans la cuisine provençale." *Medievales* 16–17 (1989): 65–75.

——— "I tempi moderni." In *Storia dell'alimentazione*, ed. J.-L. Flandrin and M. Montanari, pp. 427–48. Rome: Laterza, 1997.

——— "Scelte alimentari e arte culinaria." In *Storia dell'alimentazione*, ed. J.-L. Flandrin and M. Montanari, pp. 512–33. Rome: Laterza, 1997.

———. "Vins d'Italie, bouches françaises." *Chroniques italiennes* 52 (1997): 119–28.

Flandrin, J.-L. and C. Lambert. *Fêtes gourmandes au Moyen Age*. Paris: Imprimerie nationale, 1998.

Flandrin, J.-L. and M. Montanari, eds. *Storia dell'alimentazione*. Rome: Laterza, 1997.

Folengo, T. *Baldus*. Ed. E. Faccioli. Turin: Einaudi, 1989.

Formenti, C. *L'alluminio*. Milan: Hoepli, 1899.

Fornari, D. *Il cuciniere militare*. Novara: Cattaneo, n.d. (1930s).

Fornari, P. *Il nuovo Carena: La casa o vocabolario metodico domestico*. Turin: Paravia, 1888.

Franceschi, G. B. and G. Venturoli. *Conservazione delle sostanze alimentari*. Milan: Hoepli, 1907.

Frati, L., ed. *Libro di cucina del secolo XIV*. Leghorn, 1899.

Frizzi, A. *La salameide: Poemetto giocoso con le note*. Venice: Zerletti, 1772.

Frugoli, A. *Pratica e scalcaria*. Rome: Cavalli, 1638.

Gallia, M. *Servire con amore: Piccolo manuale di istruzioni pratiche per le domestiche*. Milan: Vita e pensiero, 1937.

Gallo, A. *Le vinti gionate dell'agricoltura et de' piaceri della villa*. Venice: Percaccino, 1569. Reprint, Venice: Borgominieri, 1575.

Gallo, G., R. Covino, and R. Monicchia. "Crescita, crisi, riorganizzazione: L'industria alimentare dal dopoguerra a oggi." In *Storia d'Italia, Annali 13: L'alimentazione*. Turin: Einaudi, 1998.

Galloni, P. *Il cervo e il lupo: Caccia e cultura nobiliare nel Medioevo*. Rome-Bari: Laterza, 1993.

Giacobone, T., P. Guidi, and A. Pansera. *Dalla casa electrica alla casa elettronica: Storia e significati degli elettrodomestici*. Milan: Arcadia, 1989.

Giardini, G. *Dizionario della cucina moderna indispensabile a qualunque ceto di persone: Vademecum del cuoco*. Milan: Brigola, 1885.

Gibault, G. *Histoire des legumes*. Paris: Horticole, 1912.

Glasse, H. *The Art of Cookery Made Plain and Easy*. London: 1770, self-published.

Goethe, W. *Viaggio in Italia*. Trans. A. Oberdorfer. Novara: De Agostini, 1982.

Gosetti della Salda, A. *Le ricette regionali italiane*. Milan: Solares, 1967.

Greimas, A. "La soupe au pistou; ou, La programmation d'un objet de valeur." In *Du Sens II*, pp. 168–69. Paris: Seuil, 1983.

Grieco, A. *Classes sociales: Nourriture et imaginaire alimentaire en Italie (XIVe–Xve siècles)*. Paris: Ehess, 1987.

———. "I sapori del vino: Gusti e criteri di scelta fra Trecento e Cinquecento." In *Dalla vite al vino*, ed. J. L. Gaulin and A. Grieco. Bologna: Clueb, 1994.

Grimod de la Reynière, A. B. L. *Manuel des amphitryons*. Paris: Chapelle et Renand, 1808.

Guerrini, O., ed. *Frammento di un libro di cucina del sec. XIV*. Bologna: Zanichelli, 1877.

Guglmayr, T. *Enciclopedia casalinga ultramoderna*. Trieste: Leitner & Wells, 1943.

Harris, M. *Good to Eat: Riddles of Food and Culture*. New York: Simon and Schuster, 1985.

Henrico da S. Bartolomeo del Gaudio. *Scalco spirituale*. Naples: Roncagliolo, 1644.

Hering, R. and F. Andreuzzi. *Lessico di cucina*. Berlin: Kirchner, n.d.

Höfler, M. *L'art culinaire français*. Aix-en-Provence: Edisud, 1996.

Humerlbergius, Dick. *Apician Morsels*. 8 vols. London: Whittaker, Treacher, and Co., 1829.

L'industria italiana del freddo. Milan, 1926–1928.

"L'Italia gastronomica . . . una carta appetitosa." *L'albergo d'Italia*, May 1932, 311.

Keys, Ancel and M. Keys. *How to Eat Well and Stay Well the Mediterranean Way*. New York: Doubleday, 1959.

———. *Mangiar bene e stare bene*. Intro. Giorgio Bini. Padua: Piccin, 1962.

La Cecla, F. *La pasta e la pizza*. Bologna: Il Mulino, 1998.

Landi, G. *Formaggiata di sere Stentato al Serenissimo re della virtude*. Ed. A. Capatti. Milan: Consorzio Grana Padano, n.d.

Lando, O. *Commentario delle più notabili e mostruose cose d'Italia e altri luoghi di lingua aramea in italiana tradotto. Con un breve catalogo de gli inventori delle cose che si mangiano e bevono, novamente ritrovato*. Ed. G. Salvatori and S. Salvatori. Venice, 1553. Reprint, Bologna: Pendragon, 1994.

Landoni, J. *La gastronomia cioè ammastramento ai bravi mangiatori*. Ravenna: Roveri, 1838.

Lastri, M. *Regole per i padroni dei poderi verso i contadini, per proprio vantaggio e di loro. Aggiuntavi una raccolta di avvisi ai contadini sulla loro salute*. Venice: Graziosi, 1793.

Latini, A. *Autobiografia (1642–1696): La vita di uno scalco*. Rome: Furio Luccichenti, 1992.

———. *Lo scalco alla moderna, overo l'arte di ben disporre i conviti*. 2 vols. Naples: Parrino e Mutii, 1692–1694.

Laurioux, B. "Cuisiner à l'antique: Apicius au Moyen Age. *Médiévales* 26 (1994): 17–38

——. "De l'usage des épices dans l'alimentation médiévale." *Médiévales* 5 (1983): 15–31.

——. *Le règne de Taillevent: Livres et pratiques culinaires à la fin du Moyen Age.* Paris: Publications de la Sorbonne, 1997.

——, ed. "Le 'Registre de cuisine' de Giovanni Bockenheyem, cuisinier du pape Martin V." *Mélanges de l'Ecole Française de Rome* 100 (1988) 709–60.

La Varenne, F. de. *Le cuisinier françois.* Paris: Anthoine de Raffle, 1686.

——. *Il cuoco francese.* Bologna: Turrini, 1682, 1693.

Le Goff, J. *L'Italia fuori d'Italia: L'Italia nello specchio del Medioevo.* In *Storia d'Italia,* II, 2, *Dalla caduta dell'Impero romano al secolo XVIII,* pp. 1933–2088. Turin: Einaudi, 1974.

Leonardi, F. *L'Apicio moderno.* 6 vols. N.p., 1790.

——. *Il cuciniere perfetto italiano.* Florence: Pagani, 1826.

——. *Dizionario ragionato degli alimenti.* Rome, 1795.

——. *Gianina ossia la cuciniera delle Alpi.* Rome, 1817.

Leyrer, Dr. *La regina delle cuoche: Cucina dei sani ed ammalati.* Milan: Manini, n.d. (ca. 1884).

Liber de coquina. See Sada and Valente, eds.

Libera, Don F. *L'arte della cucina: Ricette di cibi e di dolci. Manoscritto trentino di cucina e pasticceria del XVIII secolo.* Bologna: Forni, 1986.

Liberati, F. *Il perfetto maestro di casa.* Rome: Bernabò, 1668.

Libro contenente la maniera di cucinare e vari segreti e rimedi per malatie et altro: "Libro di casa" di una famiglia reggiana del Settecento. Ed. G. Bizzarri and E. Bronzoni. Bologna: Il lavoro editoriale, 1986.

Lopez, R. S. *La nascita dell'Europa.* Turin: Einaudi, 1966.

McNair, J. *Pizza.* San Francisco: Chronicle, 1987.

Maestro Martino. *Il libro de arte coquinaria.* In *L'arte della cucina in Italia,* ed. E. Faccioli, pp. 131–218. Turin: Einaudi, 1987. (Transcriptions of other Maestro Martino manuscripts can be found in C. Benporat, *Cucina italiana del Quattrocento* [Florence: Olschki, 1996].)

Maestro Martino da Como e la cultura gastronomica del Rinascimento. Milan: Terziaria, 1990.

Mangiare meglio per vivere meglio: Guida practica a una nutrizione razionale per una buona salute. Milan: Selezione dal Reader's Digest, 1989.

Mantegazza, P. *Almanacco igienico-popolare: Igiene d'Epicuro.* Milan: Brigola, 1872.

——. *Almanacco igienico-popolare: Igiene del lavoro.* Milan: Brigola, 1881.

——. *Almanacco igienico-popolare: Piccolo dizionario della cucina.* Milan: Brigola, 1882.

——. *Giornale della mia vita.* Manuscript in the Monza Public Library, vol. 48, 1895.

Mantovano, G. *L'avventura del cibo: Origini, misteri, storie e simboli del nostro mangiare quotidiano.* Rome: Gremese, 1989.

Manzoni, A. *I promessi sposi.* Milan: Principato, 1990.

Marchese, P. *L'invenzione della forchetta.* Genoa: Rebettino, 1989.

Marchesi, G. *La cucina regionale italiana.* Milan: Mondadori, 1989.

Marchi, E. *Il maiale.* Milan: Hoepli, 1897.

Marchi, E. and C. Pucci. *Il maiale.* Milan: Hoepli, 1914.

Marinetti, F. T. and L. Fillìa. *La cucina futurista.* Milan: Sonzogno, 1932. Reprint, Milan: Longanesi, 1986.

——. *The Futurist Cookbook.* Trans. Suzanne Brill. San Francisco: Bedford Arts, 1989.

Mariotti, G. *Gastronomia alla ventura.* Rome: Mercurio, n.d.

——. *Quando siam dall'oste insieme.* Rome: Treves, n.d.

Martellotti, A. "The Parmesan Pie." *Petit Propos Culinaires* 59 (1998): 7–14.

Martellotti, A. and E. Durante, eds. *Libro di buone vivande: La cucina tedesca dell'età Cortese.* Bari: Schena, 1991.

Massialot, F. *Le cuisinier royal et bourgeois..* Paris: Charles de Sercy, 1691.

——. *Il cuoco reale e cittadino.* Venice: Baseggio, 1773.

Massonio, S. *Archidipno, ovvero dell'insalata e dell'uso di essa.* Venice: Brogiollo, 1627. Reprint, Milan: Artes, 1990.

Mattioli, P. A. *Commentarii in libros sex pedacii Dioscoridis.* Venice: Officina erasmiana, 1554.

——. *I discorsi di M. Pietro Andrea Matthioli.* 6 vols. Venice: Valgrisi, 1557.

Mazzarino, S. *Aspetti sociali del quarto secolo: Ricerche sulla società tardo-romana.* Rome: L'Erma di Bretschneider, 1951.

Mazzei, L. *Lettere a Francesco Datini*. Ed. C. Guasti. Florence: Le Monnier, 1880.

Meldini, P. "La tavola pitagorica." *La Gola*, April 1986, 6.

———. *Pranzi di carta: I menù tra storia della cucina e storia dell'arte*. Rimini: Orsa Maggiore, 1990.

Mennell, S. *All Manners of Food: Eating and Taste in England and France from the Middle Ages to the Present*. Oxford: Blackwell, 1985.

Menon. *La cuisinière bourgeoise*. Paris: Guillyn, 1746.

Messedaglia, L. "Leggendo la cronica di frate Salimbene da Parma: Note per la storia della vita economica e del costume nel secolo XIII." *Atti dell'Istituto veneto di scienze, lettere ed arti* 103 (1943–44): part 2, 351–426

———. *Il mais e la vita rurale italiana*. Piacenza: Federazione italiana dei consorzi agrari, 1927.

———. "Per la storia delle nostre piante alimentari: La melanzana." *Annali dell'Accademia di agricoltura di Torino* 94 (1951–52): 119–34.

———. *Vita e costume della Rinascenza in Merlin Cocai*. 2 vols. Padua: Antenore, 1974

Messisbugo, C. *Libro novo nel qual s'insegna a far d'ogni sorte di vivanda*. Ferrara: Buglhat and Hucher, 1549 (as *Banchetti, compositioni di vivande et apparecchio generale*). Reprint, Venice: Giovanni Eredi Padovano, 1557..

Milham, M. E. "Toward a Stemma and Fortuna of Apicius." *Italia medioevale e umanistica* 10 (1967): 259–320.

Monelli, P. *Il ghiottone errante*. Milan: Treves, 1935.

Montagné, P. *Larousse gastronomique*. Paris: Larousse, 1938.

Montaigne, M. de. *Travel Journal*, in *The Complete Works*. Trans D. Frame, pp 867– 1039. Stanford: Stanford University Press. 1943.

———. *Essays*. in *The Complete Works*, pp. 2–857.

Montanari, M. *L'alimentazione contadina nell'alto Medioevo*. Naples: Liguori, 1979.

———. *Alimentazione e cultura nel Medioevo*. Rome: Laterza, 1988.

———. *Convivi e banchetti*. In *Strumenti, tempi e luoghi di comunicazione nel Mezzogiorno normanno-svevo*, Atti delle XI Giornate normanno-sveve, pp. 323–44. Bari: Dedalo, 1995.

———. *Convivio: Storia e cultura dei piaceri della tavola dall'Antichità al Medioevo*. Rome: Laterza, 1989.

———. *Convivo oggi: Storia e cultura dei piaceri della tavola nell'età contemporanea*. Rome: Laterza, 1992.

———. *La fame e l'abbondanza: Storia dell'alimentazione in Europa*. Rome: Laterza, 1993.

———. "I luoghi della cultura alimentare." In *Centri di produzione della Cultura nel Mezzogiorno normanno-svevo*, Atti delle XII Giornate normanno-sveve, Bari, October 1995, pp. 355–72. Bari: Dedalo, 1997.

———. "Maometto, Carlo Magno e lo storico dell'alimentazione." *Quaderni Medievali* 40 (1995): 64–71.

———. *Nuovo convivio: Storia e cultura dei piaceri della tavola nell'età moderna*. Rome: Laterza, 1991.

———. "Le posate: Un'ovvietà?" In *Posate*, ed. M. Ferreri, pp. 9–15. Mantua: Corraini, 1997.

Morelli, L. *La casa che vorrei avere*. Milan: Hoepli, 1931.

———. *Massaie di domani: Conversazioni di economica domestica per le scuole secondarie di avviamento professionale a tipo industriale femminile*. Turin: Lattes, 1935.

———. *Nuovo ricettario domestico*. Milan: Hoepli, 1935.

Moretum: Appendix virgiliana. Turin: Paravia, 1960.

Morpurgo, S. *LVII ricette d'un libro di cucina del buon secolo della lingua*. Bologna: Zanichelli, 1890.

Moulin, L. *La vita quotidiana dei monaci nel Medioevo*. Milan: Mondadori, 1988.

Mulon, M. *Deux traités inédits d'art culinaire médiévale*. In *Actes du 93e congrès des sociétés savantes* (Tours, 1968), vol. 1, *Les problèmes de l'alimentation*, in *Bulletin philologique et historique*, 1971, 369–435.

Narrazione delle solenni reali festi fatte celebrare in Napoli da Sua Maestà il re delle due Sicilie Carlo Infante di Spagna Duca di Parma, Piacenza . . . per la nascita del suo primogenito Filippo Real Principe delle due Sicilie. Naples, 1749.

Naso, I. *Formaggi del Medioevo: La "summa lacticiniorum" di Pantaleone da Confienza*. Turin: Il Segnalibro, 1990.

Nebbia, A. *Il cuoco maceratese*. Macerata: Chiappini e Cortesi, 1781. Reprint, Macerata: Eredi Pannelli, 1786.

Nelli, G. *Il re dei cuochi: Trattato di gastronomia universale*. Milan: Legros, 1868. Reprint, Milan: Carrara, 1889.

Nievo, I. *Le confessioni di un italiano*. Milan: Mondadori, 1981.

Nigro, G. *Gli uomini dell'Irco: Indagine sui consumi di carne nel basso Medioevo. Prato alla fine del '300*. Florence: Le Monnier, 1983.

Nisbet, A. M. and V. A. Masséna. *L'Empire à table*. Paris: Birot, 1988.

Notari, U. *Il giro d'Italia . . . a tavola*. Perledo: Edizioni d'Italia, n.d. (after 1931).

Il nuovo economico cuoco piemontese e credenziere napoletano. Milan, 1822.

Odescalchi, A. *Il cuoco senza pretese*. Como: Ostinelli, 1834.

Olio ed olivi del Garda veronese: Le vie dell'olio gardesano dal medioevo ai primi del Novecento. Ed. A. Brugnoli, P. Rigoli, and G. M. Varanini. Cavaion: Turri, 1994.

Osterie romane. Milan: Ceschina, 1937.

Ottolini, G. *Il digestore di Papino: Ridotto ad uso di cucina*. Opuscoli scelti sulle scienze e sulle arti. Milan: Marelli, 1783.

Ottonelli, G. *Annotazioni sopra il vocabolario degli accademici della Crusca* (Venice, 1698). In vol. 9 of S. Battaglia, *Grande dizionario della lingua italiana*. Turin: UTET, 1975.

dagli Orzi, Galeazzo. *La massera da be*. Ed. G. Tonna. Brescia: Grafo, 1978.

Paleari-Henssler, M. *Bibliografia latino-italiana di gastronomia*. 2 vols. Milan: Chimera, 1998.

Pandolfini, A. *Del governo della famiglia*. 1446. Reprint, Florence: Pietro Fraticelli, 1847.

Panzini, A. *Dizionario moderno: Supplemento dei dizionari italiani*. Milan: Hoepli, 1905.

——. *Dizionario moderno: Supplemento dei dizionari italiani*. ed. Milan: Hoepli, 1923.

——. *Dizionario moderno: Supplemento dei dizionari italiani*. 8th ed. Milan: Hoepli, 1942.

Papin, D. *La manière d'amolir les os et de faire cuire toutes sortes de viandes en fort peu de temps & à peu de frais*. Paris: Michallet, 1682.

——. *A New Digester or Engine for Softating Bones*. London, 1681.

Parmentier, A.-A. *Della pentola americana del Sig. Parmentier, Mém. d'agric. de la soc. R. de Paris 1786*. Opuscoli scelti sulle scienze e sulle Arti. Milan: Marelli, 1787.

——. *Dei pomi di terra ossia Patate*. Belluno: Tissi, 1802.

——. *Estratto delle opere del conte di Rumphort sulla maniera di comporre minestre sostanziose ed economiche colle esperienze fatte dalla Società agraria, ad istruzione e vantaggio del popolo piemontese*. Turin: Pane e Barberis, 1800.

——. *Rapport au ministre de l'intérieur par le Comité général de Bienfaisance sur les soupes de légumes dites à la Rumford*. Paris, 1800.

Parmentier, J.-M. *Il re dei re dei cuochi*. Turin: Bietti, 1895.

Paulus Diaconus (Paolo Diacono). *La storia dei Longobardi (Historia Langobardorum)*. Ed. and trans. A. Zanella. 6 vols. Milan: Rizzoli, 1971.

Pesce, P. A. *Macelli moderni*. Milan: Hoepli, 1910.

Petronio, A. *Del viver delli romani e del conservar la sanità . . . Libri cinque dove si tratta del sito di Roma, dell'aria, de'venti, delle stagioni, delle acque, de vini, delle carni, de pesci, de frutti, delle herbe*. Rome: Basa, 1592.

Petronius, A. *De victu romanorum*. Rome: In aedibus populi romani, 1581.

Picco, C. *Nuovo lessico di cucina abbreviato*. Bologna: Cappelli, 1965.

Piovene, G. *Viaggio in Italia*. Milan: Mondadori, 1957.

Pirenne, H. *Mahomet et Charlemagne*. Brussels: Nouvelle Société d'Editions, 1937.

Pisanelli, B. *Trattato della natura de' cibi et del bere*. Rome: Bonfadino e Diani, 1583. Reprint, Venice: Imberti, 1611.

Planhol, X de. *L'eau de neige: Le tiède et le frais*. Paris: Fayard, 1995.

Platina, B. *De honesta voluptate et valitudine*. Rome: Uldaricus Gallus, n.d. (ca. 1473–1475). Reprint, Venice: Impressum Uenetiis per Ioannem de Cereto de Tridino alias Tacuinum, 1503.

——. *Il piacere onesto e la buona salute*. Ed. E. Faccioli. Turin: Einaudi, 1985.

Pontormo, J. *Diario*. Florence: Le Monnier, 1956.

Prato, C. *Manuale di cucina*. Graz: Libreria Styria, 1902.

Prezzolini, G. *Maccheroni e C*. Milan: Longanesi, 1957.

Pulci, L. *Il morgante maggiore*. 3 vols. Venice: Antonio Zatta, 1784.

Puoti, B. *Vocabolario domestico napoletano e toscano.* 2d ed. Naples: Stamperia del Vaglio, 1850.

Il quattrova. See *La cucina elegante.*

Queyrat, E. *Los buenos quesos argentinos.* Buenos Aires: Hachette, 1974.

Rajberti, G. *L'arte di convitare spiegata al popolo.* In *Tutte le opere.* Milan: Berardoni, 1850–1851. Reprint, Milan: Gastaldi, 1964.

Il re dei cuochi, ossia l'arte di mangiare al gusto degli Italiani. Florence: Salani, 1881.

Reale Fusoritto da Narni. *Aggiunta fatta al Trinciante del Cervio.* Florence: Il Portolano, 1979.

Rebora, G. "La cucina medievale italiana tra Oriente e Occidente." *Miscellanea storica ligure* 19, nos. 1–2 (1987): 1431–1579.

Redon, O. "La diffusione in Italia di una tradizione culinaria senese tra Due e Trecento: Les Douze Gourmands; ou, La bande prodigue." *Bollettino senese di storia patria* 100 (1993, but 1995): 35–46.

Redon, O. and B. Laurioux. "L'apparition et la diffusion des pâtes sèches en Italie (XIIe–XVIe siècles)." In *Techniques et économie antiques et médiévales: Le temps de l'innovation,* ed. D. Meeks and D. Garcia, pp. 101–8. Aix-en-Provence: Errance, 1997.

——. "La constitution d'une nouvelle catégorie culinaire? Les pâtes dans les livres de cuisine italiens de la fin du Moyen Age." *Medievales* 16–17 (1989):. 51–60.

Redon, O., F. Sabban, and S. Serventi. *A tavola nel Medioevo.* Rome: Laterza, 1994.

Regimen sanitatis: Flos medicinae scholae Salerni. Salerno: Azienda autonoma di soggiorno e turismo, 1973.

Roanelli, M., M. Laudani, and L. Vercelloni. *Gli spazi del cucinare.* Milan: Electa, 1990.

Robuchon, J. *Larousse gastronomique.* Paris: Larousse, 1996.

Rodinson, M. "Recherches sur des documents arabes relatifs à la cuisine." *Revue des études islamiques* 17 (1949): 95–165.

Roggiero, G., G. Ricchieri, and A. Ghisleri. *Testo-Atlante scolastico di geografia moderna.* Bergamo: Istituto di Arti Grafiche, 1910.

Roggero, S. *Piatto unico all'italiana.* Milan: Mondadori, 1977.

Romagnoli, D. " 'Guarda no sii vilan': Le buone maniere a tavola." In *Storia dell'alimentazione,* ed. J.-L. Flandrin and M. Montanari, pp. 396–407. Rome: Laterza, 1997.

Romano, R. *Paese Italia: Venti secoli di identità.* Rome: Donzelli, 1994.

Romoli, D. *La singolar dottrina.* Venice: Tramezzino, 1560.

Rosenberger, B. "La cucina araba e il suo apporto alla cucina europea." In *Storia dell'alimentazione,* ed. J.-L. Flandrin and M. Montanari, pp. 266–81. Rome: Laterza, 1997.

Rosselli, G. de.' *Opera nova chiamata Epulario.* Venice: Zoppino, 1516.

Rossetti, G. B. *Dello scalco.* Ferrara: Mammarello, 1584.

Rossi, A. *Elogio del formaggio di grana piacentino.* Piacenza: Maserati, 1964.

Rovetta, R. *L'industria del pastificio.* Milan: Hoepli, 1908.

——. *Il pomodoro: Cultivazione, industria e fabbricazione delle scatolette di latta.* Milan: Hoepli, 1914.

Rumford, B. *Essais politiques, économiques et philosophiques.* Geneva: Manget, 1799.

——. *Estratto delle opere del conte di Rumphort sulla maniera di comporre minestre sostanziose ed economiche.* Turin: Pane e Barberis, 1800.

——. *Saggi politici, economici e filosofici del conte di Rumford che hanno servito di base allo stabilimento di Monaco per i poveri.* Prato: Vestri, 1819.

——. *Saggio sopra l'alimento de' poveri.* Opuscoli scelti sulle scienze e sulle arti. Milan: Marelli, 1796.

Sabban, F. and S. Serventi. *A tavola nel Rinascimento.* Rome: Laterza, 1996.

——. *La gastronomie au Grand Siècle.* Paris: Stock, 1998.

Sacchetti, F. *Il Trecentonovelle.* In *Opere,* ed. A. Borlenghi. Milan: Rizzoli, 1957.

Sada, L. *Spaghetti e compagni.* Bari: Edizioni del Centro Librario, 1982.

Sada, L. and V. Valente, eds. *Liber de coquina: Libro della cucina del XIII secolo. Il Capostipite meridionale della cucina italiana.* Bari: Puglia Grafica Sud, 1995.

Salza Prina Ricotti, E. *L'arte del convito nella Roma antica.* Rome: L'Erma di Bretschneider, 1983.

Samarelli, D. *Omegna paese di pentole e caffettiere.* Omegna: Edizioni città d'Omegna, 1990.

Sangiorgio, A. *La macchina di Papinio riformata all'uso economico e farmaceutico. Opuscoli sulle scienze e sulle arti.* Milan: Marelli, 1778.

Santi Puppo, P. *Il cuciniere moderno ossia la maniera di ben cucinare*. Lucca: Baroni, 1849.

Savonarola, M. *Libreto de tutte le cosse che se magnano: Un'opera di dietetica del sec. XV*. Ed. J. Nystedt. Stockholm: Almqvist & Wiksell, 1988.

Scappi, B. *Opera dell'arte del cucinare*. 6 vols. Venice: Tramezzino, 1570. Reprint, intro. G. Roversi, Bologna: Forni, 1981.

Schiavone, A. *Italiani senza Italia: Storia e identità*. Turin: Einaudi, 1998.

Schookius, M. *Tractatus de butyro*. Groningen, 1664.

Scopoli, G. A. *De diaeta litteratorum*. Innsbruck: Wagner, 1743.

Scully, T. *L'arte della cucina nel Medioevo*. Casale Monferrato: Piemme, 1997.

———. "The 'Opusculum de Saporibus' of Magninus Mediolanensis." *Medium Aevum* 54 (1985): 178–207.

Sercambi, G. *Novelle*. Ed. G. Sinicropi. Bari: Laterza, 1972.

Sereni, E. "Note di storia dell'alimentazione nel Mezzogiorno: I Napoletani da 'mangiafolia' a 'mangiamaccheroni.' " *Cronache meridionali* 4–6 (1958). Reprinted in *Terra nuova a buoi rossi*, pp. 292–371. Turin: Einaudi, 1981.

Sergent, E. and G. Giorini. *Nuovo vocabolario italiano domestico*. Milan: Pagnoni, n.d.

Sermini, G. *Le novelle*. Ed. G. Vettori. Rome: Avarizini and Torraca, 1968.

Simmons, Amelia. *American Cookery*. Hartford, 1796.

Il "sollazzo" e il "saporetto" con altre rime di Simone Prudenzani d'Orvieto. Ed. S. Debenedetti. In *Giornale storico della letteratura italiana*, supp. 15. Turin, 1913.

Sorrentino, F. "Maccaroni romaneschi." *L'Accademia italiana della cucina* 64 (1996): 11–12.

Stefani, B. *L'arte di ben cucinare, et instruire i men periti in questa lodevole professione*. Mantua: Osanna, 1662.

Storia d'Italia, Annali 13: L'alimentazione. Ed. A. Capatti, A. De Bernardi, and A. Varni. Turin: Einaudi, 1998.

Suor Germana. *Quando cucinano gli angeli*. Casale Monferrato: Piemme, 1983.

Tanara, V. *L'economia del cittadino in villa*. Bologna: Monti, 1644. Reprint, Venice: Brigonci, 1665.

Tarugi, G. *Prerogative dell'acquaticcio*. Macerata: Piccini, 1685.

Tasso, T. *Dialoghi: Il padre di famiglia*. Milan: Bompiani, 1945.

Tissot, S. A. *Della salute de' letterati*. Venice: Caroboli e Pompeati, 1769.

Touring Club Italiano. *La guida gastronomica d'Italia*. Milan: TCI, 1931.

———. *Manuale dell'industria alberghiera*. Milan: TCI, 1923. 5th ed. Milan: TCI, 1954.

Tozzi, F. *Pennino l'oste*. Signa: Masso delle Fate, 1996.

Trattorie d'Italia 1939. Ed. Federazione Nazionale Fascista Pubblici Esercizi. Rome: Federazione Nazionale Fascista Pubblici Esercizi, 1939.

Ulivi, P. *L'industria frigorifera*. Milan: Hoepli, 1912.

Valvassori, C. *Enciclopedia domestica*. Florence: Marzocco, 1940.

Vanzetti, E. *Il doppio quattrova ovvero la cucina elegante*. Milan: Domus, 1936.

Vasselli, G. F. *L'Apicio overo il maestro de' conviti*. Bologna: Dozza, 1647.

Veronelli, L., ed. *Il carnacina*. Milan: Garzanti, 1961.

Vialardi, G. *Trattato di cucina pasticceria moderna*. Turin: Favale, 1854.

I vini d'Italia giudicati da Papa Paolo III (Farnese) e dal suo bottigliere Sante Lancerio. Leghorn: Bastogi, 1890.

Voltaire. *Les anciens et les modernes; ou, La toilette de Madame Pompadour*. In *Mélanges*. Paris: Gallimard, 1961.

Weiss, U. H. *Gastronomia: Eine Bibliographie der Deutschgesprachigen Gastronomie*. Zurich: Bibliotheca Gastronomica, 1996.

Willan, A. *I maestri cucinieri*. Milan: Fabbri, 1977.

Wymann, W. *Des maîtres de l'art culinaire du monde entier vous parlent*. Paris: Comptoir français du livre, 1954.

Zacchia, P. *Il vitto quaresimale*. Rome: Facciotti, 1636.

Zambrini, F., ed. *Il libro della cucina del sec. XIV*. Bologna: Romagnoli, 1863.

Zampieri, M. and A. Camarda. *Sotto il segno dei maccheroni: Rito e poesia nel Carnevale Veronese*. Verona: Cierre, 1990.

Zannoni, M. *A tavola con Maria Luigia*. Parma: Artegrafica Silva, 1991.

Zingali, G. "Il rifornimento dei viveri dell'esercito italiana." In R. Bachi, *L'alimentazione e la politica annonaria in Italia*. Bari: Laterza, 1926.

INDEX